THE DUKE OF YORK'S FLANDERS CAMPAIGN

THE DUKE OF YORK'S FLANDERS CAMPAIGN

FIGHTING THE FRENCH REVOLUTION
1793–1795

by
Steve Brown

FRONTLINE
BOOKS

**The Duke of York's Flanders Campaign
Fighting the French Revolution 1793–1795**

First published in Great Britain in 2018 by
FRONTLINE BOOKS

An imprint of
Pen & Sword Books Ltd
Yorkshire - Philadelphia

Copyright © Allen George Packwood

ISBN: 978-1-52674-269-8

The right of Allen George Packwood to be identified as Author of this work has been asserted by him in accordance with the Copyright, Designs and Patents Act 1988.

A CIP catalogue record for this book is available from the British Library

All rights reserved. No part of this book may be reproduced or transmitted in any form or by any means, electronic or mechanical including photocopying, recording or by any information storage and retrieval system, without permission from the Publisher in writing.

Typeset in Palatino 10.5/12.5 by Lapiz Digital

Printed and bound by
TJ International Ltd

Pen & Sword Books Ltd incorporates the imprints of Pen & Sword Archaeology, Atlas, Aviation, Battleground, Discovery, Family History, History, Maritime, Military, Naval, Politics, Social History, Transport, True Crime, Claymore Press, Frontline Books, Praetorian Press, Seaforth Publishing and White Owl

For a complete list of Pen & Sword titles please contact

PEN & SWORD BOOKS LTD
47 Church Street, Barnsley, South Yorkshire, S70 2AS, England
E-mail: enquiries@pen-and-sword.co.uk
Website: www.pen-and-sword.co.uk
Or
PEN AND SWORD BOOKS
1950 Lawrence Rd, Havertown, PA 19083, USA
E-mail: Uspen-and-sword@casematepublishers.com
Website: www.penandswordbooks.com

Contents

Foreword ix
Conventions xiii
    Characters xiii
    Naming Conventions xiii
    Ranks xv
    Regimental Titles xv
        Austria xv
        France xv
        Hanover xv
        Hessen-Darmstadt xv
        Hessen-Cassel xv
        Dutch Republic xv
        Britain xvi
    Place Names xvi
    Distances xviii
    Map Legend xviii
Prologue: Frederick and Frederica xix

PART 1 – 1789 TO 1792: THE ROAD TO WAR

Chapter 1 – A Thousand Feudal Elements 3
    The Estates-general 3
    The Right of Peace and War 6
    The Declaration of Pillnitz 11

Chapter 2 – The First Coalition 16
    Mons to Valmy 16
    Lille to Trier 23
    Fraternity and Assistance 28

Chapter 3 – War is at Our Very Door 30
    Seditious Societies 30
    The Militia is Called Out 32
    The Most Perfect Union 34

Chapter 4 – The First Coalition Force 39
    Led by a Single Will 39
    Hanover and Hessen-Cassel 43
    Guardian Angels 44

Chapter 5 – Phoney War 51
    A Convenient Place to Assemble an Army 51
    With the Utmost Vigour 54
    Unfit for Service 57

PART 2 – 1793: COALITION OF THE UNWILLING

Chapter 6 – Advance to Contact 67
    Raismes 67
    Famars 76

Chapter 7 – Valenciennes 82
    The Seige 82
    The Capture 88

Chapter 8 – Linselles to Dunkirk 92
    Caesar's Camp 92
    Linselles 95
    Dunkirk 98

Chapter 9 – The Channel Ports 104
    Hondschoote 104
    Maubeuge and Wattignies 116
    Menin and Nieuwpoor 119

Chapter 10 – Winter Quarters 124
    1793 in Review 124
    A Mettlesome One 128

PART 3 – 1794: A NEW CAMPAIGN SEASON

Chapter 11 – Good Cavalry Country 138
    Catillon and Le Cateau 138
    Menin and Willems 152

Chapter 12 – Tourcoing 159
    Annihilation Plan 159
    The First Day 164
    The Second Day 175

Chapter 13 – Tournai 186
    Pont-à-Chin 186
    The Emperor Goes Home 191

Chapter 14 – Exit Austria 194
    Enter Moira 194
    Fleurus 200

Chapter 15 – Defending the United Provinces 207
    Farewell to the Austrian Netherlands 207
    Boxtel 216

Chapter 16 – Every Disgrace and Misfortune 222
   Nijmegen.. 222
   New Broom 230

PART 4 – 1795: THIS MOST UNHAPPY EXPEDITIONARY FORCE

Chapter 17 – Winter on the Waal... 243
   Geldermalsen 243
   Half-Starved Carmagnols.. 246

Chapter 18 – Retreat to Bremen 250
   Legions of Vultures 250
   Homeward Bound 256

Chapter 19 – Ringed with Enemies... 260

Chapter 20 – Torpor and Treachery 265

APPENDICES 272-337
     I.   The Crimp Riots... 273
    II.   Biographies 276
          France 276
          Great Britain 278
          Austria.. 279
          Hanover.. 280
          Hessen-Cassel... 281
          Prussia 281
          Netherlands 282
   III.   Commanders of the Armée du Nord 1791–1795 283
   IV.   The British Expeditionary Force 1 May 1793 285
    V.   The Hanoverian Auxiliary Corps April-June 1793 287
   VI.   The Hessen-Cassel Auxiliary Corps June-July 1793 290
  VII.   The French Garrison of Valenciennes 30 May 1793 292
 VIII.   The Duke of York's Command 13 August 1793 294
   IX.   The Duke of York's Command at Dunkirk 25 August 1793.......... 296
    X.   Freytag's Dispositions South of Dunkirk 5 September 1793 299
   XI.   The Duke of York's Command at Le Cateau 16 April 1794 301
  XII.   French Forces at Tourcoing, 17–18 May 1794.................................... 303
 XIII.   Coalition Forces at Tourcoing, 17–18 May 1794 309
 XIV.   Lord Moira's Reinforcements at Ostend June/July 1794................ 315
  XV.   The Duke of York's Command 15 August 1794 316
 XVI.   The Coalition Garrison of Nijmegen 1 November 1794.................. 322
 XVII.   Reorganisation of the British Infantry Brigades
          13 November 1794 323
 XVIII.   British Regiments Present in Flanders 1793–1795............................ 325
 XIX.   The Nursery: Eminent British Officers Who Served in
          Flanders 1793–1795... 331

Bibliography 338

Notes 346

Index 368

Foreword

Say the word 'Flanders' to the average Briton and the inevitable response will conjure up images of mud-stained khaki-clad Tommies of 1914–1918. But the British Army has fought longer and harder in Flanders than any other place on earth. Starting in 1658, Cromwell's time, an English Commonwealth army fought there alongside the French against the Spanish army and English Royalists.[1] This resulted in the Battle of the Dunes near Dunkirk, in a location fought over again in the campaigns described in this book. The French and Cromwell were victorious and as a reward, the English Commonwealth was gifted the port of Dunkirk.[2] In 1670 King Charles II signed a secret treaty with France against the Dutch, then sent an army there in 1672 (comprising both Scots and English regiments) where they campaigned (in part under the great Turenne), fighting in the Low Countries and Germany until 1678. English and Scots troops were there again in Marlborough's campaigns from 1705 to 1713, then in 1745 and 1746, the aforementioned First World War, 1940, 1944 and 1945. So, the presence of a British army in Flanders from 1793 to 1795, the period covered by this book, was merely the latest episode in a long military association. To borrow a phrase, there are more Englishmen lying in some foreign field in Flanders than anywhere else outside Great Britain.

The Duke of York's Flanders Campaign was not, is not and will never be considered one of the British Army's premier achievements. There are no Waterloos to be found in its dusty annals. The depth and breadth of English-language writings on the campaign pales in comparison to the volume of writings in French, Dutch and German. (Indeed, this book would not have been possible without reference to these non-English sources.) For this campaign was not a British campaign, much less an English War. Only 17 per cent of the troops who served in the Coalition armies in the 100 Days campaign of 1815 were British; 68 per cent spoke German. The Coalition army assembled on 16 April 1794 to kick off the new campaign season contained 7 per cent English speakers and 83 per cent German speakers.[3]

Yet if it was not a British war, it was a war that shaped the British Army. Many ensigns, lieutenants and captains of 1793 became the colonels, major generals and lieutenant generals (even a field marshal) of the Waterloo campaign in 1815. The Duke of York, that much maligned and misunderstood commander-in-chief in Flanders, went to become Commander-in-Chief of the Forces and according to Fortescue, 'did more for the army than any one man has done for it in the whole of its history'.

The miniscule size of the British expeditionary force at the outset was offset by the arrival of what could be called the King's Germans – the Hanoverians and subsidised levies from Hessen-Cassel and Hessen-Darmstadt. These proved to be some of the expeditionary force's best troops and their efforts have often been masked within English-language accounts. Hopefully within the book I have treated them as equals. Many of their officers, later serving as émigrés, went on to become familiar names in the Napoleonic era, particularly within the King's German Legion between 1803 and 1815.

Those familiar with the Waterloo campaign or the First World War will find this book liberally peppered with familiar place-names. Between 1793 and 1795 Ypres was besieged; Menin was fought over; Mons was frequently occupied. A small battle was fought at Mont St Jean; a larger battle was fought at Ligny; the Austrians retreated through Wavre. What will be less familiar was the style of making war. The Imperial, which is to say Austrian, method was to concentrate mainly on besieging fortresses, and doing it all as if time was not of the essence. The Duke of York saw it differently, itching to go 'in for the kill', but he was a minor partner. The French, driven by their National Convention and the fear of the guillotine, were evolving into a different species altogether. Once Carnot organised them into shape at the end of 1793, they were, in retrospect, unstoppable.

I wish to point out that this is not a history of the French Revolution. The chronicling of that Europe-shattering event could fill a book in itself. This narrative covers only as much detail concerning the history of the Revolution and political events in Paris as is necessary to provide context to the campaign in Flanders. Those wishing to read more deeply into the causes and effects of the revolution are advised to seek out Christopher Hibbert's *The French Revolution*, or Simon Schama's *Citizens* as excellent background reads. I can also recommend Paddy Griffith's *The Art of War in Revolutionary France*

FOREWORD

1789–1802 as essential reading for those wanting to know more about the formation and performance of France's armies at this time.

I owe my thanks in writing this book to my publisher John Grehan for once again encouraging me to see this project through, and to him and Martin Mace for agreeing to photograph specific sites, leading to some of the images within this book. I also owe a debt of gratitude to Diana Mankowitz for photographing the Henry Clinton and James Moncrieff papers at the University of Michigan; to the staff at the University of Nottingham for granting me access to the William Cavendish-Bentinck journals; and mostly to Stuart Reid and Bob Burnham for their helpful advice and review comments, allowing me to correct some obvious and not-so-obvious (to me) howlers and oversights. Any errors, mistranslations or omissions remaining are of course all mine.

Conventions

Characters
The Duke of York's campaign in Flanders started twelve years before Napoleon's first campaign as Emperor, being his march eastwards from the English Channel to the celebrated battlefield of Austerlitz in 1805. Most of the commanders who participated in the 1793 campaign were products of eighteenth-century warfare, belonging to a generation that was almost obsolete by 1805. Their names, usually long and convoluted ones, therefore, may not be familiar. I have adopted the convention of describing them by their full name and title on first appearance in the text; thereafter, I have generally reverted to a shorter version of their name (or title) to avoid becoming tedious and long-winded. I have also provided a short biography of many of the leading lights of the era at the rear of this book, in the hope that this may assist the reader when momentarily trying to sort out who-is-who – and also, to describe their ultimate fate.

Naming Conventions
I decided from the outset to impart as much historical flavour to this work as I could. In keeping with the multi-national complexion of the forces arrayed against Republican France, I elected to use national (as distinct from Anglicised) forms of names, titles and places, wherever possible.

This has resulted in potentially unfamiliar terms to the general reader, I am sure, but has hopefully imbued the work with a broad sense of the era and of the multitude of nationalities involved.

The Germanic prefix 'von' is used whenever a character first appears, but thereafter omitted; however, the French 'de' has been retained where linking between a title and surname.

CONVENTIONS

Modern Rank	British Army	French Army	Austrian Army	Prussian Army
Field Marshal / General of the Army	Field Marshal	Maréchal	Feldmarschall	Feldmarschall
General	General	Général d'Armee	General der Kavallerie / Feldzeugmeister	General der Infanterie / Kavallerie
Lieutenant General	Lieutenant General	Lieutenant-général / Général de division	Feldmarschalleutnant	Generalleutnant
Major General	Major General		Generalmajor	Generalmajor
Brigadier / Brigadier General	Brigadier General	Maréchal de camp / Général de brigade		
Colonel	Colonel	Colonel	Oberst	Oberst
Lieutenant Colonel	Lieutenant Colonel		Oberstleutnant	
Major	Major	Chef de Bataillon	Major	Major
Captain	Captain	Capitaine	Hauptmann / Rittmeister	Kapitän
Lieutenant / 1st Lieutenant	Lieutenant	Lieutenant	Oberleutnant	Leutnant / Premierleutnant / Oberleutnant
2nd Lieutenant	Ensign	Sous Lieutenant	Leutnant	
Sergeant Major / Warrant Officer	Sergeant Major	Adjutant-Chef / Adjutant Sous Officier	Oberwachtmeister	Feldwebel
Sergeant	Sergeant	Sergent	Wachtmeister	Unteroffizier
Corporal	Corporal	Caporal	Korporal	Korporal
Lance Corporal	Chosen Man		Gefreiter	Gefreiter
Private	Private	Soldat	Gemeiner	Musketier

xiv

CONVENTIONS

Ranks
The various rank systems used at the time were confusing, and some armies (i.e. the French) changed theirs in mid-campaign. The preceding table attempts to add clarity by comparing the various ranks used at the time with the modern equivalents. It is at best an approximation.

The Hanoverian, Hessen-Cassel and Hessen-Darmstadt contingents generally followed the Prussian style.

Regimental Titles
I will readily admit that I like seeing regiments described in their national form rather than by Anglicised titles. Thus, to my eyes, 'k.k. Linien-Infanterie-Regiment Nr.1 (Kaiser Franz II)' is far more appealing than saying '1st Austrian Infantry Regiment (Kaiser Francis)' which feels somehow flat and anglophile. Therefore, the following conventions appear through the work (typical examples only are shown):

Austria
'k.k. Kavallerie-Regiment Nr.20 Kurassier (Freiherr Mack)' which might be abbreviated to 'Kurassier Regiment Nr.20'.

France
'7ème Régiment de Hussards' which might be abbreviated to '7e Hussards'.

Hanover
'10.Infanterie-Regiment (von Diepenbrock)' which might be abbreviated to '10.Infanterie-Regiment'.

Hessen-Darmstadt
'Hessisches Leibgarde Infanterie-Regiment' which might be abbreviated to 'Leibgarde Infanterie-Regiment'.

Hessen-Cassel
'HK Füsilier-Regiment von Lossberg' which might be abbreviated to 'Füsilier-Regiment von Lossberg'.

Dutch Republic
'Infanterie Regiment No.2 (Van Maneil)' which might be abbreviated to 'Infanterie Regiment No.2'.

Britain

British regimental names are reproduced exactly as appeared in the Army List of the relevant year, although shortened after the first mention in the following fashion:

'14th (Bedfordshire) Regiment of Foot' which might be abbreviated as '14th Foot'.

Or: '15th (The King's) Regiment of (Light) Dragoons' which might be abbreviated as '15th Light Dragoons'.

Since history has remembered the events of this book as 'The War of the First Coalition Against France' I have preferred the word 'coalition' to describe the alliance of non-French nations in this book in preference to 'Allies'.

Place Names

British writers of the era tended to use the French version of place-names in Belgium and the Netherlands, leading to (in some cases) quite distinct variations from town and city names used by the inhabitants.

Many place-names are unchanged (for example, Paris) and are therefore used completely in accordance with modern usage. However, some exceptions to this, necessary to align the text with 18th century usage, has led to the need for the following explanation:

18th CENTURY	**MODERN**
Bois-le-Duc	's-Hertegenbosch
Courtrai	Kortrijk
Flushing	Vlissingen
Helvoetsluys	Hellevoetsluis
Menin	Menen
Tiel	Tuil

National boundaries have also changed. What we now know as Belgium more-or-less equates to the eighteenth-century Austrian Netherlands (with some changes). However, the occupants referred to themselves as Belgians. Therefore, I have used the term Austrian Netherlands when referring to the nation under coalition or Austrian rule, and Belgium when independent. The occupants are referred to throughout as Belgians.

The Netherlands was known as either the United Provinces or the Dutch Republic (Republiek der Zeven Verenigde Nederlanden), a situation which had existed since separation from Spanish rule in 1588. It was a deeply-divided nation in 1792, with the population sundered along Patriot (pro-Coalition) and Republican (pro-French) lines. It did not survive the campaigns described in this book, becoming the French-leaning Batavian Republic in early 1795.

CONVENTIONS

The Holy Roman Empire was a geographic entity of more than 500 states, which had existed for about a thousand years, but was in its dying days during the Revolutionary Wars. It was by tradition (in the eighteenth century) ruled by the reigning Habsburg Emperor seated in Vienna. In 1792 the Empire consisted of 6.5 million Germans, 3.4 million Czechs, 2 million Flemings and Walloons, 1 million Poles, 0.9 million Croats and 0.7 million Serbs, plus smaller populations in places such as the Tyrol and northern Italy.[1] The Empire was dissolved on 6 August 1806 when Emperor Franz II abdicated under pressure from Napoleon. Franz became Emperor of Austria and King of Hungary instead, a situation which existed until the fall of the Habsburgs in 1918.

The term 'Imperialists' was often used in British language literature at the time to describe the armies of the Holy Roman Empire, which were essentially Austro-Hungarian. The term Austria is used to describe the Archduchy of Austria (Erzherzogtum Österreich), a Hapsburg kingdom which ran from the River Thaya north of Vienna south to Croatia, and westward to the Tyrol. It abutted on the east the Kingdom of Hungary (Magyar Királyság) which was also ruled by the Habsburgs; as such Hungarian troops were integrated into the Austrian army alongside the other elements.

Germany did not exist at the time and was an amalgam of many kingdoms, grand duchies, duchies, principalities and free cities – not counting Hanover, which belonged to King George III of Great Britain. Some were not even contiguous geographically; many existed across several tiny enclaves. The history of how they came to be this way could fill a book. All that needs be said is that the Kingdom of Prussia was the largest, most populous and most militaristic of all. What are collectively described as 'Hessians' in this book came from the pocket-sized Landgraves of Hessen-Darmstadt and Hessen-Cassel. Hessen-Cassel had been an ally of Great Britain for fifty years, famously hiring out 17,000 of their troops to fight in the American War of Independence and would continue to fight for Great Britain in Flanders – so long as the subsidies were paid. Hessen-Darmstadt was a member of the Holy Roman Empire and would therefore support Imperial interests in Flanders alongside Austria.

The Electorate of Brunswick-Lüneburg, more commonly referred to in English as the Electorate of Hanover, was technically ruled by King George in London, the king being Prince Elector of Hanover in addition to his other titles. Hanover had (in 1793) its own governmental bodies but had to sign a treaty with Great Britain whenever Hanoverian troops were required to fight in King George's wars. Its army was therefore largely modelled and clothed on British lines, without forming part of the British army, and certain of its institutions were rather more Prussian in nature.

The Kingdom of Great Britain included England, Scotland and Wales. Ireland had its own legislature, nobility and legal system, but was ultimately under the rule of the monarch of Great Britain.

The extent of France in 1792 was (with some only some minor exceptions) much the same as today.

Distances

The metric system was not formally adopted in France until 1799, later than the events described in this book. Therefore, keeping with the theme of adherence to historical norms I have adopted the older system of miles to describe distances, and yards to describe shorter distances, with metric equivalents shown in brackets.

Map Legend

COALITION	
▙	Coalition headquarters
▶	Coalition divisional staff
▬ ∶ ▮ ∗	Coalition infantry (initial position)
▬ ∶ ▮ ∗	Coalition infantry (final position)
◣ ▌	Coalition cavalry (initial position)
◣ ▌	Coalition cavalry (final position)
‖‖‖‖‖‖	Coalition artillery
..... ∴	Coalition skirmishers
FRENCH	
▯	French headquarters
▷	French divisional staff
▭ ▯▯▯	French infantry
◣ ▯	French cavalry
‖‖‖‖‖‖	French artillery
∘∘∘∘∘ ∘∘∘∘	French skirmishers

Prologue

Frederick and Frederica

The White Hall of the Schloss Charlottenburg was a hive of activity on Thursday 29th September 1791. Preparations were underway for the intended marriage of Princess Friederike Charlotte Ulrike Katharina, the eldest daughter of King Friedrich Wilhelm II of Prussia and his wife, Princess Elisabeth of Brunswick-Wolfenbüttel. Frederica, as we shall call her in the Anglicised form, was twenty-four years old, quite small even for the age, with petite hands and dainty feet. Somewhat plain, with bad teeth, she exhibited an attractive demeanour, was a good musician and singer, loved animals beyond description, and liked to be well-informed about the events of the day. No doubt it was these qualities which attracted the eye of her suitor and intended; Prince Frederick, Duke of York and Albany, the second son of King George III of Great Britain.

Not that George's wishes had much to do with the occasion. It had been decided that the Protestant royal houses of Britain and Prussia should be joined, and this couple were the insurance. Prince Frederick was an impressive fellow. Six feet tall, big and burly, with (somewhere under the powder) brown curly hair, his father's round face, dimpled chin, ski-slope nose, and green eyes with laughter wrinkles at the corners. He was no intellectual but cultivated a large circle of friends attracted by his affability and generosity. He laughed a lot, a big, hearty chuckle. Those who knew him considered him generally 'a good egg' and knew him as someone who liked to work hard and play harder. When not playing soldier, he could generally be found, if in England, at the racetrack; a pastime the Germans found incomprehensible.

Frederick's birth and social position had accelerated his military promotions significantly beyond his age and experience. Brevetted colonel at age seventeen, he became a major general at nineteen, and lieutenant general at age twenty-one. His active military career had consisted entirely of drilling his beloved Coldstream Regiment of Foot Guards (of which he was the regimental colonel) in barracks. But he had at least a good military education, and some of the best possible mentors. From the beginning of 1781 until July 1787 he had lived in Hanover, studying at the University of Göttingen. His maternal uncle Karl Wilhelm Ferdinand, Prince Elector of Brunswick-Wolfenbüttel, took the lad under his wing, and in 1783 took young Frederick to Potsdam to introduce him to King Friedrich II of Prussia, known to history as Friedrich der Große – Frederick the Great. King Friedrich[1] liked his young English namesake and invited him to attend Prussian reviews and field days. Prince Frederick wrote to his father on 8 June 1783.

'He [the King] is short and small but wonderfully strong made. Not very well upon his horse, but on horseback Your Majesty would be astonished to see him ... He has exceedingly the air of a gentleman and something exceedingly commanding in his look.'[2] The prince became an enthusiastic supporter of the Prussian style of training, making war, instinctively following orders, and enforcing discipline.[3] On 27 November 1784 he was appointed Duke of York and Albany, and Earl of Ulster, upon passing his twenty-first birthday. From this point forward, we shall refer to him as the duke. In 1785 he requested permission to attend the great Prussian military review in Silesia, and the aged King Friedrich gladly assented. The duke wrote gushingly home of the experience:

> The day before the King arrived the 29 battalions marched in one line, which never was attempted before, and I suppose never will be again. The distance from one wing to the other was 7446 paces. It succeeded surprisingly well ... the cavalry is infinitely superior to anything I ever saw... One day the King decreed without any previous notice that the 35 squadrons of cuirassiers and dragoons should charge in one line. Never was there seen so finer [sic] sight. There was not a single horse out of its place until the word Halt was given, when, as the commander was at the head of the right squadron, it was impossible for the squadron on the left to hear in time enough, so they advanced about twenty paces too forward.[4]

King Friedrich der Große died in his armchair at Potsdam on 12 August 1786. The duke had been present at a dinner-party a few nights before, at which the king had taken ill. By this time the duke was agitating his father for permission to come home, having not set foot in England for nearly six years.

He had learned a great deal in Hanover. He spoke fluent German, as well as French, which would serve him well in years to come. He had visited the Holy Roman Emperor Joseph II in Vienna in 1784, where he had lived a heady social life, making the useful acquaintance of the future Emperor, Franz, nephew of Joseph, almost his same age. He was a crack shot and an expert horseman. 'I have often run five or six miles as hard as I could on foot with my gun on my shoulder after a stag' he boasted to his older brother.[5] But foundations for problems in later life had also been laid – he had started to gamble excessively. Perhaps this is unsurprising, since in the words of childhood tutor, he and his brother George 'could never be taught to understand the value of money'.[6]

The duke finally arrived home on 2 August 1787. His first action was characteristic, to dash a note off to his older brother, George, the Prince of Wales: 'My Dear Brother, I am at this very instant arrived.' The two were almost exactly a year apart in age, and extremely close, at least in fraternity if not in personality. George was as feckless and unpredictable as Frederick was disciplined and affable. As boys they had re-created the battles of Frederick the Great in the gardens of Kew House, watched over by Lieutenant Colonel Gerard Lake, a learned and trusted Guards officer. Despite the seven years apart, the two became inseparable again. They were often to be found at Newmarket, usually losing vast amounts on the horses. The duke and his younger brother, the Duke of Clarence, gave a dinner party, at which twenty guests drank sixty-three bottles of wine.[7] On 27 October that year he was promoted to lieutenant general and given the colonelcy of the Coldstream Regiment of Foot Guards. On 20 May 1789 he fought a duel on Wimbledon Common with Lieutenant Colonel Charles Lennox of the Coldstream Guards (later the Duke of Richmond, whose soiree the Duke of Wellington so famously attended on 15 June 1815). The exact reasons for the dispute are somewhat vague; they revolve around certain things said by Lennox at certain clubs concerning his disapproval of the royal prince's actions during King George's recent illness. Lennox fired first and shot off one of the duke's powdered curls. The duke declined to fire. And that was that.

After four years away, the duke returned to Berlin in May 1791. Events in France appeared so serious as to suggest that a continental war against France might break out. One source asserts that he travelled to Prussia to offer his services to King Friedrich Wilhelm II; this may well be true, as it is entirely in character. But we know for sure that he travelled with another goal in mind. On 28 August he wrote home:

> You knew that for many years the Princess Frederique has been a flame of mine ... You will not forget that that when we left Berlin

four years ago I told you that I should be very glad to marry her if it could be brought about ... I can safely say that I have never lost sight of my object ... I have no doubt of being perfectly happy. The Princess if the best girl that ever existed and the more I see of her the more I like her.[8]

Which brings us back to the Royal Wedding. In late afternoon of 29 September 1791, the assembled dignitaries took their places in the White Hall at Potsdam. It was a family affair, even a somewhat extended family. King Friedrich and Princess Elisabeth were present, obviously. Also attending were Prince Friedrich Ludwig Christian of Prussia; Willem Batavus, the hereditary Prince of Orange and his wife, Frederika Sophia Wilhelmina of Prussia; Prince Friedrich Heinrich Ludwig, the younger brother of Frederick the Great; the bride's siblings Prince Friedrich Wilhelm Karl and Princess Augusta; Karl August, Grand Duke of Saxe-Weimar-Eisenach, brother-in-law to King George; Princess Augusta Frederica, Duchess of Brunswick-Wolfenbüttel, elder sister of King George. The ruling families of Britain, Hanover, Prussia, Brunswick and Saxe-Weimar were inter-married to an extent that their family trees resembled a modern railway map. But these were relationships that would establish the course of the next twenty years in Europe and be of great significance in 1815. At about six o'clock in the afternoon:

> All the persons of the blood royal assembled in gala, in the apartments of the dowager Queen, when the diamond crown was put upon the head of the Princess Frederica; the generals, ministers, ambassadors, and the high nobility, assembled in the white hall. At seven o'clock the Duke of York, preceded by the gentlemen of the chamber, and the court-officers of state, led the princess, his spouse, whose train was carried by four ladies of the court, through all the parade apartments, after them came the King with the Queen Dowager, Prince Lewis of Prussia, with the reigning Queen, and others of the royal family, to the white hall, where a canopy was erected of crimson velvet, and also a crimson velvet sofa for the marriage ceremony.
>
> The royal couple placed themselves under the canopy before the sofa, the royal family stood round them, and the upper counsellor of the consistory, Mr. Sark, made a speech in German. This being concluded, rings were exchanged, and the illustrious couple kneeling on the sofa, were married according to the rites of the reformed church. The whole ended with a prayer. Twelve guns placed in the garden fired three-rounds, and the benediction was given. The new-married couple then received the congratulations bf the royal family, and returned in the same manner-to the apartments where the royal family and all persons present sat down to card tables;

after which the whole court, the high nobility, and the ambassadors, sat down to supper at six tables: the first was placed under a canopy of crimson velvet, and the victuals were served in golden dishes and plates.[9]

The happy couple were re-married at Buckingham House,[10] London, on 23 November following, after a peaceful visit to King George's Hanoverian realm but an eventful transit across France, during which their carriage was stopped, and a mob required them to remove all royal symbols before being allowed to proceed. They arrived in London on 29 October. Frederick's first action, as always, was to contact his beloved elder brother George. The Duke of York was already extremely popular, and Frederica's tiny high-heeled court shoes caused a sensation. Soon women everywhere in London were squeezing their feet into replicas. The couple eventually moved into a house in Piccadilly previously belonging to Lord Melbourne, and a country estate near Weybridge called Oatlands.

In August 1792, the duke resumed his military career, principally attending to the regimental matters of the Coldstream Guards. No doubt they marched beautifully, but like the rest of the British army, the Guards had not seen active service in over ten years, since the regrettable campaigns in North America. Outside of the Guards, the duke must have been acutely conscious of the comparison between the magnificent Prussian and Austrian armies he had watched first-hand on the continent to the small and badly-equipped British model.

But things were stirring just across the Channel, and the Duke of York must have sensed that his barrack-yard days were about to become something far more momentous.

PART 1 – 1789 TO 1792: THE ROAD TO WAR

Chapter 1

A Thousand Feudal Elements

The Estates-general
Louis-Auguste de France, more correctly King Louis XVI of France, was aged 34 in 1789. Shortish (about five-foot-six or 1.65m) and dumpy, he had the bearing and gait of a farmhand. His eyesight was so bad that he had to hold documents up to his nose to read, yet he refused glasses. Introverted to a great degree, he loved practical jokes and childish pursuits. He was not too concerned with affairs of state. His natural kindness and generosity were hidden behind a cold formality probably brought on by shyness. As a second son, he had never expected to be King as a boy, nor had been educated to act as one.[1] Timid and indecisive, he had ascended the throne in 1774 upon the death of his grandfather, Louis XV:[2]

> Louis the XVI himself ... entered on the task of government with a heart full of piety, philanthropy and public spirit. He was earnest, and pure minded, penetrated by a sense of his own dignity and the responsibilities attached to it; and firmly resolved to close forever the infamous paths in which his predecessor had walked. But, unhappily, his capacity bore no proportion to his goodwill. He was incapable of forming a decision; his education was deficient; he was awkward both in person and speech, and slow of comprehension. As he had a very limited knowledge both of the people, and the condition, of his empire, the selection of his ministers was, from the very outset determined by accident — the influence of his aunts, his queen, or the contending court factions; and as he was immovable wherever morality was concerned, but utterly helpless in the practical execution of his ideas, his was just a case, in which almost every thing depended on the aid of his nearest advisers. He possessed just sufficient sense of justice and benevolence to encourage every effort for useful reforms; but lacked entirely

that firmness of an enlightened judgment, which knows how to bring about a positive result, in spite of the opposition of existing interests.[3]

By 1774 he had been married for four years to Maria Antonia Josepha Johanna, the youngest daughter of the Holy Roman Emperor Franz I. History remembers her as Marie Antoinette. She was not popular in France, being a foreigner and daughter of the Holy Roman Empress Maria Theresa, over whom France and Austria had gone to war in 1740. The new king inherited a throne that had become tarnished during the latter reign of his grandfather. Louis XV had long been a popular king, and French culture and art had reached a high point during his reign. But France in 1774 had a glorious gloss of civility hiding a very old-fashioned and somewhat backwards agrarian economy, as described by one historian:

> In the eighteenth century France afforded an example of a state, the surface of which was covered with modern institutions, but which still rested on a feudal foundation, and preserved within it a thousand feudal elements.[4]

Neither the king nor the nobility saw any reason to change the status quo, and the divine right of kings permitted King Louis XV to do as he pleased, which included acting more playboy than monarch, excelling mainly only in hunting and womanising. Excesses at court and failed wars were paid for through increased taxation, levied upon those outside the nobility and clergy. The vast bulk of the population who paid these taxes slaved away on tiny farm lots under serf-like conditions. Unlike Britain, France had no budding industrial revolution to guarantee jobs, skills or future prosperity. Foreign travellers commented frequently upon the apparent poverty of French farm-folk and the backwardness of rural French society.

France had a fine army with a long and illustrious history, one of the best in Europe, if not the world. But it was divided along the same social lines as the society it served. No man could be an officer unless he could prove four generations of noble descent. Countless sums were employed in salaries and rich endowments for nearly 1,200 generals. At the other end of the scale, common soldiers starved on pay of 10 sous a day. Recruitment followed feudal lines, as officers recruited on their estates and entered into 'private contracts' with their dependant peasantry. This ensured some degree of loyalty, and generally low desertion rates; but it hampered the rapid expansion of the army in times of war. On paper there were 103 line infantry regiments, of which seventy-nine were French and twenty-three Foreign.[5] Each regiment had two battalions with about 600 men each. There were also six Chasseur regiments (light troops) each with four companies of green-coated light infantry and four squadrons of mounted chasseurs à cheval. Various militia regiments (*Troupes Provinciales*) provided 75,000 reserves, parimarily for garrison duty. Top of the tree was the *Maison Militaire du Roi*, the household contingent. The infantry component was four battalions of *Gardes Suisses* and six battalions of *Gardes Francaises*. The cavalry arm was provided by the *Gardes du Corps du Roi*. The household troops were responsible for guarding the royal palaces and maintaining public order in Paris.

It took from 1774 until 1788 for King Louis XVI to sense that social changes were in the wind – not inconsiderably influenced by the American War of Indepenence. He tackled the matter by assembling an Estates-General, an institution that only met whenever the monarch needed to get the advice of his subjects.[6] The opening was fixed for the 5 May 1789 in Versailles, and we may date the commencement of the French Revolution from this day. The three estates (clergy, nobility and bourgeoisie) met in equal numbers but separate chambers. Voting would be done separately, with each having a third of the vote. It must have been obvious that 95 per cent of the population who comprised the third estate could be outvoted by a combination of the clergy and nobles, the other 5 per cent of the population.

Thereafter followed weeks of debate over how voting for the estates should be conducted; in the end, the king permitted the third estate to double in size. Attendees of the third estate began to talk about declaring themselves a national body and taking the law into their own hands. On 17 June a motion passed for the third estate to now call itself a National Assembly. Another motion declared all taxes illegal, allowing them to continue until a new system was invented to replace them; it was carried unanimously. The National Assembly had evolved from challenging the first and second estates, to challenging the sovereignty of the king by taking responsibility for the laws on tax. Two days later the entire first estate – the clergy – voted to join the National Assembly. That left the second estate, the nobility, out in the cold. On 20 June the doors of the National Assembly were locked and guarded by troops, so the members decamped to a nearby tennis court and declared the 'Tennis Court Oath' – that all would not disperse until their business was done.

On 23 June the king was conducted into the hall with great pomp 'to make known for the last time his royal pleasure.' What he said – or mumbled – surprised many. The department of finance was put entirely into the hands of the National Assembly. The king declared himself ready to abolish the most oppressive taxes, to reform the army and the courts of law, to institute provincial assemblies and to do away with the censorship of the press. All these matters were to to be decided and regulated by the Estates-general but must be done by the three estates in separate consultation, not by the National Assembly. The Assembly rejected the royal authority imposed over it and proclaimed its members free from arrest. The king backed down. On 27 June the king ordered the estates to meet in common and vote by head. All remaining nobles were ordered to join the National Assembly, and the Estates-general was no more. It caused riotous celebrations, but the fact remained that half of the National Assembly still only represented 5 per cent of the population and would not be voting to change their way of life anytime soon.

King Louis, smarting from his rejection in the eyes of the Assembly, caved in to his advisers and ordered six regiments from around Paris to Versailles to quell the reform movement, whilst another ten regiments ringed Paris. A petition from the National Assembly to disperse the troops was rejected on 10 July. The following day the king dismissed Finance Minister Jacques Necker, a man widely admired for his apparent transparency with figures and the fact he had staved off financial ruin several times.[7] Riots broke out across Paris. King Louis sent for the Duke of Luxembourg, the president of the second estate, and ordered him to affect a union with the commons:

> 'I have no money,' [the King] said, 'and the army is full of mutiny; I cannot protect you, for even my own life is in danger.' 'To do that,' cried the duke in astonishment and terror, 'is, in the present state of public opinion, to proclaim the omnipotence of the States-general; the nobles are ready to die for their King.' 'I do not wish,' replied Louis, 'that any man should lose his life for me.'[8]

The fate of the monarchy was decided on 13 July 1789. Paris was in uproar. Colonel Pierre Victor, baron de Besenval, who commanded the troops in the Champ de Mars, could have quelled the revolution by displaying firmness and occupying the city. But he did not. After vainly sending messenger after messenger to Versailles, he at last decided, in the morning of 14 July, to withdraw his regiments from the capital. The loss of Paris, the overthrow of the aristocratic party and the ancient monarchy had now become a certainty.

The Right of Peace and War
The storming of the Bastille on 14 July was only a side-show. It is only notable because the Bastille was an unpopular symbol of the divine

right of kings, royal tyranny and arbitrary rule, and therefore became a symbol of the revolution. In reality the storm was a damp squib. The Bastille held seven prisoners, of whom four were incarcerated for the crime of counterfeiting, and one who was a lunatic. They were guarded by thirty-two Swiss mercenaries of the Salis-Samade Regiment and eighty-two Invalides (pensioners) – in all, sixteen guards for each petty criminal. The defenders surrendered and the governor, Bernard-René de Launay, was the first victim to have his head carried around Paris on a spike. What is less known is that the Hôtel des Invalides was stormed at the same time, and that nearly 5,000 royal troops encamped on the Champ de Mars did not intervene in either affair. 'Is it a revolt?' King Louis XVI asked the next morning, to be told: 'No sire, it's not a revolt. It's a revolution.' Two days later John Frederick Sackville, the British ambassador to France, reported to Secretary of State for Foreign Affairs, the Duke of Leeds:

> Thus, my Lord, the greatest revolution that we know anything of has been effected with, comparatively speaking – if the magnitude of the event is considered – the loss of very few lives. From this moment we may consider France as a free country, the King a very limited monarch, and the nobility as reduced to a level with the rest of the nation.[9]

Nothing of course was ever going to be so simple. The king and the nobility had no intention of being mere observers in this process. On 16 July the crowd declared that if the king did not come to Paris, '80,000 of the National Guard[10] would go to Versailles, fetch him, and scatter the swarm of aristocrats to the four quarters of the world.' On 17 July King Louis' younger brother Charles Philippe, Comte d'Artois left Paris with his family, bound for his wife's family estates in Savoy. King Louis wanted d'Artois to act as foreign spokesman for the monarchy in case he himself was muzzled. On 12 October d'Artois wrote to Holy Roman Emperor Josef II – Marie Antoinette's brother – to intervene militarily in French affairs on his family's behalf. The Emperor became actively involved in the planning of a rescue attempt. These plans came to nothing, largely because King Louis did not want to become a fugitive monarch (not yet, anyway) and Marie Antoinette refused to leave her children behind in favour of a faster carriage.

In Paris, the newly-renamed National Constituent Assembly busied itself creating new laws. On 26 August it released its singular most important document, the *Declaration of the Rights of Man and of the Citizen*, based in part upon the U.S. Declaration of Independence.[11] 'Men are born and remain free and equal in rights. Social distinctions can be founded only on the common good' ran the first article. However, this declaration was only intended to apply to 'active' citizens – male landowners over the age of 25. In other words, those who could wield political clout, some 4.3 million out of a total population of 29 million. All others were 'passive' citizens – all women, children, foreigners and those without property.[12] On 19 October the National Constituent Assembly relocated to Paris and declared a state of martial law to prevent future protests. Two weeks later they decreed the confiscation of all church property. Religious reform was a major agenda item. The day before Christmas, non-Catholics (primarily Protestants) were given eligibility for election to government office and be employed in all workplaces, civil and military.[13]

The year 1790 saw the rise of political clubs. The Société des amis de la Constitution had already been established on 6 November 1789 by anti-royalist deputies from Brittany; it later became famous as the Jacobin Club. Four months later the radical Société des Amis des droits de l'homme et du citoyen was formed in a convent in the the Cordelier suburb of Paris. The National Constituent Assembly continued administrative reforms. On 15 January provinces were replaced by 83 *departements*, a regional naming style that continues to this day. A month later monastic vows are suppressed by decree; monks and nuns were to return to civil life, with a pension. By this stage the Vatican had become so alarmed as to condemn the Declaration of Rights of Man. Elements of the population were equally unhappy, leading to pro-Catholic riots across France in April, May and June. The Assembly deemed, on 12 July, that clergymen should lose their special status, being required to take an oath of allegiance to the government. They were mere citizens like everybody else, paid by the state. King Louis authorised this 'Civil Constitution of the Clergy' on 24 August. What is more, members of the clergy were now to be elected by the people. Protestants could determine the appointment of a Catholic.[14] The open enmity of the Catholic church to accept these new laws prompted the Assembly to demand an oath of obedience from the clergy to this decree. Pope Pius VI officially condemned the Civil Constitution of the Clergy on 10 March 1791. The region of Avignon, the seat of the Popes in the 14th century and still a Papal possession (since 1309), did not belong not to France; anti-Papal riots ensued, but the Assembly took no action, wishing to avoid further confrontation with Pope Pius VI. Avignon was eventually annexed back to France again on 14 September 1791.

Religious and administrative reforms aside, there was much work to do in the sphere of foreign affairs. Overseas colonies were not forgotten, particularly those in the West Indies. The Assembly agreed to continue the institution of slavery in French colonies on 8 March but permitted the establishment of colonial assemblies.[15] Three weeks later all free men older than 25 years were given the right to vote, even in the colonies. On 22 May the Assembly issued the Decree of Right of War and Peace (*Décret de Déclaration de paix au monde*). Article I read:

> The right of peace and war belongs to the Nation. War cannot be determined upon but by the decree of the Legislative Body, which shall be passed upon the formal and necessary proposition of the King, and afterwards sanctioned by his Majesty.[16]
> Article IV read;
> ...the National Assembly hereby declaring that the French Nation renounces the undertaking of any war with the view of making conquests, and will never employ its forces against the liberty of any people.

However, a few of the Assembly were surely keeping an eye on events north of the border. The so-called Brabant Revolution had broken out in October 1789, ostensibly in response to reforms imposed by Holy Roman Emperor Josef II but inspired by events in France. The provinces which now constitute modern Belgium (with the exception of the bishopric of Liege, which was until 1795 an ecclesiastical principality) were known in the eighteenth century as the Austrian Netherlands. What had been previously known as the Spanish Netherlands passed at the Treaty of Utrecht in 1713 to Austria, then the chief rival of France on the Continent, with the caveat that certain fortresses on the southern border were to be garrisoned jointly by the Dutch and the Austrians as a barrier against French aggression. The Brabant Revolution, centered in Belgium, aimed to overthrow the incumbent Habsburgs and showed that a determined force of revolutionaries could defeat the established armies of Europe. On 27 October 1789, a force of Belgian rebels clashed with an Austrian brigade in the town of Turnhout and beat them. The Austrian force withdrew into Luxembourg. Notable Belgian towns and cities such as Brussels, Ghent, Diest, and Tirlemont fell to the rebels. Brabant declared its independence on New Year's Eve 1789 and was joined the following month by many other parts of Belgium, leading to the creation of the United Belgian States. Austria realised that her grasp on Belgium was weak and so determined to do something about it.

Diplomats from Austria, Prussia, the United Provinces (Netherlands) and Great Britain met in Reichenbach in Silesia on 26 June 1790 to discuss possible military intervention against the French Revolution, and to discuss the situation in Belgium. Austria and Prussia were not natural allies; their interests clashed in Poland. Whereas the Austrians wished to preserve a harmless neighbour, the Prussians wanted to partition large tracts of Polish territory to expand East Prussia. The Prussians also had their eyes on the rebellious region around Liege and offered to send troops there to settle things. However, the Austrian annexation of Ottoman lands to the east had caused friction which needed to be resolved. This resulted in the Declaration of Reichenbach, signed on 27 July 1790, and ratified at The Hague Conference in October 1790. Austria agreed to restore all conquered territories to the Ottoman Empire; but more importantly agreed to grant the rebellious Belgians amnesty and return their old constitution, in return for increased Austrian military presence. Prussia lost out on the deal. King Friedrich Wilhelm II was forced to abandon plans for expansion, as well as any attempts to acquire strategic benefits from Austria's losses. Austria did not delay. The following day the Assembly in Paris refused to allow Austrian troops to cross French territory to suppress the uprising in Belgium. They would have to march through Prussia instead. It was a good thing they had put their differences behind them.

On 21 October 1790, the Assembly in Paris decreed that *Le Tricolore* would replace the white flag with fleur-de-lys emblems as the official flag of France. Red and blue were the traditional colours of Paris, added to the traditional white of France. The three colours could also represent the Three Estates – the nobility, red; the clergy, white, and the bourgeoisie, blue.[17] Next they turned their attention to the reform of the army. These were announced to the citizens on 1 January 1791. The 'Royal Army' was now the French Army. Feudal traditions were to be eliminated immediately; line regiments were to lose their *ancien régime* titles and be known by numbers only; the rank of officer was to be open to all citizens, not just nobles; recruitment was centralised in municipalities. A code of military justice was introduced. Regimental structures were fixed at two white-coated battalions of nine companies each per regiment, one of which was to be grenadiers in bearskins. The Chasseur (green-coated light infantry) battalions were likewise re-structured to eight companies each, each company having a complement of Carabiniers (light infantry grenadiers).[18] By May 1791 the army had a paper strength of 138,000 men, down from 189,000 in 1789, a drop-off that prompted a call to place the Gardes Nationale on a national footing, which ultimately created 169 battalions for the regular army.

In February 1791 a rumour circulated that the royal family were about to flee France. King Louis' aunts had recently left France, bound for Rome. The Assembly debated a decree that would outlaw emigration; this led to the Day of Daggers (*Journée des Poignards*) on 28 February. Alarmed by the lack of Gardes National in Paris (a riot in Vincennes lured 1,200 guardsmen there), 300 to 400 armed nobles gathered outside the Tuileries, ostensibly to guard the monarch and seeking to petition the king to recall his aunts. An offer to allow a smaller contingent of twenty delegates into the palace to see the king was stone-walled. The returning Garde Nationale remained resolute in not allowing anyone in, and dispersed the crowd following a three-hour stand-off. In the eyes of the nobles, the king had sided with the Gardes National, even though they only had his interests at heart. The noble's respect for the monarchy was seriously degraded. It was probably at this point King Louis realised he had no friends left and made plans to escape.

Friday 3 June 1791, was an important day for the French people, for all the wrong reasons. The Assembly adopted a proposal that decapitation should be the new form of capital punishment, using a new device proposed to them by Dr. Joseph-Ignace Guillotin.[19] Some 17,000 Frenchmen would ultimately die by this invention in the coming few years.[20]

By this time the Comte d'Artois had left Turin and travelled via Mainz to Trier. In conjunction with Louis Joseph, Prince of Condé, he was planning a counter-revolutionary invasion of his homeland. His hand was stayed by a letter from his sister-in-law, Marie Antoinette, begging him to take no action until the royal family had secretly escaped from Paris. Their rendezvous point was to be the royalist stronghold of Montmédy commanded by Général de Bouille, north of Verdun. But the royal family never made it, being arrested en route at Varennes during the night of 20–21 June 1791. Their credibility amongst all classes of French society was by this time at a low ebb. The Assembly issued a decree of 15 July that Louis would only remain king under a constitutional monarchy. On the Champs de Mars in Paris two days later thousands of protesters, organised by the Club des Cordeliers through a petition, demanded the abdication of the king. The Mayor of Paris, Jean-Sylvain Bailly, ordered the Garde Nationale, commanded by Lieutenant-général Gilbert du Motier, Marquis de Lafayette, to open fire. Some fifty or so (the exact number is very uncertain) were seriously injured or killed. Lafayette, the hero of the American War of Independence, effectively ended his popularity at home, and very nearly his career, and so did Mayor Bailly. Bailly eventually mounted the guillotine.

The Declaration of Pillnitz

> His Majesty the Emperor and His Majesty the King of Prussia ... declare together that they regard the actual situation of His Majesty the King of France as a matter of communal interest for all sovereigns

of Europe. They hope that that interest will be recognised by the powers whose assistance is called in, and that they will not refuse, together with aforementioned Majesties, the most efficacious means for enabling the French king to strengthen, in utmost liberty, the foundations of a monarchical government suiting to the rights of the sovereigns and favourable to the well-being of the French. In that case, aforementioned Majesties are determined to act promptly and unanimously, with the forces necessary for realising the proposed and communal goal. In expectation, they will give the suitable orders to their troops so that they will be ready to commence activity.[21]

Thus ran the Declaration of Pillnitz, issued from Pillnitz Castle on 27 August 1791. Its co-authors were the Holy Roman Emperor Leopold II and King Friedrich Wilhelm II of Prussia. The emperor had a very personal stake in the fate of the French monarchy; he was the older brother of Marie Antoinette. The vague indirect language was intended as a sop to the many French émigrés who had taken refuge in the Empire and were calling for foreign assistance to rescue their homeland.[22] The role played by Prussia in the Declaration was less clear, since Prussian and Austria were not natural coalition partners, but welcome nonetheless since the rest of Europe seemed disinterested. Perhaps King Friedrich was hoping to emulate his famous uncle:

> Friedrich Wilhelm was eager to bear the brunt of the punitive expedition and thus to reap the presumably easy laurels of victory; but surprisingly the 'revolutionary hydra' proved too difficult to kill for the highly militarized states of Austria and Prussia. It required a pan-European coalition and almost a quarter of a century to cut off all its heads.[23]

In fact, Emperor Leopold did not intend to go to war at all. Austria had no intention of re-establishing the French *Ancien Régime*. Vienna hoped to establish a stable constitutional monarchy that would disable France as a European power. He also knew that British Prime Minister William Pitt did not support war with France. But he had to do something, so the Proclamation went out, calling on other European powers to intervene if the life of the King Louis was threatened.[24] Indirect language or not, the French National Convention interpreted the declaration as the Holy Roman Empire's intention to go to war.

The *Declaration of the Rights of Man* became the preamble to the new French Constitution on 3 September 1791. The new document still distinguished between the propertied 'active' citizens and the disenfranchised 'passive' citizens. Women had few rights, with no entitlement to education, freedom to worship, or freedom to speak or publish. It also stated that 'the king's person is inviolable and sacred,' principles that would be broken and torn within a few months. King Louis signed the new constitution on 14 September in front of the Assembly.

By late 1791 French émigré nobles were fleeing France by the score. Their favoured destinations were the Austrian Netherlands (where at least part of the population spoke French) and the smaller German states close to the French border. Émigrés were ordered to return to France before January 1, 1792 by an Assembly decree of 9 November, under penalty of losing their property and a sentence of death. King Louis XVI vetoed the declaration two days later, but asked his brothers (Louis, Comte de Provence, and Charles, Comte d'Artois) to return to France. They refused, citing 'the moral and physical captivity in which the King is being held,' and thus became criminals in the eyes of the Assembly, guilty of treason. The king wrote a secret letter to King Friedrich Wilhelm II of Prussia on 3 December, urging him to intervene militarily in France 'to prevent the evil which is happening here before it overtakes the other states of Europe.'[25]

But the king was clearly playing a double-game. On 14 December he addressed the Assembly and told the house that he had given the Electors until 15 January 1792 to break up all émigré-led gatherings of troops within their realms. To fail to do so would make them enemies of France. The King then went on to say that he had also written to the Holy Roman Emperor Leopold II, putting him on notice he was prepared to declare war in case his demands not be met. Then Defence Minister Louis-Marie-Jacques-Almaric, Comte de Narbonne-Lara, addressed the Assembly and told them of his plans to camp an army of 100,000 men along the Rhine, in three armies under the leading active generals of France. Running north to south, these were:

Armée du Nord – Marèchal Jean-Baptiste Donatien de Vimeur, comte de Rochambeau, aged 66 who had been commander-in-chief of the French Expeditionary Force that sailed to provide aid to the American colonies in 1780. This army was organised into three 'departements' (Nord, l'Aisne and Pas-de-Calais) with (by April 1792) sixty-nine battalions, forty-six squadrons and about twenty-four companies of artillery under command.

Armée du Centre – Lieutenant-Général Marie Joseph Paul Roch Gilbert du Motier, marquis de Lafayette, at the age of 34 far and away the youngest of the three. The famous Lafayette, the renowned hero of the American War of Independence and close friend of George Washington, had his reputation badly stained by the Champ de Mars massacre. This army was organised into three departements (Moselle, Meuse and Meurthe) and had forty-three battalions, fifty squadrons and twenty artillery companies under strength three months later.

Armée du Rhin – Marèchal Johann Nikolaus Luckner, a 69-year-old Bavarian who had served in the French army for nearly 30 years. His command contained five departements (Bas-Rhin, Haut-Rhin, Haut-Saone, Doubs and l'Ain) with sixty-six battalions, fifty-four squadrons and four battalions of artillery camped along the Rhine by April 1792.[26]

These armies were just the start and would need more men. On 28 December the Assembly voted to summon an army of volunteers to defend the borders of the France Republic.

The Holy Roman Emperor, Leopold II, signed a military convention to invade France with Prussia's King Friedrich Wilhelm II in Berlin on 7 February 1792. Three weeks later he was dead; Leopold died suddenly in Vienna on 1 March 1792 at the age of 44. The throne passed to his 24-year-old son, Franz (Francis) II. Where Leopold was conservative, moderate and enlightened, Franz was immature, distrustful and violently anti-Jacobin. In Paris, the Girondin ministry began agitating for war. King Louis attended a session of the Legislative Assembly on 20 April and sat through speeches calling for a pre-emptive strike, before rising and formally declaring war against Austria and the Emperor Franz, his wife's nephew. The declaration of war was met with tumultuous acclaim. Again, the king was playing a double-game. The invasion of combined Austro-Prussian and émigré forces might expel the revolutionaries from power and restore his divine right.

King Louis appointed a new minister for foreign affairs on 15 March; the 53-year-old Lieutenant-général Charles-François du Périer Dumouriez. Born in Cambrai, Dumouriez considered himself a Wallonian and was passionately devoted to the liberation of the Austrian Netherlands. He had been employed in the secret diplomacies of King Louis XV and in so doing gained a wide knowledge of international politics. He fervently wished for a war with Austria, to rid his homeland of the hated invaders. On 20 April 1792, he presented to the Assembly the proposal that war should be declared against Austria. It was carried by acclamation. Dumouriez naturally intended to start proceedings with an invasion of the Austrian Netherlands. Fearing a backlash from Britain, he sent a member of the National Assembly, Charles Maurice de Talleyrand-Périgord, to London in January 1792 with assurances that, if victorious, the French would not annexe any territory. The main goal was to keep Britain from allying with Austria.

Talleyrand returned home without a definite answer; Prime Minister William Pitt was keeping his options open.

Austria and Prussia had signed a treaty, so a declaration of war against the King of Austria, the Emperor of the Holy Roman Empire, was a declaration of war against Prussia. And so, the emperor turned to the Prussian Generalfeldmarschall Karl Wilhelm Ferdinand, the Duke of Brunswick, at 56 years of age the premier soldier in Europe, who drew up plans. A 50,000-strong Prussian army would concentrate at Koblenz (the de facto émigré headquarters), advance along the Moselle into Luxemburg and then invade northern France, on the way by-passing Metz before advancing into Champagne. This would be supported by two Austrian flanking operations; the Imperial army in the Austrian Netherlands would cover the Prussian right by advancing southward along the River Meuse, whilst the troops in Anterior Austria would protect the Prussian left flank. All told, the Duke of Brunswick would command some 90,000 men, possibly aided by as many as 20,000 émigrés. But the maths was flawed. The Austrians could only contribute 14,000 men in the Austrian Netherlands (after accounted for garrisons), and only 15,000 men were immediately available in Anterior Austria. A pattern was set; time would show that military planning in this campaign always looked considerably better on paper than in reality.

Chapter 2

The First Coalition

Mons to Valmy

The French decided they should invade the Austrian Netherlands at three points simultaneously, starting on 28 April 1792, with thrusts against Namur, Mons and Tournai. The Belgian town of Mons, so crucial in the opening year of a much later war, was the site of the first clash between the French invaders and Austrian defenders. It was not an auspicious start for the French. In the morning of 28 April Lieutenant-Général Armand-Louis de Gontaut, duke de Biron, marched from Valenciennes at the head of 7,500 men and thirty-six guns, pushing back some Austrian vedettes he encountered near the border:

> The 29th he appeared before Mons, near which he saw the enemy most advantageously posted on rising grounds, and much more numerous than he had reason, to expect. M. de Biron immediately sent off a courier to the commander-in-chief, to acquaint him with his position, and passed the night under arms. While he was waiting for orders, he was Informed that the Queen's regiment had deserted, and as they fled, had given out that the general was gone over to the enemy.[1]

The 6th Dragoons (formerly the Régiment de la Reine) had indeed withdrawn. Biron followed and forced the deserters back into line:

> The Austrians, perceiving the confusion amongst the French troops, attacked them, and obliged them to retreat. Whole regiments ran away, only one corps behaved with intrepidity, it was the second battalion of Parisian volunteers ... General Biron had his horse shot under him on the onset; the colonel of Esterhazy's regiment was taken prisoner with his thigh shot off.[2]

The French lost 400 men, dead, wounded and captured; the Austrians lost thirty men. The Austrian commander Feldmarschalleutnant Johann

Peter Beaulieu, by birth a Belgian, did not take advantage of his success; he deemed his orders were to defend his homeland, not invade France. That same day the Irish-born Maréchal de Camp Théobald Dillon led a second French column east from Lille towards Tournai. His small division – four battalions, eight squadrons and six cannon – ran into an Austrian brigade commanded by the French-born Generalmajor Ludwig Franz Civalart d'Happoncourt near the village of Marquain. As at Mons the French, mostly regulars, panicked and fled with barely a shot fired. Before they even reached Lille, Dillon's troops murdered their commander, believing that their defeat was due to some form of conspiracy. Given the calibre of the regiments involved, there may have been some truth in this. An anonymous 'witness', writing from Lille to William Pitt, recorded the horror:

> The soldiers charging their Colonel (Dillon) with having betrayed them, seized him, cut off his head, legs, and arms, and burnt his body in the Grand Place at Lille. That the Chief Engineer, with three other officers, who had endeavoured to protect their Colonel, had also been murdered. As had been a French Abbe who happened to pass the Grand Place at the moment of the murder of Colonel Dillon; and that the French soldiers had roasted three Austrians, whom they had made prisoner in their retreat.[3]

The projected attack on Namur did not even get going. These botched opening skirmishes forced several changes. The Governor of the Austrian Netherlands, Prince Albert Kasimir August Ignaz Pius Franz Xaver von Sachsen-Teschen, decided on a strategy of 'offensive defence' – to raid and unbalance the French, rather than waiting to be attacked. Successful actions at Bavay and Rumegies on 19 May and Florennes on 23 May convinced him of the soundness of this approach.

The French were being repulsed at every turn with minimal Austrian losses. Something had to be done. In Paris on 5 May, the Assembly ordered the raising of thirty-one new battalions for the army.[4] But quantity was not the problem; it was quality and leadership. So, an alteration was forced by the retirement of the commander of the Armée du Nord, the venerated Marèchal Comte de Rochambeau. The post went to Marèchal Luckner who was ordered to take his 43,000-man army north and capture Ghent and Brussels.

Luckner's Avantgarde under the command of Maréchal de camp Francois Jarry[5] advanced north from Lille on 17 June and easily captured the village of Menin, just east of Ypres. Pushing eastward, the following day Luckner's men overwhelmed a weak Austrian garrison at Courtrai. Feldmarschalleutnant Beaulieu managed to assemble a division-sized force from local garrisons and repulsed Luckner's Reserve brigades at the village of Harlebeke, just north of Courtrai, on 23 June. Luckner fell back to Courtrai, and Beaulieu attacked him there six days later. Despite his numerical superiority over the Austrians – at least two-to-one – Luckner fell back to Lille. The first French invasion of the Austrian Netherlands was over.

The pedestrian Luckner was removed from command of the Armée du Nord on 12 July[6] and the post given to Lieutenant-Général Marquis de Lafayette. Lafayette lasted five weeks in the command. He was anti-Jacobin, already unpopular, and his denunciations in Paris in June had seen him branded a traitor in some quarters. On 14 August, before the Armée du Nord could go back into action, Minister of Justice Georges Danton put out a warrant for Lafayette's arrest. Lafayette escaped to the Austrian Netherlands but was taken prisoner by Austrian troops near Rochefort. His goal, to flee to the United States, was not to be granted. But at least he escaped with his life; Luckner was not so lucky. After agreeing with Lafayette to support a constitutional monarchy, he was sent to Châlons-sur-Marne to help build a Reserve Army. He unwisely travelled to Paris in October 1793 to explain his political views, but gaining no acceptance, he resigned and returned home. Fate came knocking; he soon found himself before the Revolutionary Tribunal and was adjudged guilty of treason. Luckner was guillotined in Paris on 4 January 1794.

Lafayette's replacement was Lieutenant-Général Dumouriez, the first real hero of the French revolutionary army. The former foreign minister, appointed on 18 August, was acutely aware of the shortcomings of his large but unskilled army and so set to training them vigorously at Valenciennes. He was determined not to invade the Austrian Netherlands again until his army was ready.

By this time the agreed strategy of the First Coalition had coalesced. The Prussians started their advance into France at a snail's pace – but at least the Army of the Rhine was on the move. Under the supreme command of King Friedrich Wilhelm II of Prussia, a nephew of Frederick the Great – an easy-going arts lover, completely unsuited to conducting military campaigns – a main army and two smaller flank forces crossed the Rhine at Coblenz. On 25 July the commander of the main column, Generalfeldmarschall the Duke of Brunswick, issued a proclamation:[7]

> Convinced that the sane portion of the French nation abhors the excesses of the faction which dominates it, and that the majority of the people look forward with impatience to the time when they may declare themselves openly against the odious enterprises of

their oppressors, his Majesty the emperor and his Majesty the king of Prussia call upon them and invite them to return without delay to the path of reason, justice, order, and peace. In accordance with these views, I, the undersigned, the commander in chief of the two armies, declare:

1. That, drawn into this war by irresistible circumstances, the two allied courts entertain no other aims than the welfare of France, and have no intention of enriching themselves by conquests.

2. That they do not propose to meddle in the internal government of France, and that they merely wish to deliver the king, the queen, and the royal family from their captivity, and procure for his Most Christian Majesty the necessary security to enable him, without danger or hindrance, to make such engagements as he shall see fit, and to work for the welfare of his subjects, according to his pledges.

3. That the allied armies will protect the towns and villages, and the persons and goods of those who shall submit to the king and who shall cooperate in the immediate re-establishment of order and the police power throughout France.

4. That, on the contrary, the members of the National Guard who shall fight against the troops of the two allied courts, and who shall be taken with arms in their hands, shall be treated as enemies and punished as rebels to their king and as disturbers of the public peace...

7. That the inhabitants of the towns and villages who may dare to defend themselves against the troops of their Imperial and Royal Majesties and fire on them, either in the open country or through windows, doors, and openings in their houses, shall be punished immediately according to the most stringent laws of war, and their houses shall be burned or destroyed...

8. The city of Paris and all its inhabitants without distinction shall be required to submit at once and without delay to the king, to place that prince in full and complete liberty, and to assure to him, as well as to the other royal personages, the inviolability and respect which the law of nature and of nations demands of subjects toward sovereigns ... Their said Majesties declare, on their word of honour as emperor and king, that if the chateau of the Tuileries is entered by force or attacked, if the least violence be offered to their Majesties the king, queen, and royal family, and if their safety and their liberty be not immediately assured, they will inflict an ever memorable vengeance by delivering over the city of Paris to military execution and complete destruction, and the rebels guilty of the said outrages to the punishment that they merit.[8]

On 11 August the Avantgarde of Prince Friedrich Ludwig Hohenlohe-Ingelfingen surprised the French garrison at Sierck-les-Baines, north-west of Thionville, capturing a regimental colour. Behind him lumbered the 24,000-man Prussian army of the Duke of Brunswick, supported by 18,000 Austrians commanded by Feldzeugmeister François Sébastien Charles Joseph de Croix, Count of Clerfayt. The force was well-supplied with artillery and carried a siege train; but the army was hampered by command inertia, poor supplies, a major natural obstacle that was the Argonne Forest, and dysentery. The main column crossed the frontier on 19 August and laid siege to Longwy four days later. The garrison, a small brigade, surrendered almost immediately. The town was primarily royalist in outlook and the garrison was massively outnumbered. The French commander committed suicide after the surrender, no doubt being well aware of the reception he could expect in Paris. Ten days later the fortified city of Verdun surrendered after a token bombardment, which cost the attackers no men at all, and the defenders only one man – their commandant, who likewise committed suicide.[9]

With the frontier fortresses secured, the Duke of Brunswick turned his attention to the capture of Paris. But not before his army camped for a few days outside Verdun in the leisurely style of eighteenth-century warfare. Enter Dumouriez, whose primary strategy had been to strike swiftly into the Austrian Netherlands, thus foiling the imminent Prussian attack and hopefully diverting their axis of advance. The Executive Council in Paris ordered him put such plans aside until the immediate threat from the Duke of Brunswick's army had been neutralised. Dumouriez correctly anticipated his enemy's movements and was at Sedan:

> From Sedan to Passavaut a forest extends, the name of which ought to be forever famous in our annals. This is the forest of Argonne, which covers a space of from thirteen to fifteen leagues, and which, from the inequalities of the ground, and the mixture of wood and water, is absolutely impenetrable to an army, except by some of the principal passes. Through this forest the enemy must have penetrated, in order to reach Chalons, and afterwards take the road to Paris. With such a plan it is astonishing that he had not yet thought of occupying the principal passes, and thus have anticipated Dumouriez, who, from his position at Sedan, was separated from them by the whole length of the forest. The evening after the council of war, the French general was considering the map with an officer, in whose talents he had the greatest confidence ... Pointing with his finger to the Argonne and the tracks by which it is intersected.

'That,' said he, 'is the Thermopylae of France. If I can but get thither before the Prussians, all will be saved.'[10]

He summoned part of the Armée du Centre under Lieutenant-Général François Christophe Kellermann to his assistance from Metz. Kellermann was a 57-year-old Alsatian who had served 42 years in the army and would become a future Maréchal d'Empire under Napoleon. Dumouriez finally settled upon a defensive position facing north and north-east, barring the Paris Road, with his left stretching down the Châlons road and his right wing on the Argonne. He positioned his thirty-six battalions and forty-four squadrons on a height behind the hamlet of Braux-Sainte-Cohiere and waited.

The Duke of Brunswick had advanced at a glacial pace through the northern defiles and had then, urged on by King Friedrich Wilhelm II, conducted a risky outflanking manoeuvre whilst short of supplies and uncertain of the French positions. He extended to his right, in a manner to bring himself to the west of Dumouriez, effectively cutting the French commander off from Châlons, or any reinforcements. But they moved too slowly. Despite having moved slowly himself, Kellermann now sprang into action. Arriving from the south, he took up a position on a height to the south of Dumouriez initially; then acting upon his own initiative, swung his twenty-five battalions and forty-nine squadrons westward onto a series of heights north and southwest of the village of Valmy, facing the impending threat to the west. More importantly, Kellermann had forty-five heavy cannon under the command of the veteran Maréchal de Camp François Marie d'Aboville, manned by regular artillerists, which he arranged along the ridge-lines to produce a wall of fire. To remind us that these were indeed strange times, commanding Kellermann's first rank was an Irishman, Lieutenant-Général Isidore Lynch; and one of Kellerman's cavalry commanders was '*Général Egalité*', a pseudonym of Maréchal de Camp Louis Philippe, the Duc d'Orléans and father of the future King Louis Philippe I of France. A Venezuelan adventurer, Maréchal de Camp Sebastián Francisco de Miranda, commanded Dumouriez's left wing.

The Prussian army advanced from the south-west, between the rivers Brionne and Auve. The Duke of Brunswick's advanced guard under the command of Prince Hohenlohe-Ingelfingen took up a position on the forward slopes of a height about a mile west of Kellermann's ridge, with a cloud of skirmishers and forty-eight 6-pounder guns to the fore. Behind them two columns of musketeers formed up for the assault, supported by dragoons and cuirassiers on either flank. A bit farther back, The duke's first rank,[11] comprising nineteen battalions and thirty cavalry squadrons, in part commanded by a Dutchman, Generalleutnant de Courbière, behind. The Austrians commanded by Feldzeugmeister Clerfayt were still some distance to the rear, as was the Armée de Condé, a division-sized force of French Royalists commanded by Louis Joseph de Bourbon, Prince de Condé.

The Prussians and Austrians represented the very best of old-school European military professionalism. The Prussians, in their blue coats and old-fashioned tricorne hats, adhering strictly to the rigid doctrines of Frederick the Great; the arriving Austrians in their white uniforms, pale blue trousers on the Hungarians, with massed battalions of grenadiers in tall bear-skin caps. Every man among them was a soldier for life. On the French side Dumouriez's men, to the east, were mainly newly-raised volunteer regiments dressed in a mish-mash of white and blue, with some green and red. In some regiments, no two men were dressed alike. But Kellermann's men on the ridge to their west were mostly regulars of the old French Army, dressed in their customary white, with black and gold helmets called casques.[12] Kellermann's first rank included the famed regiments of Picardie, Navarre, and Dauphin. If the Duke of Brunswick expected that he could dislodge them from that ridge in a matter of minutes, he was mistaken. These Frenchmen were not the raw recruits so easily beaten at Mons and Tournai.

At face value, the battle was an anti-climax; a tactical draw. The battle started with an artillery duel, which swathed the battlefield with smoke, but caused few casualties. It was at this point that the Prussians expected to see the French tumbling rearwards. But they did not. So, a Prussian advance was ordered, and still the French did not budge. So the Prussians withdrew, and the artillery duel re-commenced. A lucky shot hit a French ammunition wagon which exploded in a massive fireball, causing consternation in Kellermann's ranks.

The Duke of Brunswick ordered another infantry assault to take advantage of the confusion, but three advancing brigades were raked by artillery fire and soon withdrew again after losing 200 men. Sensing the moment, Kellermann raised his hat and cried '*Vive la Nation*!' The French did not advance but instead started singing patriotic songs. It was their way of letting the advancing Prussians know that no backward steps would be taken. To their amazement, the Prussians started to retire.

The superior French artillery had done all the hard work. Total casualties did not exceed 500. Two Coalition supporting columns, Austrians and French emigres, did not even manage to reach the field in time. The average Prussian *soldaten* were disgusted: 'That very morning they had thought of nothing short of spitting the whole of the

French force and devouring them ...' volunteer Johann Wolfgang von Goethe wrote, 'but now everyone went about alone, nobody looking at his neighbour, or only to curse or swear.'[13] But on a deeper level, Valmy caused shock-waves, and promulgated a series of actions in other theatres of war, as we shall see. The professional armies of old Europe had been beaten by a citizen army of new Europe, and one buoyed entirely by political idealism. The day the news of the victory arrived in Paris, the French Republic was declared. It was the start of Year One of French Liberty.

The two armies sat in position for ten days. Dumouriez ordered Kellermann to Sainte-Menehould and ordered roads and fields to be wasted in case the Prussians attempted a further advance. Dumouriez then attempted negotiations with the Duke of Brunswick, hoping to persuade him to leave the First Coalition. But King Friedrich Wilhelm II was present, had just heard the news of the French Republic, and would have none of it. The king insisted that King Louis be restored before he would even discuss the matter. The French countered by demanding that the Prussians leave French soil before they would continue any negotiations. By this time the Duke of Brunswick's army was riddled with dysentery, his supplies were low, the French still held the road to Paris, the weather was foul, and the French were clearly increasing in numbers. If he advanced west on Paris, or sat where he was, he risked becoming surrounded. The only option was to retire back across the frontier. So, on the night of 30 September, the Austro-Prussian army retired the way it had come, back towards Coblenz, giving up everything it had gained on the campaign. Verdun was handed back to the French by peaceful negotiation on 14 October. The one great Coalition chance to end the war in 1792, using the best armies continental Europe could offer to capture Paris, had failed.

Lille to Trier

On 21 August the Austrians had about 25,000 men near Mons, commanded by Beaulieu; 12,000 near Tournai, commanded by Clerfayt; and 7,000 in two camps of observation on the frontier. The combined Prusso-Austrian forces on the Rhine numbered 52,000, not including the émigré contingent. In Alsace-Lorraine, another 34,000 Austrians and 7,000 Prussians camped on the east bank of the Rhine, awaiting developments.

Four French armies were arrayed to meet them. Lieutenant-Général Arthur Dillon[14] (in place of the absent Dumouriez) commanded the 50,000-man left wing of the Armée du Nord between Dunkirk and Valenciennes, about half of whom were strung out across the frontier to keep watch on the Austrians to their north. The right wing, another 50,000 men, were between Valenciennes and Landau, mostly in garrisons; Luckner's 44,000-man Armée du Centre was between Landau and Metz; Kellermann had 12,000 between Metz and Strasbourg; the Armée du Rhin had 44,000 near Strasbourg under Lieutenant-général Adam Philippe, Comte de Custine. In the south of France, the Armée du Midi under Lieutenant-général Anne-Pierre, marquis de Montesquiou-Fézensac commanded 44,000 men facing Savoy.[15]

Prince Albert von Sachsen-Teschen, the Governor of the Austrian Netherlands, decided to take offensive action to divert French forces away from the main Coalition thrust on the Rhine – a thrust which, unknown to him, had already failed at Valmy. He laid siege to the fortress of Lille, some 5 miles (8km) beyond the frontier, with 14,000 men and fifty-two cannon on 25 September, five days after Valmy. The French garrison of 10,000 men, a mixture of regulars and Gardes National, was never seriously threatened. Reinforcements arrived with ease over the next two weeks. Sachsen lifted the siege on 8 October once news of the Coalition retreat from Valmy filtered through and retreated to Courtrai. Such was the 'Valmy effect.' Another example occurred on 30 September. Brimful with confidence after the glorious news of the victory, the Armée du Rhin swung into action with orders to 'secure the natural frontier of France along the Rhine.' A part of Lieutenant-Général Custine›s force driving north towards Mainz trapped Oberst Winkelmann's Austro-German garrison of 3,600 men at the town of Speyer on a loop in the Rhine, about 10 miles (16km) south of Mannheim. The Austrians fought hard, but the encircling river and lack of boats gave them no chance of retreat, and the majority were taken prisoner. Five colours were taken and later taken in triumph to Paris.

Three weeks later the city of Mainz fell to Custine. Lacking available forces in the area, the city had been abandoned by the Coalition, leaving a scratch force of 5,400 to defend against Custine's advancing columns. The Austrian contingent managed to break out and escape to the east, leaving the rest of the garrison (Kur-Mainzers, Nassauers, armed peasants and university students) to be taken prisoner, then paroled on the basis that they would not fight again for one year. At least no lives were lost in the capture, nor were any lost the following day when the free city of Frankfurt surrendered to the French. It considered itself neutral and had no garrison. Custine put French garrisons into both Mainz and Frankfurt.

By this time the French armies had undergone some structural changes. On 1 October a decree from the National Convention split the four French armies into seven. The left wing of the Armée du

Nord remained the same, but the right wing became the Armée des Ardennes. The Armée du Centre became the Armée de la Moselle, at last giving it a geographical base. The Armée du Rhin had a portion divided off to become the new Armée des Vosges. The left wing of the Armée du Midi became the Armée des Alpes, and the right wing the Armée des Pyrénées. These seven armies ringed France, in an eastwards arc from Dunkirk circling clockwise right down to Bayonne. On 1 November a further decree split the Armée des Alpes into two new entities, the Armée de Savoie and the Armée d'Italie, later made so famous under Napoleon.

The new Armée des Ardennes received its baptism of fire at Latour on 22 October. The 5,000-man Avantgarde commanded by Lieutenant-général Jean-Baptiste Cyrus de Valence collided with a garrison of Austrian musketeers and jägers at the village of Latour, about 2 miles (3km) north of the French border in the south-eastern corner of the Austrian Netherlands. Bad weather forced a draw, which was repeated the next day at Virton, slightly to the west. By this time the garrison town of Longwy had been handed back over to the French by the retreating Prussians, and so the campaign season in the Ardennes theatre closed for the year.

But bad weather or not, Dumouriez was not going to let it stop his planned invasion of the Austrian Netherlands, a task that so occupied his mind it almost blinded him to other eventualities. His 45,000-strong Armée du Nord advanced from Valenciennes and crossed the frontier on 2 November, headed towards Mons. His Avantgarde was commanded by the youthful Maréchal de Camp Auguste Picot, Comte de Dampierre, comprising eleven battalions of line infantry, ten battalions of light infantry, seven light cavalry regiments and two companies of artillery, 22,000 men all told.

The Austrian forces in the Austrian Netherlands were commanded by the governor, Prince Albert von Sachsen-Teschen. He had over 20,000 men, albeit defending a long frontier. He had placed five grenadier battalions and four line infantry regiments around his headquarters at Mons, with fifteen companies of jägers employed close to the border to act as a kind of trip-wire. Another five infantry regiments were at the time en route from Namur to Mons. Two more infantry regiments, several companies of jägers and a regiment of hussars were deployed in an arc between Saint-Hubert and Dinant, with similarly-sized garrisons in Bury and Namur. But from dispositions, it is evident his major concern was in West Flanders. Three infantry regiments, two regiments of jägers and ten squadrons of light cavalry defended Tournai. Four infantry regiments, four companies of jägers and a regiment of uhlans (lancers) defended the region around Ypres. Six more infantry regiments and support services defended various fortresses in the interior, back from the frontier.

The first clash did not go well for the French. On 3 May the Chasseurs Belgiques (light infantry) and two squadrons of the 2e Hussards ran into an Austrian advanced post between the villages of Wilheries and Elonges. The inexperienced chasseurs were caught out in the open by the veteran Blankenstein Hussars and cut to pieces; 200 were killed and wounded and another fifty captured in a matter of minutes. The Avantgarde nonetheless completely outnumbered the small and isolated Austrian garrisons and so pressed on towards Mons as the Austrians withdrew. The following day they clashed with an Austrian brigade at Boussou, 2 miles (3km) further east along the high road to Mons. This time the superior French artillery decided the day, and the Austrians withdrew towards Mons having lost 350 men. Prince von Sachsen-Teschen was outnumbered by three- or four-to-one by the invading force, but could not give up Mons without a fight, for to possess Mons was to possess the high road to Brussels. He decided to defend the five-mile-long ridge running from Mons on his left to the village of Jemappes on the right. It was a stone's-throw from the site of the first action of the war on 28 April, six months earlier. Then, the French had panicked and ran at the first volley. Perhaps they would do so again. The only problem with the position was that the position backed onto a flood plain bordering the Trouille and Haine rivers, which involved crossing two causeways. The only practicable route for a retreat was through Mons.

The Austrians occupied the ridge and village of Jemappes with 11,600 infantry, 2,170 cavalry and 56 guns. Feldmarschalleutnant Franz Freiherr von Lilien commanded the right wing from the heights south of Jemappes, with 3,000 infantry and nearly 300 cavalry, including seven companies in the village itself. One of his brigades was commanded by the 21-year-old Generalmajor Archduke Karl von Österreich, Herzog von Teschen, younger brother of the Emperor Franz II. The centre was entrusted to Feldzeugmeister Clerfayt with 1,700 infantry and 600 cavalry, arrayed along the ridge. The left of the ridge was commanded by Feldmarschalleutnant Beaulieu, 3,000 infantry. Various other small units, mostly cavalry, held the vulnerable extreme left, which had the potential to be outflanked from the south. Two infantry regiments were kept in reserve in front of Mons. Twenty cannon in redoubts and regimental regimental guns (mostly small calibre) were arrayed along the ridge. Prince von Sachsen-Teschen had done the best possible with the available forces, but it was not going to be enough.

Dumouriez had 32,000 infantry, 3,800 cavalry and 100 guns, supported by another 4,000 men and fifteen guns under Lieutenant-Général

Louis-Auguste d'Harville. He had spotted the weakness in the Austrian left and planned an outflanking movement on his right, commanded by Lieutenant-Général Pierre de Ruel, marquis de Beurnonville, supported by d'Harville.

Beurnonville was to attack first and surround the weak Austrian left. His much stronger left wing under Maréchal de Camp Jean Marie Begais Ferrand was ordered to capture Jemappes on the Austrian right, after which Beurnonville would move left to attack the Austrian centre while d'Harville captured Mont Palisel in the Austrian rear, cutting off their retreat.

It all sounded good on paper, and with a three-to-one superiority, ought to have succeeded handsomely. For Napoleon, it would have been no more serious than the affair of a *déjeuner*. But Dumouriez was not Napoleon, and the battle was not well-managed.

After an artillery bombardment just after dawn on 6 November, the attacks on both flanks went in and soon ground to dead stops. On the French right Beurnonville failed to capture the villages which would have completed his outflanking movement. On the left Ferrand's men could not take Jemappes. Clerfayt was forced to reinforce the Austrian right wing, weakening the centre of the already slender line.

At noon a French attack went in all along line. Eight battalions in column from Beurnonville's right wing attacked the Austrian line on the ridge and captured five guns before being put to flight by the Coburg Dragoons. The gallant *Général Egalité* rallied a group of units, dubbed them 'the battalion of Mons' and re-directed them to the fight along with other units nearby, finally overcoming the outnumbered Austrians on the ridge. By this time Ferrand was making some headway around Jemappes, largely because some French troops had crossed the river Haine in boats to attack the Austrian positions from the rear. The Austrian right was forced to retreat across the river Trouille towards Mons, and the Austrian centre soon followed. The left wing remained in place long enough to cover the retreat, and then withdrew. The French left and centre did not mount a pursuit. It seems that d'Harville only arrived after the action was over and did not influence events.

The Austrians lost 305 dead and 513 wounded and missing. Another 423 men and five cannon were captured. The French lost about 650 dead and 1,300 wounded; despite the large superiority in forces they had only inflicted modest losses on the Austrians and failed to prevent them withdrawing in good order. Some French generals had been inspirational, the artillery was as professional as always, but the volunteer infantry had been reluctant and shaky in the advance. It was, perhaps, a modest French tactical victory, and by later Napoleonic standards would have been about as significant as (say) Roliça in 1808. But in the context of what had come before it, Jemappes caused a sensation. The Republican French army had beaten an army of European regulars and had forced them from the field. Confidence in Paris shot to new heights. The French had prevailed at Valmy by simply standing their ground. Jemappes proved the new French army could win if it initiated aggressive warfare by acting boldly. A new template had been discovered.

Mons opened its gates to the Republicans the following day. On 8 November the Austrian administration fled from Brussels and ordered the army to fall back on Liège. Dumouriez remained in Mons until 12 November, then advanced north on Brussels entering the city in triumph two days later. Thereafter the major fortresses of the Austrian Netherlands fell easily. On 17 November a French warship entered Ostend without opposition, and the French captured Mechelen on the road to Antwerp. Ten days later they occupied Liège. The last Austrian units evacuated the country on 28 November. Antwerp fell on 29 November, and Namur capitulated to the Armée des Ardennes after a three-week siege on 2 December.

Thus, the Austrian Netherlands belonged to Republican France on this date, but as a nation it was very different to France. Whilst glad to be free of their Austrian overlords, they found them replaced by plundering and ill-disciplined French volunteer units. In the next few months the Republicans managed to alienate the deeply conservative population, who did not share the same history, experiences or loathing of the established order as their neighbours to the south.

On 15 December the National Assembly in Paris decreed that all French Revolutionary institutions would apply equally in Belgium as they did in France. On 26 January 1793, it was decreed that Belgian troops should be integrated into the French army. By the end of January 1793, the only government in Belgium was the military one established by the French, and they planned to use the army to force the Belgians to vote for incorporation with France.[16]

Fraternity and Assistance
After the fall of Brussels, the National Convention was brimful of confidence. On 19 November 1792, it issued the famous Decree of Fraternity, and ordered that it be translated into and printed in other languages:

> The National Convention declares, in the name of the French nation, that it will grant fraternity and assistance to all people who wish to recover their liberty; and it charges the executive power to send the

necessary, orders to the generals to give assistance to such people, and to defend those citizens who have suffered or may suffer in the cause of liberty.[17]

These were eventful days in Paris. The following day the scandal of *l'armoire de fer* (the iron chest) broke. Allegedly an iron chest was found hidden behind wall panelling in the Tuileries Palace, containing a document which demonstrated the duplicity of the king's advisers and ministers, and implicated military men such as Dumouriez and Lafayette. Some documents were made public, others discretely destroyed. There are even theories that the chest was planted by Republicans to make the king's standing even more tenuous than it was. Either way, it had the intended effect. On 3 December, Pierre Robespierre addressed the National Convention: 'Neither prison nor exile can make public happiness indifferent to the existence of a dethroned king ... a king whose name alone attracts the scourge of war on an agitated nation ... I state with regret the fatal truth: Louis must die, because the country must live.'[18] It was decreed that Louis XVI should be tried by the National Convention.

King Louis's trial commenced on 11 December. His charges were read, all thirty-three of them, including the damning one, high treason. Louis was interrogated by the presiding officer Bertrand Barère de Vieuzac, being required to respond to and justify each charge. The king was granted a *conseil de défense*. He told his lawyers that he knew a guilty verdict was inevitable and that he would be executed but advised them to prepare and act as though they could win. He signed his Last Will on Christmas Day, before presenting his defence on 26 December: 'By speaking perhaps for the last time, I declare that my conscience does not reproach me, and that my defence counsel has told you the truth.'[19] This was the last time the king personally appeared at his trial. His pleaded not guilty on all thirty-three counts.

On 15 January 1793, the National Convention voted. The guilty verdict was as inevitable as the king had expected; 693 deputies voted for guilty, none for acquittal, and twenty-three abstained. The following day they voted on the punishment. 361 voted for immediate execution, 288 voted against death, while 72 voted for death only with certain delaying conditions and reservations. One of those who sensationally voted for the death penalty was the king's cousin, *Général Egalité*, the duc d'Orléans. Immediate execution won the day, by a margin of 361 votes to 360.

King Louis XVI was guillotined in the Place de la Révolution on Monday 21 January 1793. His corpse was buried in an unmarked grave in the Madeleine cemetery. Now no crown in Europe was safe. War between France and every monarchy in Europe seemed inevitable.

Chapter 3

War is at Our Very Door

Seditious Societies

'The King of France, Louis XVI, inhumanly & unjustly beheaded on Monday last by his cruel, blood-thirsty Subjects – Dreadful times I am afraid are approaching to all Europe – France the foundation of all of it – The poor King of France bore his horrid fate with manly fortitude & resignation – Pray God he may be eternally happy in thy heavenly Kingdom. And have mercy upon his Queen.'[1] So recorded a British parson in January 1793 upon hearing the news of the demise of King Louis XVI.

In the early part of the French Revolution Great Britain had looked upon events in France as intriguing; Britain and France had been traditional enemies since the thirteeth century. There was no love for the Bourbon dynasty in Britain, and many hoped their replacement might prove a more congenial neighbour. The mood swung the other way in late 1792 upon news of King Louis's arrest and trial. News of his execution brought crowds out onto London streets wearing black arm-bands and mourning clothes. Their neighbour, it appeared, had turned into a barbarian.

Prime Minister William Pitt (the Younger), a colourless 32-year-old workaholic, took swift action and immediately expelled the French Ambassador, Bernard-François, marquis de Chauvelin. He needed to be seen to be decisive; up until that point he had mis-read the seriousness of events on the continent. 'Unquestionably there never was a time in the history of this country,' he had declared in the House of Commons in February 1792, 'when, from the situation in Europe, we might more reasonably expect fifteen years of peace, than we may at the present moment.' He then cut back the annual budgets of both the army and Royal Navy, despite considerable opposition.[2] Radicals and reformers in coffee-shops and society meeting-houses across Britain had been delighted.

On 12 May 1792, Home Secretary, the Right Honourable Henry Dundas, arose in the House of Commons and delivered a message from King George, informing them that seditious practises had been carried on by societies in London. They had allegedly been in correspondence with other foreign societies, intent on assembling a convention to represent the people of England in defiance and opposition to Parliament. This, he pointed out, was on principles subversive of the laws and constitution of the kingdom, and 'introductory of the anarchy prevailing in France.' Their papers had been seized and would be laid before Parliament. He recommended all to examine them, and to adopt such measures as might appear necessary. The papers were produced on the following day. Pitt moved an address of thanks to the king for the communication received and proposed that the papers should be referred to a 'Committee of Secrecy' consisting of twenty-one members, chosen by ballot.

This committee met and produced a report three days later. It contained the proceedings of the two societies for the previous eighteen months. This was, however, not new information. Most of it had been already published in public newspapers by the societies themselves.

The king felt compelled to take action. Five days later he issued a proclamation aimed at stamping out the 'seditious societies' that had sprung up over Britain in the wake of the French Revolution:

> Whereas divers Writings have also been printed, published and industriously dispersed, recommending the said wicked and seditious Publications to the Attention of all Our faithful and loving Subjects: And whereas we have also Reason to believe that Correspondences have been entered into with sundry Persons in Foreign Parts, with a View to forward the criminal and wicked Purposes above mentioned ... We, therefore, being resolved, as far as in Us lies, to repress the wicked and seditious Practices aforesaid, and to deter all Persons from following so pernicious an Example, have thought fit, by the Advice of Our Privy Council, to issue this Our Royal Proclamation, solemnly warning all Our loving Subjects, as they tender their own Happiness, and that of their Posterity, to guard against all such Attempts, which aim at the Subversion of all regular Government within this Kingdom, and which are inconsistent with the Peace and Order of Society... And We do further charge and command all Our Sheriffs, Justices of the Peace, chief Magistrates in Our Cities, Boroughs and Corporations, and all other Our Officers and Magistrates throughout Our Kingdom of Great Britain, that they do, in their several and respective Stations, take the most immediate and effectual Care to suppress and prevent all Riots, Tumults and other Disorders, which may be attempted to be raised or made by any Person or Persons.[3]

This quelled the activities of these 'seditious societies', at least for a while. However almost six months later, on 19 November 1792, The National Convention in Paris issued their decree of 'fraternity and assistance,' as we have seen. The decree soon found its way into the English language and onto hand-bills and posters across the length and breadth of the British Isles.

The Militia is Called Out

There was at this time no police force in Great Britain, and only soldiers could keep the peace. But the army was small and mostly in overseas garrisons; it was dangerously thinly-spread at home. More policing required more troops. Out of sheer necessity on 1 December 1792, the King issued a proclamation embodying the English militia:[4]

> It is enacted, That it shall be lawful for Us … if no Parliament shall be then sitting, to order and direct the Drawing out and Embodying of Our Militia Forces, or any Part thereof … We therefore, being determined to exert the Powers vested in Us by Law for the Protection of the Persons Liberties and Properties of Our faithful Subjects… And We do hereby, in pursuance of the said recited Act, notify to all Our loving Subjects Our said Intention and the Causes and Occasion thereof.[5]

Mobilisation of the militia proceeded without delay. Militiamen were drawn by ballot – all men between the ages of 18 and 45 had to register in each parish, and a list of names was affixed to the door of the parish church – and when selected, serve full-time for twenty-eight days per year, or be permanently embodied in a time of national crisis. By the end of the month some 7,680 militiamen had assembled in England, with some 6,410 ordered embodied, 14,900 English and 1,849 Welsh not yet ordered, for a grand total of about 30,839 militiamen.

They did things differently in Scotland; at the beginning of March, seven Scottish fencible regiments (from the term 'defencible') were embodied. These were formed by the leading clan chiefs and landowners in the areas where they were recruited. A fencible regiment was also embodied on the Isle of Man.

That left Ireland. On 9 April 1793, The Catholic Relief Act was passed through the Irish Parliament in Dublin. It granted Catholics the franchise, so that all forty-shilling freeholders had the right to vote for members of Parliament. Almost all civil and military positions were opened to them, and they could enter Trinity College, Dublin, and obtain degrees. Higher classes of Catholics were allowed to carry arms. However, in order to have the benefit of the Act, they had to take the oath of allegiance. Despite these long sought-after reforms coming to fact, many restrictions remained. No Catholic could be Lord Lieutenant or Lord Chancellor; and no Catholic could sit in Parliament. Simultaneously, three other acts were passed; the Convention Act against unlawful assembly, intended to prevent meetings of delegates such as the 'Back-Lane Parliament';[6] the Gunpowder Act to prevent the importation and sale of gunpowder and arms (and Magistrates had the power to search for arms whenever and wherever they pleased); and the Irish Militia Act. This last was intended to raise 16,000 militiamen and to increase the army establishment in Ireland from 11,000 to 17,000 men. There was nothing sinister in this act. The 11,000 regular troops stationed in Ireland might be required to be withdrawn for the war with France, and therefore someone had to take their place.

People in Ireland misunderstood the Militia Bill. At the lowest level, they saw it as a way of leaving families fatherless at a time of crisis; some saw it as a way of providing Catholics to be led by Protestant officers in a foreign king's war. The Bill was not popular amongst the English community in Dublin, either. The government was seemingly 'arming the natives' who were often restless.

The first Irish militia was ordered to be embodied on 20 April. But then trouble started. Seven people were killed by dragoons at Carrick-on-Shannon in County Leitrim on 9 May, trying to liberate prisoners who had refused to take the militia oath. On 21 May the 41st Regiment of Foot was attacked by rioters near Manorhamilton in County Leitrim. The day of 30 May was particularly bad. An anti-militia riot occurred at Athboy (County Meath); ten were killed, twenty wounded. A similar riot in Enniskillen saw seven killed and 100 rioters taken prisoner. On 7 July, four soldiers and forty-six rioters were killed during a riot at Erris, County Mayo. The worst day of all was 11 July, when Major Charles Valotton and his garrison of fifty men of the 56th Foot in Enniscorthy, County Wexford, found themselves surrounded by a crowd of 2,000, who had earlier demanded that two rioters taken in earlier disturbances be released. If not, the rioters would attack the town. The troops immediately opened fire; eighty rioters were killed and five were later hanged.

The riots did not prevent the Irish militia regiments from forming. Where recruits were slow in coming forward, the government filled their places with volunteers, substitutes, and eventually, English and Scots volunteers. The Irish militia thereafter played its part in allowing the percentage of regular soldiers on the Irish establishment to be reduced, freeing regular regiments of the British army to act on the continent, should it come to that.

The Most Perfect Union

The term 'British Army' only came into being in 1707 due to the Acts of Union between England and Scotland, with the monarch as the titular Commander-in-Chief, to whom all ranks were expected to swear allegiance. But the monarch required Parliamentary consent to maintain a standing army in peace-time, thereby ensuring civilian rather than royal control of the nation's army.[7]

Civilian departments seeped their way into the military machine of Great Britain to support this policy. The army's rations were dispensed by a civilian Commissary-general. Troop movements at home were ordered by the Secretary-at-War's department (politicians and civil servants); troop movements abroad depended upon the (civilian) Transport Board, which provided merely the sea-borne transport – once ashore the troops depended upon transport provided by the (civilian) Commisssary-General. The same civilian mentality applied to the planning of military strategy. This indeed was the one area where a competent Commander-in-Chief ought to have come into his own, studying how the army might be applied to reinforce British foreign policy. But this rarely happened. Instead, the Secretary of State for Foreign Affairs planned campaigns in Europe, whilst the Home Secretary planned them in the colonies (or potential colonies). In February 1793, these posts were held by The Right Honourable William Grenville and The Right Honourable Henry Dundas respectively. Grenville was aged just 33, the son of a former Prime Minister and a cousin of Prime Minister William Pitt. Dundas was a 50-year-old Scottish barrister, a workaholic who liked to keep a finger in every pie, usually to the disadvantage of the fillings.

Despite the monarch holding the nominal title of Commander-in-Chief, it was customary in times of crisis to appoint someone to the post of Commander-in-Chief of the Forces of the Crown. The role of Captain-General had been created for Sir Thomas Fairfax after the outbreak of the English Civil War in 1645. The post gave him no military superior in the kingdom, and the ear of Parliament. His lieutenant general, Oliver Cromwell, succeeded him in 1650 and held the role until being appointed Lord Protector in 1653. George Monck assumed the post in 1660 (with the title of General-in-Chief Command, which included a seat in Cabinet) following the accession of King Charles II, and thereafter the role was intermittently filled, most notably by John Churchill, 1st Earl of Marlborough, from 1690 until 1691, and again from 1702 until 1708. There was no appointment between 1714 and 1744, from 1759 until 1766, or from 1769 until 1778.[8] Jeffery Amherst, a 61-year-old former Commander-in-Chief in North America with a dubious record that seemingly involved using biological warfare to exterminate the local tribes, was appointed in 1778. He resigned the post in 1782 and retired to his estate in Kent, probably expecting to see out his days as Colonel-in-Chief of the 2nd Troop of Horse Guards. His successor, General Henry Seymour Conway, served as Commander-in-Chief until his retirement on 21 January 1793 at the age of 71. His timing was inauspicious.

The by now, quite elderly Lord Amherst was appointed General on the Staff four days later with the new title of Commander-in-Chief of the Forces. As had always been the case, the post provided the appointee authority over discipline, supplies, training and promotions within the infantry and the cavalry, but no authority whatsoever over the artillery and engineers – they reported to the Master-General of the Ordnance – or any authority over the Royal Navy, which reported to the Admiralty.

But at the age of 76, Amherst had neither the energy nor the remaining wits to implement a common system of drill, let alone supplies or organisation. Every regimental colonel drilled his men as he saw fit, and any manoeuvre involving multiple units was a free-for-all of differing speeds, commands and formations; in fact, the opposite of what the duke had seen in Silesia. Promotions 'became the playthings of politics.'[9] Any cashed-up young gentleman could buy an officer's commission and work his way up through the ranks by purchasing the next available vacancy in a regiment; as a result, officers hopped their way between regiments as they greased their way up the seniority list. Eminent individuals organising complete regiments could find themselves starting their military careers with the rank of lieutenant-colonel, leap-frogging over hordes of older officers with twenty year's experience but little cash or influence.[10]

The military administration at Horse Guards revolved principally around two senior officers, who split between them the tasks involved in running the army. Lieutenant General William Fawcett, a 66-year-old Lancastrian was Adjutant-general to the Forces, responsible for discipline, strength returns, regulations and standing orders; whilst the truly ancient Lieutenant General George Morrison (aged 89) was Quartermaster-General to the Forces, responsible for quartering and accommodation of the army, movements and transportation. Local commanders-in-chief (usually lieutenant generals) commanded garrisons in the East Indies, West Indies, North America, Quebec, Lower Canada, and Gibraltar; whilst the Lord Lieutenant, a civilian post, commanded the garrisons in Ireland.

On 31 January Georges Danton rose to his feet in Paris and lashed the Convention with a fiery speech, 'Let us fling down to the Kings the head of a King as a gauge of battle!' He urged the deputies to decree an act of political union with the Belgians, who he believed 'were already one at heart with them'.[11] To do so would alienate the countries most concerned with preserving the Austrian Netherlands and turn them into enemies. Such as it was, the French Republic declared war against Great Britain and the United Provinces the following day. It was to be the sixth war between the two countries since 1702. News of the declaration arrived in London on 7 February. Four days later William Pitt rose to his feet in the Commons: 'The event is no longer in our option, for War has not only been declared, it is at our very door.'

Their attention turned to the army. But the army was not exactly in a state of war-time readiness. Of the regiments of household cavalry, the Life Guards, had not seen action since 1743, nor the Royal Horse Guards since 1762. One of the seven regiments of Dragoon Guards had not been on active service since as long ago as 1695. Three of the twenty dragoon regiments had never seen active service at all, while another three had last drawn their blades in the Jacobite Rebellion of 1746. Britain's 79 infantry regiments of the line were mostly dotted around the globe. Eleven were in Canada, twenty-three in Ireland, sixteen in the West Indies, eight in the East Indies, the rest Gibraltar, the Channel Islands, Scotland and New South Wales. The forty companies of Royal Artillery were similarly dispersed.

Only ten line infantry regiments were available in England for any kind of service – the 2nd, 3rd, 11th, 14th, 25th, 29th, 30th, 54th, 57th and 59th – and the majority were re-building after prolonged service overseas. Most were cantoned in towns and villages, there being few regular barracks at this time.[12]

The 2nd (Queen's), 11th, 25th, 29th and 30th had been ear-marked for service aboard ships of the Royal Navy to do duty as marines, and so were camped outside harbourside towns. The 57th Foot was headquartered in Tynemouth in Northumberland, too far away for easy movement to the continent, whilst the 54th and 59th were en route to Guernsey and Jersey respectively. This left the 3rd and 14th as the only possible employable units.

The whole of Scotland was defended by four infantry regiments; the 19th, 37th, 42nd and 53rd, of which the 42nd (the Black Watch) were very far north at Fort George and in various widely-spread garrisons across the highlands. The availability of the cavalry was better overall, with thirteen regiments 'at home' in England and two in Scotland. But other than the Life Guards (who rarely left London), all were cantoned in cities and market-towns the length and breadth of the isle, acting, as was customary at home, as the nation's proxy police force.

Only 3,990 line infantrymen, 2,933 Foot Guards and 2,769 cavalrymen were available in England and Scotland.[13] This was Lilliputian by comparison with France, Austria and Prussia; and vastly inferior in quality to the latter two. Whitehall 'solved' this issue the day after war was declared by increasing the establishments of infantry regiments from 355 men to 850 men.[14] This solved nothing; it merely meant that every infantry regiment suddenly had to recruit, train, house and feed an additional 495 men, plus officers in proportion.[15] In desperation regiments turned a blind eye to many a man's age, criminal record or deformities in their haste to get them into red coats.[16]

Pitt and Grenville then got down to the business of forming alliances. A treaty with Hanover was signed on 4 March for 15,000 men, to be augmented by 5,000 more in January 1794. A commercial treaty was agreed with Russia in London on 25 March 1793, promising trade restrictions against France but no troops. On 25 April a treaty was signed with Sardinia in which the King of Sardinia promised to keep on foot an army of 50,000 men during the war, receiving a subsidy of £200,000 per annum.[17] Great Britain was to send a fleet into the Mediterranean in return.

A month later Spain signed a commercial agreement in which both countries were to shut their ports against French vessels and to prevent neutral vessels from aiding French commerce. A treaty with the King of the Two Sicilies on 12 July required them to provide 6,000 soldiers, four ships of the line, and four smaller vessels, in return for which Great Britain undertook to maintain a respectable fleet in the Mediterranean. Then came the two big ones. A treaty between Great Britain and Prussia was signed at the camp before Mainz on 14 July, for the 'most perfect union and confidence in carrying on the war against France', subsequently converted into a treaty of subsidies. Then came a treaty signed at London on 30 August between Great Britain and the Holy Roman Emperor. Portugal entered the Coalition by a treaty signed at London on 26 September, in which it undertook to shut its ports against the French during the war. Treaties for troops were also concluded with some of the smaller German States. The Spaniards decided to join the Coalition upon hearing the news of the execution of a fellow Bourbon monarch; the French Ambassador was dismissed, and the Convention in Paris unanimously declared war against Spain on 7 March 1793.

The primary British war aim was not to quell the Republicans and place the hated Bourbons back on the throne; far more practical goals were uppermost. The French must be kept out of the United Provinces, and Channel ports must be protected so as not to endanger trade. The fall of the United Netherlands might mean the loss of the Cape of Good Hope as a friendly victualling port on the sea route to the East Indies. It was clear from the outset therefore that any British expeditionary force could always be expected to occupy the right flank of the line in the Austrian Netherlands, protecting West Flanders and the Channel ports. Neither Austria nor Prussia shared these strategic concerns, however:

> Austria pursued the war with France chiefly with the object of gaining Bavaria and parts of Eastern France, Belgium (with Lille and Valenciennes) being allotted to the Elector uprooted at Munich. Prussia and Russia promised to abet this scheme as a set-off to their prospective plunder of Poland; but, obviously, after securing their booty in the summer of 1793, they had no interest in aggrandizing the House of Hapsburg. Further, England entered on the Flemish campaign with motives widely different from those of Austria. Pitt and Grenville sought to plant her more firmly at Brussels by girdling her with the fortresses of French Flanders; but she sought to recover Belgium only to fling it to the Elector. Finally neither Russia nor the German Powers cared an iota about the security of Holland. Their eyes were fixed on Warsaw or Munich. In truth, despite all their protestations as to the need of re-establishing the French monarchy, they were mainly bent on continuing the territorial scrambles of former years. The two aims were utterly incompatible.[18]

The war aims of all parties being at cross-purposes as they were, Pitt and Grenville nevertheless constructed the First Coalition. Their strategic aims being so diverse, the term 'coalition' is almost a misnomer. It was an alliance held together by the frayed ropes of national self-interest. On paper, the armies of this coalition numbered some 314,000 men. With such forces arrayed against a France in disarray, Pitt declared, the war could not last long.

Prime Minister William Pitt – in common with his 1914 counterparts - mistakenly believed that the war would be short. He underestimated France's sense of patriotic identity, and the esprit de corps of her citizen armies. His financial measures were based upon short-term thinking, as indeed was British strategic thinking for many years to come. The plan to defeat revolutionary France rested on three strategic pillars; firstly, supporting European allies – Austria, Prussia, the United Provinces and Hanover – with cash and troops; secondly, using the Royal Navy to capture French colonies; and thirdly, offering practical aid to opponents of the Revolution, many within France itself.

Chapter 4

The First Coalition Force

Led by a Single Will
The wars that lasted from 1793 until 1815 were known, in nineteenth century Britain, as the 'Great War'. That is, before the name fell out of fashion at the end of the Victorian era and was later appropriated for what we now know as the First World War, at least up until 1939. But in France they were called *Guerres de Coalitions*, in Germany *Koalitionskriege*, and in the Netherlands *Coalitieoorlogen*; the Wars of the Coalitions. For there were in fact seven coalitions arrayed against France in the period. The first two ran from 1792 until 1797, then from 1798 until the Peace of Amiens in 1801. The next four were face-to-face with Napoleon as the ruler of France and contained the momentous campaigns of Austerlitz (1805), Jena and Friedland (1807), Wagram (1809) and the campaign in France (1813 to 1814).[1] The seventh coalition was the shortest, lasting from March to July 1815 and incorporating the Waterloo campaign. Twenty-two empires, nations, or nation-states participated in the various coalitions, but only one was present in all seven; Great Britain.[2]

The French Republic declared war against the United Provinces on 1 February 1793, the same day as against Great Britain, and against Spain (also ruled by the Bourbons) on 7 March. Portugal joined the First Coalition by signing a treaty with Spain in July. The Holy Roman Empire joined on 23 March, Naples in September, and Tuscany in October. The United States declared itself neutral on 22 April.

As we have seen, the first foreign contingent to fall in beside Austria and Prussia in the First Coalition was the Armée de Condé, a French émigré force commanded by Louis Joseph de Bourbon, Prince de Condé, a cousin of King Louis. Senior commanders within the army included the prince's grandson the Duc d'Enghien, and the two sons of Louis XVI's younger brother, the Comte d'Artois. Thus, the army was sometimes referred to as the Prince's Army.[3] Family connections meant everything. The new Emperor Franz II was a nephew (by marriage) of Louis XVI; Wilhelm IX of Hessen-Cassel was cousin to King George III of Great Britain and Hanover, and to the stadtholder Willem V of the United Provinces; Willem V was also a cousin to King George. The phrase 'the enemy of my enemy is my friend' held as firm and true in 1793 as it did in 1914.

Nations allied to the signatories soon found themselves involved in the action. In October 1792, as the Austro-Prussian army started its retreat from Valmy and the fortress of Mainz capitulated, soldiers on leave were summoned back to their regiments in the nearby Electorate of Hanover. Hanover occupied a unique position on the continent. It was ruled by King George III of Great Britain, a monarch who never visited this part of his domain. Yet it was also one of the select number of German states forming the electoral colleges that chose the Holy Roman Emperor. The fact that the vote was a foregone conclusion – the electors always chose a member of House of Habsburg, the ruling house of Austria as Emperor – did not diminish this exalted responsibility. And part of this responsibility was to provide troops for the emperor's wars, as well as for King George.

A German-born Austrian, Feldmarschall Friedrich Josias von Sachsen-Coburg-Saalfeld[4] was nominated Commander-in-Chief of Coalition forces in Germany. He duly ordered the Hanoverian Ministry to set their expected contingent (nearly 4,000 men) on the march to join him. He did not like the reply he received from Hanover:

> That His Majesty [King George] had already placed his contingent in marching order, but seeing the incredible dilatoriness of formation of the national [coalition] army, thought he had the best reasons for making use of his own army corps, which His Majesty had ordered to march to defend the United Netherlands from the danger which threatens them, whereby in the holding and repelling of the common enemy, it (the army corps) would do the greatest immediate service to the German fatherland.[5]

King George had determined to place a British army in the Austrian Netherlands, and to include in this an Auxiliary Corps of approximately 13,000 Hanoverian troops in British pay. Prussia made vigorous efforts to make the Hanoverians march to the Rhine instead. But that was not in Britain's interests, and King George replied that: 'he would only let his contingent advance with a national army, to which all states contributed; moreover, that he did not recognise the "protective" policy of the Allied Powers (Austria and Prussia) in their operations.'[6] The First Coalition was already an unstable one. 'After long negotiations, protracted through the jealousy of divided interests, and mutual mistrust of the Powers, after the lamentable issue of the campaign of 1792, the great coalition against the French Republic was called into existence in the early part of 1793.'[7]

The French strategic situation to the north at the end of 1792 was this. Dumouriez and his Armée de la Belgique (his private name for his portion of the Armée du Nord) was to act against Holland and Cleves, with 62,000 men. The Armée de la Moselle (also 62,000) was to lay siege to Coblenz. The Armée du Rhin (also 62,000) was to commence operations in Swabia. A reserve of 25,000 men was to be concentrated at Châlons. Dumouriez had planned to conquer the Dutch whilst keeping Great Britain neutral, always a slim hope at best. This neutrality was purloined when France declared war on Great Britain. One of the National Convention's first military edicts was to order him to overrun the United Provinces. His original plan was to send two columns north, one under his own command to take Maestricht, whilst Miranda laid siege to Venlo, after which both armies would join and advance to capture Nijmegen.

The Coalition forces for the re-conquest of Belgium at the start of 1793 looked impressive. On or near the Rhine were 55,000 Austrians under Prince Coburg, flanked by 11,000 Prussians commanded by General Friedrich Augustus, Prince of Brunswick-Wolfenbüttel-Oels, and 13,000 Hanoverians, destined for Gelderland. In reserve were 33,000 Prussians under General Friedrich Ludwig Hohenlohe-Ingelfingen. King Friedrich Wilhelm of Prussia marshalled near Frankfurt a force of 42,000 of his own troops together with 14,000 other German allies. Further south was the Imperial Army of the Rhine, General der Kavallerie Dagobert Sigmund von Wurmser with 24,000 Austrians. The constituent minor states of the Holy Roman Empire had promised a force of 120,000, and further east loomed the Russians.

The Coalition met in Frankfurt at the start of February and agreed that the newly-appointed Austrian commander, Prince Coburg, should march to the relief of Maestricht immediately with 40,000 men. Meanwhile the Prussians had advanced from Aachen and reinforced the Austro-Dutch-émigré garrison of Maestricht. This caused Dumouriez to change his plans. He ordered Miranda to lay siege to that place while he led an expeditionary force (which he dubbed l'Armée de Hollande) aimed at Dort (Dordrecht), which could then drive directly north towards Amsterdam.

A Coalition army of Austrian, Prussian, Dutch and English-Hanoverian-Hessian forces was to assemble along the Franco-Belgian frontier, approximately along the line from Valenciennes to Dunkirk. Under the overall command of Coburg, the Austrians, far and away the largest contingent, were commanded by Feldzeugmeister Clerfayt and the young Archduke Karl. This 'Imperial Army' had 142,000 infantry in sixty-two regiments, 11,000 jagers (light infantry), and 21,000 cavalry in 206 squadrons. This was a considerable force, for the most part experienced and well-trained; the cavalry was particularly good. The Imperial weakness was leadership. Austrian generals tended to be slow and timid; fear of displeasing the emperor usually outweighed any dashing displays of initiative. Attached to the Imperial army was a division-sized force of 6,000 émigrés commanded by the Prince de Condé, and a Saxon legion of 3,500 infantry and 1,500 cavalry.

The Prussians also had an impressive contingent. Under Generalleutnant Alexander von Knobelsdorff (who had recently assumed command from the sick Karl, Duke of Brunswick), they comprised 50,000 infantry and 13,000 cavalry in ninety squadrons. The infantry adhered to the precise and highly-disciplined military theories of Frederick the Great. It was a wonderful army to look at, but like the Austrians, usually let down by their leaders, as was the case at Valmy.

Frederick, Duke of York, was to command the Anglo-Hanoverian-Hessian army. Britai's contribution was to be paltry, 2,000 Guardsmen at the start, shortly rising to 4,200 infantry and 3,000 cavalry. Their Hanoverian allies (7,600 infantry and 2,500 cavalry) were led by the 73-year-old Feldmarschall Wilhelm von Freytag. On his staff was the 19-year-old Prince Adolphus, Duke of Cambridge, seventh son of King George. The Hessians, a contingent from the tiny German landgrave of Hessen-Cassel were yet to join. These soldiers-for-hire were a contingent of 8,000 men commanded by Generalmajor Ludwig von Wurmb. The Dutch contingent was commanded by their monarch, Willem V, Prince of Orange-Nassau. It was a token force of 1,200 infantry and 3,000 cavalry.[8]

The French suffered no problems of multiplicity of language, command structure or political motivation. They were led by a single will, that of the National Convention; and powered by most active arm, the Committee of Public Safety. Facing the Coalition along the Belgian frontier was the Armée du Nord under the vain and ambitious Lieutenant-général Dumouriez. He had 40,000 regular infantry, 6,500 chasseurs (light infantry), 106,000 Gardes Nationale and Fédérés,[9] 9,000 Volontaires de la réserve, 10,000 heavy cavalry and 18,000 light cavalry. To his right he was supported by the Armée des Ardennes

(25,000 men) with the strong Armée de la Moselle (66,000 men) farther east.[10] These impressive numbers conceal the fact that morale was low and desertions commonplace. The men had been neither paid nor provisioned properly for months. They were lacking 30,000 pairs of shoes, 25,000 blankets and camp equipment for 40,000. In December 1792 alone, 60,000 men packed up and headed for home.[11] Training and discipline in the newly-raised units were sketchy. The line regiments did not trust the new republican units, and vice versa. The regulars had great difficulty recruiting, since most preferred to join the new volunteer regiments, where the pay was better and the term of service shorter. The line regiments retained their *ancien régime* white uniforms, but the republican units dressed in whatever was at hand, more often than not civilian clothing.

Hanover and Hessen-Cassel

These internal problems generally did not exist within the Coalition contingents, but they did have other issues. An order was received in Hanover from London to have the Hanoverian contingent in marching order by 15 March. Many regiments were under-strength, and additional recruits were hurriedly drafted in, some taken from regiments that were not marching, but mostly numbers were made up by recently recruited peasants.

In most respects the Hanoverian army was a replica of the British, the infantry dressed in red eighteenth-century style open-fronted coats with different facing colours per regiment. Officers and NCOs wore yellow sashes. The Leibgarde-Cavallerie-Regiment wore red coats, but all other cavalry wore dark blue. Artillery wore dark blue coats with red facings. All troops except grenadiers wore bicorne hats; grenadiers were distinguishable by their bearskin caps. The White Horse of Hanover adorned their colours. The 14.Infanterie-Regiment was a light battalion, dressed in grey trimmed with dark green, with Corsican hats turned up on the left side; the light infantrymen carried short-barralled muskets.

Regimental organisation followed the German model rather than the British. The Hanoverian force eventually sent to the Austrian Netherlands included four 'combined' cavalry regiments (four squadrons each of 150 men.)[12] The infantry comprised six infantry regiments of two battalions, each with four musketeer companies of 156 men. In addition, three combined grenadier battalions (four companies each of 176 men) provided an elite element. The two battalions of Garde-Regiment zu Fuß (Foot Guards) and two battalions of the 10.Infanterie-Regiment donated their grenadier companies to form the 1.Grenadier-Bataillon. Combined Grenadier battalions had four companies each of 158 men.

The Hanoverian artillery was organised into a regiment of two battalions each of five companies. Two companies were horse artillery batteries, and the remaining eight companies were used to form four heavy batteries. The Hanoverian contribution was therefore much stronger than the British expeditionary force at the outset. Their cavalry was particularly good, expert in outpost duties and renowned for the quality and care of their mounts.

Hessen-Cassel was probably the most militaristic state in Europe, even more so than Prussia, whose influence was obvious. Indeed Hessen-Cassel, like Prussia, could be described as 'not a country with an army, but an army with a country.' The mercenaries of the landgraviate dressed nearly identically to the Prussians, in open-fronted dark blue coats with various regimental facings. Officers and NCOs wore crimson and silver sashes. Grenadiers wore tall metal mitre caps, fusiliers had similar caps but shorter, and musketeers sported tricornes. Each regiment comprised one battalion of grenadiers (four companies) and two of musketeers, but the grenadiers were always detached and combined into converged grenadier battalions. The dragoons were dressed in light blue, with large bicorne hats, whereas the *gensd'armes* wore white coats, and the *kuirassiers* straw yellow. Artillerymen wore dark blue faced red. The army of this tiny state was solid, disciplined and professional. The green-coated Jäger-Bataillon was particularly good; the cavalry reliable but on the whole not as good as the Chevauxlegers and Garde du Corps of their Hessen-Darmstadt neighbours.

Guardian Angels
Sir William Eden, Ambassador to the United Provinces,[13] wrote to Pitt on 15 February 1793 and requested that the Duke of York come to the Netherlands, without troops if necessary, to take command of the Dutch Army.[14] The following day, the French invasion started, as they advanced north from Antwerp. The Dutch fell back to the line of the River Maas, and the first major action was fought five days later when a division of the Armée du Nord under the elderly Maréchal de camp Jean Claude d'Arçon besieged Breda. The garrison, commanded by Major General Alexander van Bijlandt, put up a lethargic resistance and surrendered three days later.[15] The fortress at Gertruydenberg on the edge of the Biesbosch wetlands capitulated on 4 March. Dumouriez was now only 60 miles (96km) south of Amsterdam.

The news from the United Provinces was all bad, and swift action was needed in London. King George, as head of the army and navy, had the right to conduct foreign policy, but he needed Parliament to pay all the expenses. The king insisted that his second son should be appointed to the command; Prime Minister William Pitt, Foreign Secretary Lord Grenville and Home Secretary Henry Dundas all agreed, although with some reservations. Therefore, command of the first tiny British expeditionary force was given to Prince Frederick, Duke of York and Albany. The duke was 29-years-old, and still to see a shot fired in anger. Such decisions might shock the population and lead to cries of favouritism today. But it was still fairly common in the eighteenth century for a Prince of the Royal Blood to command armies on the continent.[16] Especially given that other commanders in the multi-nationality Coalition were of similar social rank. It would be very difficult for a commoner to reprimand or criticise a prince for a perceived failing – a problem that Marlborough often encountered. In addition, the duke had close personal contacts and relationships with the leading figures in the Prussian and Austrian armies, not to mention a good understanding of how they operated. He had spent seven years engaging with the best military staff system in Europe, and spoke and read excellent German, which could not be under-estimated. His personal staff, called his 'family', was carefully hand-picked. As an antidote to his inexperience he was given the assistance of his old mentor from his childhood days, the commander of the Brigade of Guards, Major General Gerard Lake. Lake was a 48-year-old ramrod-straight Guardsman and an early advocate of total war. He had been a soldier for 35 years during which he had seen active service in Germany and at Yorktown.

An anonymous account of the early months of the war (probably from an officer of the Guards) recorded as follows:

> The royal assent was obtained for the embarkation of a detachment from the Brigade of Foot-Guards, about one o'clock, on Wednesday the 20th of February, 1793; and the Duke of York having ordered the seven Battalions to parade in St. James' Park, informed them it was his Majesty's pleasure, that three Battalions should go upon foreign service, and that consequently many men would be wanted from the second Battalions to complete the first. His Royal Highness added, that he did not wish to have any of them drafted, but desired such as were willing to serve, under his immediate command, would turn out volunteers; the whole Brigade, to a man, immediately advanced with a regular step.[17]

Britain's army had fought in North America from 1775 until 1783 without a single household regiment seeing active service.[18] But now the three Guards regiments were to form the leading element of a British commitment to the Continent. The Guards were the only troops fit to send overseas. 'For so minute was this force at the outset,' Alfred Burne writes, 'that it could be contained within the limits of Horse Guards Parade.'[19] The command had been so sudden that officers serving outside of London on recruiting duty barely had time to re-join their regiments. The companies of the Guards were augmented, by re-allocating the best men from companies staying at home, to four serjeants, four corporals, two drummers and fifty-six privates per company.[20] At 06.00 hours on the morning of Monday 25 February, the Brigade of Guards, commanded by Lake, was reviewed by the king in Saint James' Park, and then marched from London to Greenwich.[21] Though Guardsmen, they were far from perfect:

> Had you witness'd the scene, you'd have thought, I am sure,
> Of Hogarth's, this march was a caricature;
> Prim'd with Whitbreads's Entire, and their bosom-friend gin,
> By driblets our men join'd their squads, to fall in…
> Our march was retarded by whiskeys and gigs,
> Mad drivers, mad oxen, and obstinate pigs;
> Men boxing, dogs barking, and women in tears,
> Harsh concert that threaten'd the drums of our ears.[22]

The brigade boarded transports via the Hospital Stairs at Greenwich, then dropped down to Long Reach and waited patiently for the tide. The transports weighed anchor the following morning at about 11.00 hours and dropped down the river to Nore. The open sea was not reached until the morning of 1 March, when the transports, accompanied by the fifth-rate frigate HMS *Iris*, sixth-rate frigate HMS *Lizard* and ship-sloop HMS *Racehorse*, entered the Channel. The transports were in very bad shape. Harry Calvert observed:

> It is much to be lamented that the first observation that must occur to every officer employed on this service, is the very unfit state the transports were in for the reception of troops, and the very small provision that was made for their health and accommodation while on board. The tonnage of the ships was so inadequate to the numbers embarked, that every bad consequence was to be apprehended had it been necessary to put on the hatches, which must have been the case had we not made Helvoet[sluys] before the gale of wind came on. There was no small species of provisions on board; no vinegar (that most essential preservative); and, lastly, neither medicines nor surgical instruments.[23]

Things only got worse at sea. An anonymous diarist recorded:

> Those on board [transport] of which, the first detachment from the brigade of guards was embarked, were peculiarly uncomfortable; the men were stowed in the holds in such numbers, that one third of them were constantly obliged to keep on deck at night, to afford the others a sufficient space to breathe freely; and the officers (though their situation is by no means of so much consequence, as they command a thousand little comforts beyond the reach of the private soldier) had only one small cabin in each vessel amongst about seven of them, on the floor of which, unable to throw off their clothes, they rested every night, wedged close together.[24]

By the evening of 1 March, the fleet was just north of Helvoetsluys. The Guards did not actually embark until noon on 4 March, when seven companies of the 3rd Foot Guards marched to Brill, and five companies of the Coldstreams occupied Helvoetsluys.[25] By this time, the command party, which had travelled much more luxuriously, was well and truly ashore. The Duke of York and his staff had disembarked at Den Haag in Flanders on 27 February and set up headquarters. His aides included a future divisional commander at Waterloo, 21-year-old Lieutenant Henry Clinton of the 1st Foot Guards, who wrote to his father on 28 February:

> The arrival of the transports is of the greatest consequence at this very sensitive moment, not so much on account of the force they contain, but from the effect our assistance has on the minds of the panic-struck Hollanders who look upon the English as their Guardian Angels.[26]

The duke had his orders, issued at the Court of St. James on 23 February, and they were oddly-worded:

> You will endeavour to as far as you can, to avoid dividing our said Troops, or placing them in the Frontier garrisons of the said Provinces. Nevertheless, in this respect you are at liberty to act as you shall judge best … You will conform yourself as exactly as possible to the tenor of our instructions given to General Lake.[27]

This was extraordinary. The duke had not seen Lake's instructions, and was to conform with instructions given only to a subordinate? He had to wait three days to find out what they were. General Lake and his retinue landed at Helvoetsluys on 2 March. It turned out that Lake's instructions forbade any operations in places 'the distance of which would prevent you from retiring hither [Helvoetsluys] in four and twenty hours after receiving an order for that purpose.'[28] In other words, do not advance more than a day's march away in any direction. His expeditionary force was to be constrained like a dog tethered to a post, in a country they had come to help save. But a secret letter sent the same day to Lake was even more extraordinary:

> Lord Auckland has been directed to communicate confidentially to the Members of the Dutch Government these Instructions, that they may be apprized of the limitations under which the Force which you command is to be employed. It may be very material that these limitations should not be known, and therefore you will be particularly careful to withhold the knowledge of them from any persons but the Prince of Orange, the Grand Pensionary and Lord Auckland, or those who may be confidentially employed by them, to concert with you the means of rendering your force as useful as possible.[29]

The duke, excluded from knowledge about the geographical restrictions upon his own force, hurried with his staff to The Hague to meet the stadtholder, Willem V, Prince of Orange-Nassau. He was astounded by what he discovered. 'I found everybody here in the greatest consternation at the news which just arrived of the Surrender of Breda, through the cowardice of the governor,' he wrote.[30] No doubt the prince was aware of the secret 'limitation' placed upon the British force and believed that they might sail back across the Channel at the slightest upset. He was also faced with the fact was that the United Provinces was in political disarray and few of his people believed the French were the enemy. The Orange-Nassau dynasty was unpopular and Republican ideals had thoroughly permeated the lower classes:

> The country ... is perfectly easy to be defended, the only danger arises from two causes, first from the irresolutions of the Prince, and from an unfortunate jealousy of his authority ... and that no one thing can be done without a written order from him, which from hurry he very often forgets to sign ... and secondly from the astonishing alarm which prevails.[31]

The general sentiment of the population made in impression upon staff officer Harry Calvert:

> On our arrival at Helvoet, we could not, without much surprise, observe the perfect tranquillity of that town, and the little preparation for defence, when we were within hearing of the enemy's guns before Willemstadt ... The cause of this total want of energy was supposed by many to be the disaffection of the people to

the Stadtholder; and the shameful surrender of Breda appeared to give grounds for this idea. When we reached Dort, there appeared to be some degree of satisfaction among the people; but we have since that time been informed that, a very few days before our arrival, there were not in the town above twenty adherents to the Stadtholder; and the difficulty we met with in providing quarters for our troops, indicated that there was no great predilection for us on the part of the inhabitants. The town of Dort is rich and very populous but has no fortifications.[32]

On 3 March, the duke persuaded William V to appoint his 19-year-old son Frederik, the hereditary Prince of Orange-Nassau to command troops between Grave and the North Sea. Then the duke went on a tour of the outposts with Prince Frederik, arriving at Dort on 6 March. Once there he heard that the fortress at Gertruydenberg had fallen, and so ordered the Guards down from Helvoetsluys. The Guards had only finished disembarkation the previous day – just in time to beat severe gales which a day earlier could have dispersed the entire fleet – and proceeded up the River Maas aboard small craft, arriving at Dort late in the day. Corporal Brown of the 3rd Foot Guards was struck by the locals:

> The streets are regular and kept remarkably clean, as well as the outside of their houses, which they are continually washing. But if we were struck with the neat appearance and cleanliness of the streets, and outside of the houses, we were much more so upon seeing the inside, where every article of furniture, whether for use or ornament, is kept in a state of cleanliness and regularity far exceeding anything we have been accustomed to see in England. The country round the town is very pleasant, being covered with gentlemen's seats and delightful gardens, watered by small rivulets cut from the rivers and canals. Two fine yachts were moored here, on board of which the Duke of York and the Prince of Orange slept.[33]

Whilst all this was going on, Maréchal de Camp Sebastián Francisco de Miranda laid siege to Maestricht with 25,000 men. But then Prince von Coburg and his 40,000 men crossed the Ruhr and caught the French advanced guard completely unaware at Aldenhoven on 1 March. The skirmish demonstrated that the French armies of 1793 were no better than 1792. Two Austrian cavalry regiments, the Nr.31 Chevauxlegers 'Graf Baillet Latour' and Nr.32 Husaren 'Esterhazy' – less than 1,000 horsemen –attacked the French reserve, killed and wounded 2,000 and captured 300, taking seven cannon and two colours. It was a fiasco. Miranda raised the siege of Maestricht, and by 3 March the French were flying in disorder westward towards Louvain and Diest.

The following day the French were driven from Liège. Perhaps 10,000 men deserted; but again, the Austrians were slow to pursue, and so the French were able to re-group. Dumouriez, who was still in Biesbosch country, hurried to his defeated and retiring army in Belgium. He rallied them at Louvain on 13 March and considered the best way to restore morale was to go on the offensive. His battered Armée du Nord took some encouragement from a successful clash with the Austrian Avantgarde (commanded by the Archduke Karl) at Tirlemont on 16 March, resulting in an Austrian retirement; but as in 1792, it looked very much as if the French volunteers were no match for the professional armies of the Coalition.

Chapter 5

Phoney War

A Convenient Place to Assemble an Army

The Duke of York's headquarters received news of the French defeat at Maestricht on 8 March and knew that the enemy had retired beyond Liège. In London, the news brought renewed optimism. Harry Calvert wrote to his uncle on 17 March, musing over where the campaign may be headed:

> The retreat of the French, and the success of the allies in Brabant, give a new face to the war. I shall be much obliged to you, if you will write me word what is the general opinion in England in regard to our destination. Are we to guard the Dutch frontiers, or to join the allies, and drive the French out of Brabant; and in that case are we to push the war to French Flanders, or on the evacuation of the Dutch provinces, is the object of our expedition completed?[1]

Spirits were high in the Coalition camp; maybe the war really could be over in six months? The Dutch population certainly did not seem too worried. Calvert was constantly amazed by the indolence and indifference of the Dutch to the situation around them:

> The hereditary Prince of Orange lived entirely on board his yacht, very seldom came on shore, and never visited the batteries erected for the defence of the island. This conduct appeared very extraordinary, when his presence was particularly necessary to animate and encourage his friends and adherents. We could not remark, without astonishment, that at this time, when the enemy were within so short a distance, no association was formed for the defence of the town, or attempt made to raise men for that purpose. It appeared yet more unaccountable to me, that some sort of defences were not erected on the dykes leading from the town to the extremities of the island, which, in case the enemy should make good their landing, would enable the British troops to defend the town till they were sufficiently reinforced to drive the enemy from the island.[2]

Worse was to come for the Armée du Nord. With the National Convention and indeed Dumouriez's own character demanding he fight a decisive action, the French turned to face the Austrians on 18 March near the village of Neerwinden, about 5 miles (8km) south-east of Tirlemont. Dumouriez had about 43,000 men to Coburg's 41,000, which included six Dutch battalions. The Austrian position extended from the Tirlemont-Maastricht road in the north to the villages of Neerwinden and Oberwinden on the Austrian left. Assuming the Austrians would be strongest on their right (the road being their supply line), he therefore planned to attack in force against their left. His split his army into eight columns, an unwieldy arrangement and difficult to coordinate. Three columns on the right were to outflank Oberwinden, attack the village head-on and capture the hill between the villages. The two central columns were ordered to attack Neerwinden. Maréchal de Camp de Miranda was ordered to use his three columns on the left to capture the village of Leau and attack along the high road.

The attack on the right began at dawn, with mixed success. The capture of the hill took until noon, whilst Neerwinden was captured early, abandoned, then re-captured by the Duc de Chartres, only to be driven out again. After some confusion due to a clash between columns, Oberwinden was captured by the French then retaken by Clerfayt. An Austrian cavalry attack on the hill in the afternoon forced the French to pull back.

By the end of the day the two sides occupied more or less the same positions in the south as at the start of the day. The attacks on the left started much later and mostly failed. Miranda began his attacks around noon, capturing the village of Dorsmael, but a determined Austrian counterattack soon re-captured it. The second column attacked the division of the Archduke Karl in a strong position on the Austrian right but failed to make any headway. An attack by Austrian troops from Dorsmael sent it into retreat. The final attack, against the village of Leau, ended in failure when the Austrian second line came into action and forced Miranda to retire his three columns back across the river pursued by the Austrians, exposing the left flank of the other five columns. Realisation dawned on Dumouriez that with the collapse of his left, he was isolated in front of Neerwinden, and retreat was his only option.

The day had not gone well for the Armée du Nord. One general officer (artillery commander Guiscard de Bar) was killed, four brigade commanders were wounded, 4,000 men had been killed and wounded, 1,000 men missing and captured, and thirty guns lost. Another 6,000 men deserted after the battle. The Austrians lost 2,800 men.

The French retreat was conducted in full daylight on 19 March, but the Austrians did not immediately pursue, and when they did, they conducted themselves at a snail's pace. After a minor defeat at Pellenberg on 23 March, the Armée du Nord retreated through Brussels the following day.

The welcome news of French disasters and the expected arrival of reinforcements bolstered the spirits of the British expeditionary force camped in the damp Dutch countryside. The first detachment of Royal Artillery personnel for service as siege artillerymen arrived in mid-March.[3]

Back at home, eleven cavalry regiments were ordered to prepare for service on the continent. However, such was the state of the army at the time, that these eleven regiments could only muster 2,500 sabres in twenty-three squadrons, well below their 'establishment' strength.

On 19 March Colonel Sir James Murray, a 38-year-old Scot, was appointed Adjutant-General to the Army on the Continent, becoming the duke's chief staff officer for all matter related to orders and discipline. The Secretary of State wrote to Murray that day, explaining Lake's 'secret limitations' on movement away from Helvoetsluys, effectively bringing them out into the open.

The first officer casualty of the campaign occurred on 21 March. He was 22-year-old Lieutenant John Western of HMS *Syren*, a relative of Harry Calvert: 'John had conducted his gun-boats close in to the opposite shore, near the Moerdyk, for the purpose of destroying some small craft lying there, when he received a discharge of musketry from a party concealed behind a dyke; a ball struck him on his forehead.';[4] He was buried in the church at Dort, with the Duke of York in attendance.

Despite actions elsewhere, March 1793 was, for the British contingent, the 'phoney war'. Conditions for the common soldier were good, as recorded by Corporal Brown on the 3rd Foot Guards:

> In consequence of an order of his Royal Highness, the commander in chief, the brigade commenced drawing bread in lieu of bread money; one pound and a half each man per day. Provisions of every kind are remarkably cheap here, and the inhabitants shew a great deal of kindness and respect for our army in general.[5]

Supreme commander, Prince von Coburg, called for British assistance to clear out Belgium and restore the Austrian Netherlands, but the orders given initially to Lake and latterly to the duke (via Murray) did not permit it. Captain Charles Craufurd of the 2nd Dragoon Guards,[6] an aide and close friend of the duke, was sent to Coburg with instructions:

> To ask (Coburg's) opinion whether the movement of His Royal Highness to Antwerp will not at this moment be of material advantage to him, by the effect of opinion, and by enabling him to employ some of his forces in other situations, and whether it will not be a convenient place for H.R.H. to assemble his Army.[7]

Coburg earnestly agreed to accept the duke's help. He now had leeway to advance to Bergen-Op-Zoom and Antwerp. It was resolved to send a second infantry brigade to support this movement, with the regiments involved brought up to strength by volunteers from independent companies. In addition, five newly-arrived light companies under Lieutenant Colonel James Perryn were added to the Guards Flank Battalion at the end of March, bringing it up to full strength. The following day the entire Brigade of Guards (less four companies of the 3rd Foot Guards to remain at Dort) embarked for Bergen-op-Zoom, 25 miles (40km) to the south, to be closer to the Coalition centre of operations at Antwerp. The duke wrote his father on 31 March, summarising his revised orders:

> I perfectly comprehend Your Majesty's intentions concerning my cooperating with the Prince of Coburg and Duke of Brunswick, without forming a junction with either of their corps, or allowing any detachment to be made from the troops under my command.[8]

The British were no longer just a garrison force and were now on their way to forming part of the Coalition army.

With the Utmost Vigour

By late March things in the French camp were going from bad to worse. Dumouriez struck up negotiations with the Austrians and offered to evacuate Belgium provided his Armée du Nord was allowed to retreat unmolested. The Austrians accepted the terms, the French withdrew to camps beyond the border, and the Austrians duly re-occupied the Austrian Netherlands. There was now no way Dumouriez could return to Paris, other than attempting to use his army as means of clearing out the National Convention. But his army had other ideas. Harry Calvert received first-hand knowledge of the news:

> Captain Crauford, one of the Duke of York's aides-de-camp, returned this morning from the Prince of Saxe-Cobourg with intelligence of such an extraordinary nature, that I cannot omit the opportunity I have of sending it to you, though you will probably have heard it through other channels before you receive this.
>
> Dumouriez demanded a cessation of arms, and a conference with the Prince of Saxe-Cobourg, which were both granted. After lamenting that the conduct of the National Assembly afforded little probability of a permanent Government being established in France, he informed the Prince that if he might confide on his Serene Highness's co-operation, it was his determination to march his army to Paris and declare for the royal cause; that to

prevent the smallest suspicion of his sincerity, he was willing to deliver Lille and Valenciennes to the Prince of Cobourg. His terms were accepted. Pending the negotiation, four deputies from the Convention arrived from Paris with orders to seize Dumouriez and give the command of the army to General Bournonville, who accompanied them. Dumouriez made them all five prisoners, and delivered them to the Prince of Cobourg, and has this morning set off with his army for Paris to put in force the plans which he has concerted with the Prince of Cobourg.[9]

Dumouriez and his staff attempted to ride to Austrian camp on 4 April, but en route they were intercepted by Lieutenant Colonel Louis-Nicolas Davout. Dumouriez ordered Davout back to the French camp, but some of Davout's men declared Dumouriez a traitor, as he had been declared by the National Convention. Dumouriez and his staff fled towards the Austrian camp as French musket-balls whistled past their ears. Dumouriez tried to rally his men against the Convention the following day, but they had largely declared for the Republic. And so Dumouriez went into exile with the Austrians. 'He escaped himself, and is now, I hear, at Brussels, with about 1000 followers.'[10] This left the French army in chaos. On 5 April, Coburg issued a proclamation:

> Desirous only of securing the prosperity and glory of a country torn by so many convulsions, I declare that I shall support, with all the forces at my disposal, the generous and beneficent intentions of General Dumouriez and his brave army. I declare that our only object is to restore to France its constitutional monarch, with the means of rectifying such experienced abuses as may exist, and to give to France as to Europe, peace, confidence, tranquillity, and happiness. In conformity with these principles, I declare on my word of honour, that I enter on the French territory without any intention of making conquests, but solely and entirely for the abovementioned purposes. I declare, also on my word of honour, that if military operations should lead to any place of strength being placed in my hands, I shall regard it in no other light than as a sacred deposit; and I bind myself in the most solemn manner to restore it to the government which may be established in France, or as soon as the brave General, with whom I make common cause, shall demand it.[11]

Three days after this bold declaration, the ambassadors of the leading Coalition powers assembled at Antwerp to agree future actions. Count Franz, Graf von Metternich-Winneburg and Count Stahrenberg attended for the Holy Roman Empire, Count de Keller for Prussia, and William Eden, Lord Auckland for Great Britain. Buoyed by recent events, that these ministers 'all imagined that the last days of the Convention were at hand; and in truth they were so, if they had communicated a little more vigour and unanimity into the military operations.'[12] It was now clear that National Convention could not be subverted from within, as evidenced by Dumouriez's failure to do so. Stronger threats were needed. The ambassadors resolved to change the object of the war; politics was to take precedence over the words of the soldiers. They openly announced the aim of providing indemnities and securities for the Coalition powers. No longer were they there to simply restore the monarchy and leave; the frontier territories of France were to be partitioned among the invading states. Coburg was left with no choice but to retract his proclamation:

> The proclamation of the 5th instant was the expression only of my personal sentiments; and I there manifested my individual views for the safety and tranquillity of France. But now that the results of that declaration have proved so different from what I anticipated, the same candour obliges me to declare that the state of hostility between the Emperor and the French nation is unhappily re-established in its full extent. It remains for me, therefore, only to revoke my said declaration, and to announce that I shall prosecute the said war with the utmost vigour. Nothing remains binding of my first proclamation, but the declaration, which I renew with pleasure, that the strictest discipline shall be observed by my troops in all parts of the French territory, which they may occupy.[13]

The three ambassadors had made a new plan, which Lord Auckland explained in a letter to Lord Grenville. The Austrians under Coburg were to capture the frontier fortresses of Condé-sur-l'Escaut, Maubeuge and if possible, Lille. The Duke of York's contingent was to be cantoned in the arc running from Ostend down to Menin, then back to Dunkirk.[14] This plan transparently conformed to the styles and wishes, political and military, of Austria and Britain. The Austrians with their view of warfare conducted as a series of sieges, and the British with their preoccupation with the Channel coast.

Coburg was not happy with this plan, preferring to have the duke at his side for operations against Le Quesnoy and Maubeuge. After discussions they agreed he would come to the duke's assistance against Dunkirk if the duke cooperated in the siege of Valenciennes. With Dunkirk captured by the end of August, September at the latest, the entire Coalition could then blockade Lille throughout the winter. A gentleman's agreement thus being in place, the campaign plan for 1793 was born.

Coburg's statements caused barely a ripple in Paris. On 8 April Général de division[15] Dampierre, was appointed to command the French Armée du Nord vice 'traitor' Dumouriez. Dampierre was only

37-years-old, a rising star of the Republican army and one of the first of a new breed of French officers, promoted on merit rather than nobility or social status. For the next ten days he reorganised the Armée du Nord in front of Bouchain, then marched them to Mont Houy near Famars, in a strategic position between the Scheldt and Rhonelle Rivers. There the French built three redoubts on the high ground south-west of the village,[16] with commanding views of Valenciennes, where Dampierre was pressed by the Convention Commissioners to send 30,000 men to the relief of Condé-sur-l'Escaut.

Unfit for Service
The second British infantry brigade for service in Flanders was formed on 9 March when Henry Dundas wrote to Major General Ralph Abercrombie in Edinburgh, ordering him to take command of a brigade comprised of the 14th, 37th and 53rd Foot, allegedly the best three of the nine regular battalions available for overseas service in England. The 14th Foot was already ear-marked to march from Chatham Barracks to Dover (and thence to Helvoetsluys), whereas the 37th was the garrison of Edinburgh Castle and the 53rd was stationed at Ayr and Stirling.

Surprisingly, at 58 years of age, this was Abercrombie's first field command, indeed his first service abroad since the Seven Years War. He had notoriously bad eye-sight, was sometimes dithering in action, but was extremely popular with the men. Present with this brigade were future Peninsula generals George Beckwith and Stafford Lightburne, both serving as subalterns in the 37th Foot; and Ronald Crawford Ferguson, a captain in the 53rd Foot. The two regiments and their commander sailed from Leith on 22 March in a convoy guarded by the Royal Navy sloop HMS *Martin*. The 37th and 53rd had been brought up to strength by raw recruits from Independent Companies, men so poor that both regiments were declared 'unfit for service' by Adjutant-General Fawcett before leaving. But so depleted were the infantry reserves at home that they went anyway. Upon arrival in Flanders they were described as 'being mostly either old men, or quite boys, extremely weak and short.'[17]

The 14th (Bedfordshire) Regiment of Foot were far and away the most experienced of this new brigade, and a near-contemporary inspection return (dated 1 June 1792) exists to permit us a glimpse into the demographics and physiognomy of this regiment. In common with all other British infantry regiments of the era the regiment was divided into ten companies of more-or-less equal strength. One company was nominally commanded by the regimental Colonel, George Hotham, although in his capacity as a desk-bound general officer responsible for the overall administration of the regiment, actual command of the company would have been delegated to a junior officer – Probably Captain-Lieutenant Hugh Perry. The actual field commanders of the regiment, Lieutenant-Colonel Welbore Ellis Doyle and his deputy, Major Alexander Ross, also commanded companies. The other seven companies were commanded by captains (William Browne, William Ramsay, William Burnett, Alexander Macbean, Edmund Viscount Dungarvan, Thomas Dyer and George Garnier). One company was designated the Light Company and another the Grenadier Company, comprising the marksmen and stormers respectively, and both were designated flank companies due to their customary positions on the left and right of the battalion respectively.

On 1 June 1792 the regiment had 326 NCOs and other ranks on the roster, an average of thirty-two men per company. Some ninety-nine had enlisted since the 1791 inspection, mostly to replace 155 men who had either died, deserted, or been discharged in the interim. Of the total regimental strength, 247 men were English, 23 Scots, 76 Irish and fouretten were 'foreigners'[18]. Two men were over 50 years of age, another twenty between 40 and 50, thirty-five 18 years and younger, but most seem to have been aged between 25 and 35. In terms of years of service, this was not a 'green' regiment. Some 86 men had 15 to 20 years' experience (with one man exceeding 30 years) and another fifty-three men had served 10 to 15 years in the ranks.

The new enlistments undoubtedly made up the whole of the eighty-one men who had served one year or less, but the median term of service seems to have been about eight years. Only a dozen men in the regiment were six feet in height or more (the tallest being six feet, one-and-a-half inches) whilst fifty-one men were five feet five inches or less. The median height seems to have been about five feet seven inches, which was fairly typical for English line infantry regiments of the era.

Despite the hard lessons of the war in North America from 1775 until 1783, much that was learned had been lost. Light infantry tactics, so important in the backwoods of Maryland and New York, still lived in the minds of senior officers but was a lost art down at company level. In this regard the British were markedly inferior to the rifle-armed Hessen-Cassel jägers, even the Austrian Grenz regiments from their wild Slavic hinterlands. British light cavalry was used almost exclusively for outpost and scouting duties, leaving the 'heavies' to act as battle cavalry (although as we shall see, the campaign changed perceptions in this regard). British cavalry was the best mounted in Europe, and perhaps the most ignorant of their work in the field; certainly, the Austrians were far superior in this respect. The Royal

Artillery, well-trained and professional, was mostly divided up into penny-packets and attached to individual infantry battalions (battalion guns) with only occasional massing into field batteries. But that is not to criticise that estimable arm, since virtually all Continental armies did likewise. The Royal Engineers were equally professional, but miniscule in numbers, being an officers-only corps. The medical services were almost non-existent. Regiments had surgeons, but few had any training, let alone knowledge of anatomy.

The transports from Leith anchored at Helvoetsluys on 1 April where Abercrombie found the 14th Foot already in garrison. The 37th and 53rd stayed aboard ship and disembarked at Antwerp on 9 April, at which point the two British infantry brigades united and marched from Antwerp to Beveren, 7 miles (11km) to the west. On 11 April Calvert witnessed the recently-ejected French garrison from Breda on their march back to France:

> I went yesterday to Antwerp, a column of the French Army arrived there from Breda; they marched in, colours flying, drums beating, bayonets fixed, and lighted matches. As a body of men, their appearance was very bad – few seemed vigorous and in the prime of life – but they were by no means so ragged, neither was their order of march so unmilitary as I have heard represented. I conversed with some of their officers, and many of them saluted us with their sword, as they passed. Is it not a most extraordinary circumstance that a body of 7000 men, totally cut off, without the most distant chance of relief, should obtain the terms of marching to their own country without being prisoners? The safety of the town of Breda appears to have been consulted more than the honour of those who granted such a capitulation ... Here are the French and ourselves, marching up the two sides of the Scheldt, the one army to attack, the other to defend the frontiers of France.[19]

The British brigades reached Ghent on 14 April, on their way south to Tournai, where the Coalition army was assembling. The Hanoverians were approaching from the east, and Oberleutnant Christian Ompteda of the 1.Grenadier-Bataillon wrote in his diary near Grave, in the morning of 15 April:

> On the 12th and 13th we made two marches through the Cleves country, a charming and fertile district, improved by cultivation, and by the benevolent hand of a Stadtholder of the province, who in former days had fine avenues made in every direction. Towards the border of the Duchy of Cleves the ground becomes unfruitful and the landscape less pleasing, until one gets over some rising ground into another district, that of Dutch Guelderland. On the

> right bank of the Maas one descries smiling meadows and pretty country houses scattered about, in the midst of which is the castle of Huen. From here I was sent to the Governor of Grave, the Dutch fortress on the other side of the Maas, to request a passage for our troops ... The place is very strong, and the prince would not have failed to make a brave defence of it. Our quarters are in the neighbourhood of the fortress, but we leave to-day in order to reach Antwerp by the 19th. There we shall halt for a while, to assemble the whole army of Hanoverians, English, and Dutch.[20]

The British reached Bruges on 17 April, the day before Adjutant-General Sir James Murray arrived from England. Murray carried with him a secret letter, written by Home Secretary Henry Dundas and dated 16 April 1793. It demonstrated that the capture of Dunkirk was to be part of the grand plan from the outset:

> In my public dispatch of this date I have conveyed to you the commands of His Majesty and the sentiments of his confidential servants, in such terms as may enable you to make any communications of that Dispatch which the Duke of York may find expedient for the success of the objects to which it is directed. I think it proper in this separate mode to communicate to you with still less reserve, some particulars which appear to merit attention.
>
> You will observe that in treating of the Expedition His Majesty wishes to be undertaken for the capture of Dunkirk, I have hinted at the propriety of the Expedition with a view of rendering more palatable to the feelings of this Country the extensive co-operation in the Low Countries which it may ultimately be advisable to adopt. But I wish in a more especial manner, to impress you with the importance of that consideration in order that it may be informed with every possible urgency. The security of the Netherlands, as a Barrier to the ambition of France, and a Frontier to the United Provinces is a motive for acting so well understood by all thinking Men, it may well be felt and stated, as truly a British Interest, but you are well aware that there exists in this Country many strong prejudices against Continental Wars, and with many a strong prepossession against the strength of this Country being directed in any other Channel than that of Naval operations. It is extremely essential to meet these prejudices on as strong grounds as possible. The early capture of Dunkirk would operate most essentially in that point of view, and the Expedition successfully conducted under the command of a Prince of the Blood, would give much éclat to the commencement of the War. I trust therefore to your own discretions to enforce this topic, with all your power, in every conference on the subject, and by that and every other argument, to urge the Prince of Cobourg to make the capture of Dunkirk on of the earliest objects of the Campaign.[21]

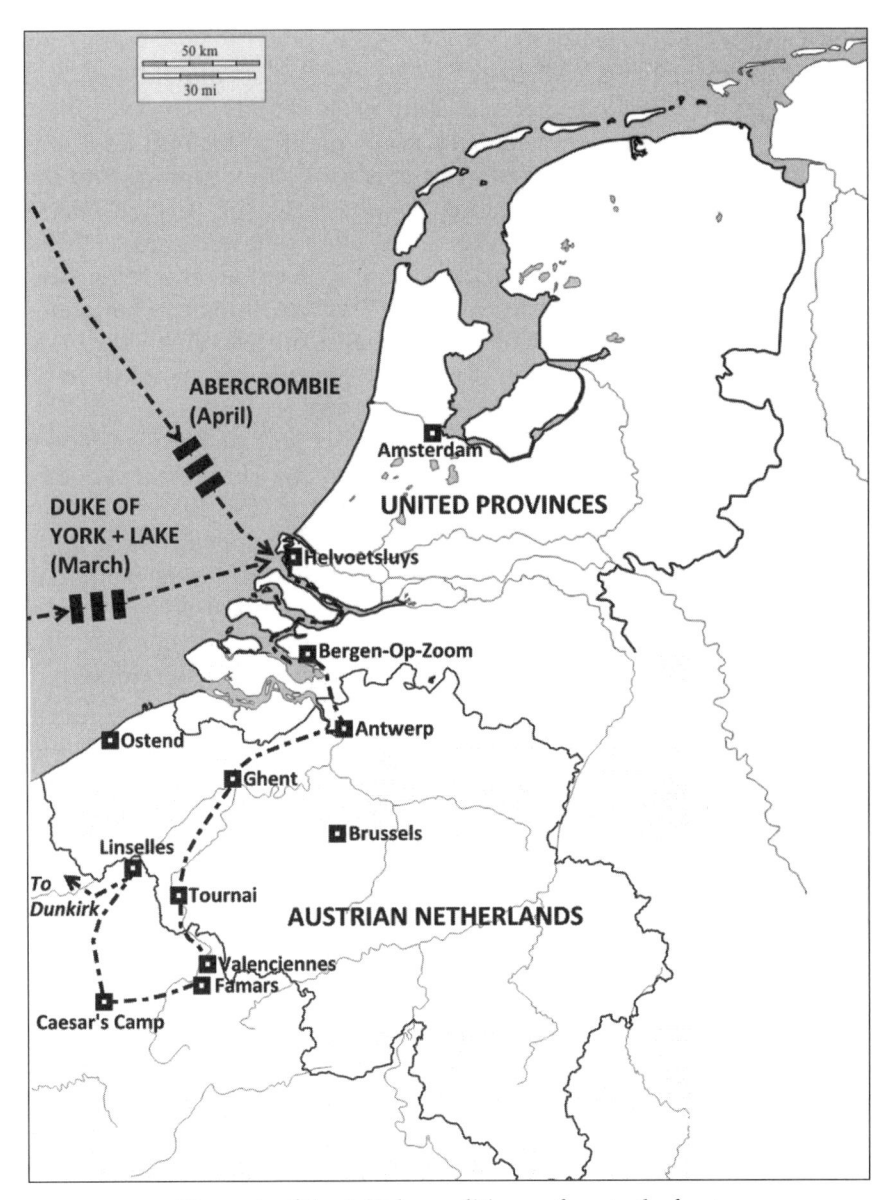

The route of the British expeditionary force to the front

But Dunkirk must wait; the duke's main priority was to get his tiny army into shape. 'All British wars opened in unreadiness and improvisation,'Corelli Barnett has written,[22] and this was no exception.

Abercrombie's brigade was very poor quality. The 14th Foot was fine, but the 37th Foot was left at Bruges for further training and the 53rd Foot sent to Ostend, being totally unfit for service. Harry Calvert was disgusted. 'The recruits that were sent to complete them, immediately before their embarkation, are worse than any I ever saw, even at the close of the American War.'[23] The remaining five battalions (four of Guards and the 14th Foot) reached Courtrai on 20 April and crossed the French frontier and reached Tournai on the 23rd. In so doing, they officially joined the Coalition army.

At Tournai the Duke of York learned that he had been promoted to full General (on 12 April). Two days later the Hanoverian cavalry under the command of Prince Ernest Augustus (the duke's younger brother) arrived. The infantry arrived the following day; but there was trouble in the Hanoverian ranks. Several companies of the 10. Infanterie-Regiment refused to march. Supplies promised to them by both the British and the Dutch had failed to arrive. Furthermore, the Hanoverians were expecting to receive the higher English rates of pay whilst in British service, but this proved to be a misconception. Close to mutiny, something had to be done. Oberleutnant Ompteda was sent to see the Duke of York:

> I was sent with a written report to the Duke of York, whose headquarters were in Tournay, to acquaint His Royal Highness with the condition of affairs. On April 24th, at eight in the evening, I mounted my horse. As I crossed the market-place, just as tattoo was being beaten, and rode through the crowd, several soldiers reached their hands out to me, while others looked at me suspiciously. From Brussels I proceeded by post-horses to Tournay, and was introduced to the cabinet of the Duke of York at eight in the morning of April 25th. His Royal Highness at once realised the importance of the matter. The Duke's first words were: 'I shall go there myself.' Shortly His Royal Highness added: 'What has been promised to the men must be fulfilled.' An hour later the Duke started off, accompanied by an adjutant. I went some distance ahead with post-horses. Two hours from Brussels I learnt that our battalion had marched, despite the ill-will of a large portion of the men, and was quartered at Hal, a town between Brussels and Tournay. The unexpected arrival of the Duke made a great impression. His Royal Highness at once assembled several companies out of the nearest cantonments, proceeded in front of the line, and made known to the troops, through General von der Bussche: 'That their conduct had

brought him thither; that the said conduct was highly criminal; that all promises made to them should be kept; that he would dispatch a courier forthwith for that purpose to His Majesty the King; but that His Royal Highness hoped, on the other hand, that the men would conduct themselves like good soldiers and brave fellows.'[24]

The partially mollified troops marched to Enghien the next day, and by 30 April they were their old selves, 'in capital condition' according to Ompteda, and occupied a frontier post at Rume. The arrival of the Hanoverians increased the duke's command from 6,500 to 19,500, to which he added 15,000 Dutchmen, and the imminent arrival of the 8,000 Hessen-Cassel troops would push the total to 42,500. By this time, he had a staff to match. Captains Harry Calvert, Lord William Bentinck and Henry Clinton were his aides-de-camp; Colonel Sir James Murray was Adjutant-General; Lieutenant Colonel John St Leger Deputy Adjutant-General; Captain Edwin Hewgill Military Secretary; the Marquis de Bouille French liaison officer. Murray was the weak link – 'indecisive, slothful, rather tactless, and consequently unpopular'.[25] 'Our little army is now again dispersed all over Flanders,' Henry Clinton wrote home on 26 April, 'and at a moment when we most want to be assembled … we occupy a position that requires at least 3 times the number.'[26]

Meanwhile Coburg, assisted by his Chief of Staff Oberst Karl von Mack von Leiberich (generally referred to as Mack), made his campaign plans as if he had all the time in the world. But then, a few days before Mack joined the army, the State Chancellery had informed him that reclaiming the Austrian Netherlands was not necessarily the highest priority. For confusion reigned at the Chancellery. The strong-willed Lacy and Thugut, as chief military adviser and foreign minister respectively, were poles apart in thinking.[27] Lacy was not a proponent of a war against France. Then he declared that Austria should exert all its strength in concert with Prussia. The violently provocative Prussophobe Thugut, however, advocated sparing Austria's own resources as much as possible and seeking the support of Britain and Russia. Views therefore oscillated between waiting for the Prussians to arrive in the Austrian Netherlands in force or waiting for the British and Russians to do all the heavy lifting. Either way, the situation could hardly be expected to generate any energy at Imperial headquarters. Mack was also smarting from being denied a promotion to generalmajor (by Thugut), and perhaps felt little motivation to act above his current pay-grade.

The Continental theory of war saw, as the first object, the possession of certain geographical targets. This was always considered more important than annihilation of the enemy's forces. Mack loved maps; 'at this game of maps and coloured labels Mack excelled,'[28] wrote Sir John Fortescue. He planned as though the enemy would sit idly by and watch whilst the Coalition manoeuvred in front of them.

France was effectively wide open before him; the Armée du Nord was in disarray, its leader having deserted. The armies of the Rhine and Moselle were retreating. Those of the Alps and Italy were expecting an attack. The coasts of Brittany and the ports of Brest and Cherbourg were threatened by the Royal Navy. The French ocean ports contained only six ships-of-the-line ready for service, whilst the French Mediterranean fleet was being repaired at Toulon. In the Pyrenees the French were without artillery, without generals, almost without bread. But Imperial planning systems ensured that sudden offensives to take advantage of weaknesses did not happen. Prince Josias was a loyal, kindly and honourable man, but he was naturally lethargic. Count Langeron described him as 'an absolute nonentity; he never gives an order, directs a single operation, and never takes a step without his director. But his birth, probity, virtue and equanimity were sufficient reason for his selection for this command where one required a Prince of a Royal House and a level-headed man.'[29] Karl Mack was almost his polar opposite, being energetic, whip-smart and somewhat domineering, leading to his unpopularity within the staff. When events were against him, he quickly became a defeatist.[30]

Prince von Coburg's natural lethargy also extended to communication with his Coalition partners. The letter from Dundas to Murray dated 16 April went on to further state:

> I must recommend to your attention another subject to be distinctly stated to his Royal Highness the Duke of York. There has appeared a backwardness on the part of the German powers to lay before His Majesty and His Ministers an explicit account of their ulterior views, either in the conduct of the War, or in the termination of it. It is impossible for His Majesty's Servants to advise His Majesty to give a blind co-operation to measures not distinctly explained.[31]

Such then were the men the duke was now subordinated to, as his tiny army sat waiting in Flanders for the plan of campaign to eke out. The important question was: when would France be invaded?

PART 2 – 1793: COALITION OF THE UNWILLING

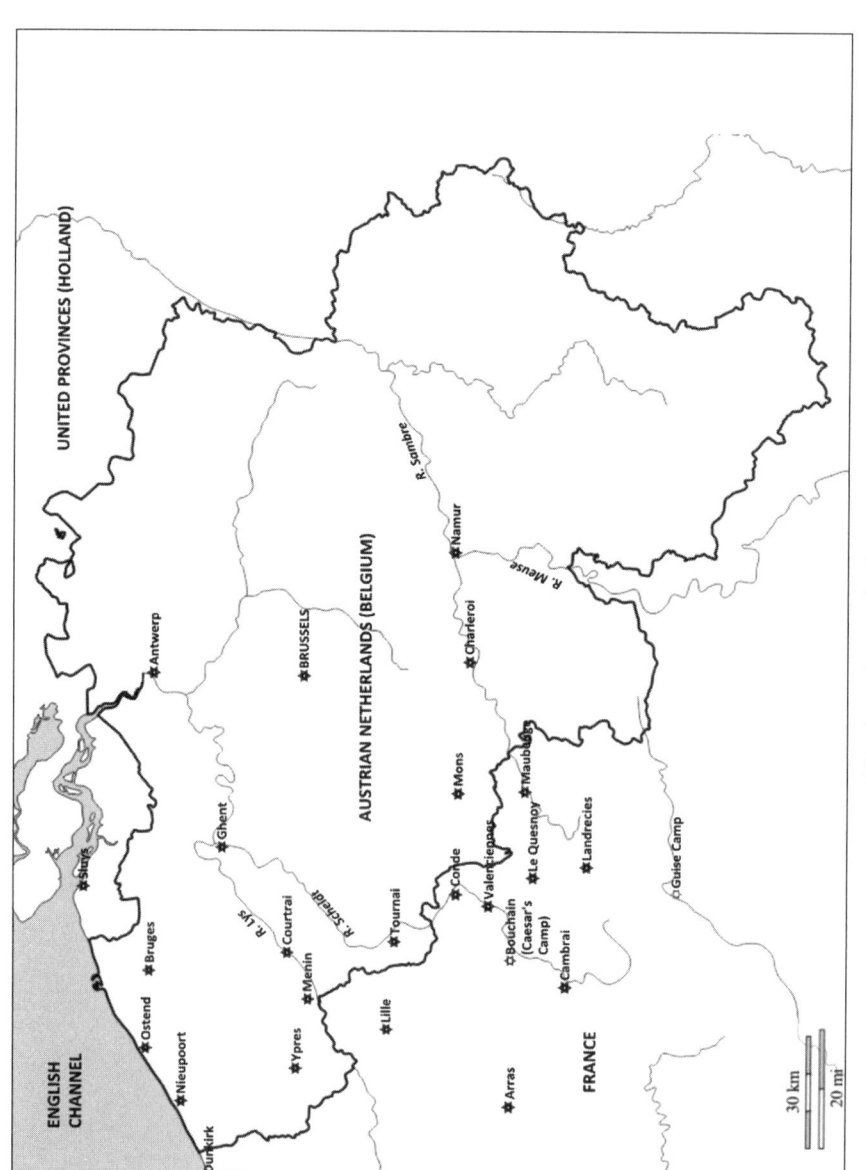

The Austrian Netherlands in 1793

Chapter 6

Advance to Contact

Raismes
Sébastien Le Prestre, Marquis de Vauban (1633–1707) was a remarkable man. Considered the foremost military engineer of the seventeenth century, he left a constructed legacy that is visible even today. Between 1667 and 1707 he designed and upgraded the fortifications of nearly 300 cities, directed the building of thirty-seven new fortresses, and fortified more than a dozen military harbours. His chain of twenty-six fortifications across northern France, from Dunkirk to the Ardennes, still existed in 1793 and formed the basis for the French defence of *La Patrie*.

The first line ran from Dunkirk on the coast through Furnes, Ypres, Menin, Lille, Tornai, Condé-sur-l'Escaut, Valenciennes, Le Quesnoy, Maubeuge and finally to Givet, on the Meuse south of Dinant. Valenciennes was at roughly the mid-point of this chain of forts and commanded the high road between Brussels and Paris. The second line, roughly parallel, ran from Gravelines on the Channel coast through Saint Omer, Bethune, Arras, Douai, Cambrai, Landrecies, Rocroi, Sedan and finally to Stenay, south of the Ardennes. A rough third line of forts, a fall-back position, existed on the Somme and Oise rivers between Amiens, Ham, Saint Quentin and Guise.

The French were widely-dispersed over a long front and adhering more to fortresses than would be the case later in the war. New commander Général de division Dampierre placed garrisons in Le Quesnoy, Valenciennes, Condé-sur-l'Escaut, Lille and Dunkirk. Ten thousand more men were between Maubeuge and Philippeville. Another 10,000 defended fortified camps between Lille and Dunkirk. His main strength was at a fortified camp at Famars on a ridge-line south of Valenciennes, about 30,000 men. And whilst the French were outnumbered, stretched very thin, and very inferior in quality to the Coalition army, they had one advantage.

The French army was a national army, with a singular purpose, system and headquarters. The Coalition army was a goulasch of self-interests and jockeying for position. The Austrians, perceiving themselves the dominant partner, mixed regiments or brigades of their troops into every division or column of the Coalition army; making even supply a nightmare, since no two national armies used the same ammunition, or system of provisioning. Perhaps it was these diversions which caused Imperial headquarters to be obsessed with maps and tables throughout April 1793, rather than attacking, when the French were at their weakest ebb of the war.

Feldmarschall Prince von Coburg produced a plan of operations on 1 May that involved putting the following quantities of troops in the field by mid-May:

Austrians	45,000 infantry, 10,000 cavalry
Dutch	12,500 infantry, 2,500 cavalry
Hanoverians	9,000 infantry, 3,000 cavalry
Hessians[1]	6,500 infantry, 1,500 cavalry
Prussians	6,200 infantry, 1,800 cavalry
British	4,200 infantry, 3,000 cavalry
TOTAL	**83,400 infantry, 22,000 cavalry** [2]

Whilst the Dutch contribution had increased, the Austrians and Prussians had reduced their commitment to the Austrian Netherlands given the reduced risk in that quarter, and their concern to keep the Rhine well-defended. The Hessians and about 5,000 of the Austrians were not expected until June.

The Coalition front line at the start of May occupied some of the Vauban forts close to the Channel and ran from Furnes and Nieuwpoort on the coast, through Ypres, Menin, Tournai, Saint Amand, and ended at Mons, north of Maubeuge. Coalition garrisons defended Ostend, Bruges, Helvoetsluys, Antwerp, Ghent, Oudenarde, Courtrai and Brussels. On the right wing were the Dutch, whose main position was at Courtrai. Three Coalition contingents in Saint Amand and Mons were involved in a blockade of Condé-sur-l'Escaut, assisted by Duke Ferdinand Friedrich of Württemberg with 5,000 Austrians to the north. Seven battalions and twelve squadrons of Prussians under Generalleutnant von Knobelsdorff were before and near Saint Amand, with two battalions and three squadrons at a fortified camp at Maulde. Clerfayt with 12,000 Austrians was to the south at Escaupont, with his right extending into the Forest of Raismes and a detached corps under Winckheim occupying the Abbaye de Vicoigne and the village of Raismes itself.

Probably amazed to have survived April without a scratch, Dampierre attacked along the Coalition line from Saint Saulve to Saint Amand on the first day of May in accordance with his orders to relieve Condé-sur-l'Escaut. His troops moved off at 04.00 hours, one column advancing along the right bank of the Scheldt, bypassing Valenciennes to Saint Saulve and Onnaing, whilst a second column skirted Valenciennes to the west and advanced to Vicoigne, Raismes and Saint Amand. Général de division Antoine Nicolas Collier, comte de La Marlière, despatched some troops from Lille to the Prussian camp at Maulde to prevent them reinforcing Knobelsdorff.

Dampierre's poorly-trained army did not do well, being burdened by the poor command decision to distribute the force across a wide front rather than mass on either bank of the Scheldt to deliver a hammer-blow. The right-hand column was easily rebuffed by the French-born Imperial Feldzeugmeister Joseph de Ferraris outside Saint Saulve, who then turned on the French garrison of Valenciennes which had advanced to the Moulin de Rouleur to support the attack. The garrison scuttled back behind the city walls. The western column established artillery batteries on the heights on Anzin from where it could bombard Raismes, then drove in the Imperial outposts in front of Saint Amand. But the fighting grew confused in the dense woodland. Clerfayt led his troops in person and repulsed four separate French attacks, assisted by the Prussians. The French fell back upon Famars, having lost 2,000 men during the day. Away to the north La Marlière confined his advance in accordance with his orders to encircle Maulde, not realising that his column greatly outnumbered the 4,000 Prussians left there; and in retiring late in the day missed a chance to crush them.

The attacks fell completely on the Austrians and Prussians, with the Hanoverians being only partially engaged. Oberleutnant Ompteda was with the Duke of York as an orderly officer, and therefore well-placed to see what was going on:

> A detachment of about one hundred and fifty French, with two guns, wanted to seize the post occupied by Captain von Low. After being harassed for a while by French chasseurs, he opened fire on them. At the same time, about ten men of the Imperial cavalry, with a lieutenant, charged and took one gun from the enemy before it had been discharged six times. Shortly before this I had joined the Duke, and we hastened to meet the victorious Austrians as they brought in the captured cannon. The French fled hurriedly, leaving two killed, and fourteen prisoners, of whom five were wounded. Our generals. Freytag and Bussche, were both present the battalion of von Diepenbroick and a squadron of Imperial cavalry were sent

in pursuit of the enemy. The latter took refuge in a wood, which we could not sufficiently reconnoitre. We sent in a few cannon balls, which accelerated the flight, and spread such alarm among the inhabitants of a French village, against which we advanced, that they followed the example of the troops, and fled too. The French did not return our fire, though they had taken away with them one of their two guns. We pursued for a considerable distance into French territory, and it was not till four in the afternoon that the troops came back, as we did not wish to expose them further in a country much cut up by woods, with which we were insufficiently acquainted.[3]

Major Jesse Wright of the Royal Artillery noted in his diary that the Austrians presented the captured cannon to the duke, 'who was near when they took it', suggesting that he was closer to the action than a commander ought to be. But this was his first general action, and we cannot blame him for wanting to see things for himself.

The National Convention ordered Dampierre to make a second attempt to lift the Coalition siege of Condé-sur-l'Escaut. The attack on 8 May was aimed at Clerfayt's positions at Vicoigne and Raismes. He had about 30,000 men at his disposal, against 43,000 Austrians, 11,000 Prussians, 3,000 Dutchmen and the Duke of York's three Guards battalions. Oberleutnant Ompteda first heard gunfire during the night of 7 May:

> On the night of May 7th - 8th I had just written as far as 'regular' in the main guardhouse at Tournay, when once more something much the reverse of regular occurred. It was the night of one of the hottest attacks of the French against the several armies - that of Prince Coburg at Quieverain, that of General Clairfait at Vicogne, and the Prussians under Knobelsdorf at St. Amand. The latter were rather near our army-corps at Tournay, and our outposts were in close touch. Had the attacks extended to us, and energetically, we might have found it a very dangerous game. Our good genius averted this, and we only heard in the distance, yet very distinctly, the ceaseless thunder of a tremendous cannonade, which even experienced Prussian officers in Tournay did not altogether like. Just as I had written the word at which I broke off, there galloped in 'reeking messenger stewed in haste,' as Shakespeare says, a non-commissioned officer sent by General Knobelsdorf. He asked for the Prussian ammunition stores in Tournay, saying, 'Good heavens! our fellows have been under fire for forty-eight hours, and fired off all their ammunition!'[4]

The Duke of York got the Brigade of Guards and the Hanoverian 10. Infanterie-Regiment on the road at 01.00 hours and arrived at Maulde at 06.00 hours. Lake put the 3rd Foot Guards and the Flank Battalion in the centre and the Coldstreams on the left.

Dampierre led an attack on Raismes at 07.30 hours while General La Marlière's troops advanced towards Saint Amand with orders to build an artillery battery to bombard Vicoigne. La Marlière managed to reach his allocated position in the forest and began to build his gun batteries; Dampierre, at the head of eight battalions, captured most of Raismes after several attempts.

Things were not looking good for the Coalition. They faced being broken apart and forced to retreat towards their respective supply bases. At 17.00 hours, Prussian General von Knobelsdorff rode up to the duke and said: 'the Austrians are giving way, our battalions are all repulsed. In the name of God, advance a battalion or we are lost!' The duke ordered the Coldstream Foot Guards lining the chaussée to advance into the Forêt de Vicoigne to their front. The Coldstreams advanced a short way, where they halted till the arrival of the elderly Prussian General Knobelsdorff, who rode up, and, with a smile, said in broken English, 'that he had reserved for the Coldstream Guards the honour, the special glory of dislodging the French from their intrenchments in the forest; that the British troops need only show themselves in the wood, and the French would retire.'[5] He however omitted to state, that the Austrians had been three times successively repulsed, with the loss of 1,700 men, and General von Knobelsdorff proposed for the Coldstream the honour of performing with 600 rank and file what 5,000 Austrians had not been able to accomplish.[6]

The Coldstreams in (probably) three-deep line along the chaussée, advanced cautiously in a south-westerly direction into the dense forest. No doubt their parade-ground line lost some order as the troops dodged trees and navigated the thick undergrowth, taking care not to tread on dead Austrians. The line inclined somewhat to the left, towards a glade facing a forest track where French chasseurs sniped from behind a lumber redoubt.[7]

Emerging from the trees at the track, with the French at their front, they could not see a well-concealed battery behind a timber rampart on their right flank, and three 9-pounders enfiladed the Coldstreams with a blast of canister at short range. A score of men went down immediately. They were pulled back into the trees and forced to absorb artillery-fire until relieved by the 1st and 3rd Guards. The Coldstreams had lost thirty-nine men killed and thirty-eight wounded; the supporting battalions did not lose a man. Major Jesse Wright recorded that he was not surprised at the casualties, given that the Coldstreams had marched through the wood 'in line and in step'. Another witness was Oberstleutnant Gebhard Leberecht von Blücher of the Prussian Red Hussars, who wrote that: 'I have never seen finer soldiers. They marched with such resolution and did everything possible to attain victory.'[8] However, their sacrifice had a positive side-effect; realising that his enemies had been reinforced, General La Marlière called off his attacks. General Dampierre was hit in the right thigh by a cannon-ball and mortally wounded during a frontal assault on the Coalition position at Vicoigne.[9] At this instant the Republican attack lost its momentum. The French withdrew from Raismes, having lost 700 men. Early the next morning the Allies captured the French positions, taking 800 prisoners in the process.

Ensign Howard of the Coldstream, who carried the colours, Serjeant-major Coleman and two serjeants were wounded, and seventy-three rank and file killed, wounded, and missing.[10] Harry Calvert rode over the battlefield four weeks later;

> This ground was occupied by the Imperial army on the 8th of May and following days. The abbey is one of the finest buildings I ever saw, totally torn to pieces and demolished by the French. There remains nothing but the walls, the noble architecture and magnificent marble of which appear to have despised their malice.[11] From the abbey we went into the Bois de Vicogne, and found out the ground where the Coldstream suffered so much. I almost wonder their loss was not greater. They were, at the same moment, exposed to a fire from a battery which plied them with grape-shot at the distance of 350 yards, and to a line of infantry which was intrenched in their front.[12]

The French retired to Famars at dawn on 10 May. The duke ordered his troops to let off a celebratory *feu-de-joie* the following day, and the whole of Courtrai was illuminated by candles the night of 12 May upon the news of the birth of a son to the Emperor Franz.[13] On 14 May the first British cavalry brigade arrived at Tournai, 900 men commanded by Major General Ralph Dundas and comprising two squadrons each of the 11th, 15th (King's) and 16th (Queen's) Light Dragoons. Ralph Dundas was a 53-year-old Scot, a lifelong cavalryman and former Colonel of the 11th Light Dragoons, a regiment on which he had devoted years of attention.

Because a mid-1792 inspection return exists for the 11th Light Dragoons, we can get a glimpse into the composition of that particular regiment on the eve of the war. The 11th was divided into six troops,[14] with one troop was nominally commanded by the regimental Colonel Studholme Hodgson, with actual command being exercised by Captain-Lieutenant William Henry Harnage. Another troop was commanded by Lieutenant-Colonel Ralph Dundas, and a third by his deputy, Major John Carnegie; the remaining three by Captains George Michell, William Trevillian and John Walbanke Childers.[15] Some changes in the regiment in February and March 1793 changed these arrangements, when George Michell was appointed Brigade-major to Ralph Dundas and Captain Alexander McKenzie took his troop; William Trevillian retired and his troop was taken by Captain Lord William Bentinck; and two new troops were formed, commanded by Captains George Lyon and George Thomas.

In mid-1792 each of the six troops comprised exactly thirty-three corporals and other ranks, in addition to the regimental complement of two field officers, four captains, four lieutenants five cornets, a chaplain, an adjutant, a surgeon, six quartermasters, twelve serjeants and six trumpeters. Nearly all the men were English, with only five Scots, five Irishman and a single foreigner in the ranks. A third of the men were aged 25 to 30, and another quarter were aged 20 to 25. The 11th were an experienced regiment, with over half the men having served seven years or more. As individuals they were physically small, with over half of the men being under five feet seven inches tall. The tallest man in the regiment was five feet nine-and-a-half inches tall, however the lack of stature was without doubt a benefit in a light cavalry regiment relying on dexterity rather than brute force for effect.

A few days after that a detachment of the Royal Artillery arrived, commanded by Major William Congreve. This comprised two companies, totalling seventeen officers and 219 men commanded by Captains Winter and Trotter. But these men had no guns. They were intended to either man the two small-calibre 'battalion guns' attached to each infantry regiment, or to serve with the general Artillery Park. Each infantry regiment's guns were crewed by two Royal Artillery NCOs and a handful of gunners commanded by a subaltern, and a captain commanded the combined guns of an infantry brigade. This penny-packet dispersal of British artillery seems odd by later standards, and opinion has been divided ever since as to its wisdom. The historian of the Royal Artillery found fault with this tactic and published his reasoning.[16] Other writers however commended the Royal Artillery for their performance in Flanders;

> I have the utmost satisfaction in informing your Grace that the zeal and ability of Major Wright and of Lieutenants Watson and Fenwick have done them the highest credit. The guns commanded by these officers were the only ones brought into action. I was myself a witness of the promptitude with which Mr. Watson's were served, and know that they had great effect.[17]

This praise was for the Royal Artillery detachment that fought at Saint Amand on 8 May, and illustrates the professionalism of the Royal Artillery officers, who, unlike their infantry and cavalry brethren were trained specialist soldiers, graduates of the Royal Armoury at Woolwich. Unfortunately, there were not many of them to go around. Of the Royal Artillery's four battalions of ten companies each, exactly half were in the West Indies, North America and Gibraltar. The remaining twenty companies were dotted across England and Scotland, many serving as fortress and harbour garrisons, with a total officer cadre of less than 100 men at company level. Like the other arms of service, and as in 1914, the Royal Artillery was much too small to perform the tasks required of it in the emerging Coalition War and would be greatly increased in strength in the years to come.

On 18 May, the duke relocated his headquarters from Tournai to Basècles, about 12 miles (19km) north of Valenciennes. His army marched at 05.00 hours, in an order of march that was typical for the era. Four squadrons of light dragoons (two British and two Hanoverian), the flank battalion of the Foot Guards and the flank companies of the Hanoverian Guards formed the Advanced Guard. Behind them rolled the Hanoverian light artillery, and then the Hanoverian infantry, left in front.[18] Behind these came the British infantry (also left in front), four more squadrons of Hanoverian cavalry, the English dragoons, then the engineers and baggage towards the rear. At the tail were 100 English and 100 Hanoverian infantry, and fifty English and fifty Hanoverian cavalrymen formed the rear-guard under the command of Major John Baird of the 53rd Foot. From Basècles they force-marched south to Estreux, which was to be British headquarters for the next three months.

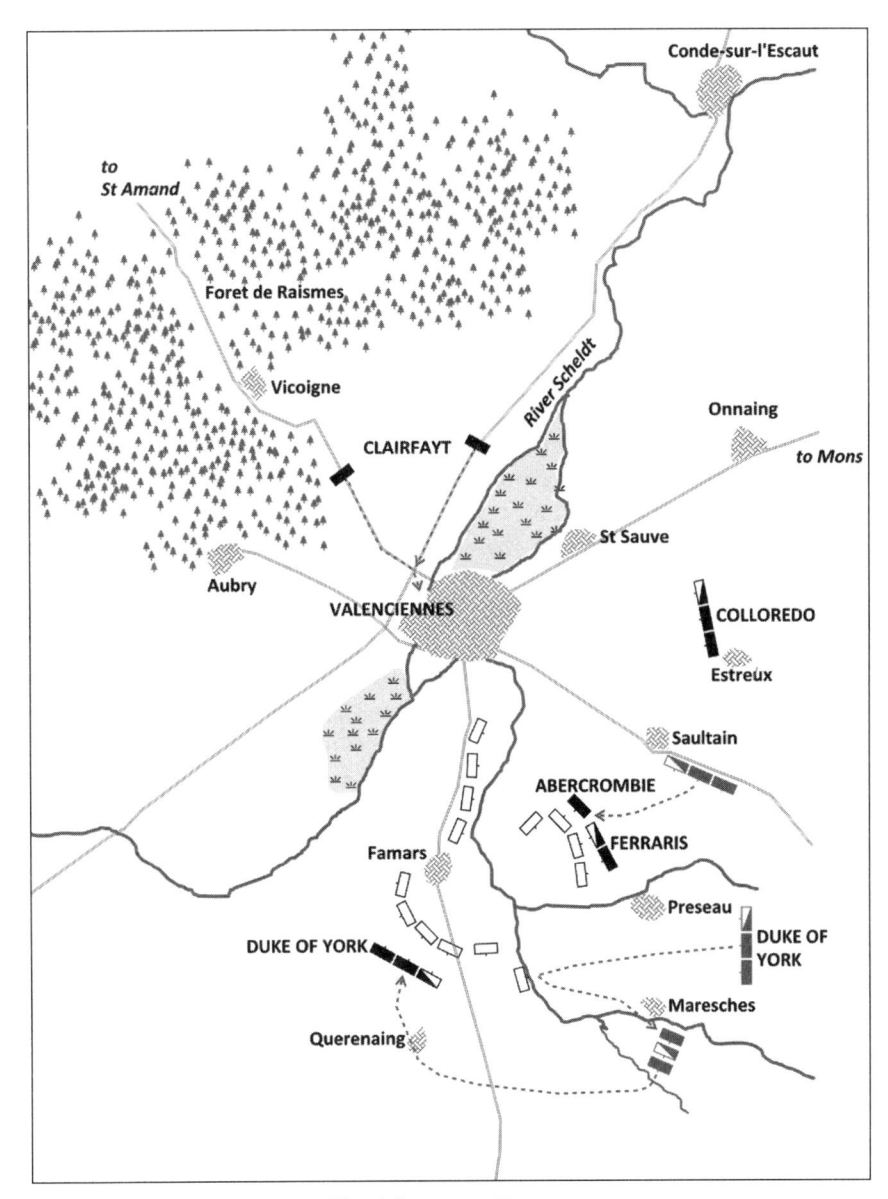

The Advance on Famars

Famars

With his Coalition army now concentrated, Prince von Coburg decided to launch an attack across a 40-mile wide front on 23 May. In the northwest, Dutch troops under Willem, Prince of Orange-Nassau were to attack Orchies, whilst his brother Frederik attacked Tourcoing. In the centre, the Prussian General von Knobelsdorff was to attack Hasnon, and Austrians under Clerfayt were to attack Anzin. More Austrians under Feldmarschalleutnant Nikolaus Colloredo-Mels were to observe Valenciennes from the north-east. To the south-east, Generalmajor Rudolf Ritter von Otto was to threaten Le Quesnoy; whilst at the end of the line, a column was to advance on the Sambre from Bavai. The duke's part was to attack the French camp at Famars, and we shall come to this part in a moment. It was an exceedingly ambitious plan; in the words of the eminent historian John Fortescue, it was completely Austrian – too much science to leave any room for sense. It had been drawn up by Imperial Quartermaster-General Karl Mack von Leiberich, the 'unfortunate General Mack' who was forced to surrender his entire army to Napoleon at Ulm in 1805.[19]

The French camp at Famars, 3 miles (5km) south of Valenciennes, was defended by 27,000 men under Dampierre's successor, Maréchal de camp François Joseph Drouot de Lamarche. It was protected by a vaguely rectangular fortified camp, built on two parallel plateaux overlooking the river Rhonelle. The plateau to the east was defended by 2 miles (3km) of entrenchments with three strong redoubts. The attack was to be made by two Coalition columns. The right-hand column under Austrian Feldzeugmeister Joseph de Ferraris was to attack the eastern side of the French camp with Abercrombie's British brigade, nine Austrian battalions, twelve Austrian cavalry squadrons and twenty-one guns. The aim was to drive the French from fortified positions east of the Rhonelle river, and then threaten to cross the river. The Duke of York's left column, with the Brigade of Guards, eight Austrian and four Hanoverian battalions, six British, four Hanoverian and eight Austrian cavalry squadrons and thirty-eight guns, was to outflank the southern end of the French position. Mack's orders to the duke read as follows:

> The destination of the first attack (York's) is to advance on the line between Presceau and Maresches as far as the River Rhonelle; then under cover of its artillery, to throw several trestle bridges in the neighbourhood of Artres, and to pass as many columns as possible over the river; thence to attack the camp of Famars by its right flank.[20]

The tiny British contingent thus found itself split between the two columns, probably done on purpose to reinforce the sense of Coalition unity. The advance began at 02.00 hours. Harry Calvert noted the splendour of the Coalition army on the march:

> The fog was so thick, that it was near half-past five before it was sufficiently dispersed to enable us to view the magnificent scene that surrounded us – the allied army, all in motion, and each column forming its march towards its point of attack, with the utmost order and regularity.[21]

Ferraris' right-hand column attacked the redoubt in the centre. A Hungarian grenadier battalion stormed them and captured the cannon within; the 14th Foot followed suit and traded musketry salvoes for the fleeing enemy. According to Abercrombie's report, the conquest of the redoubt was mainly due to the agility and activity of an Hanoverian artillery captain, called Schuessler, who had directed his battery specifically against the redoubt. At about the same time the flanking redoubts were taken by the Hungarian grenadiers and the I/4.Infanterie-Regiment. Several cannon and 200 men were captured.[22] The Hanoverian Garde du Corps was active in driving off a much larger force of French cavalry attempting to outflank the Coalition column, losing seventy-five men in the process:

> Here were suddenly three large enemy squadrons (from the heavy Cavalry Regiments Berry and a Dragoon Regiment) who, without being noticed, had formed behind a hill to receive their infantry with the greatest evil, but moved in perfect order. The Garde du Corps, although only 220 men strong, did not hesitate for a moment to meet the much larger enemy. Oberstlieutenant von Bülow rushed to the front of Major von Schulte's second squadron, and both parties attacked one another with equal devotion, lasting for a time, man to man. A squadron of Barco-Husaren, on the right wing of the Garde du Corps, could not resist the heavy enemy riders; these now rode to the Garde du Corps' flank and rear, and the Garde also had the disadvantage of having to make a charge downhill. Nevertheless, the enemy was at last completely driven off, and several officers and men were made prisoners.[23]

Ferraris then halted to wait for news from the Duke of York's column. But the duke's left-hand column had barely moved. The fog did not clear until 07.00 hours, five hours after the march started, and as a result the column reached the river near Artres in full daylight and in plain view of French picquets. The river crossing was defended by five French gun batteries:

> The first cannon-shot I saw fired at us made a quite different impression on me to that which it made on older soldiers, according

to their admissions to me. It was a misapprehension on my part. I thought the range was too great, and laughed at it, and I was wrong. The balls went right and left over our heads and inflicted some losses on the Prince of Wales' Light Dragoons. They even carried as far as the second line, where the Grenadier companies of the 5th and 6th [Hanoverian regiments], who had served in Gibraltar, and were au fait at that sort of thing, ducked their heads, and let the projectiles pass. Our Grenadiers stood very steadily, and as nearly all the lower classes, particularly the peasantry, have surprisingly long sight, they all regarded what was going on before us with the greatest attention, and my neighbours often helped me to verify observations I despaired on making, though my own eyesight is not bad.[24]

The duke sent a column – the Guards, two battalions of Austrians, six squadrons of British cavalry and two squadrons of Hanoverian light cavalry – on a long outflanking movement to the east, via Maresches where his men crossed the river at 11.00 hours, after which put they instead of the men had a two-hour stop; and then in a giant loop westward, ended up at Quérénaing, 2 miles (3km) south-west of Famars not long before dusk. His diversion had brought him to the strongest part of the French lines, on the steep southern slopes of the plateau. He sent his light dragoons out to the west to scout for redoubts on the French left.

There were a handful of daylight hours left, and an attack was still possible, aimed at three large redoubts south of the village of Famars. But the duke's cavalry and infantry had advanced well in advance of his artillery, which would take time to come up. His column was also accompanied by the new Coalition quartermaster-general, the 71-year-old Feldzeugmeister Friedrich Fürst zu Hohenlohe-Kirchberg;[25] and Hohenlohe deemed it too late in the day to assemble a suitable attack. The duke dutifully complied. It must wait until the morning. The army camped, gloriously if uncomfortably:

> We bivouacked for the night in the neighbourhood of Querimain [sic], and as the different corps mostly camped out just in the order of their arrival, they presented a highly variegated spectacle. On our immediate right was the Hungarian regiment Sztaray, one of the most distinguished in this war. Their appearance, and their half-savage customs (for the Hungarian soldier, although brave and well disciplined, has a tincture of wildness), made a striking contrast to the elegance of the English Guards thirty paces behind them. But among these various nations, united by a mighty, just, and honourable cause in common brotherhood in arms… there was one feature common to all - fatigue and gnawing hunger.[26]

Corporal Brown observed:

> The troops which displayed their valour and activity most, were the Hanoverian flying [horse] artillery, with the British light cavalry, and those of the several other nations, as the nature of the engagement, were chiefly adapted to their mode of warfare, in pursuing a flying enemy in an open country, where very few impediments occur to obstruct their progress.[27]

Maréchal de camp Lamarche and his aide-de-camp Lieutenant Michel Ney [28] rode into Valenciennes at 16.00 hours that afternoon to meet with the Convention Commissioners and garrison commander Général de division Jean Henri Becays Ferrand. His news was not good; that the camp at Famars was nearly surrounded, and greatly outnumbered, and so must be evacuated.

Lamarche gave seventeen battalions to Ferrand and then withdrew from Famars during the night as the duke's tired men were settling down to a good night's sleep. The French rear-guard was a party of 150 men under the towering Capitaine Adolphe-Édouard-Casimir-Joseph Mortier[29] who stayed in position for six hours and did not retire until sunrise.[30] The French retreated to Bouchain, 10 miles (16km) to the south-west of Valenciennes, reinforcing that town as they went. En route, their baggage train was captured by Captain Robert Craufurd[31] at the head of two squadrons of the 11th Light Dragoons, an action that earned Craufurd the approbation of the duke.

French losses for the day had been 3,000 men, seventeen guns and three colours. The Austrians had sustained most of the casualties amongst the Allies, 1,100 men against eighty-three Hanoverians and thirty Britons, mostly lost at the bridge at Artres and in cavalry skirmishes late in the day.

The duke's force south of Famars was roused before 03.00 hours and was ready to march an hour later. His troops formed line on some rising ground at 05.00 hours as the artillery went forward to bombard the French camp; but it was empty. At 09.00, the Brigade of Guards occupied the deserted camp, and four hours later the baggage train arrived, to the relief of all. The troops had not been re-supplied for fifty hours and were starving.[32]

Oberleutnant Ompteda had received his baptism of fire, and was jubilant:

> We have been so fortunate yesterday as to have fought a victorious battle, and now occupy the strong position on the heights where the French were yesterday, surrounded by several entrenchments, on which they reposed their last hopes. Our troops fought with their

old courage, which has attracted fresh attention on the part of the Austrians and English. The Garde du Corps distinguished itself extremely. Being unexpectedly brought into contact with several squadrons of French cavalry of greatly superior strength, a fierce encounter took place in which the hostile cavalry were completely repulsed. But this victory has cost us dear. Adelepsen was killed; Oberstlieutenant von Bülow, Kapitaines (of cavalry) von Bülow and von Zedwitz are wounded. Bock has got two sabre-cuts on the arm, which are, however, not of importance. The most unfortunate thing is that, as far as we can ascertain, Scheither, William Bülow, and the youngest Kielmansegge[33] must be prisoners. It is stated that the French prisoners say they saw two of these officers being taken to Valenciennes.[34]

From the elevated captured camp at Famars the troops could plainly see Valenciennes spread out below them. That place was now ringed by Coalition forces, and so the siege could commence.

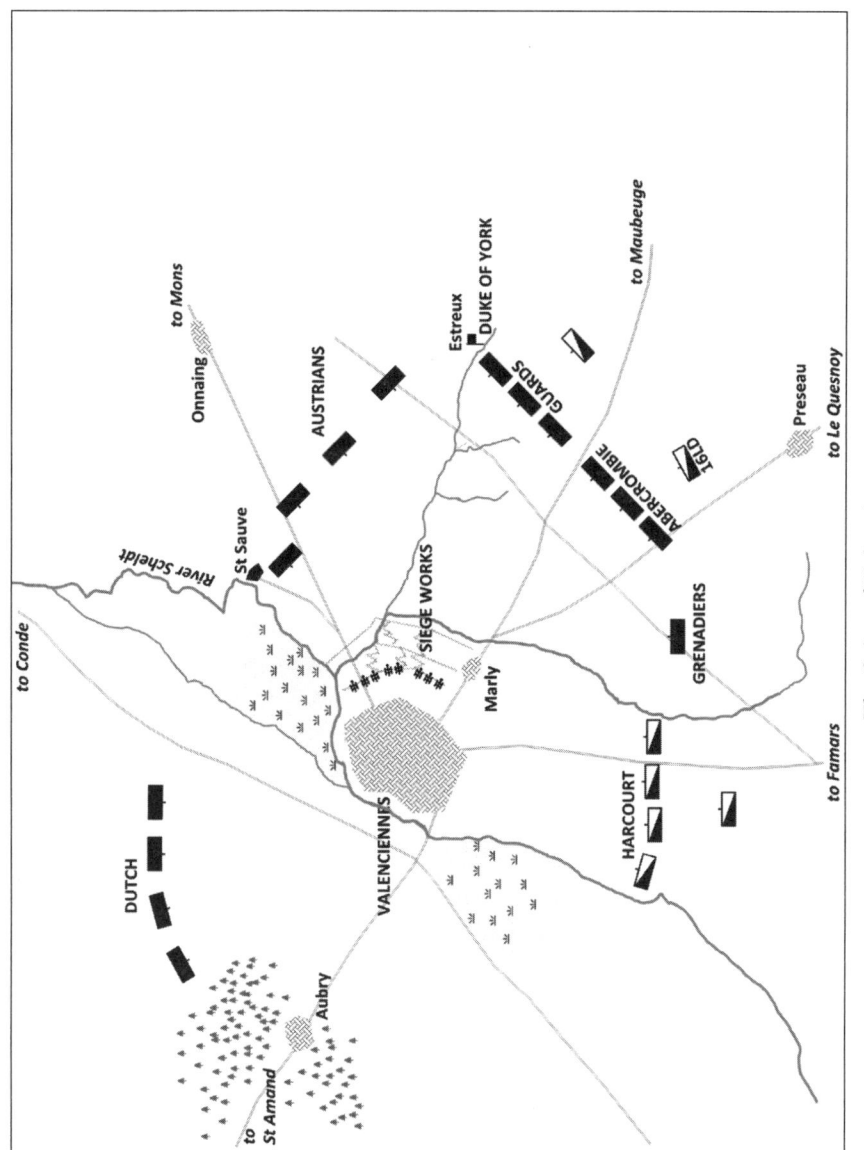

The Seige of Valenciennes

Chapter 7

Valenciennes

The Seige
The prevailing eighteenth-century notion of warfare was as a series of sieges, followed by a big decisive battle once the enemy was out in the open. It did not occur to the Coalition that they could take advantage of the weak condition of the French forces and simply march on Paris. No, all the frontier fortresses must be reduced first; and the priority was to be the very city where some enemy troops from Famars had taken refuge – Valenciennes.

The Duke of York was given command of the siege, his first major military appointment. The British Cabinet had been concerned that this would prevent him from attacking Dunkirk, which was becoming the main British target, but eventually decided to accept the offer. The duke's besieging force comprised 25,000 men, of whom 14,000 were Austrian. In recognition of this, Prince von Coburg appointed Austrian Feldzeugmeister de Ferraris to the duke's staff. Preliminaries to the siege commenced on 24 May when garrison commander Général de division Ferrand opened the locks of the Scheldt and commenced a flooding of the plains south of the city. However, the locks were in poor condition and the water level rose slowly; it took five days to reach the highest point. On 25 May the Royal Artillery bombarded the village of Marly, just outside the walled city. Oberleutnant Ompteda was witness to the start of the main siege on 27 May:

> Before we marched out of the camp at Famars we were eyewitnesses of the beginning of the siege of Valenciennes. At daybreak a numerous siege artillery opened fire. This spectacle I saw from the highest part of the ground at Famars, at the foot of which our battalion had been encamped. On the summit of this rising ground the French have erected a memorial to their General Dampierre, who was killed in one of the fierce combats

at the beginning of the month. It is a triangular pyramid, decorated with trophies, and with a medallion portrait of the general. On the three sides of this pyramid are three inscriptions. On the side next [to] France one reads: *Il aima sa patrie*. On the side obliquely towards Belgium: *Il detesta les traitres*. This is an allusion to Dumouriez, who would not follow Dampierre. On the side bearing the medallion is written over it: Ses vertus, lui assurent l'immortalite. Lower underneath: Soldats de la liberte! Francois Republicains! Il fut pour vous un bel exemple de valeur et de civisme. This immortal monument was made of painted canvas, supported by wooden stakes. The word civisme was in tatters. But the position of the monument was unique ... From this point I noticed Valenciennes at three o'clock in the morning, in a thick mist, which was every moment lit up with the flash of heavy guns. On the right one of the suburbs was in flames. At six fire broke out in the middle of the city, and spread more and more as we marched hither.[1]

Corporal Brown of the Guards liked the countryside:

This is a fine, open, fertile country, delightfully variegated with gentle rising hills, and pleasant vallies [sic]; in one of which lies Valenciennes on the river Scheldt. This river washes the northwest part of the town, where there are also some marshy ground, which might retard the approach of an enemy; but the other side, viz. the south-east, is a dry, chalky soil, and more level: here the chief scene of action during the siege was carried on: the trenches extending from near the river fide on the east, to Marley, a considerable village, with a fine piece of water on the south: in this village a great number of the enemy made a stand, it being under the cannon of the town. A considerable quantity of firelocks, pouches, and other warlike instruments were found in the houses of the country people. Every house was plundered in a most unfeeling manner, by the Austrians and others of the foreign troops; whose hardened hearts, neither the entreaties of old age, the tears of beauty, the cries of children, nor all the moving scenes of the most accumulated distress, can touch with pity; nor do they content themselves with taking whatever may be useful to them, but destroy whatever they cannot carry away. It would seem the Austrians are not allowed by their laws to plunder in such a degree; for this day one of their officers detected a soldier plundering a poor woman's house of all she had, when, moved with compassion, he ordered him to desist; but he refusing, the officer drew his sword and killed him instantly on the spot.[2]

Slowly, reinforcements trickled in from home. On 29 May, a second British cavalry brigade arrived at Ostend, this time the 'heavies' under the command of Major General William, the 3rd Earl Harcourt. Four regiments that later fought at Waterloo – two squadrons each of the Royal Horse Guards, 1st (Royal) Dragoons, 2nd (Royal North British) Dragoons and 6th (Inniskilling) Dragoons. Accompanying them was the Loyal Emigrant Regiment under the command of Lieutenant Colonel Claude-Louis, Comte de Chârtres-Nançay. This was a unit made up on French royalists recruited in the London area. Two companies of chasseurs were added at Ostend from local royalist recruits. Also new on the scene were two squadrons each of the 7th (Queen's Own) Light Dragoons and the 2nd (Queen's Bays) Regiment of Dragoon Guards.

On 30 June the Dragoon Guards participated in a joint Anglo-Austrian raid on a French encampment. The French were taken completely by surprise and fled, then decided to make a stand when they came to a field of high corn. The Dragoon Guards and the Austrians charged and broke them once more, but some tried to surrender. Captain John Le Marchant of the Bays was appalled by the actions of his Austrian allies:

> I am just returned from a scene, that, on reflection, makes my soul shrink within me; but it is one of the horrors of war. What gave me most pain was to see that the Austrians gave no quarter. Poor devils on their knees, merely begging for mercy, were cut down. My own people, thank God! were as merciful as possible; and I think, destroyed none in the pursuit, except such as would not give themselves up. Dive's party had taken five men alive, but leaving them for an instant in pursuit of others, some Austrians came up and butchered them.[3]

Calvert plainly did not think much of his Dutch allies either, although he had a high opinion of the Austrians:

> I conclude you have heard of the exploits of the Dutch. At Turcoin [sic], half the detachment taken prisoners. On the approach of the enemy, three battalions, with their cannon, &c., &c., retired from Furnes; the post was retaken in a couple of days by two squadrons of Hussars. I think it high time the Meinheers should return to their bogs. From such friends and allies, may the Lord deliver us. I really believe that half a dozen battalions of Austrians and as many squadrons of Hussars, would drive them all out of the country.[4]

Writing to his sister in mid-June, upon learning that a junior officer of his acquaintance was coming out, he wrote: 'At his age, I think the more he sees the better, and he cannot learn in a better school than from our Austrian allies, who are the very best troops I ever saw.'[5] And as to the Prussians, they were seemingly in decline: 'The Prussians have a great deal of lee-way to make up, to regain the military character they established under their late king.'[6] This hero-worship of the Austrians had however a serious consequence – it seemed to be assumed they knew better in all things military. The duke's chief engineer, Colonel James Moncrieff, and indeed the duke himself, both favoured an immediate assault on Valenciennes, a *coup de main*, and argued strongly for such a tactic at a conference on 8 June; but the Austrian Ferraris reverted to type and insisted on a slow regular siege in the Imperial fashion. He won the debate and even made sure Austrian engineers had overall direction of the works.

The siege was conducted by Oberst Fromm, Imperial Chief Engineer. The artillery was under the Command of Generalmajor Leopold von Untenburger. Major Jesse Wright RA and Colonel James Moncrieff RE were reduced to subordinates and oversaw trenching and gun-siting around Valenciennes for the next six weeks. Some of the goings-on were noted by Captain Henry Clinton who reported to his father on 11 June:

> A very clever fellow, an Austrian officer of Pontonniers has thrown across the inundation about a mile above Valenciennes such a dam, with a bridge of 700 yards, that we are now under the apprehension of having our communication cut by fear of the sluices of Bouchain. It is nearly in the same place as that made by Turenne 150 years ago, except he made use of floating fascines. We have many high bridges. The dam is raised in proportion as the water increases.[7]

Some 4,500 soldiers in six brigades toiled in the trenches doing twelve-hour shifts, with 3,000 men to cover them. The main Coalition attack was planned to go in on the east side of Valenciennes. However, the ground was not broken in front of these defences until the evening of 13 June:

> His Royal Highness, the commander in, chief ordered that a working party, consisting of 750 men, under the command of a field officer, from the brigade of British infantry, should parade this evening on the right of the British encampment: they assembled about half past six o'clock, and marched about eight, with a covering party of 500 men, composed of light dragoons, Austrian heavy cavalry, and Hanoverian grenadiers; they marched towards our works and immediately began to open the trenches upon the town: the enemy were very quiet during the night.[8]

The following day the town was summoned but refused to surrender. On 16 June the garrison sent two observation balloons up; pot-shots failed to bring them down. The French garrison was hardly homogenous, and Ferrand had to cope with defenders who were adherents of Dumouriez, as well as the low-grade 'reinforcements' left behind by Lamarche. The population lived mostly underground and diseases were rife. A first French sortie by the garrison near Marly on 17 June was repulsed. William Bentinck thought the raiders looked as if they were drunk.[9] Calvert wrote to his sister:

> Our first parallel is complete, and I think nothing can prevent our guns opening on the town to-morrow at daybreak. You may picture to yourself the sort of salute it will be, when I tell you that only in the parallel on the eastern side of the town are thirteen batteries, each containing eight pieces of cannon; two of these batteries will fire hot shot. I cannot help feeling much for the poor women and children. I hope they are well secured in cellars, &c. Nothing can have been more prosperous than our approaches hitherto; we have thrown up communications and works, I dare say to the extent of near three miles, with very small loss indeed; that of the English is only three men slightly wounded by splinters of shells.[10]

Over 1,000 shells were fired during the night of 18 June.[11] By 21 June the attackers could plainly perceive a breach made in the side of the steeple of the great church. It only got worse for the defenders:

> Between twelve and one o'clock this June morning we perceived the large buildings on the left of the great church to be on fire; it continued burning with great fury till it was consumed to the ground, the fire of which communicating with the main body of the church, set it all on a blaze: this church was one of their principal magazines, for forage, arms, &c. about four o'clock the roof fell in, when the flames burst out with greater fury than ever ... This morning a shell burst close to a Hanoverian soldier, as he was asleep in the trenches; his body was blown all to atoms, and never seen more, except one arm, which was found in the trench.[12]

It had rained for most of June, and the men waded through trenches in calf-deep water. The wetness delayed the arrival of the heavy siege guns. But the weather in July turned hot. The troops turned out each evening to hear the Austrian bands play, although a British Guards officer thought them 'very inferior to that of the Coldstream.'[13] Shot and shell continued to rain every day, which led to unfortunate incidents:

> An accident happened to a soldier of the 16th regiment of light dragoons this day; he had got a shell into the camp by some means

or other, and curiosity excited him to try to get the fuse out, in doing of which it caught fire between his legs, and tore one thigh and the other leg entirely off; he died soon after.[14]

On 10 July Condé-sur-l'Escaut surrendered to the Austrians, after a siege lasting eleven weeks. The garrison of 4,000 men marched out on 13 July with all the honours of war and then marched into captivity. The duke rode there and was witness to the capitulation, probably hoping to see how it was done. 'I found the Troupes de Ligne, of whom there were three Battalions, better in point of Men than I had imagined, but the Gardes Nationales were worse than I could have had an idea of.'[15] The British fired a *feu-de-joie* the following day. In mid-July several mines were laid under some French horn-works on the northern road leading to Valenciennes. The preparations for the siege of Valenciennes were continuing at a snail's pace, much to the duke's chagrin:

> The parallels (trenches) have been open for some days, and the commandant of Valenciennes summoned to surrender. He had the impertinence to address his reply to 'Frederick York' sending him at the same time his oath and a French national cockade. Moreover, they have been trying to send despatches to the National Convention by means of small air-balloons, which fortunately fell into our hands. The fire of our batteries began to play on the place, and parts of the city were set on fire, which were, however, extinguished by the besieged. A brisk fire was returned by the fortress, by which, as yet, very few soldiers are wounded. The day before yesterday a horde of Carmagnoles made a sortie on us from the fortress, shouting: '*Vive la nation!*' But they were boldly received, and although I was unable to observe anything closely, I gather that Colonel von Bothmer with a detachment of our Guards gave them some heavy volleys. They left twenty-four dead on the field without having killed any of our men.[16]

A detachment of Royal Artillery with a battery of long 6-pounders arrived at Valenciennes from Ostend on 22 July.[17] With their help the last of the siege artillery around Valenciennes was sited, and the guns in the third parallel commenced firing on 23 July. The siege battery now comprised forty-eight twenty-four pounders, eight twelve-pounders, ten six-pounders, thirty-six mortars and sixteen howitzers. According to William Windham, the soon-to-be Secretary of War present at the siege as a private observer, the siege batteries fired off 45,000 shells and 76,000 cannon-shot between 18 June and 26 July; about 1,250 per day, or nearly one a minute.[18]

By 24 July, it was obvious the siege was entering its final phase. Ompteda recorded that day:

> For a few days the fire of the besieged has diminished markedly. Deserters inform us that they lack ammunition, particularly shot and shell. In the meantime ours drop plentifully into the unfortunate town. Our fire is much the hottest at night-time. Nearly every night there are more or less serious conflagrations, which fill the city with loud lamentations clearly audible in our trenches. Two nights ago I saw from my picket the notable church tower of Valenciennes in flames. An officer and some men were placed in the tower for the purpose of making observations. These unfortunate persons are said to have all perished in the flames, or by a hazardous leap. It is further stated that the women of the city besought the commandant on their knees to give up the fortress, or they would not have a roof left, but that Ferrand replied that in that case he would pitch tents for them.[19]

The Duke of York visited the trenches often and did not shy away from danger. On 25 July a cannon-ball took the head off an Austrian walking a few paces behind him, and later another killed a nearby guardsman whilst the duke was standing observing a battery. His personal bravery was perhaps meant as setting an example to the Hanoverians, who were mutinous again (two cavalry officers had actually encouraged their men to desert and were duly sent home) and whose behaviour under fire was drawing criticism from their British allies. The arrival of the Hessen-Cassel force in two divisions between 10 and 19 July increased the siege force by 7,600 men, albeit with only thirty rounds per man, no spare ammunition, and poor quality horses.[20]

The Capture

Three mines[21] were exploded at eight-minute intervals from 21.00 hours on 25 July. Immediately a storming party made up of 150 men from the Brigade of Guards, 150 men from Abercrombie's line brigade and 150 Hanoverians went into the salient angle of the ravelin of the French horn-works at bayonet point. They were supported by two Austrian columns (Generals Count Erbach and Wenkheim), with 450 Hessen-Cassel (Oberst von Lengerke) and Hanoverians (Oberstleutnant Offeney) supporting the British in the second line. The horn-works were captured, and some French artillery put out of action for the loss of nineteen men.

The Duke of York sent an aide to summon the city to surrender the following morning and announced that this would be the last such summons. The garrison commander Général Jean Ferrand asked for a twenty-four-hour truce at 20.00 hours. After negotiations the garrison surrendered the following day at 16.00 hours.

The French were allowed to march out of Valenciennes with honours of war and allowed to return home – as long as they agreed not to serve against the Allies for the rest of the war. It was not all plain sailing however; the citizens pelted their defenders with fruit and stones as they departed before running up the Bourbon flag. French losses during the two-month siege were about 1,000 (mainly due to sickness), 130 cannon, forty-three mortars, eleven howitzers and 68,000 rounds of ammunition. Austrian losses were thirty-six officers and 1,269 men; British were 146 and Hanoverian 206, virtually all caused by artillery fire on the trenches.

The final terms of the surrender of Valenciennes were agreed at noon on 28 July. The Imperial Feldmarschalleutnant Karl Freiherr von Lilien was named as commandant in the name of the Emperor, and a detachment of 200 Guardsmen under Colonel Sir James Duff (1st Foot Guards) occupied the town as the band of the 14th Foot played 'British Grenadiers' and the March from Handel's *Scipione*.[22] Captain Harry Calvert was lucky enough to be entrusted with the victory despatch:

> The next night, his Royal Highness sent me with despatches, containing accounts of this important event, to the King, royal family, and the Ministers. In the night of the 30th I arrived in London, and the next morning had the honour of delivering his Royal Highness's despatches to his Majesty at Kew. I was on this occasion promoted to the rank of Major.[23]

The population of Valenciennes were no doubt glad to be free of the deadly bombardment:

> During the armistice the fair ladies of Valenciennes showed themselves on the ramparts, and made a number of polite and inviting signs to the English and Hanoverian officers, but not to the Austrians, against whom the French display a deadly hatred.[24]

The French garrison marched out of Valenciennes with their wives and children in tow, a column of 6 or 7,000 people bound for new homes. The Austrians took up residence in their place:

> According to the conditions of the capitulation, the 6,000 men, composing what remained of the garrison, were to march out through the Cambray gate, and pass before us with all military honours and the pomp of a parade, and were then, at a little distance

further from the city, to lay down their arms and be escorted by two divisions of Imperial cavalry to the nearest French post, which was the village of Avesne-le-sec, a good hour's distance. At the appointed time I placed myself, with Captain von Low, by the Cambray gate. The greater part of the besieging army, amounting all together to 20,000 men, was drawn up in two lines on both sides of the road. It seemed as if the corps of the different nations were vying with one another in splendour of appearance.[25]

The victors were a coalition army, and contained officers from many nations:

Midway between the two lines stood all the generals of the different army corps employed in this part of France, and they, with their numerous staff, as well as a number of officers from every European army, formed a most brilliant and interesting gathering round the distinguished personages who had played so conspicuous a part in this war. Among several other persons who have become known in more recent history, my attention was especially directed to Prince Poniatowsky, a nephew of the noble and unfortunate King of Poland. He commanded for some time with credit an army of his own nation, which was unfortunately overcome by the superior forces of the Russians. This Poniatowsky is a man in the prime of life, finely built, with a noble, manly, agreeable, and resolute countenance.[26]

Two hundred and fifty miles (400km) to the east, a similar operation had been going on at the city of Mainz. A Coalition force started a siege of that place on 10 April, attempting to recapture the German city lost to Custine the previous October.

Unlike Valenciennes, Mainz was held in great force. Maréchal de camp François-Ignace d'Oyré had 23,000 men and 312 cannon within the city walls, against which the Duke of Brunswick could array 37,000 Prussians, Austrians, Saxons and Hessians. The preparatory siege works took an eternity; the bombardment did not commence until 18 June. The French finally surrendered on 23 July after losing 4,000 men. They were paroled and allowed to return to France on the condition that they did not fight against the Coalition again for one year. The National Convention got around this by sending them (and their brigadier Chef de brigade Jean-Baptiste Kléber, temporarily in disgrace) west to the Vendée to put down a pro-Royalist revolt.

The long, slow sieges of Condé, Valenciennes and Mainz were Coalition tactical victories only. The Coalition gained merely real estate, and a few thousand prisoners and combatants on parole.

The French gained the one thing they needed most – time. Time to recruit, re-organise and re-supply. Had Colonel Moncrieff got his way with his *coup de main*, Valenciennes might have fallen a month earlier. But the Coalition partners were thinking about things other than time – their own national and political interests. What should have been France's darkest hour was at last admitting daylight, as one commentator observed:

> Happy were the French, because the united powers did not act with the concert that is the strength of coalitions! If misunderstandings had not kept the cabinets of Europe divided in their efforts to to dissolve the Republic, what would have been the fate of France? But to have hesitated when it was necessary to strike great blows, the foreign powers did not perceive that in war even more than elsewhere, lost time never repairs.[27]

Chapter 8

Linselles to Dunkirk

Caesar's Camp

Custine had fatally failed to capture the besieged fortress of Condé, and then let Valenciennes fall. The Revolutionary Tribunal[1] was not impressed and brought a charge of treason. He was replaced by the tall and fervently patriotic Général de division Jean Nicolas Houchard, his face badly disfigured by old wounds. Houchard considered his appointment a curse. He arrived at his new headquarters on 11 August to find that a representative of the Convention had arrested his entire staff and had sent all the Armée du Nord's headquarters records to Paris. Custine was guillotined in Paris on 28 August 1793; Houchard's tenure would be even shorter than Custine's.

With such command uncertainty, and the French army in disarray after defeats at Valenciennes and Mainz, not to mention the loss of the Austrian Netherlands, Coalition unanimity and decisiveness at this point could have proven deadly to the Republicans. But singular interests and nationalistic politics carried the day. The historian Sir Archibald Allison summarised it the best:

> If the conduct of the Allies had been purposely intended to develop the formidable military strength, which had grown up in the French Republic, they could not have adopted measures better calculated to effect their object than were actually pursued. Four months of success, which might have been rendered decisive, had been wasted in blameable inactivity; after having broken the frontier line of fortresses, and defeated the covering army of France in a pitched battle, when within fifteen marches of Paris, and at the head of a splendid army of 130,000 men, they thought fit to separate their forces, and instead of pushing on to the centre of republican power, pursue independent plans of aggrandizement. The English, with their allies, amounting to above 35,000 men, moved towards

Dunkirk, so long the object of their maritime jealousy, while 45,000 of the Imperialists sat down before Quesnoy, and the remainder of their vast army was broken into detachments to preserve the communications. From this ruinous division may be dated all the subsequent disasters of the campaign. Had they held together and pushed on vigorously against the masses of the enemy's forces, now severely weakened and depressed by defeat, there cannot be a doubt that the object of the war would have been gained.[2]

The decision to lay siege to Dunkirk had not been made by any military man. Prime Minister William Pitt, under the influence of Secretary of State for the Home Department Henry Dundas, not to mention the king, coveted Dunkirk for political reasons, as we have seen. It could be, as it had long ago once been, a potential British base in Europe. It could also be a useful bargaining chip in any post-war peace negotiations. Control of West Flanders and the Pas de Calais would give the Royal Navy a variety of strong harbours on the French coast and a multitude of safe landing spots for reinforcements, as well as denying these ports to the French navy. Any Coalition force in this region would always be a significant diversion for the French, directing troops away from the main Coalition thrust towards Paris from Valenciennes and Maubeuge.

The downside was that the proposed Dunkirk operation would create a gap in the Coalition line, weakly manned by the wavering Dutch army. The perceived positives outweighed the matter of the tenuous gap, and the order arrived for the duke to march for the coast. The duke undoubtedly knew this was a problem; but had not yet the experience or command confidence to do other than as ordered. The historian Alfred Burne was scathing about the decision:

> Unfortunately, the English Government still clung blindly to their Dunkirk project. Now, this project would have been perfectly sound in April, when the Allies were dispersed, but the situation in August had changed; the Allies were fairly well concentrated in the centre of the line, where a breach had just been made, and to disperse the striking force just when an outstanding victory was within their grasp was fatuous … The Duke was strongly opposed to the Dunkirk venture, but the English Government was obdurate, and York – always a pattern of loyalty to his seniors – regretfully parted company with Coburg and marched north for Dunkirk, taking with him a force of 10,000 Austrians, while Coburg turned placidly to besiege the minor fortress of Quesnoy.[3]

Tuesday 6 August 1793 was a very hot day. The duke had three columns under his command. The first, British, was commanded by himself; the second, seven battalions and six squadrons of Hanoverians was under Feldmarschall von Freytag; the third, four battalions and ten squadrons of Austrians, was commanded by Feldzeugmeister Hohenlohe-Kirchberg. His own small British command had been boosted by three additional light companies, one each from the three Guards regiments, plus a draft of 600 Guardsmen which had arrived at the end of July. Fresh troops did not guarantee order; in fact, they seem to have added to a general air of confusion. Lieutenant & Captain William Knollys of the 3rd Foot Guards recorded his impressions on the march:

> When our business is over no one can possibly tell, for our orders are given one Hour, and we march the next, & even our Field Officers are ignorant ... the villages through which we march are plundered, find Edifices destroyed, so that we sleep in Stables, Churches & whatever we can find – I am sorry to tell, that the Combined Armies distinguish neither Friends nor Enemies in their Progress, and Devastation marks our advance, indeed it is almost impossible to avoid it, for when our soldiers starve & literally we have no Provisions provided, it is impossible to stop them from taking what they can.[4]

The British cavalry was seriously engaged for the first time in a skirmish south of the so-called Camp de César[5] just outside Bourlon, 5 miles (8km) west of Cambrai, on 7 August. The campsite extended from 3 miles (5km) north of Cambrai to the Bourlon Wood, about 3 miles west of that place, and occupied by 35,000 Frenchmen commanded by the Irishman, Général de division Charles Kilmaine.

The duke was given a column of 25,000 men and orders to sweep clockwise to the south of Cambrai and catch the French in the western flank, as they were reeling from the main assault delivered by Coburg's 15,000-man Austrian column. The advance started at 03.00 hours across open country, fine cavalry country. However, the duke's route of march was long; so long in fact as to give plenty of warning to the French, and to exhaust the infantry on a boiling hot day. By dusk they were little more than half-way to Bourlon Wood; Jackson's rapid flank march at Chancellorsville it certainly was not. Kilmaine held a council of war that night and decided to retreat westwards, leaving a French cavalry force to delay the Coalition columns at Bourlon Wood.

The duke's column stuttered forward again at daybreak on 8 August, accompanied this time by the Austrians, who had caught up overnight. From a ridge west of the wood the duke spotted the French cavalry rear-guard near the village of Marquion and sent his aide Captain Herbert Taylor to appeal to the Austrians for cavalry support, but they politely declined. So, the Duke gathered around him a mixed force of some infantry and (mostly) cavalry and marched off towards the distant French. Little did the duke know that the isolated French cavalry were about to be reinforced by Kilmaine and his main column, just out of view. Count Louis Alexandre Andrault de Langeron, a French émigré serving as an observer with the Austrians, was on hand to witness what came next:

> This day I had the happiness to save the life of the Duke of York. On arrival at the Agache he ordered the Austrian cavalry on the left to make for the bridge of Saing-les-Marquion and intended himself with the English cavalry to cross at Marquion, where we had captured the bridge. The village was on fire, and we were so roasted by the fumes that it was impossible to cross. The cavalry halted. The Duke of York who was leading with a single orderly and myself, dashed through the burning village. However, at a gallop, and a hundred yards beyond it reached a small height from which we saw, only 20 yards away, two lines of French cavalry. As they wore practically the same uniform as the Hanoverian cavalry, the Duke, who had more personal bravery than experience of war, cried: 'There are my Hanoverians!' He continued to advance and almost reached the line of enemy officers, when I cried out to him 'Monseigneur, those are the French!' and seizing his horse's bridle turned him and led him back to Marquion. But for me he would have been killed or taken – which would have been the same thing for him, for the Convention spared no Englishman.[6]

Major General Ralph Dundas' brigade (11th, 15th and 16th Light Dragoons) and the Hanoverian cavalry fought off 200 French cavalry, isolated two enemy battalions and took forty-six prisoners for the loss of ten men. However French cavalry rescued their infantry and allowed the French to slip away without seriously engaging the Coalition troops, albeit in some confusion and haste. The Austrian cavalry, which was numerous and could have harassed the French retreat, was stuck somewhere to the rear of the Austrian columns to the east. Thus, as at Famars, the French had escaped with minimal loss, and another opportunity had been missed.

Linselles

The duke brushed off his near-capture and conducted his column in its inevitable transit towards Dunkirk.[7] The French were initially bewildered as to his manoeuvres and hoped that perhaps he was retiring from the campaign to sail home to England. The recently-arrived British heavy cavalry brigade was not even with them, doing garrison duty at Ostend. On 18 August the Prince of Orange-Nassau and his Dutch forces attacked

French outposts at Mauvaix, Blaton and Linselles (about 8 miles or 12km north of Lille) with four battalions. He took the village of Linselles and then lost it again to a determined French attack commanded by Général de division Jean-Baptiste Jourdan. The prince asked for help, and the duke ordered Major General Lake and his Brigade of Guards northwards to help them. Arriving at 18.00 hours after a four-hour march, 1,100 Guardsmen found that the Dutch had retired completely, leaving them unsupported. Harry Calvert was on the scene:

> The army marched in two columns – the left by Roucq, crossing the Lys on a bridge of pontoons about a mile above Menin, the right through Neuville and Halluim, crossing the river at Menin. They encamped in two lines on the Ypres road with their left on Menin. In order to cover the march, the Dutch made an attack on the enemy's posts at Lincelles and Blaton, situated on the road from Werwick and Lille, which the enemy had fortified but did not defend. In the evening, however, the enemy attacked both these posts in great force. The Dutch retired from Blaton to Lincelles. On the enemy's approach, they abandoned Lincelles, leaving their guns and ammunition. At this moment, the brigade of Guards, under the command of Major-general Lake, who had marched on the first notice of the attack, made their appearance. The General in vain endeavoured to persuade the Dutch to stand and rally under cover of the Guards, but nothing could persuade them to show the smallest countenance. He therefore resolved to attack the enemy with the three battalions he had with him, who, marching at a moment's warning out of camp, did not exceed 1200 men. The intrepidity of the troops made up for the smallness of their numbers, and under a most galling fire of grape, they stormed and carried the redoubts, &c., and took ten pieces of cannon, tumbrils, &c., and 70 prisoners.[8]

Corporal Robert Brown was present with the 3rd Foot Guards:

> General Lake having made the proper disposition, the attack began. The 1st regiment being in front of the column, began the attack, and the 3d regiment and Coldstream forming on their left with the utmost celerity, the whole line then rustled in upon the enemy with irresistible force, amidst showers of grape shot from their redoubts; and after discharging a volley or two of musketry, made a furious charge, accompanied with a loud huzza, mounted their batteries in the face of the enemy, and devoted all they met with to the bayonet. The French, who had been accustomed to the cold lifeless attacks of the Dutch, were amazed at the spirit and intrepidity of the British, and not much relishing the manner of our salute, immediately gave way, abandoning all that was in the place, and in their flight threw away

both arms and accoutrements. We took one stand of colours, ten pieces of cannon, with two pieces which they had taken from the Dutch, and a number of prisoners. We suppose the number of troops in that place to have amounted to between 5 and 6,000; ours were short of 1,200.[9]

The duke was especially pleased for his old friend and mentor Lake: 'Upon the first intelligence of what had happened, I sent six Battalions to General Lake's support, and went there myself, but before We arrived everything was over and the enemy was completely gone.'[10] The senior British casualty of the day was Lieutenant Colonel Thomas Bosville of the Coldstream Guards, one of the tallest men in the British army at six feet four inches tall. His height did for him; he was hit in the head by a musket-ball.[11] Linselles (mis-transcribed by the War Office as Lincelles) was the first British battle honour of the war. The following day the newly-arrived Lieutenant General Sir William Erskine was given command of the British heavy cavalry brigades of Harcourt and Mansell. Nick-named 'Woolly', Erskine was a 65-year-old Scot who had served in the Army for over fifty years.

All this local excitement inspired no special notice in Paris. Everyone had bigger concerns; events unfolding there would have dramatic consequences for the French. On 14 August Lazar Carnot had joined the Committee of Public Safety, with control over the formation, training and movements of the armies of the Republic. Carnot was an inspired workaholic, with massive powers of productivity, vast organisational skills, and the ability to enforce discipline. Two days after his appointment he issued his famous decree calling for a *levée en masse* of the male population. It was to ultimately produce an army of 1,500,000 men in late 1794, as compared to 650,000 in June 1793. This was the first employment of mass conscription in history, to create the largest army the world had ever seen:

> The young men shall march to the combat; the married ones shall forge arms and transport provisions; the women shall fabricate tents and clothes, and attend the military hospitals; the children shall make lint to serve as dressings for the wounds of the patients; while the old men shall cause themselves to be carried to the public squares to excite the courage of the warriors, to preach the unity of the republic, and inspire hatred against kings.[12]

Carnot knew Dunkirk well. He had been in the army for twenty years, had been an Engineer officer, and understood the mechanics of fortification. That Dunkirk was badly in need of repair he had known for years. In early April 1793 he had rushed there to throw his enormous energy behind the necessary improvements. The fruits of these labours were shortly to flower.

Dunkirk

The Duke of York drove his men hard after Linselles, covering 35 miles (56km) in two days, and in sweltering heat. He established his headquarters at Furnes, then commenced his grand manoeuvre of Dunkirk on 22 August.

His force advanced along the dunes towards the fortified camp at Ghyvelde, 6 miles (9km) east of Dunkirk, harassed all the time by French gunboats. On the night of 22–23 August, the French abandoned the camp and the Coalition captured eleven cannon for the loss of fifty Austrians. Général de division Houchard was disgusted by the feebleness of the resistance. 'The soldiers are good,' he wrote to the Convention, 'but the cowardice and crass ignorance of the officers make them learn cowardice, and to fly before the enemy is nothing to them.'[13]

The duke's plan was to place a siege cordon around Dunkirk. On 19 August he split his army into a Covering Force and an Observation Force. Feldmarschall von Freytag's column, all the Hanoverians with ten British cavalry squadrons and two battalions (plus detachments) of Austrians – 14,500 men – was to approach Dunkirk from the south, and to protect the Coalition left flank as the 'Army of Observation.' Generals Abercrombie and Erskine commanded the British Covering Force in the centre, under the eye of the duke. Feldmarschalleutnant Baron Alvinczi commanded the Austrian contingent on the right flank. Generalleutnant von Buttlar commanded the Hessen-Cassel brigade in support on the left. By 24 August the Coalition force was defending a twenty-mile cordon around Dunkirk, starting close to Ypres and headquartered at Hondschoote. However, encirclement by land was useless if the defenders could reinforce from the sea, and in this the duke was reliant upon the support of the Royal Navy, daily expected. Even the French expected the town to fall as soon as the Royal Navy appeared.

Local French garrisons had shown traces of resistance, though mostly feeble. On 21 August, the advanced guard of Freytag's Hanoverian force had stumbled across small French garrisons at Rexpöede and Oost-Cappel, about 10 miles (16km) south-east of Dunkirk. The raw French militia fled at the first shot; Hanoverian losses were about forty killed and wounded. A more serious skirmish occurred on 24 August at Rosendael, a coastal town one mile east of Dunkirk. The duke's reserve column comprising Austrian troops plus the flank companies of the British Guards and Hessen-Cassel 3.Grenadier-Bataillon under Austrian Feldmarschalleutnant Graf Eduard d'Alton[14] attempted to establish a siege position near the town:

> The battle was very violent; the enemy, superior in number and favoured by the cannon fire from the ramparts of Dunkirk,

repeatedly conquered the terrain which the Allies had won in rapid succession. It seems that d'Alton had made the mistake of not attacking with all his might from the outset, but only thrusting it into action piecemeal...

So, the fight went on and on for several hours. Around 9 o'clock in the morning the two Hessian grenadier battalions of Eschwege and Wurmb received reinforcements. Count d'Alton, a still youthful, knightly hero, dismounted and personally stood at the head of both battalions. In a few powerful words he invited them, by a courageous attack, to end the murderous and long-lasting engagement. A loud cheer went to answer him, and with courageous warlike cries and irresistible impetuosity, the two battalions crowded into one another, making a quick start towards Rosendahl. The enemy was completely knocked over, and a gun was captured by the grenadier battalion of Wurmb. At the village exit of Dunkirk, however, the enemy had placed guns whose fire drove the battalions back some distance. D'Alton, with a bare sword everywhere at the head of the grenadiers, pursued them to the foot of the glacis of Dunkirk.

At this moment, however, an enemy column of 4,000 men, supported by numerous artillery, exited from the dunes and attacked the village from the north. The small group of Hessian grenadiers, together scarcely 700 men strong, could not resist this new attack. D'Alton was mortally wounded in the head by an enemy sniper, and the grenadiers were completely pushed back from Rosendahl. Meanwhile, however, General Lieutenant v. Wurmb's command arrived with the regiments Prince Karl and Kospoth as reinforcements, and so just arrived when the French had reconquered Rosendahl again. He immediately took command of d'Alton's troops and sent them on another assault. In the meantime the enemy had once again left this corpse-filled place, and had occupied the outermost row of houses opposite Dunkirk, from which, however, in spite of all his efforts, because of the supportive fire from the fortifications, he could not be expelled. The battle ended in the late afternoon, when the rest of the village, maintained by the regiments of Prince Karl and Kospoth and two battalions of English light infantry, was occupied.[15]

The 5,000 strong French garrison was eventually forced out, Austrian losses were 170 men, British and Hessen-Cassel 129. D'Alton was killed towards the end of the action and Lieutenant Colonel George Eld of the Coldstream Guards was killed by a cannon ball through his chest. The duke's report makes it clear that most casualties were caused by the French artillery:

> We suffered very little from their musketry, because they never attempted to dispute the ground with us, but kept firing and retreating; but they no sooner got under cover of their own guns,

than they began to open upon us with both grape and round shot, and in our retreat to a convenient cover, we suffered considerably. Unfortunately the ardour and gallantry of the troops carried them too far in spite of a peremptory order from me, three times repeated, they pursued the enemy upon the glacis of the place when we had the misfortune to lose many very brave and reliable men by the grapeshot from the town.[16]

The Coalition was able to take up new positions, which ran from the coast south to Téteghem. The northern part of the Coalition line was in the sand-hills along the coast, the villages all poor and covered in sand-drifts, while the southern part was in an area of swamp known as the Great Moor. More difficult terrain to defend would be hard to devise:

> The position itself was in many respects disadvantageous. It was much broken up by innumerable little ditches, hedges, and patches of of brushwood, all of which the troops had to clear away with their side-arms for wants of better tools; it was wholly destitute of drinking water, that in the canals being brackish, and that found in wells unpalatable; and finally, it lay open to the minutest inspection from the tower of Dunkirk Cathedral.[17]

The construction of redoubts before Dunkirk commenced, and thus the siege started. Infantrymen toiled in the sandy trenches under the direction of Major of Trenches Captain John Sontag.[18] All the Coalition needed now was for the promised Royal Navy blockading fleet to arrive. The defences of Dunkirk were ancient and in very poor condition. The occupants intended to surrender – until the Commissioners arrived from Paris and put a stop to the idea.

Meanwhile in Paris, the French army, under the inspired management of Carnot, was in the process of re-inventing itself. The French Army officially adopted blue uniforms in place of the traditional (Royalist) white on 24 August. Knowing that a rebuff at Dunkirk would be humiliating and demoralising for the British, he ordered up as many troops as could be found to the sea-side town. Soon Houchard had 23,000 men in a fortified camp at Cassell, some 17 miles (27km) south of Dunkirk, assisted by 4,000 men approaching from Lille and another 15,000 marching from the Moselle. Dunkirk itself was defended by (initially) 5,000 men under Général de brigade Joseph Souham, later boosted to 8,000 once a reinforcement under Jourdan arrived.[19] The very able Jourdan was then transferred to command the Cassell camp and replaced by Leclaire. With so many men on hand, the defences were soon dramatically improved; morale soared. And still the Royal Navy blockading fleet had not arrived.

French gunboats appeared off-shore and began bombarding the Coalition coastal right flank with impunity. The duke's army was desperately short on fire-power – he had no siege artillery. Eleven transports arrived offshore on 27 August, but high tides meant that only two of them could disembark at Nieuwpoort, the rest having to sail to Ostend. Those at Nieuwpoort discharged Major William Orchard Huddlestone of the Royal Artillery with sixty-three heavy artillerymen, but the ten 24-pounders they were intended to serve were still aboard ship. In the end the duke took cannon from a frigate. The commander of the Royal Navy Channel fleet, Rear-Admiral John Macbride, arrived without his fleet on 30 August, but then was scattered in the storm like the rest of his ships, and did not re-appear until the siege was over. Only at the start of September was the duke able to start bombarding the walls of Dunkirk. A Royal Navy frigate, HMS *Brilliant*, eventually arrived to add firepower support to the siege, but was blown away by a storm three days later. The siege of Dunkirk was therefore not a blockade, and the French could re-supply the place from the sea unimpeded. Notwithstanding, the mood in the Coalition camp was positive. 'For my own part I think every thing is going on extremely well,' Murray wrote to Henry Dundas on 3 September.[20]

The storms which gave way to continuously rainy weather in early September were an ominous sign, and the Coalition optimism waned as little things started to go wrong. Another company of the Royal Artillery (Laye's) arrived, but without its guns, which were still at Nieuwpoort.

Souham opened the town sluices, which inundated the fields east of Dunkirk and filled British trenches with two feet of water. 'The inundations increasing daily, rendered the ground, on which the British encamped, a perfect swamp ... An epidemical disorder called the Dunkirk Fever, soon broke out amongst the troops, increased daily, and carried off the soldiers rapidly.'[21] On 5 September Freytag's men attacked a French advanced post at Arnecke without success, during which Oberleutnant Ompteda was wounded:

> Attack by the battalion on a French post at Coffre, half an hour from Cassel, at which latter is placed a corps of 16,000 men. Several casualties. General Fabry of the Imperial army, in command, was wounded at the beginning of the action. Two other columns which should have also attacked this position were two hours late, on account of which the battalion had to bear the heavy brunt of the day. Surrounded in flank and rear by the enemy, we were delivered from otherwise unavoidable defeat by the determination of Captain von Bremer to cut the way through to the right to Eskelbeck. The

> battalion got back in the evening to Wormhout, after defending itself without cannon against a very numerous enemy, and for a long time occupying the position it was ordered to take. Killed, Captain Schlüter and 4 Grenadiers; wounded, Lieutenants von Ompteda and Bodecker and 74 Grenadiers.[22]

Ompteda was taken to Bruges where he made a slow recovery.[23]

Meanwhile, far to the south-east at Le Quesnoy, the Austrians busied themselves with their own operations, aimed at securing the frontier in front of Mons. Prince Coburg had hoped to capture Cambrai, but seeing it too strongly fortified, opted to take the lesser fort of Le Quesnoy instead. Being a small town, the garrison was commanded by a mere lieutenant-colonel, François Goullus. Around his modest walls Feldzeugmeister Clerfayt had 18,000 men; Prince Josias covered the operations with the remainder of the Austrian force.

The bombardment commenced in the morning of 2 September. At 17.00 hours Clerfayt summoned the garrison to surrender. Goullus refused. Clerfayt ordered a bombardment which lasted for six days without slackening. Late on 10 September Goullus sent an officer to negotiate surrender terms, hoping to arrange an honourable capitulation. By this time, aware of the French tendency to find loopholes around promises of parole, Clerfayt insisted that the garrison should be taken as prisoners of war. The garrison marched into captivity on 11 September. From now on, there would be no more honourable capitulations and parole with promises of 'not to fight again'. Warfare was moving away from the eighteenth-century model, a game of gentlemen. The nineteenth-century version of war was slowly forming.

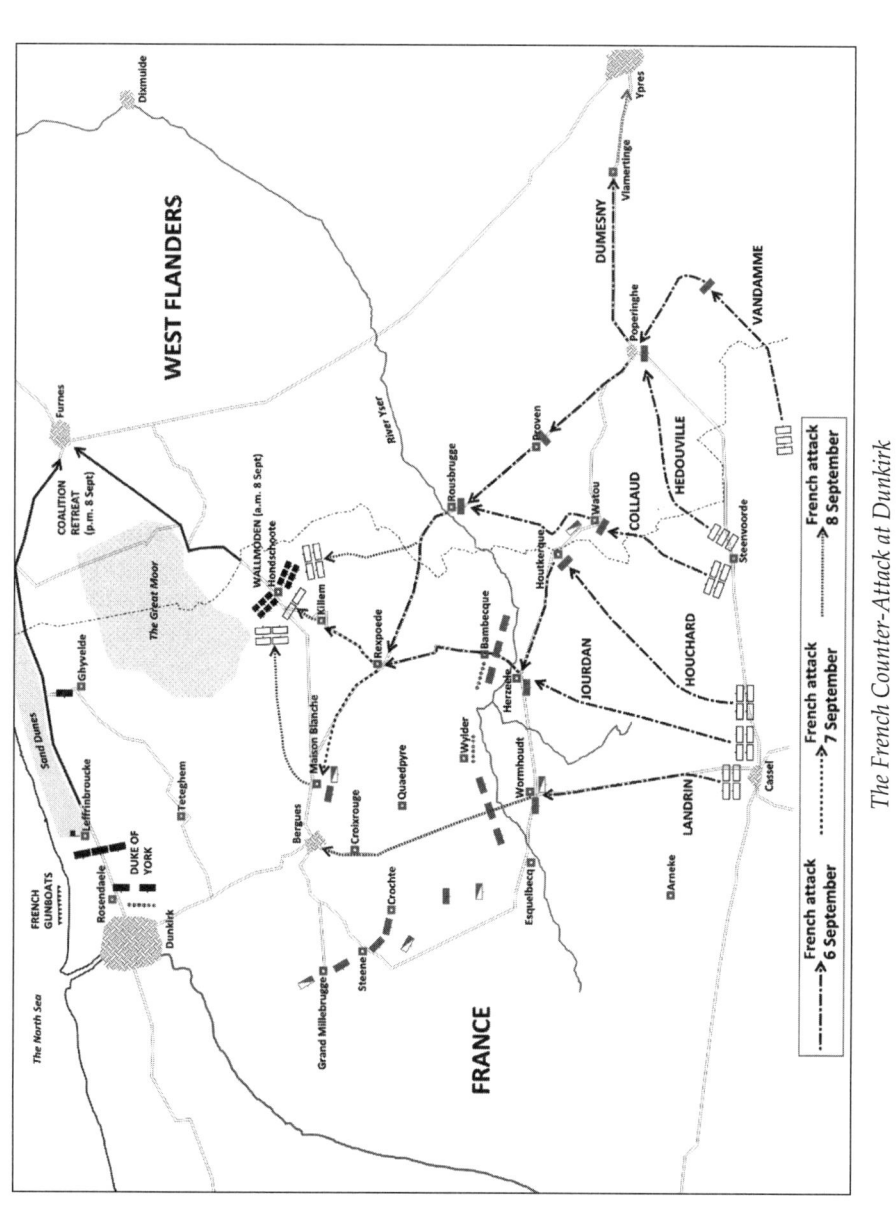

The French Counter-Attack at Dunkirk

Chapter 9

The Channel Ports

Hondschoote
Aware of his predecessor's fate (Custine was guillotined in Paris on 28 August), Général de division Houchard suddenly found a burst of energy and on 6 September ordered a massive attack against Freytag's Austro-Hanoverian covering force in front of Hondschoote, 10 miles (16km) south-east of Dunkirk, with 42,000 men in six columns, plus a diversionary force attacking from Bergues. Out on the right flank, the 1st Column under Lieutenant Colonel Dominique Vandamme (4,400 men) attacked northwards from Bailleul towards the Hanoverian outposts in Reningelst and threw them back to Ypres. The 2nd Column under Général de brigade Gabriel Marie Joseph, comte d'Hedouville (7,400 men) attacked the Hanoverian occupants of Poperinge from Steenevorde, conquered the place, and pushed the Hanoverians back eastwards as far as Vlamertinge, whereupon a part of the column turned northwest against Roesbrugge. The 3rd Column under Général de brigade Claude Sylvestre Colaud (strength included above) conquered Watou, advanced to Proven, and cut off the Hanoverian troops in Poperinge from retreating to Roesbrugge. These three French columns together amounted to about 12,000 men, and the posts they attacked were all defended by companies, so that the defenders in total were not more than 1,500 men. At Proven a part of the 2nd Column joined the 3rd, both then moving northwest together towards Roesbrugge, and drove Hanoverian Generalmajor Carl von Dachenhausen back to Rexpoëde.

The 4th (Houchard), 5th (Jourdan) and 6th (Landrin) columns (about 24,000 men) all attacked northwards from Cassel. Houchard's 4th drove on to Houtkerke, Jourdan's 5th to Herzeele and 6th to Wormhout. Houchard easily captured Houtkerke from the tiny garrison and sent Jourdan a sizeable column as a reinforcement. The Hessen-Cassel Jäger-Battaillon commanded by Oberst Moritz von Prüschenk encountered Jourdan near Winnezeele and captured a cannon but was eventually forced to retreat through weight of numbers. The Grün-Loudon Freikorps was sent towards the Houtkerke as reinforcements.

The French soon renewed their attacks, but the Hessen-Cassel Jägers defended the southern edge of Herzeele until late in the evening, and only when the village had been bypassed on all sides did Oberst von Prüschenk order the retreat to Bambecque. The Grün-Loudon Freikorps was forced off the track and into bushy terrain, losing a cannon. The cavalry found themselves compelled to retreat with much loss to Bambecque. Feldmarschall von Freytag set up several battalions of artillery at Wylder, Bambecque, and and Kruystraete as a rallying line for the Avantgarde. But since Bambecque was threatened on the eastward left flank and rear by the French 2nd and 3rd columns advancing from Roesbrugge, not to mention the 4th and 5th columns fiercely attacking from the south, Freytag had no choice but to order a general retreat to Rexpoëde.

Generalmajor Diepenbroick led a spirited counter-attack west of Esquelbecq against Landrin's 6th Column, which involved British and Hessen-Cassel dragoons fighting on foot due to the roughness of the country. Landrin retreated back to the south of Wormhoudt and readied himself for another advance the following day. Général de brigade Theodore Francois Leclaire deployed his 6,000-man diversionary force after mid-day outside Bergues and attacked the left wing of the Coalition position outside Dunkirk, at Bienkes Mille. After heavy losses on both sides, Leclaire retired back into Bergues at 17.00 hours to await fresh orders for the morrow.

Freytag's right wing was firm, but his left was in disarray, and there was a very real chance the French could cut the duke's force outside Dunkirk off from it's supply base at Furnes. At 20.00 hours, he issued orders for his tired troops to retire upon Hondschoote, astride the main road to Furnes. The French advance in the centre and right had been lightning fast, and even those fancying themselves behind the lines suddenly found themselves in danger. HRH Prince Adolphus[1] and Freytag unwittingly strayed into the path of a French cavalry picquet in Rexpoëde:

> Field Marshal Freytag, convinced that Dachenhausen still held Rexpoede… was advancing quietly with the Prince Adolphe of England (later Duke of Cambridge), his staff, General Trew, Captain Scharnhorst, 24 dragoons and 100 men of the Guard, when suddenly, at the entrance of the village, a squadron of French cavalry charged this group who were seemingly unaware of their presence. General Freytag, wounded in the head, losing blood, fell

from his horse and sank into a ditch; he was taken prisoner. Prince Adolphe succeeded in escaping only thanks to the devotion of his aide-de-camp, Lieutenant de Wangenheim.[2]

Temporary command fell to General der Kavallerie Graf Ludwig von Wallmoden-Gimborn who made it his first task to rescue his superior officers and evict the French from the town:

> The [French] artillery ... obstructed the highway, and the [Hanoverian] cavalry, hastily called, could not in the darkness force them out of the way. Hanoverian Guards, under Colonel Mylius, arrived finally, but, greeted by a terrible fire from the the edge of the village, he was forced to turn around; then the whole column was thrown to the left of the road... and began to wander the countryside in disorder. Meanwhile, Walmoden who was in person at about the middle of this column, was joined by Adjutant-general Spörken and Quartermaster-General Lieutenant-colonel Kuntze, who hastened to tell him that Freytag was a prisoner. Realising at once that in this situation his column, composed of cavalry and artillery, would be powerless to clear a passage, Walmoden immediately went to the left column and gave General de Bussche the order to attack Rexpoëde with the 2nd Battalion Grenadiers, the 1st squadron of the 7th Cavalry Regiment, a division of the Austrian Brentano regiment and some companies of Grün-Laudon. These infantrymen had fought all day long, and marched in the rain on broken roads; they had only eight rounds per man, but Walmoden exhorted them to understand that the right-hand column must be cleared at all costs.[3]

Wallmoden tasked the 2.Grenadier-Bataillon with re-capturing Rexpoëde:

> Although the grenadiers had spent the whole day under fierce fire ... they needed just an encouraging word, a reminder of their duty and the necessity to save their comrades at the 1st Column. These braves, each with barely 8 rounds, attacked the enemy with the greatest bravery, in the face of their superior strength. After a few shots from small rifles and some salvos, the brave grenadiers fired. Sustained by the other troops, they charged Rexpoede with the bayonet, drove out the enemies and thereby not only opened the way for the continuation of their march to the 1st Column on the other side of the village, but also freed the Feldmarschall from his imprisonment.[4]

The wounded Freytag had been escorted to Rexpoëde and shut up in a house in the village, then left behind by the French:

> It was there that he was found, much to his surprise, and delivered by Lieutenant von dem Bussche, son of the general and by Ensign

> Arentschildt, who had given themselves the task of finding their leader. As Freytag was weary and wounded, he was laid on a caisson which transported him to Veurne.[5]

Despite success at Rexpoëde, the Hanoverians were isolated and surrounded by swarms of advancing Frenchmen. There was no alternative but to continue the retreat to Hondschoote. The detachments of generalmajors Wangenheim and Dachenhausen had already retreated there. With all choices gone, von dem Bussche marched his exhausted grenadiers northwards through the night, and they arrived at Hondschoote at 06.00 hours on the morning of 7 September.

The most grievous loss to the Duke of York on 6 September was the mortal wounding of his Chief Engineer, Colonel John Moncrieff, during Leclaire's attack.[6] The following morning was quiet, as the exhausted foes snatched some rest. But Houchard did not let up, and at f16.00 hours attacked the Hanoverian defenders of Killem, less than a mile south of Hondschoote. Generalmajor von Diepenbroick commanded there with the 2. and 3.Grenadier-Bataillons, two battalions of the 5.Infanterie-Regiment, and two battalions of the 10.Infanterie-Regiment:

> Although some of the men were bleeding from several wounds, no-one wanted to give way, and yet the Hanoverian troops would have to succumb to the increasing deployment of the enemy with little battalions ... Diepenbroick, with the 2nd and 3rd Grenadier Battalions and the 2nd Battalion of the 10th Regiment, approached the French with the bayonet, and fell back with a considerable mass of dead and wounded.[7]

Houchard knew he had to give one more push on 8 September. The day opened with a diversionary attack by Général de division Pierre-Joseph Dumesny's division towards Ypres at 05.00 hours in the morning. The ground was difficult, and progress was slow; so slow that at dusk all the division could do was camp within a mile of the ramparts of the city.

At night three siege batteries (one consisting of 16- and 12-pounders, another of light artillery and the third howitzers) were constructed. Meanwhile, over on the left, Houchard ordered Général de division Jean-Noël Landrin's division to march on Dunkirk, and sent his adjutant-général, Capitaine Pierre-François-Joseph Durutte[8] of the 19e Dragoons to Bergues to coordinate the attack between the divisions of Landrin and Leclaire. Leclaire proposed to unite both in a single attack on the left of Hondchoote, but Landrin declined to take the advice of an inferior officer and spent the day advancing northwards from Wormhout at a snail's pace, arriving under the walls of Bergues only at dusk and thus taking no part in the fighting of 8 September.

Houchard's grand plan on the 8th involved the divisions of Colaud, Jourdan, Vandamme and Leclaire in an encircling movement directed on Hondschoote. At 04.00 hours, Vandamme left Killem and pushed his skirmishers along the road to Rexpoëde close to the western side of Hondschoote, concealed behind hedges and copses. The main body marched at about 03.00 hours and halted at the crossroads of Six-Paths about half a mile south-west of Hondschoote by 07.00 hours.

Houchard and Jourdan were astonished not to have seen any enemy detachments covering the main position of the Hanoverians. Houchard asked some peasants if Hondschoote was occupied by the enemy. They gave him some vague answers from which he concluded that the Coalition had left in the town about 5,000 men and a few pieces of artillery. Suspicious of this answer, Houchard ordered Adjutant-général Simon François Gay de Vernon to make a reconnaissance. De Vernon was able to very accurately ascertain the disposition of the Hanoverians, and even count their guns.[9] He rode back to advise Houchard that the enemy's left was resting in country entirely cut up by hedges and ditches, that his right was covered by the Bois d'Hondschoote and by wetlands. Houchard therefore to decided to attack against the centre, despite the presence of a 12-pounder battery on a hill overlooking the Killem road, and another eight cannon in two redoubts flanking the hill. Vandamme's and Jourdan's skirmishers were sent forward as the 12-pounders opened fire on the French infantry in column along the Rexpoëde road. Houchard declined to attack until the divisions of Colaud and Leclaire arrived; his columns therefore absorbed artillery fire for two hours as swarms of French skirmishers harassed the Hanoverian battalions, now visible.

The harassment was such that Wallmoden ordered Generalmajor von Cohenhausen to execute a counterattack with a battalion of the Hessisches Gross und Erbprinz Infanterie-Regiment and two companies of the k.k. Linien-Infanterie-Regiment Nr. 35 (Brentano). They succeeded in driving back Vandamme's chasseurs but were stopped in turn by a deep ditch bordered by a hedge behind which the French could fire with impunity. They then retreated to the outskirts of Hondschoote, where they restocked their ammunition. A second attempt by Jourdan's division met the same fate.

At that moment, Houchard believed the battle was lost. His staff and subordinates argued against retirement, knowing that a retreat would soon degenerate into a free-for-all flight. The men needed to be kept moving forward. There would be an all-out attack, echeloned from the right.

In the centre, Jourdan and Delbrel were barely keeping their men in the ranks as the Hanoverian artillery rounds fell amongst them, when another advance by the II/Gross und Erbprinz, and about forty Hanoverian grenadiers commanded by Major Mallet up the appropriately-named Killem road, caused a general retirement. The quick-thinking Jourdan rode to a battalion held in reserve, guarding the regimental *tricolores*, put some reliable cavalry on their flanks and marched them forward at the double-quick, herding the retiring infantry forward again to the firing-line. 'Our column, like a snowball, will grow larger as it moves forward,' Jourdan said; 'we will be seconded in our attack by the division of the left, which has the order to advance as soon as we start the charge.' Jourdan was disobeying Houchard's orders, since he was required to wait for the movement from the right. But the movement activated everybody, and all three columns advanced against the Hanoverian batteries and entrenchments.

Meanwhile, over on the left, the division of Général de division Leclaire had spent the morning marching eastwards from Maison Blanche at a snail's pace along a flooded road-way. His column came into view at Hondschoote about 400 yards from the village:

> I put a battery on a small bridge, the two pieces of the 32nd division of gendarmerie that I had marched to the head of the column. I ordered the strongest fire, convinced that the enemy would be intimidated to be attacked unexpectedly on this side and that it would revive the right [main] columns, which surely could not have expected that I would arrive at this point. When I was certain that the columns on the right must have heard the fire, I said one or two words to the gendarmes, at the moment when one of the two pieces had been dismounted. They threw themselves, bayonets in front, on the enemy's entrenchment, knee-deep in water ... The entrenchment was carried and the pieces taken. Out of 400 gendarmes, I lost 117 killed or wounded. At this moment, the 1st Battalion of the Orne, which followed the gendarmes and supported them, the 1st of Calvados likewise, suffered much ... A horrible butchery was made of the enemy.[10]

Leclaire took a squadron of the 5e Chasseurs à Cheval into the centre of the village, routed some Coalition squadrons and made 300 Hanoverians captive. A little after noon, Leclaire and his troopers entered the Place d'Hondschoote, as Hanoverians fled in every direction.

Over on the right flank, the division of Général de brigade Colaud had arrived, but had halted opposite the Hanoverian left flank, unable to advance. Houchard placed himself at their head with the 17e Régiment de Cavalerie and drew his sword; with a cheer, Colaud's men advanced against the entrenchments at the bayonet. In the centre, Jourdan had been wounded and taken to the rear, and his attack was losing impetus. Représentant en mission Pierre Delbrel rallied the men and moved them forward once again. Timing in warfare is everything, and Delbrel's assault coincided more or less exactly with Colaud's advance on the right, and Leclaire's capture of the village on the left. Merely a civilian, he nonetheless acted at precisely the right moment.

Wallmoden knew that further defence was useless and decided to retreat to Furnes. Moreover, his men's ammunition was almost exhausted. The duke had already decided upon a fall-back position (if it came to that) – it was south of Furnes, the right leaning on the Furnes canal at Bergues, near Buiscamp, the left at the Loos canal at Steinkerke.[11] The Hanoverians retired in two columns, that on the right via Leysele and Ysemberg; the left, following the canal, reached Bulscamp by Houthern. The cavalry, more-or-less unused until then because of the nature of the ground, followed as a rear-guard. Another rear-guard was left behind in the village – the II/Gross und Erbprinz, plus one company of the I/Gross und Erbprinz. Two Hanoverian batteries commanded by Oberstleutnant von Behr and Kapitan Gerhard David von Scharnhorst[12] volunteered to stay behind also. All ran the risk of being taken prisoner but managed to escape due to considerable confusion in the French ranks.

The confusion was understandable. It was by then 13.00 hours; Houchard's young, raw troops had been on the march for ten hours and fighting for the last four. The scene in Place d'Hondschoote was chaotic:

> I found General Houchard, he ran to me, kissed me, saying that I had saved him from a great embarrassment. I replied that it was necessary to put the columns in order at once because everything was pell-mell. I do not think he took that into account or that he did not hear me ... All the volunteers asked me for their battalions; I formed platoons as and when. I was glad at that moment that we felt the need for diversity of uniforms. I thought and expected that the enemy would be pursued, but there was no question of it. I waited patiently, gathering as much as possible our troops who could no longer be hungry and fatigued, when I received the order to establish them around the village.[13]

The Hanoverians would have been easy pickings as they retreated eastwards in considerable disorder, but the French were too exhausted to pursue. It had been a chastening experience for the defenders. Every French attack had been preceded by what von Diepenbroick referred to as 'little battalions' - clouds of skirmishers firing from concealment in hedge-rows, within canals or from behind stone walls. The Hanoverians and Hessians fought in their traditional way – a three-rank-deep line, firing volleys by platoons (half-companies), advancing with the bayonet to drive away any troops who came too close. The Hanoverian contingent alone had lost 226 killed, 1,144 wounded and 961 missing.[14] The valiant Generalmajor von Cochenhausen lay mortally wounded, riddled with grape-shot, and died in Hondschoote on 10 September. The French losses were not recorded. Houchard wrote that he thought he had 700 wounded, which sounds too low.[15]

The siege-force at Dunkirk heard the roar of battle to their rear on 8 September. To keep them occupied, Houchard had ordered Général de brigade Jacques Ferrand to make sorties. The first, between nine and ten in the morning, had captured Rosendael and destroyed a battery in front of the village. A second, at two in the afternoon, was made on the duke's right wing with the aid of the gunboats. The duke learned of Wallmoden's retreat between 15.00 and 16.00 hours:

> In the middle of the last Sortie I received the unfortunate intelligence that after doing everything that Troops could do, Count Walmoden had been overpowered through numbers, and that he had been obliged to retreat close to Furnes, by which means the Enemy had got possession of the roads which led down from Hundschoote upon my rear, and had it in their power to bring down any force they chose, after over-powering the 53rd Regiment, to cut Me completely off.[16]

A council-of-war was called immediately. The duke and Marquis de Bouille[17] wanted to bring away the artillery, but they were opposed by the other general officers, who feared it would slow down the retreat. The guns were to be left behind. The heavy baggage was sent away at 18.00 hours, and the army moved away in some disarray between 23.00 hours and midnight (an hour late), with Lieutenant General Erskine commanding the rear-guard. The dilatory commencement was due to the troops not being ordered to fold the tents until too late, and some companies who had done trench-duty during the day being asleep when the order to retreat was given.

The path followed by the right column was halted by a British convoy blocking the road. The horses were stranded, the drivers drunk or absent. It took a long time to clear them away. Some thirty-two heavy guns, lately arrived, and 500 barrels of powder, had been left behind. The duke's columns did not reach Furnes until 10.00 hours on the morning of 9 September, having taken ten hours to march 12 miles (19km). The siege of Dunkirk was over, for no gain whatsoever.

The duke put on a brave face but was personally gutted: 'I confess I have been exceedingly hurt at having been obliged to retire from before

Dunkirk,' he later wrote to his brother, 'however, being convinced that it was not owing to my own fault ... I bear it with all the philosophy and resignation I am master of.'[18] He was much more forthright to his father:

> Your Majesty's Ministers undertook to furnish a complete Naval force, and desired me to leave it totally to them ... During the first four days I was encamped before Dunkirk, nothing arrived from England though the wind was perfectly fair. At last One Convoy arrived containing only half the Artillery and Stores ... As for the Naval force, none appeared until the very night that I was obliged to retire, so that whenever the Enemy chose to make sorties, their Gun Boats advanced and fired into the rear of our works.[19]

The duke's own staff officers were equally abject: 'Upon the undertaking and the raising of the siege of Dunkirk,' Captain Bentinck wrote, 'it may be proper to observe that the siege of Dunkirk was contrary to the opinion of all the General's military people, but solely the plan of the Ministry of England ... our ill success may in no small degree be attributed to the want of cooperation of the British fleet, which arrived the day after our retreat.'[20]

Houchard and Souham made no effort to harass or attack the retreating army. The siege had cost the Duke of York 3,000 casualties (plus many more caused by disease), three colours and five light cannon, thirty-two heavy cannon, 10,000 cannonballs, 60,000 powder charges, 120 oxen and some artillery horses. The entire loss of the Hanoverian corps was ninety-five officers and 2,236 men. 'In the evening a great number of wounded Hanoverians came in from the army,' James Russell recorded in his diary, 'likewise a quantity of baggage and 4 wagons loaded with money, escorted by a party of Light Dragoons – same day Prince Ernest arrived wounded in the face and shoulders by a stroke from a sword.'[21] Colonel John Moncrieff was buried 'near the flagstaff on the ramparts' on 10 September.[22] The sick and wounded were sent to Bruges in cattle carts, attended by far too few surgeons. This all led to confusion: a wagon of sick men, accidentally left between the high and low water marks on the sands near Nieuwpoort, was submerged by the high tide. All those who could not move were drowned.[23]

The Coalition army reunited at Furnes at noon on 9 September. The French did not celebrate. They considered they had been given a reprieve, not a victory. The Coalition forces in West Flanders were once again concentrated, in a strong position, and had not suffered significant losses. Houchard had failed to pursue, and this would have serious consequences for him in a few short weeks. His 18,000 men at Hondschoote had allowed the 7,000 Hanoverians to get away unmolested, not counting Hedouville's 4,000 cavalry and Vandamme's 9,000 light infantry who were not far away. Furthermore, Landrin's division at Bergues had not marched far that day and ought to have been able to take the duke in the left flank at Dunkirk.[24]

The following day, the duke received some alarming news:

> I have this day received the Intelligence that the French have made an attack upon Ypres and were bombarding the town; at the same time I have been informed that the Hereditary Prince of Orange has as usual taken fright and means to retire from his present position at Menin, by which movement I find myself completely abandoned by every body. I have therefore resolved to try if possible to save the Troops under my command towards Ypres; should I find it possible, I intend to attack the French Army; if that is impracticable, I shall fall back and take up a position between Nieuport and Dixmuide.[25]

On 11 September Rear-Admiral John Macbride's fleet arrived off Ostend, three weeks too late to be of any service. Totalling fourteen vessels, loaded with 282 cannon and 2,100 sailors; it was of not inconsiderable size and fire-power, and could have made all the difference at Dunkirk.[26]

The French siege-force at Ypres bombarded the city for a day then retired precipitately after a Dutch column was spotted reinforcing the place from Menin. Dumesny ordered the retreat at 20.00 hours on 9 September and were pursued along boggy roads by the Austrian Blankenstein Hussars. Dumesny's men, ill-disciplined and voracious looters, made a ragged retreat back to Bailleul.

With the Duke of York falling back on Ypres, Houchard was free to turn his attention upon the shaky Dutch division positioned near Menin. The Dutch had been retreating since 28 August, when they had given up Tourcoing, Watrelos and Lannoy in the face of a French assault, virtually without firing a shot. 'Our good friends the Dutch have again behaved with their usual cowardice,' the duke wrote to his father in disgust.[27] He was forced to send the Prince of Orange-Nassau six squadrons of Hessen-Cassel cavalry to bolster the Dutch force. On 13 September, part of the Armée du Nord under Dumesny fell upon the Dutch garrison at Werwick (2 miles or 3km west of Menin), and totally destroyed it, sending it into headlong flight north. At the same time two divisions of the Armée du Nord (22,000 men) destroyed the main wing of the Dutch army at Menin itself, commanded by the teenager Willem George Frederik, youngest son of the Prince of Orange-Nassau. Dutch losses were five generals (including Frederik, wounded), eighty-eight officers, 3,000 men and forty guns.

The Dutch army fled north-east in great haste to Courtrai, and the French entered Menin, thus capturing the high road between the Duke of York at Furnes and Clerfayt's Austrians around Le Quesnoy. From Menin, they could strike at either Courtrai or Ypres. The duke sent Harry Calvert to the Prince of Orange-Nassau with a message imploring him not to abandon Courtrai. Before he left, Calvert wrote from Dixmuide: 'Yesterday evening they [the French] attacked the Dutch posts of Messines, Werwicke, and Commines upon the Lys, but I fancy nothing decisive occurred on either side.'[28] He was dead wrong about nothing decisive having occurred. In fact, the situation was now very serious for the Coalition, and Calvert's diary entry betrays some of this anxiety. From a position of holding all the advantages at the start at the beginning of August, the Coalition in northern France six weeks later found itself divided and the two wings almost cut off from each other due the large French salient around Courtrai. It was all because the British and Austrians had parted ways to concentrate on 'pet projects'. If the duke was to plug this gap in the Coalition lines, he needed more men.

Luckily, a brigade commanded by Lieutenant General Sir Charles Grey landed at Ostend in the evening of 14 September, having been despatched upon receipt of the news from Dunkirk. It had come from Portsmouth, part of a proposed reinforcement for the West Indies, dressed for summer climes and patently unprepared for campaigning on the Continent. Nonetheless, they were welcome. Comprising the 19th (1st Yorkshire North Riding), 42nd (Royal Highland, or Black Watch) and 57th (Middlesex) regiments of foot. They joined the duke's army at Torhout that evening, which was auspicious timing. The duke was in a council of war, considering his options, which were basically to provide support to the Dutch whilst safeguarding his own communications with home, via Ostend and Nieuwpoort. The council decided to attack Menin. At the same time, Beaulieu with six battalions and six squadrons of Austrians occupied Courtrai.

Hearing the news about Courtrai in the morning of 15 September, local commander Général de brigade comte d'Hédouville sent a brigade down the Lys river to threaten that town, then left Menin with part of his division headed for Lille. The Duke of York was apprised of this whilst on the march near Roeselare and immediately sent his advance guard of Hanoverian infantry and British cavalry to assist Beaulieu's Austrians at Courtrai.

Still despondent after the fiasco at Dunkirk, the duke needed luck, and good news. He got both. He received news from Prince Coburg that Quesnoy had fallen, and he was bringing his army west to co-operate with the duke once more. A few days later Abercrombie's brigade re-joined the army from Dixmuide, and two more regiments arrived from home – the 3rd (East Kent, The Buffs) and the 27th (Enniskillen) regiments of foot. By 16 September Coburg was at Cysoing (about 5 miles or 8km south-east of Lille) and if both columns attacked the French salient simultaneously, they might be able to put the Armée du Nord 'in the bag'.

As it turned out, events outran this possibility. Some French troops had been left outside Menin to hold the Coalition off until night, but the garrison, commanded by Dutch Patriot officer Herman Willem Daendels, defended the place for a while, then panicked and abandoned the town. Many drowned in the River Lys in their desperation to escape. The French re-capture of Courtrai failed also. At the French approach, Beaulieu led a sortie out of the town and drove them back. D'Hédouville brought up reinforcements to no avail. Before long the entire French force was in retreat to Lille, pursued by the Austrians, whilst the duke's army 'encamped under the walls' of Menin. French casualties were 400 killed and wounded, 200 prisoners and two guns. From a position of strength, they had been repulsed thanks to an extremely mediocre military performance, one which soon came to the attention of the National Convention.

The Coalition troops had a wretched time at Menin. The weather had turned, and it rained incessantly: 'For the last two days and nights we have been exposed to an incessant rain, which we fear may have bad effects,' an anonymous officer wrote, 'as many of the regiments are uncovered, and those that have a sufficient number of tents, are entirely unprovided with straw to lie upon.'[29] On 6 October Major General Lake returned to England, very ill.

The duke's force increased in strength, but only in fits and starts. In August the York Rangers (also called Ramsay's York Chasseurs) had arrived at Ostend, comprising two companies of (mostly) German riflemen under French and Irish officers. They comprised the only green-clad rifle-armed unit in the duke's army at the time. Also 200 men from the Royal Irish Artillery disembarked, a sister formation to the Royal Artillery.

In October a subsidiary treaty between the Duchy of Baden and Great Britain promised 750 men for the campaign. One company of the 1st Battalion, and the entire 2nd Battalion of the Baden Leib-Infanterie Regiment with four cannon subsequently arrived. The Baden contingent had no investment or interest in the campaign and suffered heavily from desertion as a result.

Houchard was arrested at Lille in late September and taken to Paris. His charges were failing to exploit his victory at Hondschoote and for the loss of Le Quesnoy; but in reality, he had to pay for the embarrassing 'defence' of Menin. He was guillotined in Paris on 17 November. His replacement was the exceptionally talented 31-year-old former private, Général de division Jean-Baptiste Jourdan.

Maubeuge and Wattignies

Harry Calvert wrote to his sister from Menin on 2 October:

> Plunder and rapine appear to be the enemy's object in all their incursions into the imperial territory, and the sufferings of the unfortunate peasants who reside on the frontiers are beyond all description. I heartily wish some of our countrymen, who do not appear to be sensible of the blessings they enjoy in residing in a land of liberty and security, and under the protection of a government which is equally the refuge of the high and the low, could be transported for a time to witness the scenes of devastation and misery that we have before us.[30]

Menin was a miserable posting. Damp and sick from three-and-a-half weeks of inactivity, the men would have been glad to be on the march again after the duke received two letters from Prince von Coburg on 8 and 9 October (the second more desperate than the first) urging him to move to Cysoing (10 miles or 16km south-east of Lille) thus shoring up the Coalition line from Nieuwpoort towards Maubeuge.[31] The duke left a corps of about 6,000 men for the defence of Menin under the command of the Austrian Feldmarschalleutnant Count Erbach, whilst Sir Charles Grey's brigade marched off to Ostend on 12 October to resume its raison d'être as an expedition to the West Indies. This left him with only about 4,000 dispersed troops, with the British cavalry, the Brigade of Guards and 37th Foot in Esperres and the 14th Foot in Courtrai.

Prince von Coburg meanwhile was busy besieging Maubeuge, 11 miles (18km) south of Mons, whilst the French built up a massive concentration of troops at Guise, 30 miles (48km) to the south. On 14 October the duke received another letter from Prince von Coburg asking him to march with all haste: 'under the circumstances He begged Me for God's sake, I would march as soon as possible and join him, with all the Troops which could be spared.'[32] Cysoing was left in the care of the Austrian Feldmarschalleutnant Baron Alvinczi.

The British contingent was showing the strain of six month's campaigning. The infantry consisted of the Brigade of Guards, reduced by service and illness to 960 men fit for duty, and the 37th Foot (300 men), plus twelve weak squadrons of cavalry.[33] The Hanoverian infantry consisted of four very weak battalions of the 6. and 11.Infanterie-Regimenter. This small force arrived at Englefontaine (17 miles or 27km east of Cambrai) just before noon on 16 October, but they were too late to be of any help.

Only too aware of the fates of his predecessors, Général de division Jourdan determined to throw himself into his work. On the 15/16 October he defeated the Austrians at Wattignies, 6 miles (9km) southeast of Maubeuge, taking heavy losses in doing so. But these were the new tactics demanded by the Republican system; better a few thousand men than the guillotine. Harry Calvert provides the best English language version of the battle:

> On the 15th, the enemy, having established themselves in a wood called La Haye d'Avesne, made an attack upon the right of the Prince of Cobourg's army, which extended along the plain on the eastern bank of the Sambre, nearly opposite Berlaimont. The Austrians retired out of some hamlets and enclosures in front of this position, and, after a heavy cannonade, the enemy being imprudent enough to commit themselves on the plain, were immediately charged by the Imperial cavalry, and repulsed with the loss of nine pieces of cannon and one howitzer. Your Royal Highness will observe that, after passing through a wood, which I believe is called Le Bois du Prince, the left of the Austrian army was formed in some degree, en potence, to the right, and extended to the village of Wattignies. This wing was commanded by General Clerfayt. The attack of the enemy on this side was repulsed, but not with the same advantage that attended the operations on the right, as the wood and enclosures in front of the villages upon the left, prevented the cavalry from being employed.
>
> On the 16th, between nine and ten A.M., the enemy renewed their attack; but, grown wiser from the experience of the day before, they showed themselves in small numbers only, in the skirts of the woods and enclosures, in front of the plain occupied by the right of the Allies; and it was soon perceived that they had carried the greatest part of their force to their right, and that General Clerfayt's left was the real point of attack. I happened to be with the Prince of Cobourg when the affair commenced, and, before I left him, the village of Wattignies had been twice taken and retaken: it was lost owing to the very severe fire of the enemy's artillery; but, in both instances, regained by the good conduct and intrepidity of the Austrians, with small arms, and once with bayonets.[34]

Wattignies cost the Austrians 365 killed, 1,753 wounded and 369 missing. French losses were probably somewhere between 3,000 and 5,000. Prince von Coburg realised he was too weak to hold the line of the Sambre, so decided to lift the siege of Maubeuge and retire across the river:

> In the evening, the fire of the enemy's artillery became irresistible, and, at night, the Duke received a message from the Prince of Cobourg, informing him that the enemy, having established themselves in Wattignies, and the other villages on his left, had so far gained his left, that he did not think his position any longer tenable, and that it was his intention to recross the Sambre in the night, and consequently raise the siege of Maubeuge. From the immense artillery of the enemy and their numbers, it was natural to apprehend that they would give some interruption to the execution of his Serene Highness's intentions; but I am happy to inform you that this service was completely performed during the night without loss. It was facilitated by a successful attack, made late in the evening, by Colonel Haddick, who drove the enemy as far as the Chateau de Solre, at the same time that General Benjowski, with the regiment of La Tour and some heavy Hussars, made a vigorous charge upon their right flank. In these two attacks the enemy lost twelve pieces of cannon, ammunition, &c.[35]

The French did not pursue. Austrian historians later criticised the duke for advancing too slowly to assist his Coalition allies; in their view, he should have arrived on 15 October whilst the battle was in full swing, rather than in the late morning of the 16th when the outcome was decided against him. But the Anglo-Hanoverian contingent had marched 54 miles (87km) in two days over muddy October roads, having had to manoeuvre around the towns of Valenciennes and St Amand en route, as pre-arranged conditions forbade British troops marching through towns garrisoned by Austrians. His men had in fact achieved a great feat, to no avail.

Once again, the French had grasped the initiative. The French Royalist émigré Langeron described the loss as inevitable due to the 'disastrous system of forming a cordon, which causes one to be weak everywhere.' Another writer wrote that: 'The Allies totally failed to see that the best way to defend the length of the frontier was to concentrate and to crush Jourdan, and although they were well informed about his collecting troops at Guise, they allowed him to bring up slowly superior forces against one link of their long chain, as if their posts were so many players, each bound to defend his own wicket.'[36]

In order to boost morale, the Duke of York ordered his army to fire a *feu-de-joie* on 20 October to celebrate the success of the Austrian attack on the lines of Weissenburg. He had every reason to celebrate, since the battle was a major success for the Coalition, forcing the Armée du

Rhin to retreat south towards Strasbourg in confusion. The Armée de la Moselle had to be rushed north to help plug the gap.

Menin and Nieuwpoort

As things unravelled at Maubeuge, the weak Coalition garrison came under pressure near Ypres. On 21 October the newly-promoted Général de division Joseph Souham with 10,000 men defeated Count Erbach's Austro-Hanoverian garrison at Menin and repeated the dose at Halluin the next day, during which most of the Hanoverian 2.Grenadier-Bataillon were taken prisoner. The Loyal Emigrants (French royalists in British service) underwent their baptism of fire on this day. That same day a sortie by Général de brigade Vandamme and his Dunkirk garrison was defeated by the Hessen-Cassel garrison of Furnes, an action at which detachments of the 27th Foot, 16th Light Dragoons and Loyal Emigrants were present. On 25 October under the cover of a thick fog, a French brigade commanded by Général de brigade Jacques Étienne Macdonald made a cross-border attack on the Coalition outposts at Wervicq, in which the Loyal Emigrants lost twenty killed and wounded and more than fifty prisoners. Two days later a much stronger French column of 12,000 men under the command of Vandamme captured Furnes and opened a bombardment on the Coalition garrison at Nieuwpoort, causing twenty-eight losses amongst the detachment of the 53rd Foot present, including Captain Ronald Crauford Ferguson, wounded in the knee.[37] The 53rd later received the battle honour 'Nieuport' to commemorate it's determined defence.[38]

Prince von Coburg maintained his headquarters at Bavai for the next week whilst the duke remained at Englefontaine. During the morning of 23 October Coburg wrote to the duke saying that he anticipated a major French effort towards Menin and ordered him to march his small force to Tournai. So, the duke put his men back on the road again, and they marched 13 miles (21km) in the afternoon. The duke rode on ahead with his cavalry and reached Tournai late on 24 October only to find that things were not as bad as the prince had made out. The Austrians had retreated from Cysoing precipitately and Coburg was once again in panic mode. The duke ordered his infantry (hot-footing behind him) to rest and wrote angry letters home to his father:

> As I have had every reason to be dissatisfied with the conduct of the Austrian generals who have commanded the detached corps of this army during my absence, I have ordered Count Walmoden, in whose talents, courage and prudence I have the fullest reliance to take command of the corps which was at Menin.[39]

The duke also wrote to Whitehall and requested reinforcements. On 27 October a squadron of the Bays (2nd Dragoon Guards) under the command of Captain James Hay encountered 150 French troops retreating towards Lezennes, 7 miles (7km) east of Loos. Major Charles Craufurd, aide and close friend of the duke, took charge of the fifty-six-man squadron, led them towards the enemy and charged. Captain Hay had his horse shot from under him, so he borrowed his farrier's grey horse. The 1st Dragoons and some Austrian Chevaulegers under the command of Prinz Ernst came up in support and helped round up the 104 prisoners of war taken. The Dragoon Guards lost two men killed and one wounded. 'Never did I see such havoc and chopping,' the duke wrote lustily home,[40] a reminder that cavalry attacking downhill into and over unformed infantry in open ground was very much to the detriment of the latter.

Then news arrived that the French had attacked Ypres (unsuccessfully), had taken Furnes and were threatening Nieuwpoort, which was only lightly garrisoned. The duke devised a plan whereby he would send Wallmoden and the Hanoverians to Menin (as we have seen above) whilst the rest of his force would create a diversion upon the French right flank at Lannoy, 6 miles (9km) east of Lille.

On 28 October the Duke sent Major General Abercrombie to Lannoy with the 3rd Foot Guards, the Guards flank battalion, one squadron of the 7th and 15th Light Dragoons, three battalions of Austrians and four guns. Abercrombie's force surprised the 5,000-man French garrison, who abandoned the village after a cannonade, and were then cut down by the Light Dragoons, losing 2,000 casualties and 1,700 prisoners. Wernecke's Austrian column came up in support and completed the rout. Coalition losses were minimal. One unfortunate casualty was First Lieutenant John Rutherford of the Royal Engineers, cut down by the British light dragoons who mistook him for a Frenchman, 'the uniform of the engineers being blue.'[41]

Count Wallmoden planned to attack Menin from the east and south, whilst a Hessen-Cassel brigade under Generalmajor von Wurmb attacked from the north. However, Wurmb decided (against orders) to march north instead towards some of his threatened countrymen at Nieuwpoort. It did not matter; the French garrison slipped away westwards before the attack could form. Wallmoden entered that town with his Hanoverians the same day. Meanwhile, events had gone satisfactorily for the Coalition at Nieuwpoort. A battalion of Hessen-Cassel troops and some artillery had reached Nieuwpoort on 27 October to bolster the defences, after which the town was defended by about 1,300 men; the 53rd Foot, three weak Hessen-Cassel battalions and a troop of Hessen-Cassel dragoons.

In the nick of time came the requested reinforcements from home. Lieutenant General Sir Charles Grey was back, thwarted once more in his desire to carry an expedition to the West Indies, landed at Ostend in the evening of 28 October with five battalions: the 3rd (Buffs), 28th (North Gloucestershire), 42nd (Black Watch), 54th (West Norfolk), and 59th (2nd Nottinghamshire) Regiments of Foot. The 3rd Foot remained at Ostend, and he sent Major General Thomas Dundas with the 42nd Foot and four companies of light infantry to Nieuwpoort, where the new commandant, Generalmajor von Wurmb had been asked to surrender by Vandamme. Wurmb refused. Reinforcements from Grey's force on 29 October greatly altered circumstances in the Coalition's favour. Realising that the relief army was near, Wurmb ordered the sluices opened on 30 October and Vandamme abandoned the siege, leaving four cannon behind.

By the end of October, the weather was deteriorating, and the end of the campaign season was near. On 30 October, the French garrison on the high road at Marchiennes (11 miles or 18km north-west of Valenciennes) was attacked by six battalions and ten squadrons commanded by generalmajors Otto and Kray. The garrison barely made an effort. They retired into the abbey, from where they sent a trumpeter to negotiate a surrender, on the conditions that their officers kept their swords. General Kray complied. The prisoners, 1,669 to in total, marched out that evening on their way to Tournai. The following day, Coalition light troops raided French outposts at Ors and Catillon-sur-Sambre (20 miles or 32km south-east of Cambrai), taking 100 prisoners.

The Coalition leaders were cock-a-hoop. From the depths of despair after Dunkirk, the tables had turned for them completely. The duke even issued a General Order on 31 October:

> H.R.H the Commander-in-Chief has the pleasure of acquainting the army, that in consequence of the gallant behaviour of the British and allied troops under his command at their different posts, the enemy has been completely beaten, foiled in all his undertakings, and been driven out of Flanders.[42]

Whatever improvements Carnot was busy implementing were yet to manifest themselves on the northern front. The last part of the year had not gone well for the French. The duke ought to have been pleased, but his temper was no doubt tested by a letter he received from Home Secretary Henry Dundas. Written apparently without seeking military guidance, Dundas took pains to criticise the duke for his handling of the campaign: 'If not [being] versant in military operations and unqualified to reason with accuracy on the subject, I was to form an opinion founded solely upon a retrospect of the last transactions of the campaign, I should be disposed to draw two conclusions,' he unhelpfully advised. He then went on the say that he thought that the enemy would profit by taking the offensive and that the duke ought to concentrate his forces rather than disperse them – as if a full general in the field and his staff had no idea about such concepts. And this from the same government that had ordered him to separate from the Austrians to undertake the Dunkirk campaign! Sir James Murray immediately replied. 'It would be in vain to disguise from you that the Duke of York is much hurt at the dispatch that has been received this day.' The duke had two reasons to be displeased. Firstly, evidently Dundas' letter had been written on the tail of the receipt of a panicky letter from Major General George Ainslie, commanding at Ostend, after hearing second-hand reports of events at Nieuwpoort which sounded like bad news for the Coalition, and which Dundas took as gospel truth. Secondly, Dundas had written to the duke three weeks earlier, stating that he approved the duke's move towards Maubeuge, because 'the troops left in the different places of Nieuport and Furnes ... will be sufficient for the protection of that part of Flanders.'[43] Vandamme's retreat had ended the danger in that quarter. It was as if people in England measured the success of the campaign purely in the ability of her troops to maintain the security of the continental Channel ports; from afar they seemed threatened, therefore, the campaign must be going badly. Sir James Murray was a lion in defending his chief, but he had a habit of rubbing people up the wrong way. His acid pen had gained him no friends at home, and his future tenure as Quartermaster-General was likely to be short.[44]

With the weather deteriorating, the Duke of York organised a defensive cordon along the frontier with his Coalition allies, then marched his weary army into camp around Tournai on 9 November. Three transports with another 500 Guardsmen and 100 line infantry drafts arrived. Two more heavy cavalry regiments had also arrived at Ostend on 9 November, the 5th and 6th Dragoon Guards, and the British expeditionary force was now significantly stronger in cavalry than infantry. This was especially true after Lieutenant General Sir Charles Grey, bound for the West Indies at long last, finally returned to England with his four regiments (19th, 27th, 42nd, 57th Foot, 1700 men), never to return. The Uhlans Brittaniques, two squadrons of French royalist lancers under the command of Lieutenant Colonel

Louis, Comte de Bouillé passed into British service. Best of all, a Hessen-Cassel brigade under Generalmajor Karl von Hanstein arrived at Tournai on 16 November, which Lord William Bentinck described as being composed of 'very fine men.'[45] A few days later they were joined by 3,200 equally fine troops from Hessen-Darmstadt and the 750 reluctant grenadiers from Baden.[46] The Hessen-Cassel troops joined the duke's army, whilst the others were sent to Menin and Ypres.

On 2 December rumours spread through the camp that Lord Moira had arrived at Ostend with eight regiments; in fact, he had only landed on Guernsey, awaiting positive news from the French Royalists in the Vendée before venturing forth to join them. A brigade of Hessen-Cassel troops under Generalmajor von Borck was added to Moira's force on 1 January, and they sailed to Cowes on the Isle of Wight (where their presence caused some political consternation) where they sat aboard ships for over a month before disembarkation started on 12 February.[47]

Winter was almost upon the frontier, and so as was traditional in the eighteenth century, both sides went into winter quarters. As they did so, the Duke of York issued an address to his troops thanking them for their exertions in 1793.[48] Tradition guaranteed that there would be little, if any, fighting until the spring came. But hang tradition; the French were showing an alarming tendency to ignore such things completely.

Chapter 10

Winter Quarters

1793 in Review

Harry Calvert wrote a letter to his sister on 19 November:

> Since our arrival here we have been quite at peace, our advanced posts have been unmolested, and from every account, the enemy's force immediately in our front is smaller than it has been at any time since the commencement of the campaign. The people of Lille are in want of every sort of comfort and necessary, particularly food and fuel. The discontent has risen to such a height as to give considerable alarm to the Convention, and twelve deputies have arrived to endeavour to appease the minds of the people. However great their dissensions may be, however adverse their political opinions, there is one subject on which, if we may judge from experience, the inhabitants of this northern frontier unite, that is, in a predilection for a republican form of government, and a determination to resist, to the utmost of their power, the attempts of the Allies on their territory. I very much doubt whether the foreign war does not furnish them with the only bond of union they have left; and whether, if the dread of the external enemy were removed, they would not now be cutting one another's throats, and perhaps in a very short time gladly have recourse to any settled form of government in preference to the anarchy which exists at present – probably, to the very system of government which is now the object of their detestation; but I am getting quite out of my element, and am deviating from the good old proverb, a cobbler to his last.[1]

In hindsight the campaign of 1793 was undertaken recklessly. It relied upon a Coalition which had no bonds and assumed a weakness within the French Republic which proved to be unexpectedly strong. All the Coalition did was goad France to fury, whilst being too weak to crush its embodiment. Ill-concealed threats of partition bound France to the cause of the Jacobins, who at any other time would have caused dismay. The Coalition drove France in upon herself. This compelled her to organise her strength to the utmost. And that strength was being marshalled dangerously by Carnot. The year 1794 might prove to be a difficult one for the Coalition.

The campaign of 1793 had exposed the weaknesses of many of those in Coalition high command. Lieutenant General Harcourt recorded in his diary that 'the cry against Coburg is great indeed. They say he had done nothing since Colonel Mack left him and that he is not equal to the command he holds.'[2] Sir James Murray was generally unpopular with the army. He was 'inclined to indecisive argument, and lacked confidence in his own opinion, while his awkward manners and "a grotesque and rather repulsive exterior" concealed the best points in his character.'[3] Murray had 'a dreamy indolence which led him too readily to surrender his own correct opinion, and to amuse himself with speculation upon the incorrect opinions of others.'[4] The Duke wrote to his father on 3 December admitting that Murray 'is not endowed with that spirit of exactness and order which are absolutely necessary in an Adjutant-General.'[5] The Duke suggested Colonel Sir James Craig as a possible replacement. Murray was summoned home to an interview with Henry Dundas on 21 December and given the colonelcy of an infantry regiment (the Scotch Brigade, later the 94th Foot) as a sop.

Craig went out to Flanders in the New Year. The duke also had reservations about the new Imperial Quartermaster-General, Feldzeugmeister Fürst zu Hohenlohe-Kirchberg – Mack had gone home in November[6] – although removing him would be far more complicated than simply writing to his father. Nonetheless, he did so anyway on 4 January 1794. Little did the duke know that the Archduke Karl also wrote to his Imperial relative – his brother, the emperor - on the very same day (4 January) demanding Mack's reinstatement: 'The Hungarian grenadiers have been much more pessimistic since they no longer see the man in the white coat riding around,' he wrote, a reference to Mack's preferred garment.[7] Magically, Hohenlohe was manoeuvered off to a field command while Colonel Mack – who, despite his short-comings, was still enormously popular with the Duke of York and his staff - returned to his old position.[8]

As to the duke himself, he was blameless for the position he found himself in. It was not his fault that he had not even commanded a company on active service, let alone a regiment; much less an army. Continental conventions of the late eighteenth century expected, nay required, a Prince of the Blood to command coalition forces. His youth and inexperience, whilst given under these conditions, were also his greatest weaknesses; leaving him blind to the effects of stocking his frequent dinner parties with young officers his own age rather than older, more senior generals (as was customary) – that led to 'bleating' in letters home from those disaffected.[9] He also developed a reputation for saying whatever he thought, and leaving private letters lying about opened in his headquarters. There were those in the army who thought him indiscreet, and 'beyond measure careless'. Nevertheless, he enjoyed a high reputation within Austrian and Prussian military circles; all the carping came from the British side.

If Coburg and Murray were indecisive, there is little evidence that the duke suffered from this complaint. Lord Bonnington, writing from the camp in front of Valenciennes during the siege, was impressed by 'the very great clearness, precision and quickness with which he [the Duke] gives his orders.'[10] We must remember that the Duke had been schooled in the German art of war, partly by Frederick the Great himself, a school which emphasised the need for a war of movement. Between the end of April and the end of October 1793 the duke moved his men more than 330 miles (530km), often keeping the French guessing as to his motives. The Austrian headquarters, on the other hand, obsessed with reducing the frontier fortresses, never moved more than 20 miles (32km) from Condé-sur-l'Escaut.

The miniscule size of his expeditionary force was almost a national embarrassment, since tiny German duchies were putting far larger armies into the field. The sad fact was that Britain had 'too many irons in the fire' requiring troop dispersals across the globe. Regiments were in the West Indies, Canada, India, and New South Wales. This is before mentioning concurrent expeditions to Toulon and the Vendée, and then adding on top the need for garrisons at home. There were far few troops and stores to send to Flanders. The duke did the best he could with his Lilliputian army, bolstered by Hanoverian and Hessian levies. The British expeditionary force had been subservient to much larger Imperial forces almost the whole time. The only independent command he had exercised was the ill-fated sideshow at Dunkirk, which had been pressed upon him by his own father and his ministers. Dunkirk had been foreseen as a mistake by nearly every officer in the expeditionary force. The historian Archibald Allison had this to say about the division of the Coalition forces to pursue folly at Dunkirk, and of the far-ranging effects of this disunity:

> The [Republican] decrees for levying the population en masse were not passed by the Convention for some weeks afterwards, and the forces they produced were not organized for three months.

The mighty genius of Carnot had not as yet assumed the helm of affairs; the Committee of Public Safety had not yet acquired its terrible energy; everything promised great results to vigorous and simultaneous operations. It was a resolution of the English Cabinet, in opposition to the declared and earnest wish of Cobourg and all the allied generals, which occasioned this fatal division. The impartial historian must confess with a sigh, that it was British interests which here interfered with the great objects of the war, and that by compelling the English contingent to separate for the siege of Dunkirk, England contributed to postpone for twenty years its glorious termination. Posterity has had ample room to lament the error; a war of twenty years deeply chequered with disaster; the addition of six hundred millions to the public debt; the sacrifice of millions of brave men, may be in a great degree traced to this unhappy resolution.[11]

The Duke of York knew perfectly well why the Dunkirk operation had failed, and summarised them in a letter to his father on 18 September;

I think therefore I am justified in saying that there were three grand causes which made this expedition miscarry; the first owing to the promises and assurances I so repeatedly received from Your Majesty's Ministers not being in any way fulfilled; the second owing to the alteration made in the plan of campaign by the Armies of the King of Prussia and of General Wurmser, by which means the Enemy was enabled to bring me the whole Army of the Moselle against the Field Marshal and Me; and the third owing to the Field Marshal's own conduct.[12]

In the first and third points he was undeniably correct.[13] 'Every man that has since perished,' wrote an anonymous officer to the *Morning Chronicle*, 'is to be set down to the score of the ministers, who have sacrificed their duty to the holiday mummery of camps or to the amusements of partridge shooting.'[14] In the second he was misinformed. The Armée de la Moselle did not detach forces to operate against the Coalition in the Austrian Netherlands; in fact, General Wurmser was quite engaged, rather successfully attacking the French along the Lines of Wissembourg, tying them down for two months.

During the winter recess, the duke sent his aide Captain Charles Craufurd on a mission to the Imperial Emperor in Vienna. Whilst there, Craufurd met with the Austrian Chancellor, Johann Amadeus Franz de Paula Freiherr von Thugut.[15] Although no soldier, Thugut was a remarkably smart, perceptive man, able to articulate five reasons for the Coalition failures in 1793. Firstly, allowing the French to escape at Famars, where a knock-out blow would have been decisive.

Secondly, the Austrian siege had been glacially slow in setting up at Valenciennes, giving the French far too much time to organise affairs and bring forward reinforcements. Third, failing to besiege Maubeuge immediately after the capture of Valenciennes; as we have seen, the Austrians concentrated on Le Quesnoy whilst the Duke marched off to Dunkirk. Fourthly, the abandonment of Maubeuge after the battle of Wattignies, on account of the Imperial line being spread too thin along the frontier. And lastly, and most criminally for all Coalition officers involved, engaging the French in terrain unsuitable for cavalry operations, given the Coalition's clear superiority in that arm. This last point was clearly not lost on the Duke of York.

A Mettlesome One

Despite the onset of winter, small actions continued along the frontier. On 28 November French troops raided Hessen-Cassel outposts under the command of Generalmajor Georg Emil von Düring at Nechin and Leers (about 10 miles or 16km east of Lille), causing fifteen casualties.[16] A garrison of Hanoverians commanded by Major Karl Kristian von Linsingen repelled another French raid at Leers two days later, losing fourteen men. The duke withdrew his best troops north to take advantage of the friendlier and better-supplied towns in the Austrian Netherlands. At Christmas 1793 the Guards and heavy cavalry were wintered at Ghent; the line battalions and the 15th and 16th Light Dragoons manned the outposts under the command of Major General Abercrombie, headquartered at Oudenarde. Major General David Dundas commanded two Austrian battalions and the 7th and 11th Light Dragoons at Courtrai. Wallmoden and his Hanoverians were at Bruges; the Hessians at Nieuwpoort, Dixmuide and Ypres.[17]

The Austrians were wintering all along the frontier. Colleredo was between Namur and Charleroi; Coburg was with his infantry at Condé-sur-l'Escaut whilst the cavalry quartered at Mons. Clerfayt was behind the Scheldt between Condé and Courtrai.

The new year 1794 rolled around on the freezing troops. Nothing had happened along the frontier for weeks. On 18 January the British fired three rounds in honour of the king's birthday. On 29 January 'several donation articles from our friends in England have been delivered out to us, which are very acceptable at this season; such as cloth trowsers, flannel waistcoats, gloves, night-caps, socks, stockings, and two pair of shoes for each man.'[18]

Newly-promoted Major General James Henry Craig arrived from home to take up his new position as adjutant-general. Craig was a 45-year-old Scot, a veteran of the American Wars, during which he had frequently commanded light troops and had advanced rapidly in rank. A biographer later characterised him as 'very short, broad and muscular, a pocket Hercules, with sharp, neat features, as if chiselled in ivory. Not popular for he was hot, peremptory and pompous; yet extremely beloved by those whom he allowed to live in intimacy with him; clever, generous to a fault, and a warm and unflinching friend to those he liked ... one of the kindest men I have ever had to transact business with.'[19] Craig took it upon himself to try and correct some of the duke's foibles:

> The only circumstance which I have observed in the Duke's treatment of the officers which I could wish changed, is with respect to the invitations to his table; in this it appears to me that sufficient attention is not paid to the field officers and those of a higher rank. I am endeavouring to bring as much as lies in my power, at present to bring about a little alteration in this respect, which if I can accomplish it I am sure will tend to increase the Duke's popularity in the army.[20]

The duke had struck up a close working relationship with the restored Imperial chief-of-staff, the Austrian Oberst Karl Mack von Leiberich. Mack advised the duke that he had devised a new campaign plan for 1794 and would like to show it to him. The duke took the unprecedented step of inviting Mack to England to explain it to the king, having taken the precaution of writing to his father on 22 January to explain all this and seek royal approval. What is even more extraordinary is that by this stage only Mack and the duke had seen the plan; Mack had not even presented it to his superior, the Coalition commander-in-chief, Prince von Coburg.

Mack met with Coburg in Mons at the start of February and, with Imperial approval secured, joined the Duke of York on a passage for London on 6 February. The aim of the trip was to brief the Cabinet on the conduct of the campaign so far and to receive further instructions. Harry Calvert went with them, recently promoted to captain & lieutenant-colonel with a company in the Coldstream Guards. They arrived in London on 9 February, the very same day that Home Secretary Henry Dundas met with the recently-returned commander-in-chief of His Majesty's forces in India: Charles, Earl Cornwallis. Prime Minister Pitt and Dundas had for some time harboured the notion that the duke ought to be replaced by an experienced soldier, and Cornwallis was, in their view, surely that man.[21] Despite his surrender at Yorktown in 1781, Cornwallis arrived home 'with his Indian military honours thick upon him; he was universally recognised as the leading soldier of his day.'[22]

Most extraordinarily of all, Oberst Mack and his assistant Oberstleutnant Merveldt were invited to a conference with Pitt, Foreign Secretary Grenville, and Dundas; the Duke of York was not present. Mack was informed of the proposed change in British command, and that the British presence on the continent would be increased to 40,000 men.[23] Pitt then demanded that the British contingent be reinforced by an Austrian corps; Mack rejected this, replying that the Imperial army needed its full strength for offensive operations. Mack also urged the replacement of the Hanoverian commander Feldmarschall von Freytag, whom he considered a thorn in the duke's side. But Mack stood up for the duke in no uncertain terms, praising him to the heavens whilst decrying his critics as a 'set of influential but inexperienced youths.'[24] Remarkably, Mack prevailed. Cornwallis was sent on a diplomatic mission to the Prussian court, whilst the duke retained his field command.

On 14 February Mack was presented to King George, who asked him to openly voice his opinion of the Duke of York. Again, Mack had nothing but praise, but used the opportunity to criticise Freytag again. King George announced that he would arrange for Freytag's Hanoverian command to be placed under Clerfayt's command, neatly solving the problem without offending the ego of Hanover's most experienced soldier. Later that same day another conference, to which the duke was invited, permitted Mack to present his campaign plan to the entire assembly in Pitt's apartments, and to recieve assent.

Back on the continent, Lieutenant General Erskine assumed temporary command of the British expeditionary force and moved his headquarters to Courtrai as the weather improved. Come the spring thaw – say, April – the new campaign season could be expected to get underway.

Erskine consolidated his headquarters at Courtrai, the garrison of which at the time comprised the Brigade of Guards, the 37th Foot, the 7th and 15th Light Dragoons, plus some foreign troops. A few days later Major General Sir Robert Laurie arrived at headquarters to take command of the 3rd Cavalry Brigade (2nd Dragoon Guards, 2nd and 6th Dragoons). Whilst the British force was still weak in infantry, there were now four excellent cavalry brigades in the line (Harcourt's, Mansel's, Laurie's and Dundas') with eight heavy and four light dragoon regiments.

Whether the French would bounce back from their reverses of late 1793 remained to be seen:

> We must finish matters this year, unless we make rapid progress and annihilate the enemy to the last man within three months, all

is lost. To begin again next year would mean for us to perish of hunger and exhaustion.[25]

On 15 February France adopted the *tricolore* (in the format we know to this day) as the official flag of the French Republic. It fluttered over a French brigade which surprised the garrison of the village of Zandvoorde, located 4 miles (7km) south-east of Ypres on 19 February and put them to flight. The garrison comprised the Hanoverian 4.Infanterie-Regiment, the Badener Grenadier Regiment, and one company of the York Rangers, a unit formed from émigré Germans with French and Irish officers in British pay. The polyglot defenders lost about 100 men. On 27 February the French crossed the River Lys at Wervicq and attempted to burn the steeple of the local church but were driven off by the Uhlans Britanniques. These were small clashes but signalled that the real action could not be far away.

The Duke of York left London in the evening of Sunday 2 March and arrived at Deal the next morning. The wind being contrary, His Royal Highness was delayed aboard the *Vestal* frigate. He landed at Ostend at noon on 4 March and proceeded that night to Courtrai, where Erskine and Feldmarschall von Freytag had their headquarters. On arrival he took temporary command of the entire Coalition army except for the corps under Feldmarschall von Coburg and started to sift through the varied business of the day. Freytag, who had never seen eye-to-eye with the duke, resigned when told about the transfer of his command the Austrians, and so the Hanoverian contingent passed to leadership of General der Kavallerie von Wallmoden-Gimborn.

The duke sent Major General Craig off on a mission to Berlin to procure some light troops, in which his force was somewhat deficient; Craig was unsuccessful. A draft of 787 guardsmen (roughly 250 men from each of the three regiments, plus NCOs) arrived two days later to reinforce the Brigade of Guards, followed a bit later by their brigade commander, the returning Major General Lake, recovered from his long illness. The Duke of York's uncle, Field-marshal HRH Prince William Henry, the Duke of Gloucester (a younger brother of King George III) arrived at headquarters at the end of March and was attached to the 1st Foot Guards as a mere captain. The Choiseul Hussars, a French émigré unit, entered British service at Courtrai; it comprised six cavalry troops and a horse artillery company.

The weather at this time was atrocious, with ten solid days of torrential rain. Continuously wet troops usually need some form of morale-boosting, and the duke was prepared. A few days later men paraded around in their new greatcoats, provided for the first time in the history of the British army, a legacy of the duke's concern for his men. At the end of March each of the Guardsmen who had fought at Linselles received a cash reward for their gallantry – twenty-one shillings for a serjeant, fourteen shillings and threepence for a corporal, and nine shillings and ninepence for a private.[26]

Reinforcements continued to arrive. On 4 April much-needed drafts for the 1st Dragoon Guards and Abercrombie's reduced brigade arrived, but Harry Calvert was not impressed: 'The recruits for General Abercrombie's brigade arrived a few days ago; they much resembled Falstaff's men, and were as lightly clad as any Carmagnole battalion.'[27]

Far to the east, the Duke of Brunswick relinquished his command of the Prussian army on the Rhine. He was sick of interference from King Friedrich Wilhelm. He wrote to Prince Ludwig of Prussia on 24 January 1794:

> I have been enveloped in circumstances as distressing as they were extraordinary, which have imposed upon me the painful necessity of acting as I have done. What a misfortune that external and internal dissensions should so frequently have paralysed the movement of the armies at the very time when the greatest activity was necessary ... I implore you to use your efforts to prevent the undue separation of the army into detachments. When this is the case, weak at every point, it is liable to be cut up in detail ... The same causes will divide the Allied Powers which have hitherto divided them; the movements of the armies will suffer from them as they have suffered; their march will be embarrassed, retarded, prevented; and the delay in the re-establishment of the Prussian army, unavoidably, perhaps, from political causes, will become the cause in the succeeding campaign, of incalculable disasters.[28]

The Duke of Brunswick was replaced by Generalfeldmarschall Wichard Joachim Heinrich von Möllendorf, a 70-year-old veteran who had started his military career in 1740.[29] This was not the only Coalition command change under consideration for 1794. Unknown to the British contingent, the Austrian brigadier Archduke Karl had travelled to Vienna to persuade his older brother, the Imperial Emperor Franz II, to personally take supreme command of the Coalition army. The emperor, frequently distrustful of his senior generals,[30] did not need much convincing and left Vienna at 05.00 hours in the morning of 2 April accompanied by his brothers Karl and Josef, Chancellor Ferdinand von Trauttmansdorff, Cabinet Minister Graf von Colloredo-Waldsee and Imperial Adjutant-General Generalmajor Franz von Rollin.[31] The emperor arrived in Brussels a week later and after a few days of attending his *Joyeuse Entrée*,[32] being annointed as Duc de Brabant and court receptions, rode to Imperial headquarters on 14 April to formally take the command.

Generalmajor Mack[33] now found himself chief-of-staff to the emperor, in a retinue that was deeply divided. Foreign Minister Baron von Thugut was there, with a clique that included the aristocratic Georg Prinz zu Waldeck und Pyrmont (who despised Mack due to his bourgeois origins) and Generalmajor von Rollin. This group favoured purely defensive warfare – simply defending the borders of the Austrian Netherlands. Mack had convinced Coburg of the soundness of his offensive plan, a strategy which put these two in direct opposition to the Adjutant-General and the Foreign Minister.

Beyond the frontier, the French were becoming more active. On 11 March French patrols attacked Coalition picquets at Linselles and Wervick and were repulsed after suffering small losses. Expecting imminent action, the duke ordered all impedimenta to the rear. Corporal Brown of the Guards:

> All the heavy baggage, spare tents, and every thing not absolutely necessary for our use, was sent back to Ghent, and a serjeant of each battalion appointed to take charge of it. Several sick men who are not able to march are also sent along with it.[34]

The French however were slow to move. On 29 March a brigade of the Armée du Nord commanded by Général de division Charles Chapuis de Tourville, crossed the Sambre at Ors and made itself master of the village of Pomereul, taking some redoubts occupied by Brunswick troops. At the same time, other brigades advanced to the heights above Le Cateau and bombarded the town. Generalmajor Franz Freiherr von Werneck with the two battalions of k.k.Infanterie-Regiment Nr.25 attacked and took the redoubts, with five pieces of the enemy's cannon, and with the assistance of a small body of cavalry, killed and wounded 500 and took 60 prisoners. The French outside Le Cateau and along the frontier retired across the river, having lost 1,200 men. All the advanced posts were re-occupied by the Allies. Hearing the news of the action, Captain Harry Calvert wrote in his diary, 'so the entertainment is begun, and a mettlesome one it will be, I dare say.'[35]

Minor actions sputtered all along the frontier. On 6 April, Hanoverian grenadiers and light dragoons skirmished with the French near ten Briel, about 5 miles (8km) south-east of Ypres, losing fifty men; French casualties included eighty-nine men captured.

A day later the York Rangers ambushed a French column near Rousbeke, killing thirty-seven.

A war council was held in Valenciennes (with the Duke of York in attendance) where Coburg prevailed with Mack's campaign plan. Emperor Franz approved the proposal to attack with eight columns in an echeloned thrust with the aim of pushing the French far enough back to permit the siege of Landrecies. The Coalition was well-supplied and rested, had a new Supreme Commander, and numbered seventy-eight battalions, 118 squadrons and twenty-seven artillery companies available for offensive action. The 1794 campaign season could begin.

PART 3 – 1794: A NEW CAMPAIGN SEASON

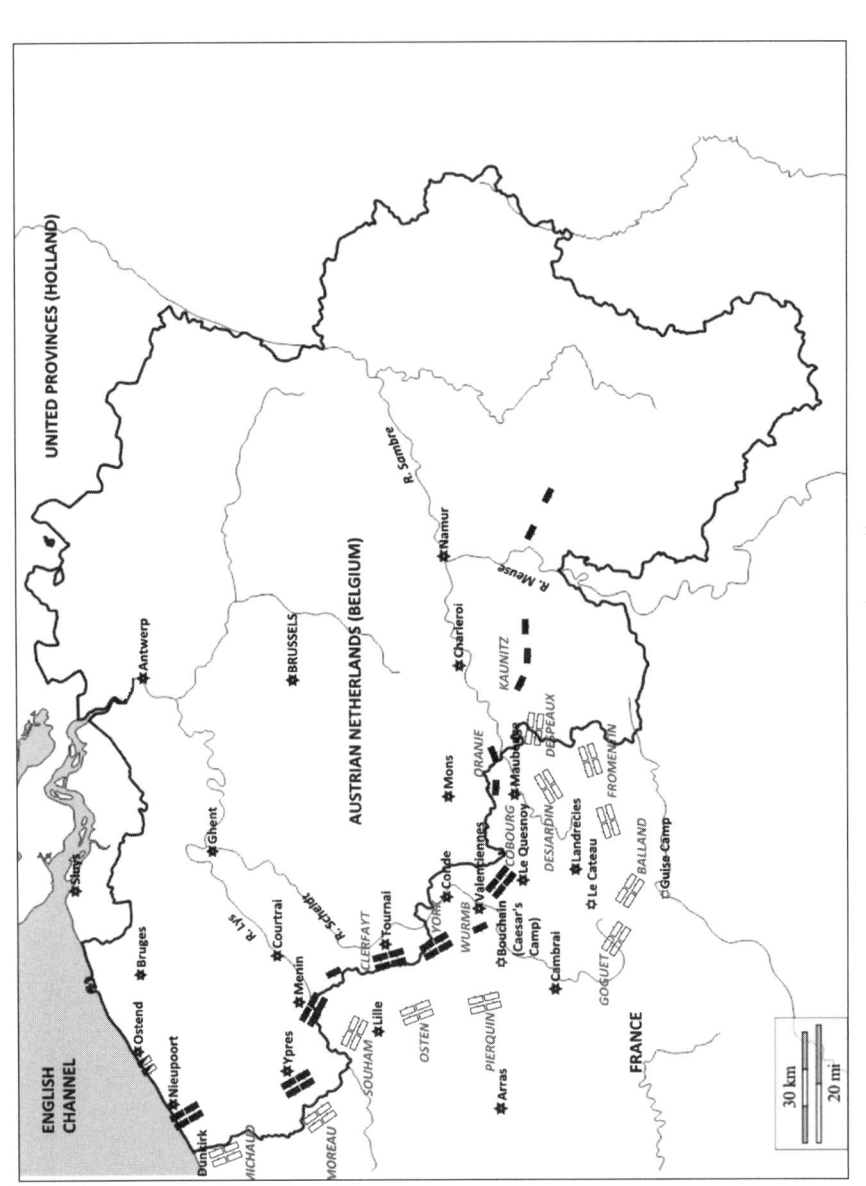

The situation in April 1794

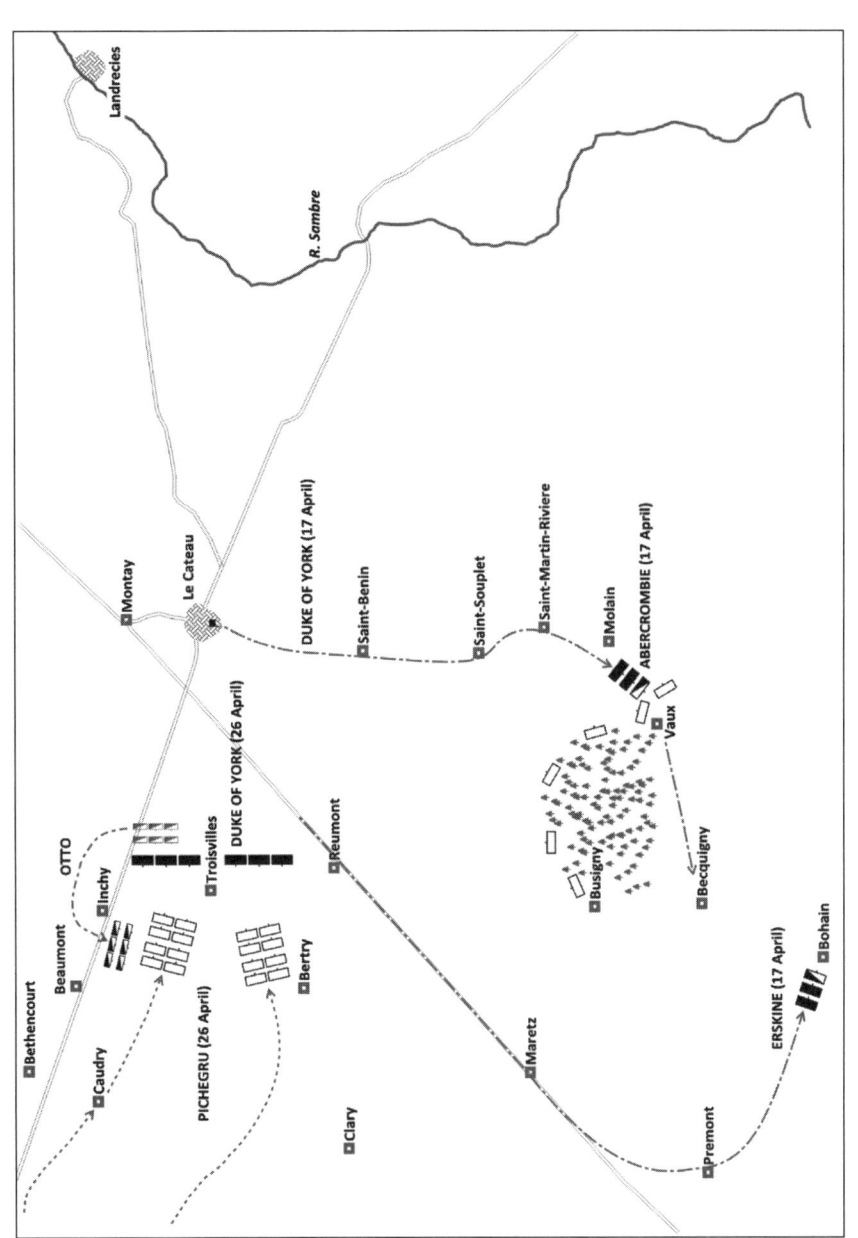

Catillon and Villers-en-Cauchies

Chapter 11

Good Cavalry Country

Catillon and Le Cateau

The Holy Roman Emperor arrived to great fanfare and assumed supreme command of the Imperial army. It was a relaxed, optimistic interlude: 'Balls and plays were likewise very common, as was indeed every other mode of gaiety.' Captain John Le Marchant, brigade-major in Sir Robert Laurie's cavalry brigade, basked in the wonder of so many continental dignitaries:

> I passed this day in company with some of the great men in the army, the Prince of Cobourg, General Mack, and others. The Prince is a thin old man, with a countenance not very expressive. Mack is a man of forty, extremely like the Abbé Mac Carty: he has some complaint in the head that keeps him in constant pain. In consequence, he wears a black caul over his skull, sewed round the bottom with thick black hair, which gives him a very grotesque appearance. He lies all day on his bed, writing with a pencil his instructions for the movements of the army: when an action takes place, he is lifted from his bed to his horse. It is singular, that with these habits, he is a passionate admirer of the sex. He is accompanied everywhere by a female attendant. I have made a sketch of his face, which is thought to be very like him.[1]

The New Year's campaign got underway in style during the morning of 16 April 1794, when the emperor inspected the Coalition army on the Heights of Montay, a mile north of Le Cateau, the same ground over which the British Expeditionary Force fought the last pitched battle in British army history on 26 August 1914. Cornet Robert Wilson of the 15th Light Dragoons was present:

> On the 16th of April the allied army, nominally one hundred and twenty thousand but not more than ninety thousand effective, assembled

on the heights above Cateau on a table-land to be reviewed by the Emperor. It was a spring day of the old seasons, and a magnificent spectacle was presented to the eye. Philosophers would perhaps have contemplated it with other feelings, but none could have been present. I thought, however, that a beautiful girl of the 14th regiment of foot dressed with English cottage simplicity, engaged more the attention of majesty, royalty, and high authority than the lines of warriors and the parade of war. Certainly she arrested the career of the Court and Staff, and fixed their gaze for several minutes.[2]

Perhaps the 14th Foot were attempting to win back some favour with the duke? Incidents of looting and murder by some individuals in the regiment had caused him to issue an order to the army on 10 April:

> His Royal Highness the Commander in Chief earnestly requests that the Generals and Field Officers, Captains and Officers commanding companies, will take pains to explain to the men of the army under their command the following order, addressed in particular to the private men of the army … His Royal Highness … announces his full determination to exert every effort of severity and rigour to put a stop to the scenes of plunder and outrage of which so many instances have lately occurred, to the dishonour of the British Army.[3]

The two offenders within the 14th were hanged in front of Abercrombie's brigade and the plundering stopped – for a while. But harsh military justice was simply a fact of life in the British Army, not an exception:

> At the same time that … British soldiers in general were maintaining with such devoted fortitude the glory of England, their camps daily presented the most disgusting and painful scenes of punishments. The halberds were regularly erected along the lines every morning; and the shrieks of the sufferers made a pandemonium, from which the foreigner fled with terror and with astonishment at the severity of our military code. Drunkenness was the vice of officers and men, but the men paid the penalty; and the officers who sat in judgment in the morning were too often scarcely sober from the past night's debauch. The highest in rank and station were often on the evening parade or on the race-ground, for races were established in the camp, in a state of flagrant inebriety; and of course, 'like master, like man' held good in all the gradations of rank, though with many most creditable exceptions.[4]

The duke's force now consisted of four cavalry and two infantry brigades, plus five companies of Royal Artillery, but he was still only a bit-part player in the Coalition cause. Feldmarschall Coburg had, with his emperor's consent, divided the Coalition army into five geographic commands, plus a reserve.[5] All of his strength was in the centre – between Tournai and Le Quesnoy – since Mack's plan was to separate the two wings of the French army by a drive on Cambrai. The commands were:

RIGHT WING
Between Channel coast and Tournai
32,000 men commanded by Clerfayt (24,000 men covering a seventy-mile front in West Flanders, and 8,000 men in garrisons at Ostend, Nieuwpoort, Ypres and Menin)
Headquarters at Tournai

LINKING FORCE
5,500 men commanded by Generalleutnant von Würmb
Headquarters at Denain

RIGHT CENTRE
Between Tournai and St Amand
23,600 men commanded by HRH Duke of York
Headquarters at St Amand

CENTRE
Between Conde and Le Quesnoy
42,900 men commanded by Prince Josias von Coburg
Headquarters at Valenciennes; garrisons at Condé and Le Quesnoy

LEFT CENTRE
Between Bavai and Maubeuge
19,000 men commanded by the Hereditary Prince of Orange-Nassau
Headquarters at Bavai

LEFT WING
Between Bettignies and Dinant
27,000 men commanded by Feldzeugmeister Count Franz von Kaunitz-Rietberg

RESERVE
Between Namur and Tréves
15,000 men commanded by Feldmarschalleutnant Beaulieu.

The new commander of l'Armée du Nord was Général de division Jean-Charles Pichegru, a former mathematics tutor whose students once included a certain Napoléon Bonaparte. He had 60,000 men in three divisions along a front extending over 20 miles (32km) in length. Pichegru was the eighteenth commander of that force since the war had started, of which seven had been guillotined or disgraced.[6] Pichegru put on his war face and immediately sent of a curt letter to Prince von Coburg:

> General
>
> I summons you in the name of the French Republic to render up immediately Quesnoy, Condé and Valenciennes, or be assured I shall attack and vanquish you.[7]

The French had not been idle over the winter break. Their army by now contained six military strata, and Carnot was determined that all should be coalesced into one enormous national army. The line regiments of the Old Régime still existed (although the Guards and foreign regiments had been disbanded), dressed in their white coats and crested casque helmets. Next came the Gardes Nationale, established in 1789 as a voluntary unpaid militia in every town, dressed in blue with bicorne hats and intended for local duties only. The Volunteers of 1791 were men extracted from the Gardes Nationale to serve with the field armies for one year, at double the salary of the regular regiments, and with elected officers. The Volunteers of 1792 were also 'one-year men' and considered themselves liable for service within the borders of France only – many subsequently deserted when forced to cross boundaries. The 'Levy of the 300,000' was the start of conscription in February 1793, with men drawn by lot. In reality, only a little over 100,000 were ever conscripted. Then came the big one: Carnot's Levée en Masse of 23 August 1793, all unmarried men aged 18 to 25, no exceptions or replacements accepted.[8]

All this effort produced a massive unwieldy army with not enough staff officers in Paris to even keep track of the strength and dispositions of thousands of new regiments. Something had to be done to unify the whole. It was determined that the Gardes Nationale battalions would be merged with the line.[9] National Guardsmen were to receive the same clothes, pay, ammunition as the regulars, and be united with them in numbered demi-brigades,[10] each comprising two battalions of Gardes Nationale and one battalion of line infantry. This provided 196 line demi-brigades. Fourteen new light infantry demi-brigades were created, differing only that each line demi-brigade carried with it six 'battalion guns', while the light infantry was without cannon. The nominal establishment of a demi-brigade was set at 3,201 men on 22 November 1793, which gave an official strength of 672,000 infantry in 210 demi-brigades. The formation of the demi-brigades was not without difficulty. The regulars showed great reluctance to join forces with the Gardes Nationale and grumbled about having to exchange their traditional white uniforms for the blue coats of the Gardes, but the union was strictly enforced. Simultaneously the propagation of the cavalry was carried on 'with the greatest zeal' despite the difficulties in securing good horseflesh. A total of eighty-three cavalry regiments were formed. Heavy cavalry regiments were established at 700 men in four squadrons, the medium and light regiments each 1,400 men in six squadrons. The artillery, based upon the core of highly-proficient regulars, was increased to fifty-four batteries, albeit with shortages in horses and equipment. On 1 January 1794, the strength of the French army stood at 760,922 men, of which 634,000 were under arms.[11]

The French plan at the start of the 1794 campaign was to attack the flanks of the Coalition position in the Austrian Netherlands. The main attack was to come in West Flanders, at the right of the Coalition line, and was designed to cut the British off from the Channel ports, and therefore their lines of supply. Dunkirk was well-garrisoned by Frenchmen, and their strong left wing in West Flanders (71,000 men) consisted of divisions under Michaud, Moreau and Souham that ran south-east towards Lille (which was also well-defended). From there Osten's division held a line southwards towards Pont-a-Marque, directly in front of the duke's position. From Arleux the line continued south-east to Etreux (south of Le Cateau), 47,000 men of the centre directly opposing Coburg and containing the divisions of Pierquin, Goguet and Balland. Etreux was the elbow of the French position, for from there the line angled north-east towards Maubeuge. This was the right wing, 36,000 men in divisions under Fromentin, Desjardin and Despeaux, whilst Favereau commanded the French garrison of Maubeuge.

The Coalition armies had approximately 160,000 men in the field, of whom it was reckoned some 120–130,000 were fit for service. The Austrians remained the senior partner. The strength of the Kaiserlich-königlich army in the Netherlands amounted to 103 battalions and 143 squadrons. The Austrian artillery array was impressive, 841 guns, which included 328 guns of siege artillery and 413 field guns (198 battalion guns, 277 guns of the Reserve Artillery and thirty-nine in the depots).[12] The Dutch could only field 16,000 men in thirty-eight battalions and twenty-four squadrons. The British, on 1 March 1794, showed a strength of 7,168 infantry, 3,276 cavalry, 554 artillerymen and seventy-nive sappers, with forty-four guns. The Hanoverians numbered 9,025 infantry, 2,108 cavalry and sixty-eight guns. The Hessen-Cassel force amounted to 5,494 infantry and 1,622 cavalry.

The Coalition troops were still, man-for-man, superior to the French in terms of experience and military efficiency. However, the one area where the French enjoyed clear superiority was in sustenance. The Imperial army relied upon food shipped along the Vistula and transported to Gdansk and from there to Amsterdam, from where the food was distributed to the army along the Maas River. The Coalition troops frequently starved in rich Belgian farmland, whereas the French lived there in the fullest abundance, living off the land, considering the fruits of the earth as their own.

The French had 154,000 men on the frontier, so evidenced a numerical advantage, which was in fact merely a superiority in quantity, not quality; most of the troops were raw recruits, levée en masse men. On 19 April the King of Prussia announced that a Prussian corps of 62,000 men, subsidised by the British, could be expected in Flanders by 24 May to even out the opposing numbers.

Pichegru was under great pressure from Carnot to do something, and so made a feeble attempt on Le Cateau on 29 March, which the Austrian defenders under Generalmajor Baron Kray easily repulsed. Pichegru reckoned his young recruits were still unready for war, and so the first two weeks of April passed by with both sides immobile on the frontier. The Coalition could not move until the emperor arrived to take command, whilst the French dare not until the green recruits were sufficiently trained. Prince von Coburg observed the strength of the French left wing and grew nervous that the Coalition strategy – to punch a hole in the French line towards Cambrai – would leave his wings denuded and allow the French to cut communications with the Channel and Namur. The French centre was still an attractive target – troops there were widely dispersed, with elements as far back as Bohain and Guise – but could that be a trap?

But marching directly at the enemy was not part of Austrian military culture. First, there were fortresses to reduce, and Landrecies on the Sambre River (9 miles or 15km south of Le Quesnoy and held by the French) must come first, in accordance with Mack's plan. The Coalition attack of 17 April was intended not as an attempt to defeat Pichegru in the field, but rather to drive the French back everywhere in the vicinity to allow the siege to proceed unmolested.

His ceremonial duties done, the emperor handed tactical command in the field over to Prince Coburg, who ordered off eight columns for the attack:

1st Column – Prince Christian von Hessen-Darmstadt (Dutch, 9 battalions, 3 squadrons)

2nd Column – Baron Joseph Alvinczi (Austrian, 12 battalions, 22 squadrons)

3rd Column – Prince Coburg (Austrian, 19 battalions, 30 squadrons)

4th Column – HRH Duke of York (Anglo-Hanoverian-Hessian, 13 battalions, 18 squadrons)

5th Column – Sir William Erskine (Anglo-Hanoverian-Hessian, 11 battalions, 27 squadrons)

6th Column – Karl, Graf Hadik von Futak (Austrian, 2 battalions, 2 squadrons)

7th Column – Prince of Orange-Nassau (Austro-Dutch, 12 battalions, 15 squadrons)

8th Column – Geisen (Dutch, 2 battalions, 2 squadrons)

The British were to support the Austrians on the right; the Duke of York to advance upon Vaux, Abercrombie's advanced guard in the van, with Erskine advancing upon Prémont. All commanders were expressly ordered to halt their troops on the captured ground. There was no intention of pursuing the enemy in the event of success.

The French were surprised on 17 April and manoeuvred out of their positions with minimal losses. Erskine's column crossed the border and easily captured Prémont, then swung east to aid the duke's column. The latter had encountered no opposition until just north of the village of Vaux-Andigny. Abercrombie's advanced guard (the Austrian Husaren Regiment Erzherzog Ferdinand, a squadron of the 16th Light Dragoons, the Austrian O'Donnell Freikorps and four horse-drawn guns, supported by a brigade of Austrian grenadiers commanded by Generalmajor Franz Petrasch) ran into a French redoubt north of the village of La Haye Menneresse. After an artillery bombardment, the three Austrian grenadier battalions[13] advanced towards the redoubt, which the French abandoned without a fight. The grenadiers then captured the village and the surrounding forest 'with the utmost violence':

> As soon as the troops had gained sufficiently the enemy's flanks the advanced guard, under the command of Major-General Abercromby, was directed to begin the attack. I immediately detached a party of the cavalry around the wood to the right, who completely succeeded in cutting them off, took four pieces of cannon and one howitzer.[14]

The Austrian Ferdinand Hussars and a squadron of the 16th Light Dragoons cut down large numbers of retreating Frenchmen. The bulk of the advanced guard ended the day in Bequigny while the light troops pushed on unopposed to Bohain. The Austrians looted and burned Vaux, so the duke spent the night in a nearby windmill. The minimal success of the day was marred by disgraceful plundering and burning on the part of the Coalition troops after the engagement; the emperor himself later confessed that his troops had set fire to thirteen villages.[15] Cornet Robert Wilson of the 15th Light Dragoons was able to verify the emperor's regrets:

> The night was a memorable one, and I have never forgotten the awful and meditative sight of thirteen villages in flames. The horizon seemed to be indeed on fire; and, inexperienced as I then was in the horrors of war, nature and education combined to make me feel unhappy at so much calamity. The distress of the poor children, amidst the tears of their parents and their burning homes, the carnage roar of cannon confusion and violence, particularly moved my pity. I commiserated the sufferers on the field of battle; but, as they had reason to anticipate their lot I have ever thought them less objects of compassion than the inhabitants; who, in all the campaigns I have since witnessed, were made the prey of friends as well as foes.[16]

The Allies lost fewer than 700 killed and wounded, nearly all of them Austrian, whilst the French lost over 2,000 men, and twenty-four guns, of which eleven were captured by the British columns.[17] The 6th, 7th and 8th columns, intended to observe the enemy beyond Cambrai, did not even engage the enemy. The Duke of York penned a victory despatch on 18 April and gave it to his aide, Captain Henry Clinton, to take home to England.[18]

Then the Austrians got down to the siege-craft so fundamental to their way of making war. The siege of Landrecies was a major investiture conducted by 23,000 Coalition troops. The left wing was commanded by Austrian Feldmarschalleutnant Alvinczi; the right by Feldmarschalleutnant Josef, Count Kinsky von Wichnitz und Tettau. The French had constructed an entrenched camp on the heights of the left bank of the Sambre dominating the fortress, with about 7,000 men present. This camp had to be captured first. On 20 April, in the presence of the emperor, a corps under the command of the Prince of Orange-Nassau attacked and took the entrenched camp by storm. The French fled to the fortress, which led to it being completely over-crowded. The siege-force began to dig trenches and construct siege batteries. Over the next week some 3,853 artillery rounds were fired into the packed fortress.

The duke's contingent formed a masking force to the west of Landrecies, holding a line between Le Cateau and Beaumont-en-Cambrésis. Four battalions of Hungarian infantry and twenty-eight squadrons of Austrian cavalry were added to the Duke of York's command. He now commanded far and away the largest column in the Coalition army.

As dreary as another siege sounds, it did have one positive effect. Pichegru moved men from his flanks to the French centre, so that the French troop massing more closely matched the Coalition's. With so many troop movements behind the front line it was inevitable that minor skirmishes occurred almost daily. On 23 April a French column, reported to be 15,000 strong, left Cambrai and marched towards the Coalition front line on the river Selle. The emperor's party was returning to the frontier after a short stay in Brussels, and Coalition headquarters feared that it had been sent out to intercept them. Generalmajor Rudolf Ritter von Otto was sent to investigate, so he took detachments of the 15th Light Dragoons and the Austrian Leopold Hussars and discovered a French column near the village of Villers-en-Cauchies, about 10 miles (16km) north-west of Le Cateau. Otto rapidly returned to his headquarters at Sainte-Hilaire and summoned reinforcements, whereupon he was given ten squadrons of cavalry; the 11th Light Dragoons, two squadrons of the Austrian Zeschwitz Kuirassiers and Major General John Mansel's brigade, with two squadrons from each of the Royal Horse Guards, 1st Dragoons and 3rd Dragoon Guards. This ad hoc brigade ran into a large force of French light cavalry near Montrecourt at 04.00 hours in the morning of 24 April and immediately attacked with his advanced guard. The French fled and then rallied, before falling back to Villers-en-Cauchies where they reined in alongside 3,000 infantry supported by artillery. Otto found himself in front of the French lines with only the 15th Light Dragoons and the Leopold Hussars; Mansel's heavy brigade had failed to follow, 'although every head was constantly turned round with anxious look[s], especially as we approached the French line, we were unable to perceive a vestige of them,' Cornet Robert Wilson of the 15th recorded.[19] Otto decided that his only chance was to attack the French line.[20] He exhorted his troops with lines such as 'Gentlemen! Remember, your numbers do not permit prisoners!' The 15th Light Dragoons and Leopold Hussars cheered and then charged, only to have the French cavalry break away to both sides, to reveal their infantry in squares. Normally squares were impervious to cavalry, but the infantry were raw recruits, and somehow the Coalition cavalry broke in. A line of French cavalry behind the infantry was swept away and a four-mile pursuit followed. 'The French were so panic-struck,' Cornet Wilson recorded, 'that they scarcely made any resistance, notwithstanding that our numbers were so few in comparison with the party engaged that every individual pursuer found himself in the midst of a flock of foes.'[21] The 15th Light Dragoons turned north and attempted to capture a convoy of artillery that was trundling towards Bouchain. They were forced to turn back due to a lack of support. The French quickly rallied. Major William Aylett brought his exhausted 15th Light Dragoons back to Villers-en-Cauchies only to find that he was cut off by retreating French columns of baggage, artillery, infantry and cavalry. Practically every man was wounded. And still there was no sign of Mansel's heavy brigade.

That particular brigade was to the south of the village, and its attack on the French position had not been successful. The 3rd Dragoon Guards had taken heavy casualties unsuccessfully attacking the French guns; they would not be able to come to Aylett's aid. But Mansel had been unlucky. 'General Mansell's conduct was entirely owing to a misconception of the order brought to him by the aide-de-camp of General Otto when on march,' Cornet Wilson explained, 'in consequence of which he carried his brigade too far to our right. When he heard the guns and volley he then discovered the mistake, but too late to correct it. Otto, however, would not receive him or hear his explanations, but desired that they might be made to the Duke of York.'[22] The French suffered heavy casualties this day; as high as 800 dead and 400 wounded. The Leopold Hussars lost ten dead and ten wounded. The 15th Light Dragoons lost fifty-eight men killed and seventeen wounded but gained a new battle honour: Villers en Cauchies. A grateful Emperor Franz II awarded special gold medals to the eight officers of the 15th present on the day.[23] But the duke, egged on by Otto, was unhappy with Mansel's performance and even talked of an inquiry. Mansel's reputation within the army diminished, at least for a while.

Pichegru had followed the plan drawn up by the Committee of Public Safety since the campaign opened. He had restricted his movements to the centre, without success. Repulsed in almost all his attacks, he had not been able to thwart the Landrecies' investment. He posted brigades on the south side of the city to protect an exit for the garrison of this place; but his efforts had been unsuccessful. Convinced of the uselessness of his relief attempts, he proposed a change to his his plan of operations to the Committee of Public Safety. In the east l'Armée d'Ardennes, commanded by Général de division Louis Charbonnier, stationed west of Philippeville, was to direct his operations towards l'Armée du Nord, first seizing the heights of Bossut, occupied by an Austrian corps commanded by Feldzeugmeister Franz Wenzel, Graf von Kaunitz-Rietberg. Moving westwards, nearly 22,000 of Charbonnier's men under Général de division Jacques Fromentin, attacked Coalition positions in densely-wooded country at Prisches and Maroilles. Prisches was taken after a long struggle. Communications between Alvinczi to the north and Count Kinsky to the south were severed. The 22-year-old Archduke Karl drew praise by leading a counter-attack which recovered lost ground. At the same time Général de division Jacques Desjardin attacked Beaumont, which the Austrians evacuated during the night. On 27 April l'Armée d'Ardennes arrived at Beaumont itself, forming a junction with l'Armée du Nord.[24]

The second prong in Pichegru's plan involved Général de division Jacques Ferrand advancing from Guise to attack the east and south of the besieging force. Feldmarschalleutnant Count Bellegarde defended the Coalition line from Oisy to Nouvion and was attacked by 23,000 French troops. The victory at Prisches enabled the young Archduke to send troops to his aid, and this second attack was also repulsed. The third prong was to be Général de brigade René-Bernard Chapuis with 30,000 men, taken from Caesar's camp and its surroundings, marching south-east from Cambrai to attack the Duke of York at Troisvilles.

The main Coalition line at this time ended at Inchy, 4 miles (7km) west of Le Cateau and came under the command of the duke. The early morning of 26 April was fine, but a thick fog lay all around. British troops, waking from their slumber on a ridge running between Inchy and Troisvilles, heard a curious sputtering sound out in front, then heard the unmistakable sound of French drum-rolls and cheering. Chapuis was advancing his men in two massive columns headed for the Coalition front line. The Duke of York rode up to the ridge and took post in either a redoubt or a windmill (sources differ) where he was joined by the tenacious Generalmajor von Otto. The duke (or Otto, again sources differ) noticed that the left flank of the French force was 'in the air', and vulnerable to a flanking attack; but he had better be quick. The duke had nineteen squadrons of cavalry, so he concentrated them all on his right flank and placed them under the command of Otto. The first line comprised six squadrons of the Austrian Zeschwitz Kuirassiers, commanded by Oberst Karl Schwartzenberg.[25] The second line was Major General Sir John Mansel's brigade, out to redeem their (or more specifically, Mansel's) reputation. The third line consisted of the British 1st and 5th Dragoon Guards and 16th Light Dragoons under Colonel Richard Vyse.

Before they moved off the duke placed himself at the head of Mansel's heavy brigade. 'Gentlemen, you must repair the disgrace of the 24th!' he called out. 'I am confident you will reclaim my good opinion of you!'[26] All must have bristled in the knowledge that their failure two days earlier was all due to poor staff work. Nonetheless, they *huzza'd* and cantered off to do their duty.

The duke ordered Colonel Congreve's artillery to keep up a hot fire on the French columns to slow them down, whilst requiring the light troops in Troisvilles to fall back through the village in order to force the French to focus their attack at this critical point. The ruse worked. The 30,000 Frenchmen, marking time as they waited for a third column of 4,000 men to join them from the south, manoeuvred feebly in front of Troisvilles as Congreve's artillery ploughed into them. Meanwhile, Otto's cavalry force, hidden by some convenient folds in the ground, rode around the northern end of the French line, capturing Général Chapuis en route, thus arriving on the left flank of the French force undetected.

The scene was set; the French were doomed. The inevitable cavalry charge presaged what historian John Fortescue called 'the greatest day in the annals of the British horse.' The six British and one Austrian regiment rode triumphantly into and over 30,000 unformed French infantry, who dispersed in one giant mass and did not stop running until they reached Cambrai. The Austrian cavalry found the third French column and routed it also. The French lost 2,500 men and twenty-six guns. The Coalition covering army lost 1,500 men during the battle, the Austrians losing nine officers and 228 men and during the cavalry attack alone. British casualties were fifty-seven killed and 100 wounded, including the gallant Major General Mansel, who redeemed his reputation at the cost of his life. His body was later found far out in advance of his brigade, having told his aide-de-camp (his son, Captain John Mansel junior) not to follow him.

Private James Russell of the 1st Dragoon Guards was a participant:

> Soon after daybreak the French army consisting of 28 thousand with 36 pieces of cannon made an attack upon our camp when (after driving in advanced piquets) the following regiments of cavalry were ordered to engage them vizt., 1st Dragoon Guards (6 Troops) 5th Dragoon Guards (4 Troops) Oxford Blues (3 Troops) and a regiment of Austrian Zelchwitz Cavalry (Cuirassiers) – our whole force did not exceed 2,500. We marched from camp and engaged them at Trois-Villes about 8 o'clock, when after a short resistance they fled with the greatest precipitation (leaving behind them a great number of killed and wounded, among the former was a General, we likewise took one General prisoner with a number of men and 35 pieces of cannon with a great quantity of ammunition. Our loss was inconsiderable (in proportion to that of the enemy) we had one General (Mansel) killed and his son (who was Aide-de

Camp to his father) taken prisoner. The loss to the King's Dragoon Guards did not exceed 10 men among which 3 were taken prisoner. Our loss in horses was more considerable as we had 95 killed, wounded and missing in the course of 3 hours – the Oxford Blues and the 3rd Dragoon Guards suffered considerably. In the evening the different regiments received the thanks of his Royal Highness the Duke of York, in person for their gallant behavior in the field- and likewise 4 pence per man to drink his Highness's health.[27]

Two days later Private Russell recorded that:

General Mansel buried (in front of the camp) the funeral attended by HRH the Duke of York, Commander in Chief and all the officers in camp, likewise the Blues, Royals, and 3rd Dragoon Guards being the Brigade he commanded in the field – after the funeral service was over a discharge of 15 pieces of cannon were fired over his grave.[28]

Major generals Abercrombie, Lake, Dundas, Whyte, Fox, and Colonel D'Oyly served as pall-bearers.

The duke penned an address to the army praising their efforts, singling out Major-of-brigade Edward Payne (15th Light Dragoons) and Captain John Beckwith (16th Light Dragoons) for their conduct, then rode around each regiment of Mansel's brigade to personally thank them. His aide Lieutenant & Captain John Murray of the 3rd Foot Guards carried the victory despatch to London and was awarded the brevet of major.[29] Eight regiments were awarded the battle honour 'Cateau'.[30] The following day, a Sunday, Corporal Brown of the Guards noted 'a *Fue de Joy* [sic] fired by the army (in honour of the victory gained over the French) beginning with thirty-eight pieces of cannon and answered by all the regiments in camp firing on horseback with pistols.'[31] There was every good reason to celebrate. The Coalition had defeated 30,000 Frenchmen in thirty minutes. A later biographer of the duke considered Cateau to be the Duke of York's equivalent of Salamanca.[32]

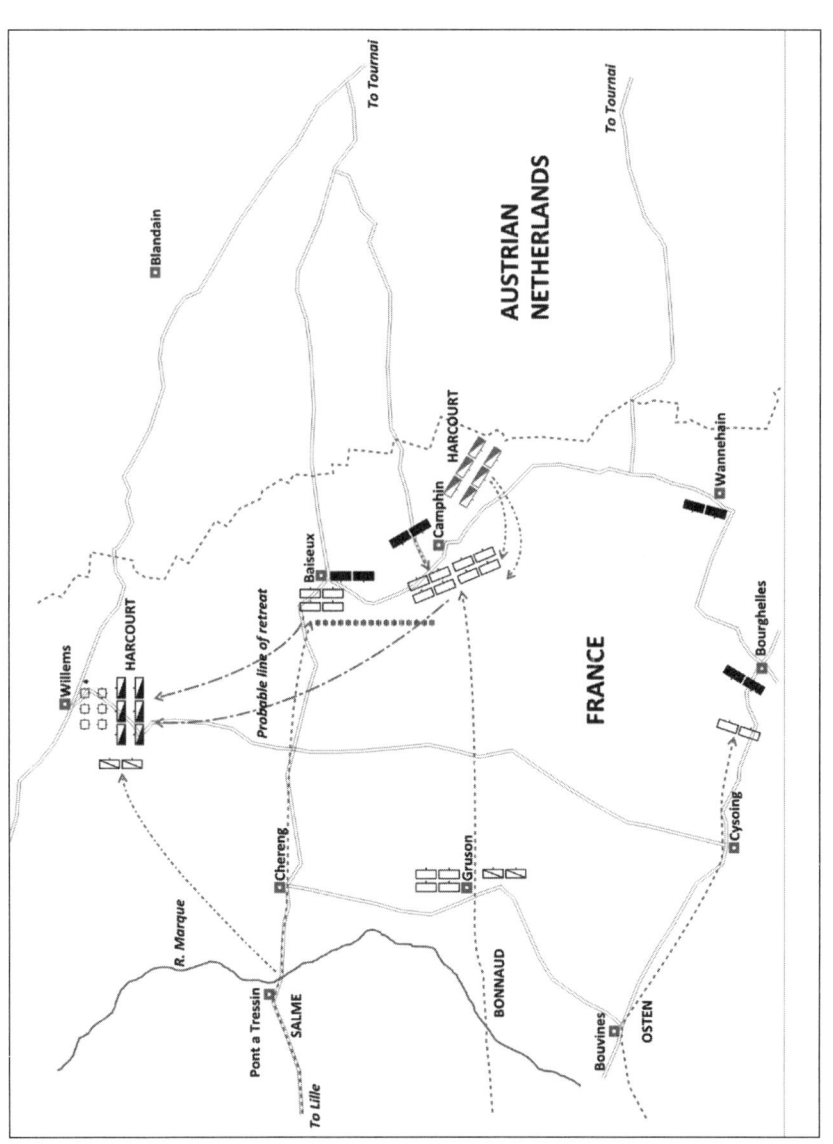

The Battle of Willems

Menin and Willems

Général de brigade Rene Chapuis was a prize capture indeed for the Coalition.[33] Especially when it was found he had a copy of Pichegru's campaign orders on him. The orders made it plain that the main French blow would fall on the right flank of the Coalition line – in West Flanders. Harry Calvert had already discerned that Coalition strategy was weak as regards protection of that flank:

> According to my idea, as long as West Flanders is without a force adequate to its protection — as long as its security must be effected by detachments from this army, we shall achieve nothing important, but shall ever be arrested in our career, perhaps in the very moment of victory, and be under the necessity of relinquishing the object of our labours from the urgency of the demand for succour on the frontier of the rich and valuable country we leave behind us.[34]

The Coalition forces in West Flanders were commanded by Feldzeugmeister Clerfayt, a native Wallonian. One battalion of the Loyal Emigres and a squadron defended Ostend; four Hanoverian battalions defended Nieuwpoort; 6,500 Hessians and Austrians garrisoned Ypres. Hessians and Hanoverians were in Menin, more Hanoverians were in Courtrai and Mouscron, and a strong garrison of Austrians and Hanoverians defended Marquain.

The French commander Pichegru had between 40,000 and 50,000 men in his main army, with another 20,000 men under Général de brigade Jacques Philippe Bonnaud at Sainghin, 5 miles (8km) south-east of Lille. At 07.00 hours on the morning of 26 April, the French attacked outposts at Dronkaard on the Lille-Courtrai road. Generalmajor von Wangenheim sent a battalion of the 1.Infanterie-Regiment and two six-pounders, and thereafter the other battalion of the 1.Infanterie-Regiment and a squadron of the 7.Dragoner-Regiment from Mouscron to their aid. Wangenheim was holding an extended line with about 1,000 men against an entire French division, which captured Mouscron. Wangenheim's men withdrew at noon to Dottignies for the loss of 42 men.

The battle recommenced at 07.00 hours the following morning when Vandamme's brigade of Moreau's division encircled Menin. On 28 April the Hanoverians re-captured Mouscron just before Clerfayt arrived with 6,000 Imperial troops. At 06.00 hours the next morning he summoned generals von Oeyenhausen, von Borrosch and Sporck to Mouscron, and in the name of the emperor and Prince von Coburg ordered his force against Menin and Roncq in order to cut off the enemy's remaining line of communications between Courtrai and Lille. The Hanoverians were forced back to Dottignies, then to Pecq, having lost 817 men in the past three days, including 299 from the 1.Infanterie-Regiment and 214 from the 6.Infanterie. The Austrians lost 903 men and eleven cannon.

A day later the French laid siege to Menin, whose garrison comprised two battalions of the 14.Leichte-Infanterie-Regiment, the 1.Grenadier-Bataillon, four companies of Loyal Emigres, some companies of Hessen-Cassel infantry and twenty-eight cannon, commanded by Generalmajor Hammerstein. Moreau sent a messenger with the usual exhortation to surrender; Hammerstein refused. But 2,400 men could only hold out so long against 20,000. Declaring that he would 'rather die in the open field than submit to capitulation,' and assisted by his chief staff officer Kapitan Gerhard Johann David von Scharnhorst, Hammerstein skilfully managed to extract most of his infantry northwards towards Roeslaere, leaving only a cadre of artillerymen behind to cover their exit.

The Hanoverians were harassed along the line of retreat. They lost 525 men, but most of the garrison made it to safety, with the exception of 179 captured Loyal Emigrants who were immediately executed.[35] Pichegru now held the line between Menin and the sea, controlled Courtrai and all the surrounding countryside, albeit in a dangerous salient, with only one escape route, through Lille to the south. He was either outrageously bold, blind to the eventualities, or prepared to risk anything to avoid the guillotine – probably the latter.

Menin had just fallen for the third time. If things continued as they were, reinforcements would be needed; the Hanoverian corp had just lost 1,300 men in four days of fighting. As fate would have it, fresh British regiments arrived at Ostend from Bristol in late April - the 8th (King's Royal Irish) Regiment of (Light) Dragoons, and the 38th (1st Staffordshire) and 55th (Westmoreland) Regiments of Foot. A week later, the 12th (East Suffolk) Regiment of Foot arrived from Ireland and along with the 38th and 55th Foot were formed into a new brigade under the command of Major General Richard Whyte before being marched to join the Duke's field army. These were very raw troops and would not spend long in the field before being returned to garrison duty.

Providentially the French garrison of Landrecies surrendered to Coburg's Austrians on 30 April. The terms were agreed during the course of the day, and before nightfall the garrison marched out as prisoners-of-war, nearly 6,000 men. The duke was now free for other duties, so the emperor ordered him to go to the assistance of Clerfayt in Flanders. Corporal Brown recorded the scene in Le Cateau:

> Accordingly orders were issued this afternoon for the whole of the troops to be in readiness to march this evening at nine o'clock, in consequence of which the tents were struck, the baggage loaded

and everything ready for marching at the hour appointed. Our route was for the camp at Famars, but we did not move off our ground before eleven o'clock, when we proceeded in the following order, viz. two squadrons 15th light dragoons, six squadrons of the brigade (late Gen. Mansel's), four battalions British guards, two battalions Winsel Coloredo, three battalions Austrian grenadiers, six squadrons Colonel Vyse's brigade.[36]

The army marched in the worst weather most of them could ever remember. Deep ditches lined the roads on both sides, and 'horsemen and guns, baggage-waggons, &c, were constantly plunging in the water.'[37] Under these conditions it is perhaps unsurprising that Major General Lake's horse fell eight feet from the ramparts of a bridge (whilst avoiding a wagon) into a ditch and Lake was thrown. He survived but was badly bruised. He went home again and was replaced by Major General Samuel Hulse in command of the Brigade of Guards.[38] As before, the British had to maneouvre around towns occupied by the Austrians, making for a long, miserable march. By 3 May the Duke of York was at Tournai. The British contingent for Clerfayt's force arrived in Marquain, just west of Tournai, the following day having splashed through the heavy rain for five days. Between the duke and Clerfayt, the Coalition army had 40,000 men positioned between Tournai and Espierres, facing west. The sun came out and several diarists recorded their impressions of the rich, rolling farmland, with good roads and cultivation as far as the eye could see – good cavalry country.

The duke saw an opportunity to put the estimated 24,000 Frenchmen in the salient south of Courtrai 'in the bag.' He urged Clerfayt to action, to no avail. The Austrian was as irresolute and obdurate as Coburg. 'No man on earth has more personal courage than General Clerfayt,' the duke wrote to his father, 'but unfortunately his lack of resolution and decision as a general is beyond all description and was the real cause of the check which he received on the 29th.'[39] The duke was so disgusted he forwarded his correspondence with Clerfayt to the emperor, who considered the matter – then ordered Clerfayt to advance.

But Pichegru moved first. He had Souham's powerful division on hand in the following locations; Macdonald's and Daendels' brigades were on the right bank of the Lys; Dewinter's brigade was at Pottelberg and the suburb of Tournai; Jardon's brigade was at Elbeke; Malbrancq's brigade was at the Moulin de Castrel. Thierry's independent brigade was at Tourcoing; Bonnaud's division was at Sainghin; and Compère's independent brigade was detached at Lannoy.

Pichegru attacked the main Coalition line in force at first light on 10 May. Three French columns were involved in the attack. Général

Souham attacked Bussche's Hanoverians at the northern end of the line, at Roncheval, Dottignies and Coyghem. Compére, with five battalions and a cavalry regiment, occupied Lannoy, whilst Thierry's brigade occupied Tourcoing. Thierry's brigade advanced on Leers and Nechin and repulsed the Coalition outposts to Bailleul.

The central column under Général de division Bonnaud, 23,000 men, advanced from the camp at Sainghin down the main road from Lille to Tournai and forced the Coalition out of their advanced posts at Baisieux and Camphin, 6 miles (9km) west of Tournai. On the right, Osten's brigade (6,000 men) advanced from Pont-à-Marque to Pont-à-Bouvines, then attacked Cysoing. From Cysoing he successively reached Bourghelles and Bachy, but could not go beyond this point, being held up by an obstinate defence by k.k. Linien-Infanterie-Regiment Nr. 20 'Graf Kaunitz-Rietberg'. The main part of Bonnaud's division, the brigades of Pierquin, Nöel, Salme and the cavalry of Baillot, passed through Gruson and Pont-à-Tressin; Nöel and Pierquin, at the head of fifteen battalions, crossed the Marque and occupied Gruson. Salme, with the remainder of the division, crossed the watercourses at Pont-à-Tressin.[40]

At this point they formed a grand battery of twenty-five guns on the heights west of the two villages and began a violent cannonade. After an indecisive fight of three hours, the Austrian grenadier division of Spleny, and the two Colloredo divisions were obliged to to yield to the numerical superiority of the French columns. At this moment, the right flank of Bonnaud's division arrived between Wannehain and Camphin and halted; the impetus of the Republicans seemed arrested. The Duke of York, again watching from a ridge-line through his trusty telescope, ordered up a strong cavalry force under Lieutenant General Harcourt made up of sixteen squadrons of the 1st, 2nd and 6th Dragoon Guards and the 7th, 11th, 15th and 16th Light Dragoons, plus two of the Austrian Leopold Hussars. Directed by the duke's Austrian liaison officer, Oberstleutnant Count Merveldt, who knew the ground well, Bonnaud's right wing was turned. At the same time, the village of Camphin was attacked by infantry. By this double movement, the duke succeeded in forcing Bonnaud's right north of Camphin. Captain Stapleton Cotton of the 6th Dragoon Guards (Carabiniers) was on the spot:

> After daybreak, the enemy descried us from the next hill, and sent a swift-flying messenger from a field-piece, which passed over us and took the ground a few yards from our front... an aide-de-camp from the Austrian general, Otto, the general of the day, galloped up to our lines (not supposing the Carabineers to be mounted) and exclaimed, 'The enemy has taken us by surprise, and surrounded

us; I fear you'll be too late.' But Sir Thomas Chapman instantly formed the regiment into close column of half troops to the left, and in a few minutes we met the enemy and stemmed his progress.[41]

As Harcourt's troopers broke out into open country the French demi-brigades formed square. But these were steadier troops than at Beaumont:

> He had formed, on our approach, a solid square of from four to five thousand bayonets, with field-pieces, with the staff in the centre and the cannon placed at intervals. The Carabineers, having formed line with intent to charge, the enemy fired a very uncourteous salute, and gave us some volleys right in the face. Here we got orders to pause, until a light six-pounder, with sixty rounds of canister, sent by General Otto, with a detachment of the 14th Foot, could be brought to bear with effect upon the enemy.

The French infantry formed square for the first time in the campaign.[42] Nine cavalry charges broke against the squares, and the Duke of York sent in Major General Henry Fox's 1st Infantry Brigade to break the deadlock:

> [The six-pounder] was placed in front, and fired a signal for the Carabineers to keep back, when Captain Crawford, aide-de-camp to General Sir William Erskine, unfortunately, without deliberation, ordered the regiment to charge; but it was impossible for cavalry to break the enemy's square; and what rendered our situation worse was that he had formed his square close to the end of a field of rape, sown in ridges with very deep furrows between. Over these we had to pass; and many of the horses having fallen in consequence, the riders were either killed or made prisoners, and some of the horses (whose owners had been killed) fell into the ranks and manoeuvred with precision till picked up by men of all corps whose horses had been shot. When the Carabineers rallied on a large plain, or flat of land (between the enemy's column and Lisle), we could muster only ten men of the Lieut. Colonel's troop mounted ... One sergeant and thirty rank and file killed, wounded, and missing, besides ninety-five horses killed; and one sergeant and several rank and file taken prisoners by the enemy, some of whom (the prisoners) joined us again.

Colonel Congreve's Royal Artillery reached the field and started to bombard the squares. The Coalition cavalry was by now reinforced up to twenty-four squadrons by the arrival of the 1st, 2nd and 6th Dragoons, later the famed Union Brigade of Waterloo in 1815. The French began to waver, and the next Coalition cavalry charge finally broke into one of the squares, when an officer of the Scots Greys charged the line, knocking three men out of place on his way in and six on the way out. This square collapsed from within, and two more soon fell. As the British infantry advanced, the remaining formed French retreated in their squares a mile north to the village of Willems, supported by a covering screen of cavalry:

> At length, a strong force of unbroken cavalry moved from the direction of Lisle, and formed a long line parallel to us. The French Carabineers were on the right, and some Hussars or light regiments on the left, which extended towards Lisle, and the right towards Tournay. Our men, having seen some of the French Carabineers before, knew them at once (by their large bearskin caps and cuirasses), and called on Sir Thomas Chapman to lead them to the charge. At that moment, our Assistant-Surgeon, Caldwell, rode up close to the front of the French Carabineers, fired his pistols in their faces, and retired zigzag at speed, while the enemy fired several rounds after him. Having rejoined us, he said that the enemy's horses would never be able to stand a charge, they were so small and light. Our men continued their solicitation for liberty to charge, crying out, 'This regiment beat us in the German war, capturing our standards and kettle-drums, and we will beat them now, if you only lead us on.' 'Patience, my brave boys,' was the major's answer. Sir William Erskine, the senior British general officer, happening to come up at this moment, Sir Thomas Chapman rode up to him, lowering the point of his sword, and saying, 'General, my boys are most anxious to charge their namesakes.' 'Sir Thomas,' answered Sir William, 'I fear you are not equal to do so; they are more than four to one of your men. However, if you are able, go on.' 'Thank you, General; I have a light troop of the Fifth Dragoon Guards with me,' replied Sir Thomas. Turning to the regiment, the commanding officer cried to the officers and men, 'Now, my boys, mind the signals for movement, and when I raise my sword to St. George, shout as loud as you are able, and into them, as quick and as close together as possible, and we'll have a glorious day yet. March, trot, canter, charge!' But the enemy did not wait to receive us, for the whole line wheeled in some way (perhaps by threes) to the left, and the Hussars got clear off, while we came into contact with the Carabineers, nearly four squadrons of whom we unhorsed in a few moments, leaving many dead on the field ...
>
> We ... followed the fugitives close to Lisle, when an eighteen-gun battery opened a smart fire with grape upon us. Having reassembled, we observed the infantry that had given us so much trouble in the morning passing between two plantations. The Oxford Blues (now Horse Guards, Blue) were ordered to charge

them; but Sir William Erskine, finding that their very heavy horses sank to the knees in the tillage ground, owing to the continuous rain that had fallen in the morning, permitted us to take their place. Sir Thomas Chapman having said, 'General, our light Irish horses will do the work,' 'Ay, and the men, too,' added Sir William. We charged, and killed about eight hundred, and as many more laid down their arms and surrendered themselves prisoners of war.[43]

The French fled in panic, suffering 2,000 casualties, while the British took 450 prisoners and captured thirteen guns for the loss of thirty-one men killed and eighty-four wounded. On the Duke's staff, Major Henry Clinton received a flesh wound in the thigh. This was another great day for the British cavalry, who were demonstrating a decided superiority over the French, and even over the highly-regarded Austrian cavalry. Eleven regiments were awarded the battle honour 'Willems'.[44]

In the north, learning that Bonnaud's attack had been repulsed, Thierry's brigade stopped and camped at Leers. Compére's brigade returned to their position in the south. By the end of the day the French were back in their original lines between Menin and Courtrai, while the Coalition line now stretched from Tournai up to Courtrai.

'The Light Dragoons are really the astonishment of everybody, and all the foreigners allow that they had no idea of such a Corps,' the Duke wrote home on 5 May. At this rate the Coalition cavalry might win the war on its own.

Chapter 12

Tourcoing

Annihilation Plan
Stung by a rebuke from his emperor, Clerfayt advanced from Ingelmünster on 11 May along the north bank of the River Lys towards Courtrai. The French garrison was surprised and could have been overpowered had Clerfayt moved his 8,500 men with alacrity, but that was not his style. By the time he had his troops in battle array the French garrison had been reinforced to nearly 25,000, troops who promptly attacked him. Nonetheless the French ended the day back inside the walls of Courtrai and Clerfayt might have claimed the victory had not Pichegru pursued him on the 12th and fought bloody battles with the rearguard at Branbielk and Ingelmünster. Clerfayt reached Tielt on the night of 13 May for the loss of 1,500 men, including Feldmarschaleutnant Freiherr von Wenkheim, who was shot off his horse on 11 May at the head of his division. Clerfayt's adverse manoeuvre split the Coalition line in two. Then Général de brigade Vandamme attacked and beat the Hessen-Darmstadt garrison at Ingelmünster over three consecutive days,[1] establishing French control over the countryside north of Courtrai.

So long as the Coalition (read: Austrian) method of war remained rooted in the 'cordon' system, stringing the army out in a long thin line of defences – troop presence everywhere, troop concentration nowhere – the French would always be able to pick off isolated garrisons at will. The duke complained of this system in a letter home to his father on 13 May:

> I humbly agree with Your Majesty that the system of Cordons into which the Austrians have fallen ever since the beginning of the War is exceedingly pernicious as well as dangerous and has been the real origin of all the misfortune to which they have been subject.[2]

At Imperial headquarters, staff officers talked about laying siege to Cambrai and Arras next. Mack disagreed; he was advocating an advance on Paris as the highest priority. Capturing Cambrai and Arras would cost time and lives, and sizeable garrisons would have to be left behind. Mack argued for the capture of smaller French cities such as Maubeuge, Avesnes, Philippeville and Rocroi, and to conquer the twin fortresses of Mezières (on the Meuse) and Guise (on the Oise). With these acquisitions, the Imperial army would have an excellent base for the march on Paris. But Mack could not prevail with this view in the face of Austrian military tradition. Then on 13 May, arrived the news of Clerfayt's defeat at Ingelmünster and Kaunitz's victory at Grandreng.[3] The Imperial left flank was sound, but the right flank was in danger. Prince von Coburg ordered the army to march west.[4] Harry Calvert could sense that the campaign was on a knife-edge: 'The moment is, in my opinion,' he wrote, 'big with events of the utmost importance.'[5]

In mid-May the French still occupied their bold salient between Tourcoing and Messines, about 15 miles (24km) deep. It was obvious to all that Pichegru was no genius, but he had some extremely talented subordinates and a clear local superiority in numbers. The French numbered about 82,000 men in the area between Lille and Courtrai. Most of these troops, 28,000 men under Général de division Souham, and 22,000 under Général de division Moreau, were on the southern banks of the Lys, between Courtrai and Aalbeke. Another 20,000 men, under Général de division Bonnaud, were in camp at Sainghin, east of Lille, and Général de brigade Osten had 10,000 men at Pont-à-Marque, to the south of the city. Other detachments were at Lannoy, Mouscron, Tourcoing and guarding the main bridges across the Lys and the Marque.

The duke saw only two possible courses of action. Either wait to be attacked; or attack first. He wrote to the emperor urging him to reinforce the sector. But before he received a reply, he decided to attack anyway, in concert with Clerfayt, on 15 May. But during the night of 14/15 May a message arrived from the emperor, advising the duke that the Imperial headquarters would be at St Amand in the morning of the 15th, with a view to planning a major Coalition attack on the 16th or 17th:

> I had before determined to attack in spite of of the great risk which I must have run, but with this information I delayed my march until I had seen the Emperor, who immediately desired me to put off my march until his army arrived.[6]

The Coalition staff met in Tournai on 16 May and hammered out a plan for a major assault the following day. 'The intention of this attack is to act upon the enemy's communications between Lille and Menin and Courtrai, to defeat his armies that he has advanced upon the Lys and to drive him out of Flanders.'[7]

The plan was signed by the duke and whilst many writers have contended it was devised by Mack – who gave it the grandiose title *Vernichtungsplan*

(Annihilation Plan), and it carried many of Mack's trademark 'scientific warfare' fingerprints – the strategic concept was probably the duke's. But on the other hand, there is evidence that the duke sketched out the same plan of attack to Clerfayt as early as 11 May, with the description, 'to envelop the enemy on all sides, and attack him everywhere.' We must remember that the duke's Anglo-Hanoverian-Hessian expeditionary force had been campaigning in Flanders for over a year by this point, without participating in a single 'big battle.' In his writings, do we detect a sense of military frustration? In any event, his desire for 'attacking everywhere' may have been watered down by Mack's dispositions, which emphasised the need for 'acting upon the enemy's communications between Lille and Menin and Courtrai', with no imperative for actually defeating them in pitched battle. It was as if simply inducing the French to withdraw would be enough. Compromise piled in upon compromise as the duke discovered on 16 May, when he was told in confidence:

> The whole plan of attack is altered and should this attack succeed it is the Emperor's intention to besiege Lisle [sic] with one hundred and eight battalions and one hundred and twenty squadrons... The intention of besieging Lisle is known to no one except General Mack, not even any one of the Austrian ministers.[8]

As if the plan had not been neutered enough already, the dispositions involved 67,000 men in six separate columns attacking roughly north-west along a front of 20 miles (32km), across difficult ground, which made communication between the columns almost impossible. The countryside was thickly forested, with many villages and poor tracks, and so unsuited for cavalry – the one arm in which the Coalition excelled. The main roads were typically lined on both sides with trees, limiting infantry movement to three-abreast columns, often waiting for guns or baggage to clear the road. The rivers were another matter. The Lys was forty to sixty yards across, with few bridges. The Marcq, though much smaller than the Lys (not being wide enough to carry a barge south of Lille), was deep, with muddy banks and a soft bottom, and no real fords. Every crossing, in other words, needed a bridge, and there were few in existence. Every column had to reach its target if the plan was to succeed, and the plan took no account of any French reaction. The six columns, sequenced from north to south, were given the following objectives;

Northern covering force – Feldzeugmeister Clerfayt, to march from Thielt with 16,000 Austrians and Hanoverians: to cross the Lys at Wervicq, objective Linselles

No. 1 Column - Generalmajor Bussche-Haddenhause with 4,000 Hanoverians: to march from Espierres by Dottignies, objective Mouscron

No. 2 Column - Generalmajor Otto with 10,000 Austrians: to march from Bailleul by Leers and Wattrelos, objective Tourcoing

No. 3 Column – Duke of York with 11,000 men (twelve Anglo-Hanoverian infantry battalions and ten cavalry squadrons): to march from Templeuve by Toufflers and Lannoy, objective Roubaix

No. 4 Column - Feldmarschalleutnant Kinsky with 11,000 Austrians: to march from Froidmont by Bouvines, objective west bank of the river Marque

No. 5 Column - Archduke Karl with 15,000 Austrians: to march from St Amand by Pont-à-Marque, objective west bank of the river Marque.

The whole force's objectives on 18 May were to start before dawn, and meet about noon in Tourcoing, directly in Souham's rear.

Columns 1, 2 and 3 were reckoned to be the main thrust and were nominally under the overall command of the Duke of York, although the majority of these troops would be well out of his visual range. The orders, reams upon reams of them, went out on the evening of 16 May. No-one seems to have considered that at dawn on 16 May the Archduke Karl had most of his force north of Landrecies, nearly 60 miles (96km) away, and although he was already marching north-west, his starting position behind St Amand on the morning of the 17th was easily a half-day's march behind the rest of the columns.[9] Clerfayt's orders traveled via a circuitous route and did not reach him until after dawn on the 17th.

The intended area of operations was massive, more directly comparable to a First World War battle rather than anything attempted in the late eighteenth century. From Thielt in the north, where Clerfayt was to start, to St Amand in the south where the Archduke Karl commenced, was 37 miles (60km). From Espierres in the east to the west side of Lille was 19 miles (30km). The battlefield of Waterloo would fit inside the Tourcoing operational area seventy-five times; that of Austerlitz, twenty times. Yet it was somehow conceived at Coalition headquarters that the armies of five nations, in six separate and dispersed columns, many years before radio communications (or even effective visual signalling systems, for that matter) could synchronise a series of coordinated attacks over an operational area of 600 square miles (1500 sqkm). 'Had the Austrians been the sworn enemies of the British instead of their allies,' the regimental historian of the 1st Foot Guards later wrote, 'they could not have devised a series of combinations more likely to terminate in their destruction, or have carried them out in a manner more certain to ensure such a result.'[10] The scientist, the novice general and the young civilian[11] had cooked up a tactical plan – arguably the most over-ambitious battle plan in history – one that a Napoleon, Wellington or Lee would surely have dismissed out of hand.

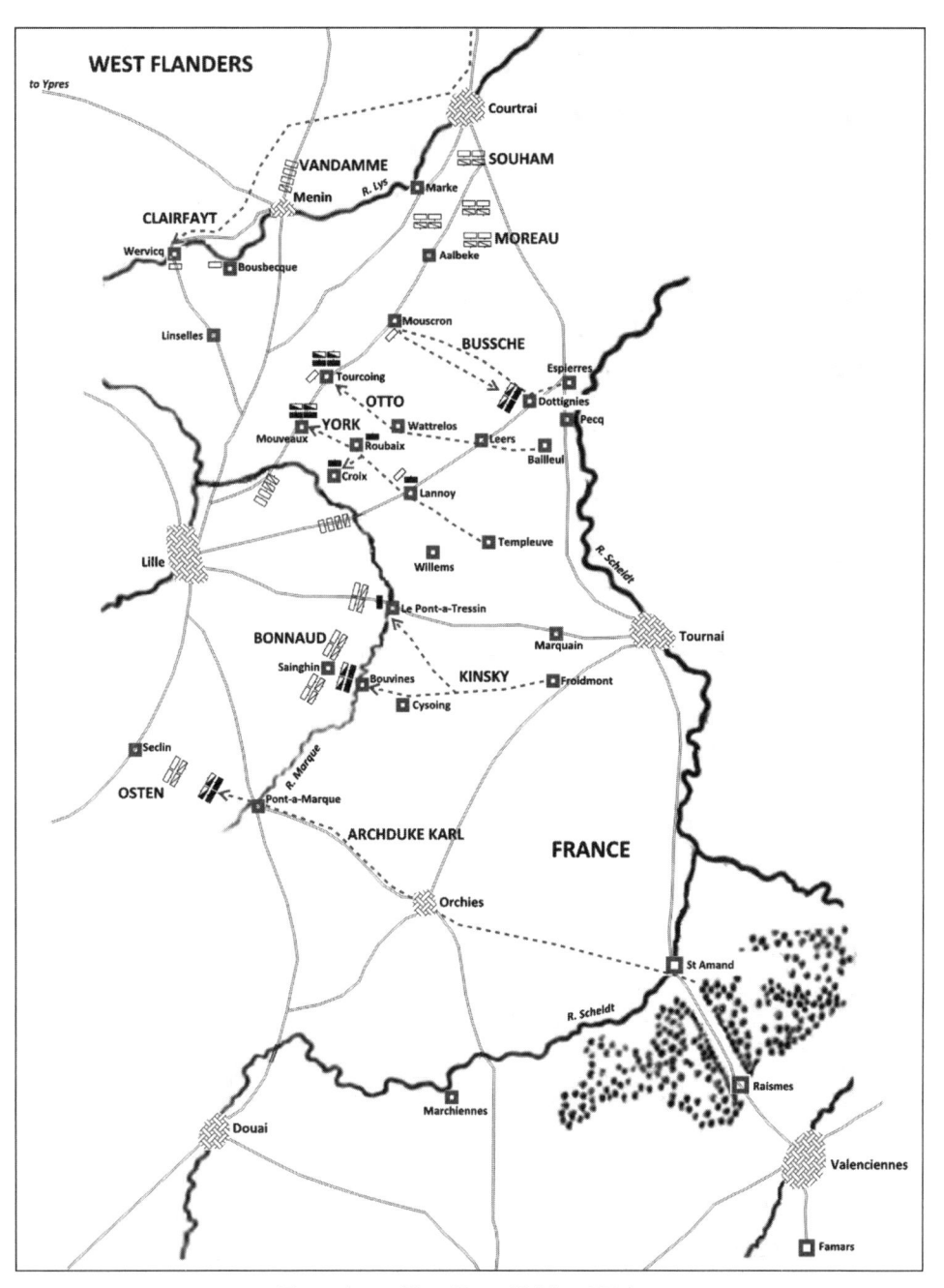

Tourcoing – First Day, 17 May 1794

The First Day

It barely needs to be stated that the plan unravelled quickly on the 17th. Clerfayt needed to move off from Thielt in the evening of the 16th in order to be in position at dawn on the 17th, but as we have seen, he did not receive his orders until twelve hours too late. The advance did not start until 06.00 hours, with his advanced guard (Hanoverians commanded by Hammerstein) in the van. They reached the chaussée from Ypres to Menin below Gheluvelde half an hour before noon, where Hammerstein separated from the main column, advanced to Gheluve, and drove the enemy out of it. Clerfayt's main column took hours to march the 3 miles (5km) to Wervicq, arriving mid-afternoon only to find the bridge fortified and defended in strength. This was the worst kind of luck with which to start a battle. The French battalion was in fact en route to Menin; half an hour later (or earlier) and the town (and river) would have been undefended. French musketry across the Lys raked the bridge and made any potential crossing appear a potential blood-bath. Clerfayt sent some troops 2 miles (3km) west to Comines to find the bridge there equally stoutly defended. The river was only sixty yards across, but his bridging train was unfortunately somewhere in the rear. It was sent for but only arrived after dark. But sometime during the night the French evacuated the town and Oberst Contrell with two battalions of the Linien-Infanterie-Regiment Nr. 38 'von Württemberg' was able to occupy the heights of Wervicq Sud without opposition before daybreak. The Nr.25 Dragoner-Regiment 'Graf Latour' scouted ahead and brought back about sixty prisoners, after cutting down several French patrols. The rest of the column did not cross until broad daylight on the 18th. Clerfayt's column was, by now, nearly twenty-four hours late.[12]

Bussche-Haddenhause's tiny No. 1 Column was reduced further before even marching by his orders, which required the Hanoverian to detach four battalions and and three cavalry squadrons as a screen to his north. As soon as the sound of heavy firing by No. 2 Column advancing against Tourcoing became audible to the south, Bussche split his remaining troops into two columns – the 1.Infanterie-Regiment and a squadron of the 7.Cavallerie-Regiment marched towards Herseaux to the south of Mouscron, whilst the right was sent on a more direct route via Dottignies and Luingne. These two columns drove the French defenders from position to position 'with the utmost rapidity', and eventually ousted the enemy from the village of Mouscron. But they were driven back to Dottignies by a heavy counter-attack from Général de brigade Louis-Fursy-Henri Compère's substantial division of Gardes Nationales. The Hanoverians were attacked from all sides.

The 1.Infanterie-Regiment in Herseaux was cut off by two enemy cavalry regiments and all captured (except for five officers and two hundred men) before it could reach safety. The right-hand column, which arrived through Luingne, succeeded in withdrawing without delay to Dottignies. The Hanoverians garrisoned Dottignies but were too weak to make much headway in a countryside plainly crawling with Frenchmen. They were only a diversion in the grand plan, which was just as well, since they were reduced to the role of by-standers for the remainder of the battle.

Otto's No. 2 Column formed up in silence before dawn on the 17th at the village of Bailleul on the main road to Leers. They did not commence their march until just after 04.00 hours, but then stopped between 06.00 and 07.00 to give the early morning mist time to burn off.[13] Two battalions of the Hessen-Cassel Garde-Grenadiere attached to this column had just been sent down from Saint Léger without their brigadier and so found themselves without marching orders; they therefore did not advance with the rest. Otto had to send an adjutant back to get them on the road, with orders to march to Cense de la Citadelle, north-east of Wattrelos, to facilitate the column's attack from the south-east. This sounded easier than it was; all the bridges across the canal-like Espierres brook were destroyed, and after unsuccessfully looking for a crossing-point, an aide ordered them to join the main column at Petit-Leers.

Otto's main force had found Grande-Leers weakly garrisoned, the defenders firing only a few volleys before fleeing north-west to Wattrelos. Otto's Avantgarde followed them up the Rue de Leers (after being told by villagers that Wattrelos was only defended by three battalions and some cavalry) but found French resistance much more determined. The Austrian Linien-Infanterie-Regiment Nr. 20 'Graf Kaunitz' and the Hessen-Cassel Grenadiere-Bataillon 'von Germann' were sent in and soon cleared the town of Frenchmen, who continued their retreat north-west to Tourcoing. Otto's Avantgarde followed and ejected them from that place – Otto's objective for the day – with ease. The Kaunitzers and the Hessen-Cassel Grenadiers followed and arrived at Tourcoing after dark. Generalmajor Eugen Freiherr von Monfrault was placed in command of the town with a company of jägers, eight squadrons of cavalry[14] and seven battalions of infantry. He placed a thin defensive cordon around the town.[15]

During the night, he received news of the failure of No. 1 Column, which had completely failed to capture Mouscron, only 3 miles (5km) to his north-east. The right flank of the column was completely open.

Otto sent the two Hessen-Cassel Garde-Grenadiere battalions to Wattrelos and left his reserve – three battalions and three squadrons – defending a height at Leers topped by a windmill. But the night passed without incident.

For No. 2 Column, the day had gone according to plan. They had captured all their objectives, and with minimal losses. But Otto made one fatal error. It did not occur to him to alert his southerly neighbour, the Duke of York, as to his advanced position. One speedy courier would have solved this. Alas, a rider was never called forward, as a result leaving the Duke of York fretful for the security of his right wing, which was in reality quite sound.

Kinsky's No. 4 Column marched at daybreak (just before 06.00 hours at that time of year) but halted at 07.00 hours in the same thick mist that was delaying Otto. Kinsky's orders were to detach three battalions and six squadrons to link up with the Duke of York on his right, and a battalion and two squadrons to maintain contact with the Archduke Karl on his left. This latter, a small 'commando force' under a Hauptmann Ochs (a battalion of Hessen-Cassel Jägers, a company of Freikorps and twenty-five dragoons of the Hessen-Cassel Leib-Dragoner-Regiment), did not get Kinsky's halt orders and carried on into the mist, marching at light infantry pace from Cobrieux to Sens de Louvil. Ochs captured the bridge across the Marque there, but when the fog lifted, and the French realised how weak his force was, they chased him back across the river to Cysoing.

The main thrust of Kinsky's No. 4 Column reached the River Marque at Bouvines at about 07.30 hours. This force comprised five Austrian battalions and two Hessen-Darmstadt battalions, five companies of Freikorps, the Husaren-Regiment 'Erzherzog Leopold' and Chevau-léger Regiment Nr.18 with the Austrian and some British guns. Kinsky's orders were to take the road to Bouvines, drive the enemy out of it, and throw them back across the River Marque. After this, the whole column would hold their positions along the Marque until the arrival of Archduke Karl on their left flank:

> The FZM [Kinsky], when reaching favourable terrain, had advanced his hussars, followed by the chevaux-legers. These were followed by the three Austrian battalions, marching with divisions out of the middle. The Infanterie Regiment 'von Kospoth' (Hessen-Cassel) and the 3rd or reserve battalions formed the 2nd Line. The heavy artillery moved in the intervals, and after the enemy outposts were driven back, in this way the advance took place on both sides of the chaussée to Chapelle aux 3 Arbres, were the troops deployed and

formed line. The enemy had a strong entrenchment about 600 paces in front of Bouvines, were the roads from Maison Blanche and Cysoing united; Bouvines itself was surrounded by a strong line, and the church-yard fortified. It was defended by 4 or 5 cannon. Behind the Marque the enemy main corps could be observed, which struck camp as soon as they saw us arrive ... After a cannonade that lasted for an hour, the Austrian volunteers which followed the battalions stormed the outwork. After the artillery had advanced closer, the enemy in Bouvines itself was attacked, and with the bayonet thrown out of it and over the Marque.[16]

Kinsky found Bonnaud's French division encamped at a hilltop fort at Sanghien on the far bank of the river, covering the Tournai-Lille road and its bridge. An Austrian attack drove the French back across the bridge as French pontoniers destroyed it. Bonnaud then erected a battery of heavy artillery on the high ground occupied by the fort of Sanghien, covering the bridge, and Kinsky declined to force the crossing until he had news of the Archduke's No. 5 Column on his left.[17]

In accordance with his orders to protect his right flank (and likely line of communication with the duke's No. 3 Column) Kinsky detached Generalmajor Wurmb (one Austrian battalion, three Hessen-Cassel battalions, a company of Tyrolean Jäger, one squadron of the Chevau-léger Regiment Nr.18 and five squadrons of the Hessian Leib-Dragoner-Regiment) down-river to the north. Wurmb's orders were to cross the bridge at Le Pont-à-Tressin, and if possible, obtain a crossing over the Marque:

> The advance guard [of Major-General von Wurmb], consisting of the Fusilier-Bataillon (Hessen-Cassel) and the Tyroler sharpshooter company, drove the enemy outposts back from Petit Baisieux to their main posts in Cheraing, were they seem to make a stand. The fusiliers and Tyroler jäger, supported by the 1tes Grenadier-Bataillon 'Von Eschwege' (Hessen-Cassel) and the volunteers of the Infanterie-Regiment No. 7 'Carl von Schröder' (Austrian), immediately attacked the village and threw the enemy back to under his cannon, to Pont à Treffin.[18]

Wurmb therefore also failed to capture the bridge. He was wounded during the afternoon, and so his younger brother Oberst von Wurmb II took over command of this wing. At about 16.00 hours he ordered a retreat from Chéreng to keep his men out of the cannon fire, and to save ammunition, which was running low, leaving the Fusilier-Bataillon as a screen at Le Pont-à-Tressin.

The action at Bouvines settled down to occasional cannon-fire and the constant crack of skirmisher fire. Many artillery horses were killed, while some captured ammunition caissons exploded. Late in the day, his Slavic irregular troops achieved the main success of the day:

> Around 4 o'clock, FZM Graf Kinsky despatched two cannon to the light troops at Sense Louvil, with the order to force the bridge. A company of the Slavonian Freikorps (Austrian) was assigned to storm the bridge, the remainder of the light troops covering its flanks by a heavy fire. But the enemy retreated when they ran to the bridge. These troops reformed on the other side of the Marque, threw the enemy out of their entrenchment, pursued them to Peronne[-en-Mélantois] and threw them out of this village also. With the enemy right wing in front of them now, they were not able to advance any further, and occupied Peronne. Here they were fired upon by our own troops for a while, which mistake was corrected as soon as possible.[19]

The village of Gruson lay roughly mid-way between Bouvines and Le Pont à Tressin in an elevated position on the Coalition side of the Marque. Kinsky detached a battalion of the Austrian Infanterie-Regiment Nr.11 'Michael Wallis' and the Hessen-Cassel Infanterie-Regiment 'von Kospoth' to drive the French skirmishers from the place, which they did at about 18.00 hours. By this time, the Archduke Karl's No. 5 Column had arrived upon their left and therefore Kinsky ordered a general assault:

> At this time, the Archduke Carl had turned the right wing of the enemy. The light troops and some infantrymen which had crossed the Marque on their own, attacked the enemy at the bridge of Bouvines with heavy fire and yelling, and drove them from there. FZM Graf Kinsky now crossed with the infantry, as soon as the bridge was repaired, after which the rout of the enemy became general. The light troops and skirmishers pursued them over Sainghin. The French retreated over Annappes, covering their retreat with a rear-guard accompanied by cannon and howitzers, and halted on the chaussée.[20]

The men of the Archduke Karl's No. 5 Column were close to dropping. They had been awake for thirty-six hours, on foot for the last twenty-four, and had just marched (and fought) for seventeen hours. Although weather is rarely mentioned in accounts of battles, Saturday 17 May 1794 was an unseasonably hot day. Starting at St Amand at dawn, they had stopped for lunch at Orchies in the sweltering heat. The vanguard under General Bellegarde drove the enemy out of Capelle. From that place the archduke detached a company of Tyroler-Scharfschützen, two battalions and four squadrons to go to Templeuve[21] and thereby made contact with Kinsky's left flank. This was difficult country, low-lying and swampy, crossed by innumerable canals and rivulets. At the same time a Dutch detachment under Prince Frederik of Orange-Nassau (five battalions and six squadrons) was ordered through Bersee to Mons-en-Pevelle. All the French divisions withdrew to Pont a Marque. The archduke's advanced guard (two battalions of light infantry) arrived at Pont-à-Marcq at about 16.00 hours, brought some artillery forward and commenced a cannonade against the French defenders on the west bank.

French reinforcements arrived from the camp at Sainghin, and it looked as though the archduke's weary men were in for a hard fight. But the detached flanking column on the right crossed the Marque at Fourneau, and with enemy between their position at Pont-à-Marcq and their main camp at Sainghin, the French defenders made a hasty retreat to Lezennes in the direction of Lille. The archduke rode with his Avantgarde to Lesquin, then ordered his troops into camp on the Coalition side of the Marque, with only some light troops guarding the French bank.

Bonnaud ceased his offensive actions for the day and retired to the village of Flers. Like Otto and Kinsky, the archduke also neglected to advise the duke of his whereabouts. His orders were to link up with Kinsky and form one large corps capable of taking Lille; but that must wait until tomorrow.

Which brings us lastly to the duke's No. 3 Column. It had gathered during the night of the 16th 'in the greatest tranquility' and under the eye of the emperor and marched at 06.00 hours. Unaccountably, Erskine's division of heavy cavalry had gone missing – it would be many hours before it was revealed they had attached themselves to Kinsky's No. 4 Column in error.[22] A miniscule French garrison in Toufflers fled without firing a shot, falling back to Lannoy another mile away. A sweep around the flanks by the cavalry as the infantry and artillery held the front did the trick; the French withdrew from Lannoy quickly, but not before a French cannon-ball struck Major Jesse Wright of the Royal Artillery and killed the duke's artillery chief.

Three miles (5km) father on, at Roubaix, their objective for the day, the Brigade of Guards forced the French garrison to abandon a strongly-held position. Corporal Brown of the Guards recorded:

> We accordingly advanced to the attack with great vigour and alacrity, from the refreshment we had received at Roubaix, and

> after some time spent in cannonading, the flank battalion which had been in front all day, having formed the line, and advancing towards the enemy, eagerly catched the word 'charge,' and rushed with the utmost impetuosity into the enemy's works, upon which they fled with the greatest precipitation, leaving behind them three pieces of cannon. In the meantime, the light cavalry wheeling round the village, overtook them in their flight, and pursued them about three miles with great slaughter.[23]

Coalition intelligence gathering during the campaign was, on the whole, lamentable, and this day was no exception. The duke sent cavalry patrols to look for Kinsky on his left with no success. The Archduke Karl and Clerfayt were so far away they may as well have been on the moon. From the north came a false report that Otto was at Wattrelos (he was much further advanced, at Tourcoing); this fallacy appeared to place the duke in a more exposed position than was actually the case. So, he decided to withdraw his main body slightly (Fox's brigade to Croix, the Hessen-Cassel Leib-Infanterie-Regiment to Lannoy) and was deploying defensive positions for the night when an Imperial courier rode up.

The emperor himself had overruled this plan and ordered both the duke and Otto to advance another 3 miles (5km) to Mouveaux; for surely there they would be able to link up with Clerfayt – who was in fact 7 miles (11km) away at Wervicq, completely immobile. The duke turned to his best troops (the Brigade of Guards and the light dragoons) and ordered them off down the road at 19.00 hours as the sun set.

The Guards repeated their success as at Roubaix, going in with the bayonet only:

> The flank battalion of Guards, supported by the battalion of the 1st regiment of Guards, led the way through a very close country. On arriving in front of Mouveaux it was found strongly entrenched and palisaded. About fifteen hundred men defended the place with several pieces of cannon. The British guns having opened a practicable entrance, the Guards stormed while the cavalry were ordered to proceed at a gallop round the work and get in the rear and cut off the flying enemy. When we moved the Guards had got got into the place. The enemy were still firing their cannon charged with grape down the road lined with an avenue of trees, and had set on fire a house on the roadside. By the scorching flames of this we were obliged to pass, as a deep ditch and fences rendered it impossible for us to break off the road till we got close to the walls. The rattling of the shot through the trees, the falling branches, the burning house, the huzzas of the infantry, and shouts of 'Go it,

Young Eyes!' (the name by which the Guards always designated the 15th [Light Dragoons], who in turn called them 'Old Eyes.')[24]

The 7th and 15th Light Dragoons enjoyed another field day pursuing the fleeing French in the almost dark, cutting down scores of men along the road to Bouderes. Mouveaux was set on fire, which had the unfortunate side-effect of alerting the French to the head of the Coalition advance, with unfortunate consequences as we shall see later. By now it was fully dark, and the Duke of York's column was strung out over 6 miles (9km) in the quadrilateral of Lannoy-Roubaix-Mouveaux-Croix.

It was clear the Coalition 'annihilation plan' was so far in tatters. The Duke of York and Otto had reached their targets, but all the other columns – Clerfayt, Bussche, Kinsky and the archduke – had failed to achieve their first day objectives. A dangerous gap of 8 miles (13km) existed between the British at Roubaix and the Austrians to their south at Bouvines. Far from enveloping the enemy on all sides, the duke and Otto's 21,000 men were in an uncomfortable salient between Bonnaud's 18,000 Frenchmen east of Lille and Souham's 27,000 north of Tourcoing. The duke wrote to the emperor by candle-light asking permission to withdraw, which was refused.

Amazingly, the French had been taken completely by surprise on 17 May. They had been marshalling their forces on the north bank of the Lys for an attack on Clerfayt, leaving only small garrisons in the towns being attacked by the Coalition. Pichegru was absent completely, visiting the extreme right wing of his army. Général de division Joseph Souham, a 27-year-old former cuirassier trooper, unexpectedly found himself in command, But Souham was a big man, as tough as old boots, and knew the penalty for taking backwards steps in the Revolutionary army. The vulnerable Coalition salient had not gone unnoticed by him or the senior French generals. They also had one piece of intelligence dated 12 May derived from three British deserters that might have convinced them of the weakness of the forces opposite them, and of the frailty of the Coalition:

> Henry Wilson, Joseph Spencer and Archibald Kars, of the 53rd Infantry Regiment named Shropshire, declare that they came from Cateau to reinforce the camp of Marquain, near Tournay; that in the battle of the 21st current [11 May] the English cavalry lost at least 1,000 men who wanted to charge the French artillery; that all crews were loaded and that the tents were taken to Tournay; lastly, that during the battle all declared a definite retreat. They also declare that there are only six English infantry regiments at

Camp Marquain, three of which are numbered 53, 14 and 37, each consisting of about 700 men, and three others numbered 1, 2 and 3, the names of regiments of the King, about 900 men each, at most; that the four or five English corps on horseback form only a body which is reduced to 1,500 men by the losses which these regiments have experienced; as to the strength at the camp of Marquain, it is impossible for them to appreciate; that the Duke of York was at the battle at Tournay, and that, according to their custom, they did not arrive until the affair was over. They report that they have a bad understanding with the Austrians, who steal from them continually, and that the English officers by their weakness do not do them justice.[25]

Souham arranged a council of war at Menin in the late afternoon of 17 May, where he, Moreau, Macdonald and Reynier met and adopted a plan put forward by an 'anonymous colonel'[26] which revolved around the fact that the Lille-Courtrai road was still in French hands and therefore direct movement between Bonnaud and Souham was altogether possible. Souham was to break off his attentions to Clerfayt's stalled northern covering force and advance southwards across the Lys whilst Bonnaud's divisions around Lille advanced northwards, likewise ignoring Kinsky's column on his right flank. Vandamme's division could hold Clerfayt in place, whilst Osten watched Kinsky. The plan relied completely upon the inertia of Clerfayt and Kinsky whilst the attack went in; but the prospect of putting all the British force, not to mention Otto's Austrians 'in the bag' was too great a temptation to ignore. The risk was worth it. French Revolutionary generals could come to decisions much quicker than the lumbering Coalition would ever manage; and could act upon their plans immediately, rather relying upon Imperial assent or the kind of slow-burn decision-making the Coalition took for granted. Rapid French action could completely reverse the Coalition strategy; 'the biter was going to be bit.'[27]

The French took their positions and awaited the hour at which a bugle-call would sound the advance – 03.00 hours in the morning of 18 May. Osten's brigade and Bonnaud's division were between Lezenne and Flers, with 30,000 men. At Wervicq, on the right bank of the Lys, was part of the Desenfant's brigade, the other part of which had retreated to Lille during the night. In Menin waited Vandamme's brigade; at Roncq, Malbrancq's brigade; on Mont Halluin, Macdonald's brigade; in Mouscron, the brigades of Thierry and Compére; at Aalebeke, the rest of Souham's division (the brigades of Daendels and Jardon). The Coalition occupied the whole Marque, by Wick, Commines, Espierre, Watreloos, Tourcoing, Mouveaux, Croix, Lannoy, Willems, and from

Pont-à-Tressin down to Pont-à-Marcq. But the duke's and Otto's forces were thinly spread out, with seven-and-a-half battalions at Tourcoing, two at Wattrelos and three at Leers, the Brigade of Guards and the 15th Light Dragoons at Mouveaux, four Austrian infantry battalions and the 16th Light Dragoons at Roubaix, and Fox's 'Little Brigade' (the old 1st Infantry Brigade) guarding the left flank at Croix. Two Hessen-Cassel battalions were in the rear at Lannoy.

The duke wrote once more to Coburg during the night seeking approval to withdraw from his dangerous position, but Mack wrote to him advising that Kinsky and the Archduke Karl would start a northwards march to his aid – ironically, also at 03.00 hours on 18 May. Kinsky, the orders advised, should be at Lannoy by noon. In theory.

The reality verged on the bizarre. Couriers carrying these orders arrived at the archduke's headquarters at Lesquin only to be told that the archduke was asleep and could not be wakened.[28] At least Kinsky was awake in Bouvines. He looked at the orders, said: 'Kinsky knows what he has to do,' and then did nothing at all for twelve hours.[29]

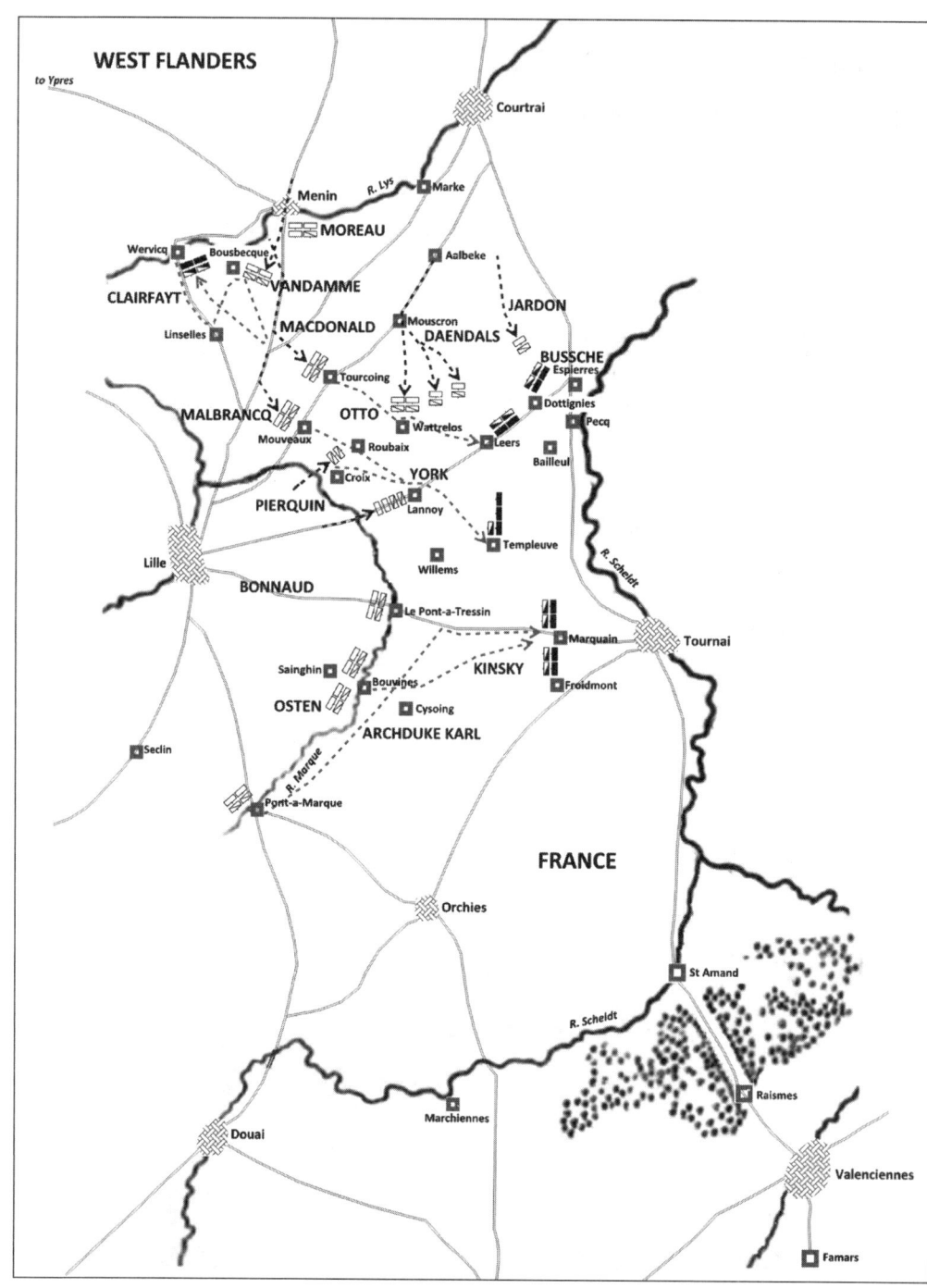

Tourcoing – Second Day, 18 May 1794

The Second Day

The French were wide awake and knew exactly what they had to do. Osten's brigade of Bonnaud's division (7,000 men) was to stay in position near Flers and Lezennes, to keep an eye on the Archduke Karl and Kinsky. Bonnaud sent his other two brigades (Pierquin and Baillot) northwards, one by L'Hempenpont upon Lannoy, the other by Pont-a-Breug upon Roubaix. These forces included Général de brigade Antoine Baillot-Faral's strong cavalry brigade (3,500 troopers from ten regiments) and a fair smattering of old French line infantry regiments. Souham's strong former division in the north (commanded ad interim by a 31-year old Dutch Patriot, Général de brigade Herman Willem Daendels) was to provide the opposite face of the pocket. Daendel's old brigade (nine battalions and a cavalry regiment) was ordered from Aalbeke upon Wattrelos; Macdonald's (thirteen battalions and two cavalry regiments) from Mount Halluin upon the western side of Tourcoing; Malbrancq's (six battalions and a cavalry regiment) from Roncq upon Mouveaux, while Général de brigade Henri-Antoine Jardon's light brigade (two battalions of chasseurs and a light cavalry regiment) was ordered from Belleghem towards Dottignies to keep the Hanoverians in check. Two strong independent brigades (Compère and Thierry, thirteen battalions, a cavalry regiment and five artillery companies) were to advance from Mouscron upon the northern front. Moreau was to keep one of his divisions (Général de brigade Nicolas-Joseph Desenfans) in reserve in the north and detach Vandamme's division to cover Clerfayt from the south side of the Lys. In all, 60,000 Frenchmen were advancing upon the six posts held by 18,000 Coalition soldiers under Otto and the Duke of York.

The duke perhaps snatched a few hours' sleep but was rudely awaken around 04.00 hours when he heard the distant rumble of artillery and musketry some 2 miles (3km) to the north at Tourcoing. Otto's advanced guard (Linien-Infanterie-Regiment Nr. 20 'Graf Kaunitz-Rietberg' and O'Donnell's Freikorps) under Generalmajor Montfrault was under attack from French troops under Généraux de brigade Compère and Macdonald. The Tyrolean Jägers kept the attackers at bay for two hours, fighting from house-to-house. The Austrians retreated to the narrow Rue du Tilleul (the road to Wattrelos) and formed a line across the road, which masked cannon firing at the French masses in the enclosed space. The French detached a battery on their right, along the Rue de l'Épidème, in front of an old chapel. It opened fire into the flank of the Austrians at the Agathon Lézy mill; this was the tipping-point. Otto's column commenced a retreat towards Wattrelos.[30]

The Duke of York sent two battalions of Austrians from Roubaix to Otto's aid on the understanding they should be returned if not needed, but they arrived too late to prevent the French from capturing Tourcoing.[31] Otto's men regrouped at Sapin-Vert and commenced a short but bloody artillery duel with the advancing French. The impasse was resolved by a pincer-movement from Daendels and Jardon, with the help of Malbrancq's division.

Otto retreated to the crossroads of Sapin-Vert and finally to Moulin-Tonton. But the French artillery kept pace and made the position untenable. With the enemy on both flanks, disorder became general. Everyone simply wanted to reach Leers, and safety. The five battalions of Kaunitz and Colloredo could only form a single strong battalion;[32] the rest were scattered. Left along the road were many wounded soldiers and twenty guns with their caissons.[33] Daendal's division subsequently completely overwhelmed the two Hessen-Cassel Garde-Grenadiere battalions defending Wattrelos. Otto's column was in disarray, but at least it managed to escape largely intact.

At 06.00 hours, and much to the shock of the duke, Bonnaud's brigades advancing from the south reached Roubaix and Lannoy, while part of his division advanced towards Mouveaux.[34] A short time later Général de brigade Philippe Joseph Malbrancq's brigade struck Mouveaux from the north; it was not hard to find, the plume of smoke acting as a telegraph to call down the French attackers. The British were split in two by the envelopment. The Brigade of Guards (now commanded by Hulse) had no trouble defending the town, and Major General Fox's now-veteran 1st Infantry Brigade was equally untroubled on the slopes west of Roubaix. But the village of Roubaix was held by three Austrian battalions and a squadron of the 16th Light Dragoons with nothing between them and two Hessian battalions at Lannoy, with Bonnaud's division bursting through the gap. The situation became desperate when one of the Austrian battalions broke and fled.

The defence of Mouveaux was by this stage completely untenable, and so at 09.00 hours the duke sent Calvert to bring the Brigade of Guards and Congreve's supporting artillery back to Roubaix. But the French had occupied some positions between these two villages as well. The duke rode forward to coordinate the retreat and found himself almost surrounded. The only way out was northwards, towards Wattrelos, where at least he might find Otto and beg for some reinforcements. But Wattrelos was in French hands, as he discovered when fifty yards from the village as a French volley unhorsed his Austrian liaison officer. He turned and rode for his life towards Lannoy with drawn sword, being pursued by French dragoons - being somewhat conspicuous in his scarlet general's uniform with the Star of the Garter on his breast.[35] He came to the Espierre brook whereupon his horse reared and refused to cross. He dismounted and waded across on foot as the French unlimbered a cannon and took pot-shots:

> The Carmagnols judging pursuit was in vain
> Like Hell-hounds still eager our lives to obtain
> An eight-pounder planted and levelling well
> Each ball they dispatched from it close to us fell.[36]

The duke borrowed a spare horse from his aide Captain John Murray on the other side and rode away to safety in Leers, completely cut off from his troops.[37]

The Brigade of Guards and Fox's 1st Infantry Brigade had no choice but to fight their way out. Fox's men held the ridge-line north of Croix, defending the main road down which the Guards retreated to Roubaix. After the Guards had passed, they commenced their retreat along to ridge-line to Lannoy. The 14th Foot attracted great acclaim for a fighting retreat in perfect order, fighting off marauding cavalry at several points until they found a French cannon behind an abbatis at Lannoy blocking the road home. Corporal Gilbert Cimitiere of the 14th, a French émigré and a local, offered to lead his regiment through some hedge-rows thus pypassing the artillery. En route the commanding officer, Brevet Lieutenant Colonel William Browne, was hit and carried in a blanket by four grenadiers, but all were taken prisoner after he asked his bearers to put him down when in too much pain.[38] Corporal Cimitiere got the 14th to safety and was rewarded with a commission.[39]

Fox's brigade managed to reach the main road beyond Lannoy, then reached safety at Leers with the assistance of a unit of French émigrés. He lost 534 of his 1,120-man command, most of them taken prisoner.

The Brigade of Guards began its retreat in good order at 11.00 hours. They passed through a dismounted squadron of the 15th Light Dragoons guarding the western end of Roubaix, the Austrian battalions having withdrawn. Cornet Robert Wilson was present with the dragoons:

> I had the command of the rearguard, which was constantly under fire from behind and from both flanks after we quitted Mouveaux and moved on the Roubaix road... By steady march and charging occasionally back we left our pursuers behind and prevented a rush upon us, which would have been fatal not only to the rearguard but

to the column obliged by flanking ditches to keep the road. Baggage-carts, and carts with the wounded enemy taken the night before, were of course soon abandoned and formed useful barricades; but I wish I could pass over the disgusting and sorrowful scene which the slaughter of the prisoners and even of the wounded amongst them exhibited. Nothing could exceed the ferocity which thus revenged itself on the helpless and of all the events of the day the most horrible was the sight of this ungenerous execution. The supplications of the victims and the fatal shots which answered their prayers rang for many days in my ears.[40]

The Guards marched up the Grande Rue in Roubaix to find that the French had sited a cannon firing directly down the street:

Roubaix had a long street at the end of which one road ran on continuing in a straight line; another road pavé turned immediately to the right at the termination of the main street. Hedges lined each side of the straight road; ditches very deep – one, indeed, a rivulet – flanked the other. Before the head of the retiring column could gain the village the enemy had made a lodgment, but were driven out. Part took post behind the hedges which lined the straight road and commanded the town into and up the pavé road; and part, on retiring along the straight road, faced about at a little distance to fire into the street and on the troops sallying out to gain the pavé road.[41]

Then the Austrian Husaren Regiment Nr. 35 rode through the column, dispersing the artillery. The civilian artillery drivers fled, after which the artillery horses were let loose. The guns, limbers and wagons littered the main street, making it impassable to the Guards. The cannon would have to be left behind. The Guards dispersed through the gardens and houses:

Thus we Went, beset on all sides, for Upwards of three miles. Immediately after our last formation, a squadron or two of some foreign hussars, instead of endeavouring to check the enemy, rode away at full speed, even through the midst of our own men, if they chanced to be in their way, and added confusion to confusion. The most part of our officers batt horses and others were so frightened at the shot, that they became quite unmanageable, and throwing off their loads, ran with the utmost fury up and down, among the soldiers. The women also, who inadvertently had been permitted to follow us, caused no small disorder; some being killed, others wounded, and some loaded with plunder, so as to be unable to keep up with the men.[42]

The Guards left the village in the hands of the single squadron of the 15th Light Dragoons, who had to run the gauntlet upon leaving by the main road to Lannoy:

> The cry of 'Charge to the right!' ran down the column, and in the same moment we were all at full speed. The enemy redoubled his efforts, and struck at us with his bayonets fixed at the end of his muskets as we wheeled round the dreaded and dreadful corner, already almost choked with the fallen horses and men which had perished in the attempt to pass. My little mare received here a bayonet-wound in the croup and a musket-ball through the crest of her neck. Two balls lodged in my cloak-case behind the saddle, and another carried away part of my sash. Our surgeon and his horse were killed close at my side,[43] and above a dozen of my detachment fell at that spot under the enemy. We still urged on ... pursued by bullets. I had got about two hundred horses' lengths distance from the town when, before the least notice could be given, the whole column of cavalry was arrested in its career, and at the same moment of course recoiled several yards. The confusion, the conflict for preservation, the destruction which ensued, baffles all description. Three-fourths of the horses, at one and the same moment were thrown down with their riders under them or entangled by the bodies of others.[44]

A few miles south-east of Roubaix the two battalions of the Hessen-Cassel Leib-Infanterie-Regiment left behind at Lannoy – perhaps assuming that rear-area duties were to be their lot in this battle – found themselves surrounded by one of Bonnaud's large divisions, some 9,000 men. The Guards were forced to skirt around to the north of the village, and the diversion this created allowed the Hessen-Cassel troops to escape to Leers.[45] The Guards headed across country to Templeuve. By the time they reached safety they had lost 137 men, mostly from the flank battalion. The 3rd Foot Guards lost a colour, but not from enemy action; a serjeant threw it away when the pursuing French got too close.[46]

The Hessen-Cassel Generalmajor Karl von Hanstein took command of a Coalition 'last barrier' position on the Espierre brook where the road between Wattrelos and Leers crossed, overlooking a swampy valley. With 100 Hungarian grenadiers and battery of 6-pounders they defended the bridge as thousands of exhausted Coalition troops made their way eastwards. But French cavalry eventually threatened their left flank, and batteries of French artillery could be seen siting themselves on the opposite bank. Otto ordered Hanstein to fall back to the heights of Leer, abandoning the line of the Espierre. Amongst the last men across were 100 of the Hessen-Cassel Garde-Grenadier Regiment under Hauptmann von Trott, and an exhausted and embarrassed Duke of York, fresh from nearly being captured out in the countryside. Several of his staff arrived bedraggled and on foot a few hours later.

Elsewhere the remaining Coalition columns were largely inactive. A staff officer tried to stir Kinsky into action at 06.00 hours:

> On the evening of the seventeenth, I received orders to go to the avant-garde of the Kinsky column. The troops ... expected the day with impatience. This came, but no marching orders - I went to Kinsky at 6 o'clock ... but he responded coldly and sadly, saying that he was ill and could no longer command.[47]

This torpor continued for the entire day of the 18th:

> It was 10 o'clock, and still no orders and no instructions; we listened calmly to the fire which displaced the Duke of Yorck, and finally at four o'clock in the afternoon, after all the troops had been lying in the field with their rifles all day, I was ordered by General Bellegarde to take the avantgarde against Croix. We marched off and were commanded at Chereng by the Prince of Waldeck to halt, because everything was lost at the Duke of Yorck. This evening we retired to Baisieux, where we went into camp.[48]

Despite the Archduke Karl's orders to move to Lannoy at three in the morning, the march did not begin until noon. Three hours later No. 5 Column finally reached the road from Tournai to Lille, still 4 miles (7km) south of Lannoy, and were then ordered to retreat eastwards to Tournai. The Archduke's column might as well not have bothered showing up. Kinsky and the Archduke used Erskine's heavy cavalry brigade which had infamously followed the wrong column as a screen to cover their retreat:

> While from a distance the cannon thunder of Tourcoing and Wattrelos rumbled over, the troops of the sick Kinsky were inactive in the fields, watching the trail of powdered smoke, getting ever closer ... and were not allowed to take any step in support of his beleaguered comrades. A similar silence prevailed in the camp of the Archduke. It is said that the instruction that he should lead fifteen battalions to Lannoy at noon had reached him at 5 o'clock in the morning, but he had a cramp and, therefore, was unable to comply with the order. the Emperor, Coburg, Mack, and Waldeck spent the morning at Templeuve, and afterwards were in Marquain, a mile from the sick Kinsky, two miles from the unencumbered Archduke,

and therefore had to have news of the obstructive condition of these generals no later than seven o'clock; and what they were discussing were the causes of honor and courage, of caution and restraint ... None of them ever sent a message; the hours went by, Tourcoing and Wattrelos became lost, Abercromby thrown, at last Lannoy was also lost. At four o'clock in the afternoon the long-awaited order to attack Roubaix came at last to Kinsky's camp, and the troops marched eagerly, in order to avert the present disaster, but a new order from headquarters, this time signed by the Prince of Waldeck, came in. The Duke of York was already completely beaten, the columns were back to the camp at Marquain. It was a statement that the day was lost, that the great offensive movement of the allies had been abandoned.[49]

Up in the north, Clerfayt acted strictly to type. His men did not start their march until 07.30 hours, (nearly two hours after sunrise), leaving two battalions, six pontoons and some light troops behind in Wervicq and Comines. Clerfayt's column marched in two wings, each of eight battalions with cavalry in proportion. Clerfayt himself commanded the right-hand wing (mostly Hanoverian, Hessian and British troops) which crossed the Lys using the old bridge and occupied the French fortifications overlooking the river. The left-hand column (under Feldmarschalleutnant Graf Sztáray de Nagy-Mihály) crossed using the pontoon bridge and proceeded with his Imperial troops down the road towards Linselles. It was by now 08.30 hours and they could hear the distant rumble of cannon-fire in Tourcoing, but it does not seem to have excited any particular urgency. Imperial generals did not march to the sound of the guns.

His opponent was Général de brigade Vandamme, outnumbered 12,000 to 21,000. So Vandamme played the smart game instead. Dilatory the day before, when his tired troops had rested on the north bank of the Lys after a long march, he planned to spend the 18th harassing the left flank and rear of Clerfayt's column from a position in and around the villages of Halluin and Bousbecque. He crossed the Lys at about the same time as Clerfayt moved off. Patrols sent out by Clerfayt confirmed that there were no French troops in either Bousbecque or Linselles, so he ordered his columns to occupy Linselles.

They were on the road to Mouveaux in accordance with their orders, but completely unaware of the plight of No. 2 and No. 3 Columns; and hours too late to be of any assistance. Then Clerfayt received the intelligence that French troops had been seen filing out of Menin to cross the Lys. He surveyed the countryside from the heights of Linselles and noticed a French 12-pounder battery on the heights south of Bousbecque, less than 2 miles (3km) to the north. As he trained his eye-glass on the hill, a column of French infantry and hussars debouched from the forest behind them, making for Linselles.

It was Vandamme. The Frenchman threatened the left rear and flank of Graf Sztáray's column, still marching down the road. Sztáray wheeled and attacked Vandamme and Clerfayt positioned a battery near Linselles to take the French in the flank. Then he detached the 55th Foot and the Hessen-Darmstadt Leib-Regiment, supported by a squadron each from the Hessen-Darmstadt Chevauxlegers and the Austrian Blankenstein Hussars, in a determined assault upon the French columns. The French fled back to Bousbecque, leaving their artillery behind, setting fire to the village of Viscourt as they did so. A squadron of the 8th Light Dragoons and one of the Hessen-Darmstadt Chevauxlegers pursued Vandamme's Gardes Nationale to the streets of Bousbecque. Vandamme himself admired their valour:

> At Bousbec the 8th Regiment of English Dragoons charged the infantry with the greatest impetuosity and broke up the battalions. They continued to charge with great temerity ... They created havoc in the park near the village. The whole of the wagons, supply-vehicles and artillery fled in disorder along the Lille Road.[50]

Heavy French cannon on the heights of Halluin annoyed the right wing of Clerfayt's column. Tired of being peppered with cannon-balls, the 55th Foot and Hessen-Darmstadt Leib-Regiment advanced to within fifty paces of the gun, fired platoon-fire and drove the gunners away. Vandamme's strategy was working to perfection. He was slowly drawing Clerfayt's column away to the north and north-east, in the opposite direction to their intended line of advance. They now had no chance of linking up with the beleaguered Coalition columns in the south.

Then a company of the Hessen-Darmstadt Leib-Regiment with some *scharfschützen* of their Leichte-Bataillon advanced east to within sight of the main road from Lille to Courtrai, and saw strong enemy columns of cavalry, infantry, baggage, and cattle, all moving in a great hurry south. They retreated to their parent battalions to report what they had seen, but Clerfayt's force was too dispersed to consider attacking them. It was now about 18.00 hours. At 19.30 hours some squadrons of French hussars and five battalions of infantry, approaching from the direction of Wasquehal (and therefore in the rear of Clerfayt's force, albeit in the intended line of advance), sent a panic through the Coalition.

A company of *scharfschützen* and the Blankenstein Hussars were ordered forward to keep them at bay, while both of Clerfayt's wings fell back to the heights south of Wervicq as the sun set, wondering why it was now all quiet to the south.

It was quiet because the fighting had ended just before 17.00 hours. The duke had finally had his 'big battle' but it had ended in disaster:

> I most sincerely hope that the heavy disaster which has fallen so undeservedly on us will be a warning to our allies; for while the same loose, unconnected, unmilitary system is persevered in, while such rashness and such childish obstinacy are the striking characteristics of their councils, nothing but loss and disgrace can attend the arms of his Imperial Majesty.[51]

Tourcoing was characterised by everything wrong with the Coalition method of making war. A plan so ambitious, over so large a geographical area, could only have been achieved by a supreme commander imposing himself utterly on the proceedings, and being present either in person or by proxy at every crisis point.[52] High-quality leadership from column commanders might have rectified some of the faults. The Duke of York, nominally in command of the three central thrusting columns, could offer no effective control over any other than his own No. 3 Column, and then recklessly allowed himself to be cut off from his troops and nearly captured. Clerfayt, Kinsky and the Archduke Karl may as well have been 'playing in a different game altogether' before charges of indolence and indecision are levelled. In the case of Clerfayt (late orders) and the archduke (unreasonable march orders on the first day) there are extenuating circumstances, but these do not excuse the inertia of 18 May. In complete contrast to the French, every Coalition column, once threatened, simply fell back upon its line of advance. At no stage did anyone venture the notion that the concentration of forces might be a good idea.

The Coalition army at Tourcoing was one of the most lethargic in history. For energy, speed and dash were the domain of youth, and the French had this quality in spades; Bonnaud was one of the older commanders at 36 years of age. Souham was only 27, Moreau 30, Compére 26 and Vandamme merely 23. Across the fence, Coburg was 56, Clerfayt 60, Kinsky 63, von dem Bussche 67 and Otto 59. The French had discovered war was a younger man's game. The Coalition would take years to learn the lesson.

'What is worse than anything,' wrote former Quartermaster-General Craig wholly inaccurately, 'is that we have lost the right to say that the British were never beaten by their current enemy.' French losses were about 2,600 killed and wounded. The Coalition lost about 4,000 killed or wounded, 1,500 captured, along with two colours and two standards, fifty-seven ammunition wagons and sixty guns.[53] British losses were 843 men, of which 200 were from the 37th Foot and 220 from the 53rd Foot. The Royal Artillery lost nineteen out of twenty-eight guns.[54] The British light dragoons got off relatively lightly. The Hessians lost 622 men, with 236 casualties (mostly prisoners) in the II/Leib-Infanterie-Regiment alone. Clerfayt's column lost 360 men but captured 400 prisoners and six cannon. The Austrian Linien-Infanterie-Regiment Nr. 20 'Graf Kaunitz-Rietberg' lost about 300 men in their fighting retreat.

And yet while Tourcoing had been a clear French tactical victory, it was in no way a French strategic victory:

> As for the Allies, those of them who took part in the battle at all, generals and soldiers, covered themselves with glory, but the inaction of two-thirds of Coburg's army was the bankruptcy declaration of the old strategical system ... Souham's victory, thanks to his geographical position, had merely given him air. The Allies, except for the loss of some 5,500 men, were in no way worse off. The plan had failed, but the army as a whole had not been defeated, while the troops of the Duke of York and Otto were far too well disciplined not to take their defeat as 'all in the day's work.' Souham was still on the Lys and midway between the two allied masses, able to strike each in turn or liable to be crushed between them in proportion as the opposing generals calculated time, space and endurance accurately.[55]

A rumour went through the Austrian camp that the British had been caught napping and then sent packing. The emperor issued an address refuting this allegation to the Coalition army on 25 May, providing a more honest appraisal of the unravelling of his army's plan than was common for such addresses in the era. The address from French headquarters was, of course, far more effusive. Paris went mad with the news.

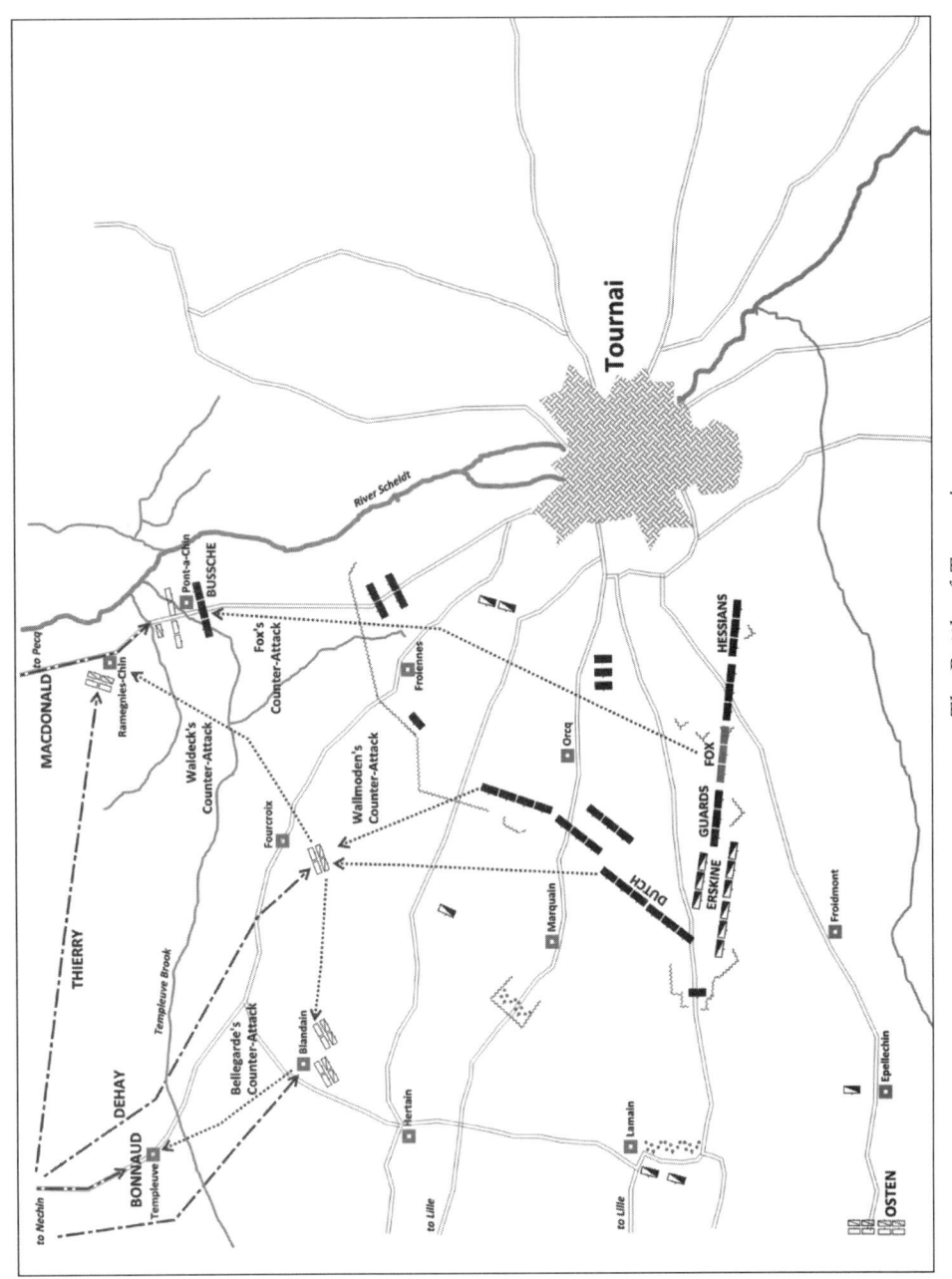

The Battle of Tournai

Chapter 13

Tournai

Pont-à-Chin

In the aftermath of the near-disaster at Tourcoing the Coalition army withdrew into an armed camp around Tournai. They formed a cordon to the west of the city, with Austrian troops manning a redoubt that ran from the river south of Pont-à-Chin as far as Marquain. From that place Dutch troops continued the defensive line to a redoubt on an elbow in the line on the main road east of Lamain. Light cavalry scouted out in front of the latter place, whilst the Duke of York's troops held the line from the redoubt running east, facing south. Hessian troops stood on their left, completing the line as far as the walls of Tournai. Although the Emperor Franz was still present in person, command of the army remained with Feldmarschall Coburg.

Respect for their Austrian allies, which had been slipping for some time, plummeted to an all-time low at the duke's headquarters. 'The English complained bitterly of the Austrians and were not wrong in complaining,' Count Langeron wrote, 'the Prince of Coburg tried to attribute to them some of his own faults.'[1] Brigade commander Major General Henry Fox, writing to his brother, blamed Mack for the recent disaster:

> The Plan was General Mack's, and was, as some of his are said to be, are too 'fine-spun' and without sufficient allowance for unavoidable contingencies, for the time was so nicely calculated that it was almost impossible that six distinct columns widely dispersed, should be able to act in such complete unison to the moment prefixed.[2]

In the aftermath of the loss, morale was low in the British camp, and as if to flatten everyone's spirits, the weather turned cold and wet. Indiscipline was everywhere, leading the Duke of York to issue this General Order:

> It is his Royal Highness the commander in chief's express order, that whenever the troops, or any particular corps, march without

> their camp equipage, no woman is upon any pretence whatever to be permitted to follow the column. His Royal Highness desires this may be considered as a standing order, and expects the commanding officers of regiments will take care it is most strictly complied with. It is necessary at the same time to warn the women and followers of the army, that the provost-marshal is hereby directed to inflict on every offender the most exemplary punishment and if the offence deserves it, even to execute on the spot, any woman or follower of the army, of any description whatever, who by cruelty, plunder, or marauding, may bring disgrace on the troops under his Royal Highness's command.[3]

And this in the heavy cavalry:

> This day four prisoners received the sentence of a General Court Martial viz. Three of the 5th Dragoon Guards and One of the 6th or Inniskilling Dragoons, the three former for plundering and drawing their swords on Sir William Erskine, Aide-de-Camp, the latter for drawing his sword on some foreign officers. The three former received (each) one thousand lashes, the latter five hundred lashes.[4]

The Duke did not write a candid letter home to his father after the battle. Instead, he sent Adjutant-General Craig to London, to explain the events of the last few days personally. In this, we sense that the duke took the loss extremely painfully and believed that only a face-to-face discussion could adequately express and flesh out the facts in a way that the written word could not. Perhaps the duke was also acutely aware that Lord Cornwallis was still in the frame as a potential replacement commander, currently attached to the Prussian army and due in Flanders at the start of June.

Général de division Pichegru, who had been absent from Tourcoing, returned on 19 May and decided to launch his own attack on the new Coalition position around Tournai. Over 62,000 French troops would be involved in the attack. The victorious Général de division Souham, with at least 30,000 troops in four brigades (Daendels, Macdonald, Malbrancq and Dehay) was to attack the northern part of the line. Bonnaud's division was to make a holding attack the north-western portion of the line with Osten's brigade carrying out a flanking movement to the south. Moreau's division was to guard Courtrai and the line of the River Lys against a possible relief effort by Clerfayt. Général de brigade Macdonald's two brigades, deployed to the right of Daendels, were to advance to Saint-Léger north of Tournai, then join Daendels on the Escaut. To his right were the brigades of Compère and Thierry.[5] But the intricacy and depth of the Coalition advanced posts, coupled with the densely-cultivated nature of the ground made accurate intelligence as to the Coalition dispositions almost impossible. Pichegru's men were going to have to wing it. Such was the confidence at French headquarters that this was not seen as a risk.

The attack began between 05.00 and 06.00 hours on the morning of 22 May. Osten's advance on the extreme French right was soon seen for what it was – a diversion. Thereupon some of the Coaliton left wing units closed in upon their centre, to reinforce harder-pressed sectors. The columns of Souham, Thierry and Compére advanced from the north-west against Ramignies-Chin and Néchin, whilst Bonnaud's large division attacked Templeuve. The Austrian Generalmajor Blasius von Kovacsevich defended Ramignies-Chin with two battalions, two companies and two squadrons, whilst Generalmajor Bellegarde defended Templeuve with ten companies. The Coalition left wing, by the Archduke Karl, had advanced to a point between Hertain and Lamain to ward off any attacks from the direction of Lille. Néchin soon fell.

The Austrian defenders fell back upon Templeuve as the French swarms surged around them and captured Blandain. Initially, the fight had only begun on a few points, but the fighting gradually expanded along the entire line of the Templeuve stream. The brigades of Thierry and Salme of Bonnaud's division crossed the brook and advanced against Blandain and against the Croisette heights, which were taken without great effort. Other French troops at Néchin advanced east, towards Ramegnies-Chin, on the river Scheldt about 3 miles (5km) north of Tournai.

The Coalition had lost three important points – Ramegnies-Chin, Blandain and height (windmill) at Croisette. Prince Coburg ordered that all be re-taken. Prince Frederik of Orange-Nassau reinforced Wallmoden and with the help of the Dutch troops, the commander of the cavalry, Generalmajor Prinz zu Waldeck und Pyrmont, retook the Croisette heights in a lucky cavalry attack. Generalmajor Karl Prinz von Lothringen-Lambesc charged the French infantry on the heights with four squadrons of k.k. Chevauxleger Regiment Nr.18 'Karaiczay', cutting down 500 men and capturing three guns.

The French not only retreated from this position, but also back over the brook. The Imperial infantry under Bellegarde followed the victorious cavalry, driving the French out of Blandain and penetrating to the first houses of Templeuve, getting involved in some ugly street-fighting with the French divisions of Malbrancq and Delhay without being able to complete the conquest of the place.

To the north, Macdonald advanced swiftly to the Escaut and linked up with Daendels, having driven Bussche's Hanoverians across the

Scheldt. Daendels thought it too dangerous to cross and advance down the east side of the river to Tournai, so Macdonald rode south down the west side at the head of the 5e Chasseurs a Cheval. At Pont-à-Chin he was fired upon by a Hanoverian battery left to defend the river crossing at the village. The rest of his brigade (3e, 24e, 68e and 200e Demi-brigades and 4e Tirailleurs) eventually came up and the Hanoverians fell back on an entrenched position beyond the village. Macdonald sent his brigade in and they were met with a hail of shot and shell. 'From ten a.m. till nine at night, the fire both of artillery and musketry was heavier than the oldest soldier on the field had ever before witnessed,' Harry Calvert recorded.[6] Souham ordered Macdonald to attack again at about 10.00 hours. His valiant troops made three frontal assaults over the course of the afternoon, losing large numbers of men each time. At 17.30 hours Pichegru (commanding from miles away at Pecq) sent an order admonishing him for his failure to capture the village; in response Macdonald's weary troops went in again. This time they were successful, as the exhausted Hanoverians tumbled back to Tournai. Some French staff officers then settled down to dinner in the village.

The only Coalition force available to counterattack were seven Austrian battalions and Major General Henry Fox's 'Little Brigade', consisting of the 14th, 37th and 53rd Foot. This brigade had suffered heavy losses at Tourcoing and numbered just under 600 men. Despite this the brigade recaptured the village at bayonet-point at 19.00 hours and secured the Coalition position, finding tables still set and food uneaten. The silver plate was very quickly souvenired.[7]

The French retreated everywhere, lost five guns in Pont-à-Chin and withdrew to their first position under the protection of three battalions that Macdonald held in reserve. At the same time, Prinz Waldeck advanced from Blandain to Ramignies-Chin and drove back everything he found from Souham's forces. The French retreated without being pursued as Bonnaud formed a rearguard at Templeuve. At this point the battle descended to desultory sniping on both sides, until the firing died away after dark.

Contrary to his usual form, Prince Coburg ordered a night attack on the French at Templeuve. Tired by the strain of the day, French troops lay drowsily in the alleyways and houses of the sprawling village. No-one had even thought to set a guard. Generalmajor Bellegarde silently entered the place at 02.00 hours with a battalion of the Austrian k.k. Linien-Infanterie-Regiment Nr. 59 'Jordis'. It penetrated the village, found the French sound asleep, and played merry Hell with the bayonet.[8]

The Battle of Tournai was fought mostly in dispersed battles. It was the classic infantryman's battle. The cavalry found little opportunity for action, and of the numerous artillery, only forty Coalition guns actually fired. Musketry had decided the outcome; disciplined, sustained volleys by Coalition troops against headlong, ferocious assaults by over-confident French infantry. It had lasted a full fifteen hours. It was almost a blueprint for the Flanders battles of August 1914, fought not far from the same spot. Prince Coburg wrote in his diary, 'the battle was stubborn and the fire unprecedented.' Cornet Robert Wilson of the 15th Light Dragoons rode over the field the next day:

> The next morning I rode over the field of battle, beginning at Templeuve which had been taken and retaken five times during the day as already stated, and which presented a tragic spectacle, all the horrors of assault having been perpetrated. One very old man with silver locks was seated at the door of a house weeping bitterly. On my asking the particular nature of his calamity, he pointed to the upper apartment. There we saw the body of a beautiful girl of about sixteen who had too evidently died under violence, and an infant sister and brother bayoneted by her side, as if they had been struck in the act of giving her help.
>
> About three miles on the right we witnessed another terrible spectacle, but of a different character. A column of eighteen hundred French had endeavoured to force its way through some orchards. When the mass was wedged in one of them which had a very small outlet, the Austrians had opened a battery of twelve guns — 12-pounders - upon it, and with such remarkable razing precision and effect that I myself counted two hundred and eighty headless bodies. The trees and branches were all indented or covered with the smashed bones and brains. Such a beheading carnage was perhaps never paralleled.[9]

The French suffered 5,500 casualties and had 450 taken prisoner (mostly from Macdonald's brigade), while the Allies lost 3,000 men. The victory at Tournai went some way towards restoring the pride lost at Tourcoing. The three regiments in Fox's battered brigade (14th, 37th and 53rd Foot) lost another 120 men this day. The duke singled them out in his despatch, noticing commanding officers brevet Major William Ramsay (14th), Captain Stafford Lightburne (37th) and brevet Major James Wiseman (53rd).[10] These three regiments were all awarded the battle honour 'Tournay'.

The constant fighting was taking its toll upon the Austrians. Despite victory at Tournai, Generalmajor Mack made it clear he no longer believed that the French could be expelled from the Austrian Netherlands. On

24 May Emperor Franz held a council-of-war; it was to prove the most eventful day of the campaign. The emperor presented three questions to his assembled generals. Kaunitz was about to fight the French again on the Sambre, and therefore the three possible outcomes were a decisive Coalition victory, the French merely pushed back but not defeated, or a clear Coalition defeat. In the event of a victory, the majority were in favour of going on the offensive again in Flanders. In the case of a draw, the prevailing view to wait until Kaunitz was reinforced, then attack again. But if beaten – the vote was to abandon Flanders (leaving a covering screen at Tournai) and retire eastwards to effect a union with Kaunitz. Mack argued that the Coalition forces were 40,000 men too weak, and even advised the emperor to start peace negotiations, unless in the next three to four weeks 40,000 reinforcements could be found. This put Mack in vehement opposition to Baron Thugut, who wanted to continue the war under all circumstances. The emperor sided with Mack. Thugut wanted Mack gone, but to do so he would need to manoeuvre the emperor away as well; so, he got into the emperor's ear about events in Poland, and the need for His Imperial Majesty to travel east to take a keener interest in them. It worked.[11]

The Emperor Goes Home
On 29 May the emperor announced that he would return to Vienna. He relinquished command, left Tournai to visit Clerfayt and did one last inspection tour of his beloved *Hauptarmee*, placing Feldmarschall Coburg once again in supreme command of the Coalition forces in Flanders. The following day, Coburg issued a general order announcing that Generalmajor Mack had received permission to leave the army due to ill health, and that 49-year-old General der Kavallerie Prinz Christian August zu Waldeck was to be his successor as Imperial Quartermaster-General.[12] Before he left, Mack presented the emperor with a memorandum outlining his view of the present situation. It was not an expert opinion but asked nineteen questions without citing their answers. From the wording it was clear that Mack believed the Austrian Netherlands could no longer be defended. Then Mack and the emperor rode across to Mons to be present at a general attack across the Sambre on either the 2nd or 3rd of June. On 3 June an Austro-Dutch force relieved Charleroi and hurled the French back across the Sambre. Afterwards the emperor boarded his carriage to Vienna, and Mack travelled home to Wiklantitz in Bohemia. Their campaigns were over.

One bright hope in the general Coalition despondency was the anticipated arrival of the promised 62,000-man Prussian contingent under Generalfeldmarschall Wichard Joachim Heinrich von Möllendorf, expected daily. Lord Cornwallis had been despatched to Berlin in February as a military liaison officer but was due in Flanders at the start of June. He duly arrived on 4 June. 'I am very happy that Lord Cornwallis is on the continent,' Harry Calvert wrote, 'for I have more reliance on his ability, wisdom, and judgment than on the collective sagacity of the whole of his Imperial Majesty's army or even Cabinet.'[13] The duke wrote optimistically home two days later; 'In the various conversations that I had with his Lordship, we thoroughly agreed in the great advantage which would arise from the Prussian army being employed in West Flanders, in preference to every other operation that had been pointed out for it.' Was the duke blotting the Austrians out from his thinking and replacing them with the Prussians? The following lines from the same letter explain why. 'I am likewise credibly informed, though I cannot assert it on my own knowledge, that M. de Thugut has declared openly that he has done everything in his power to persuade the Emperor to give up this country.'[14]

On 26 May, sensing the Coalition disunity irrevocably gave them the upper hand, the National Convention in Paris issued a proclamation:

> England is capable of every outrage on humanity; and of every crime towards the republic. She attacks the rights of nations and threatens to annihilate liberty. How long will you suffer to continue on your frontier - the soldiers of the most atrocious of tyrants? He formed the congress of Pilnitz and brought about the scandalous surrender of Toulon. He massacred your brethren at Genoa and burned our magazines in the maritime towns. He corrupted our cities and endeavoured to destroy the national representation. He starved your plains; and purchased treasons on the frontiers. When the event of battles shall put in your power either English or Hanoverians, bring to your remembrance the vast tracts of country English slaves have laid waste. Carry your view to La Vendee, Toulon, Lyons, Landrecies, Martinique, and St. Domingo, places still reeking with the blood which the atrocious policy of the English has shed. Do not trust to their artful language, which is an additional crime, worthy of their perfidious character and Machiavellian government. No, no, republican soldiers, you ought therefore, when victory shall put in your power, either Englishmen or Hanoverians, to strike; not one of them ought to return to the traitorous territory of England, or to be brought into France. Let the British slaves perish, and Europe be free.

On 7 June, the Duke issued his own response to the decree:

> His Royal Highness the Commander-in-Chief thinks it incumbent on him to announce to the British and Hanoverian troops (under

his command) that the National Convention of France (pursuing that gradation of crimes and horrors which it has distinguished the period of its Government as the most calamitous of any that has occurred in the history of the World) has just passed a decree that their soldiers shall give no quarter to the British and Hanoverian troops. His Royal Highness anticipates the indignations and horrors which will naturally arise in the minds of the brave troops whom he addresses on receiving this information. His Royal Highness desires (however) to remind them that mercy to the vanquished is the brightest gem in a soldier's character and he exhorts them not to suffer their resentment to lead them to any precipitate act of cruelty on their part ... In all wars (from the earliest times) between the British and the French nations they have been accustomed to consider each other in the light of generous as well as brave enemies - while the Hanoverians (for centuries the allies of the former) have shared in this reciprocal esteem. Humanity and kindness have at all times taken place the instant opposition ceased and the same cloaks have commonly been seen covering wounded enemies while discriminately borne to the hospital of the conquerors.

The British and Hanoverian armies will not believe that the French nation (even under the her present infatuation) can so far forget their former character as soldiers as to pay any attention to the decree (as injurious as it is disgraceful to the persons that passed it) In his confidence His Royal Highness trusts that the soldiers of both nations will continue their sentiments of resentment and abhorrence to the National Convention alone... and his Royal Highness is confident that it will only be (on finding contrary to every expectation that the French army has relinquished every title to the fair character of soldiers and as men by submitting to and obeying such an atrocious order) that the brave troops under his command will think themselves justified and indeed under the necessity of (themselves) adopting a species of warfare to which they will stand acquitted to their country, to their own conscience and to the world, in such an event the French (army alone) will be answerable for the tenfold vengeance which will fall upon their wives and children and their (unfortunate) country already groaning under very calamity, which the accumulated armies (of a principle ambition) can keep upon their devoted victims. Fredk. Duke of York.[15]

To their credit, the French armies in the field completely ignored the proclamation handed down to them by their own government. The National Convention rescinded the proclamation in mid-June and decreed that any French soldier guilty of inhumanity towards any English, Hanoverian, or Hessian prisoner would be executed.

Chapter 14

Exit Austria

Enter Moira

Lord Cornwallis left Flanders, bound for further negotiations with Generalfeldmarschall Möllendorf. But he, and the rest of the Coalition, were in for a disappointment. The uprising in Poland which had drawn the emperor away had also attracted the close attention of Russia and Prussia, all intent on getting a slice of any geographical gains to be made whilst simultaneously squashing the desires of rivals. The 'Polish Problem' in fact provided more security to the borders of France in 1794 than any French army could. The promised 62,000 Prussian troops were never going to arrive in Flanders. They only ever had one possible direction of march – east. Lord Malmesbury wrote to Grenville:

> The disgraceful failure of every military operation His Prussian Majesty has undertaken since the year 1791 has destroyed the reputation of the Prussian army; and the duplicity and versatility of his Cabinet put an end to all confidence and good faith.[1]

The Coalition had achieved some success on the plains of northern France, which, being excellent cavalry country, played completely to their strengths. But the low-lying canal-crossed countryside of Flanders negated this advantage. Pichegru knew that if he was going to defeat the Coalition, it must be in that theatre, in which the Armée du Nord now had a marked superiority in numbers. Pichegru laid siege to Ypres with 35,000 men on 1 June, establishing a camp at Passchendaele.

Clerfayt called for reinforcements but Coburg sent few and seemed reluctant to intervene.[2] The duke took matters into his own hands and sent Hanoverian Generalmajor Hammerstein with a force of 11,000 men to attempt the relief of Ypres on 6 June. They clashed with the French at a fortified post at Vry-Bosch, just north of town. The 8th Light Dragoons, 12th Foot and Loyal Emigrants were present at the action and the 38th Foot arrived as reinforcements after the post was captured. Total Coalition losses were eighty men. The duke made another appeal to Coburg on 12 June, which led at least to a partial effort. This attempt to raise the siege of Ypres involved an attack from the north at Hooglede on 13 June, about 3 miles (5km) north-west of Roeselare. An Austro-Hanoverian force of 19,000 men clashed with Souham and Macdonald's 24,000 Frenchmen. Generalmajor Hammerstein, who had gathered his division at 06.00 hours before Torhout on the main road, received orders from Coburg at 07.30 to commence the attack.

Hammerstein arrived in good time with the vanguard of the 2nd Column in front of Gits; two Austrian grenadier battalions of the 2nd Column went through the village. The British and Hanoverian infantry had to go around the village and attack it in the flank. The enemy soon returned. The Coalition infantry and Hammerstein's cavalry then had to endure a violent cannonade. After an hour the French cannon-fire eased a little, and the Austrian grenadier battalions resumed their advance through the village. They pushed on to Hooglede in three columns, a mile west, defended by Souham's entire division. Malbrancq's brigade on the left of the French position was routed almost immediately. Hammerstein pushed back Souham's right wing; but Sztarray's column in the centre encountered stiff opposition. To the south, the 4th and 5th Columns captured Roeslaere, but were too far away to assist the hard-pressed columns in Hooglede.

As French pressure grew at Hooglede, Clerfayt ordered a retreat to Tielt. Total Coalition losses were thirty-five officers and 886 men, of whom 130 were taken prisoner. The British and Hanoverian losses amounted to 264 men, of which the Hanoverian grenadier battalions took 133, and the Loyal Emigrants lost fifty-five. The single British brigade present (38th Foot, 55th Foot, 8th Light Dragoons) played only a minor part. The relief attempt failed.[3]

As always, Harry Calvert summed up the strategic implications and relayed them in his regular correspondence with Colonel Sir Hew Dalrymple:[4]

> You will observe that, should Ypres fall, and the enemy get possession of Tournay, there is no single fortress from hence to the mouth of the Scheldt, which will prevent them immediately over-running the country and taking possession of the left bank of the Scheldt, from this place quite to the sea... The Scheldt would become their frontier, and their industry and activity would soon render it a most formidable one; and the accession they would acquire of coast, and of one of richest countries in Europe, would

give them advantages which can hardly be computed; while their vicinity to Holland must excite the greatest alarms for the safety of that country, where, as you know from personal observation, the hateful doctrines of French republicanism do not excite the horror they deserve.[5]

Coburg finally shook himself into action on 18 June, but it was too late; the Austro-Hessian garrison of Ypres had surrendered that same day and marched out with all the honours of war.[6] As Calvert feared, the French now had control of the whole of West Flanders, with 80,000 men between Ypres and the sea.

On 19 June Général Jourdan crossed the Sambre and once again laid siege to Charleroi. Prince Coburg duly marched his Austrians towards the Sambre, leaving the Duke of York with a weak force around Tournai to hold the centre of the line. Following the loss of Ypres, Clerfayt retreated to Deynse, where the following day troops under Pichegru attacked him and forced him back to Ghent. Imperial Chief-of-Staff Waldeck was sick, and no-one had been appointed in his place; the Austrian contingent was rudderless.

French control of all Channel ports such as Ostend and Nieuwpoort now seemed possible, if not extremely likely. The Duke of York received news of Clerfayt's retreat in West Flanders on 22 June. A general retreat northward was ordered, and the British headquarters left Tournai, never to return, as the populace panicked, despite the presence of four Austrian battalions entering the town as a garrison. The British marched 15 miles (24km) north-east to Renaix.

Luckily a substantial force of British reinforcements was on its way. In view of heavy losses in May, plus Austrian vacillation, Secretary at War Henry Dundas ordered the force under Major General Francis Rawdon-Hastings (latterly and more popularly known as Lord Moira) currently camped on the Isle of Wight, to embark for Ostend. Their first mission was to reinforce Clerfayt's embattled corps in West Flanders, ensuring a semblance of communication with the Channel coast. This force, which included three regiments plucked from the Irish establishment, embarked at Southampton on 18 June. Some of the regiments (19th, 27th, 28th, 42nd, 54th, 57th, 59th) had previously been part of Sir Charles Grey's mobile force in 1793. An anonymous officer recorded:

> We sailed immediately to Spithead, our Fleet consisting of between 40 and 50 Transports; these vessels were all fitted up purposely for the accommodation and health of the Troops; upon a new plan the contrivance of Sir Jeremy Fitzpatrick; each Vessel was provided with a ventilating Machine, which by means of tubes, was so contrived, as to expel the foul air at the moment it admitted

the fresh, to every part of the Vessel. At Spithead, we joined our Convoy; which consisted of several Ships of the Line, Frigates; Gun-Boats and floating Batteries; which last were Old Ships of War cut down, and carrying 36 and 42 pounders; which were at this time supposed to be intended for the reduction of Dunkirk, which had already been unsuccessfully attacked by the Duke of York; and with whose Army we were to co-operate.[7]

Four days later, and in advance of Moira's force, reinforcements arrived at Ostend. These were the 8th (King's) and 44th (East Essex) Regiments of Foot, following only a few days later by one squadron of the 14th Regiment of (Light) Dragoons and the 33rd (1st Yorkshire West Riding) Regiment of Foot, commanded by a young officer going on active service for the first time, Lieutenant Colonel Arthur Wellesley. Lord Moira's main force arrived at Ostend on 26 June, having sailed through Lord Howe's fleet on their way home from the naval action of Glorious 1st of June. His 'division' consisted of about 7,800 men in three brigades (Brigadier-generals Lord Cathcart, Charles Graham and Peter Hunter) but as impressive as this sounds, most of the troops were raw recruits. Moira's men marched through Ostend to join the 8th, 33rd and 44th, all commanded by Colonel Richard Vyse. The reinforcements were intended for the defence of Ostend but could be used by the Duke of York 'in any measures he decided upon'.

The duke learned of their arrival on 27 June. Since their employment was in his hands, he had to make the difficult decision: to keep control of Ostend, or to bolster his own depleted and badly outnumbered force in East Flanders? He decided upon the latter, and immediately dashed off two letters, one to Henry Dundas – declaring it was 'absolutely necessary that the force under Lord Moira should join me' – and the second to Moira asking him to unite his force with all possible expedience, travelling by sea to Antwerp then marching overland. Moira nonetheless decided to make the whole march overland, and the following day headed for Bruges. This movement was sudden and unexplained. Officers left their spare clothing and camp equipage behind, assuming they would return.

The French were well aware of their arrival. Quartermaster-General Wellbore Ellis Doyle pulled a neat trick by riding into Bruges and ordering the Burgomeister to prepare 30,000 rations. This intelligence was transmitted to General Vandamme, who refrained from attacking so apparently large a force. No one had any idea of where they were headed:

> This day proved extremely hot, insomuch that the Men (unaccustomed to marching so heavily loaden,) could with difficulty be kept up, as from the weight of their Arms, and Sixty rounds of

> Ammunition, together with their knapsacks, which they had brought tolerably well loaden from England, they found it very difficult to get forward; they however soon found means to rid themselves of part of their burthen, by throwing away great part of the contents of their knapsacks; and near Bruges, the Road was absolutely strewed with Shirts, Shoes, Stockings, &c. &c. which would no doubt, prove a valuable prize to the Neighbouring Inhabitants.[8]

The citizens of Bruges were glad to see them:

> [We] were received by the Inhabitants, with the greatest apparent joy; the Bells for which Bruges is famed, were ringing most melodiously to welcome our arrival; and (being Sunday,) every individual was dressed out to the utmost advantage; the Ladies especially, who crowded the Windows applauding and shaking their handkerchiefs; the Priests, and Fryars too, pronounced their Benedicites with great earnestness as the Troops passed them. At every door was a Female with a bottle and glass, who seemed happy when a Soldier would stop to drink with her, at the same time endeavouring by every means in her power, to convince him that he was welcome to it.[9]

The 42nd Highlanders in their kilts were to the astonishment of the Belgian population and were given the nickname 'the Vrouws'[10] which they affectionately retained for the rest of the campaign. Unfortunately, the ill-disciplined British troops did not repay the welcoming Belgians with any grace:

> Lord Moira is exceedingly distressed by the complaints which have been made to him from inhabitants plundered by the British soldiers. He calls upon the officers commanding regiments, by every sense they have of military discipline or national credit, to exert themselves in suppressing a conduct so disgraceful to the army.[11]

As was common to most continental armies, every infantry regiment in Moira's force had two attached 'battalion guns' intended to provide local fire support to the regiment:

> It may be necessary to observe, that to every Regiment of Foot, are attached two light Brass Six-pounders, to each of which belong twelve Artillery-Men, and three Horses with their drivers; besides an Ammunition Waggon and Tumbril, to each Regiment, which were very heavily laden; the Horses were brought over from England, and were of the most spirited kind, and in the highest keep, otherwise they would not have been able to have

gone through the hardships and fatigues which they continually underwent.[12]

Lord Moira's corps joined the Coalition army just outside Ghent on 1 July, going into cantonments alongside their Hanoverian and Hessian allies as part of Clerfayt's army in West Flanders. Lacking tents, the men built huts (the troops called them wig-wams) from tree boughs and scrounged for vegetables. They were put back on the road the night of 3 July, and marched to Dendermonde, then to Alost.

The French attacked Coalition outposts early in the morning of 6 July, and Lord Moira's men had their baptism of fire. Lord Moira led a counter-attack, principally with the 8th Light Dragoons, and repulsed the Frenchmen:

> The skirmish then became general in the very heart of the Town of Alost, to the no small consternation of the Inhabitants. Our party consisted only of a few Officers with their attendants, and the were completely surrounded by the French, they however cut their way through, though not without some loss, as our party had in the whole affair twelve killed and wounded; of the latter description were two Officers, Col. Vandeleur, of the 8th Light Dragoons;[13] and Col. Doyle, of the 87th Foot,[14] this last Gentleman was dangerously wounded by a sabre in two places. A detachment of Light Dragoons coming up, soon put an end to the contest, in which the French suffered considerably, leaving behind them in the Town, a number of Men and Horses, killed and wounded. A picquet of the 87th Regiment was in the place during the skirmish, but they could not be of any service, as the parties were so intermixed that it was not possible to fire, without the danger of killing some of their own Country-Men.[15]

Mistaking a party of French Hussars for Hesse-Darmstaft dragoons, Colonel John Doyle of the 87th Foot had ridden innocently up to a French officer to enquire as to the news of the day, 'and got for answer a cut on the head'.[16] The grenadier company of the 87th, placed in houses around the town square, opened fire and drove the Hussars away, sweeping Doyle away with them. Once back behind the French lines Doyle was ignored (perhaps assumed to be a paroled prisoner), and so he bolted cross-country at the first opportunity, found his own lines and started the long journey back to England for medical recovery.

The freshly-blooded force marched from Alost to Malines on 9 July, where they joined the rest of the Duke of York's army in the afternoon, to the rejoicing of all. The duke himself had spent the last few days of June at Renaix, anxiously reading incoming reports of Moira's progress. Then, like a bomb-shell, he heard the news about Fleurus.

Fleurus

The talented and energetic Général de division Jourdan, former commander of the Armée du Nord, was given a new command in late May - the Armée de Sambre-et-Meuse. This was formed from the old Armée des Ardennes, two divisions from the left wing of the Armée de la Moselle and two divisions from the right wing of the Armée du Nord. It was a massive force, over 95,000 men, and its goal was the capture of Charleroi.

The city was invested on 12 June. Four days later a large Austro-Dutch force, some 41,000 men commanded by the Prince of Orange-Nassau, attacked out of a heavy mist at Lambusart and tumbled the French back cross the Sambre for the loss of 3,000 men. The new commander of the Armée de Sambre-et-Meuse was 'encouraged' by Representative Louis de Sainte-Just with every sort of penalty if he could not capture Charleroi immediately.[17] The city itself was only lightly defended, by a single Austrian brigade under Oberst Reinach. Jourdan smartly turned the Representative to his own devices and had Sainte-Just threaten ten types of Hell upon the head of Reinach. The garrison and its terrified commander surrendered on 26 June and all defenders were made prisoners-of-war, just as Prince Coburg approached to raise the siege.

Coburg had 32,000 infantry with 14,000 cavalry and resolved to attack there and then. His army comprised five columns, arrayed from west to east; the 1st under the Prince of Orange-Nassau on the right, then the 2nd under Prince Feldmarschalleutnant Peter von Quosdanovich, the 3rd under Feldzeugmeister Count Franz von Kaunitz-Rietberg, the 4th under Archduke Karl, and the 5th under Beaulieu on the left.

The Prince of Orange-Nassau had some success with his Dutch troops, pushing back the divisions of Anne Charles Montaigu and Guillaume Duhesme on the French left. Beaulieu's Austrians likewise pushed back the division of François Marceau on the French right. But the French centre under Général de division François Joseph Lefebvre[18] held firm between the villages of Fleurus and Ligny, and then counter-attacked. Colonel Jean Baptiste Bernadotte[19] of the 17e Demi-brigade led his men in a brilliant attack against Austrians in a wood and was awarded the rank of Général de brigade on the battlefield.[20]

Lefebvre's Chief of staff, Colonel Jean-de-Dieu Soult,[21] described it as 'fifteen hours of the most desperate fighting I ever saw in my life'.[22]

Sir Ralph Abercrombie
(National Portrait Gallery)

Charles William Ferdinand, Duke of
Brunswick-Wolfenbüttel (Courtesy
A.S.K. Brown)

Harry Calvert (National Portrait Gallery)

1 THE DUKE OF YORK'S FLANDERS CAMPAIGN

William Schaw Cathcart, 1st Earl Cathcart (National Portrait Gallery)

François Sébastien Charles Joseph de Croix, Count of Clarfait (Courtesy A.S.K. Brown)

Prince Frederick Josias of Saxe-Coburg-Saalfeld (Courtesy A.S.K. Brown)

Charles Cornwallis
(National Portrait Gallery)

Prince Frederick, Duke of York and Albany
(National Portrait Gallery)

The old walls of Bergues still surround the centre of the town. (Courtesy John Grehan)

Helvoetsluys, the site of the original landing and first HQ of the expeditionary force (Courtesy of Arjen Kranse)

Another view of the canal at Helvoetsluys (Courtesy of Arjen Kranse)

Hondschoote Windmill. (Courtesy Robert Mitchell)

Part of the walls of Valenciennes Citadelle. (Courtesy of Peter Potrowl)

Though considered only a minor fortress during the Flanders Campaign, Le Quesnoy's fortifications are hugely impressive. (Courtesy John Grehan)

The flat open country to the north of Willems (Courtesy Robert Mitchell)

The River Waal at Druten (Courtesy Robert Mitchell)

Sir James Craig (National Portrait Gallery)

Auguste Marie Henri Picot de Dampierre (Courtesy A.S.K. Brown)

The Hon. John Thomas de Burgh
(National Portrait Gallery)

Welbore Ellis Doyle (National Portrait Gallery)

David Dundas (National Portrait Gallery)

William Erskine
(National Portrait Gallery)

The Duke of York at the siege of Valenciennes (Courtesy A.S.K. Brown)

Emperor Franz II at the Battle of Tournay (Courtesy A.S.K. Brown)

Battle of Hondschoote (Courtesy A.S.K. Brown)

Wilhelm von Freytag (Courtesy A.S.K. Brown)

Henry Fox (National Portrait Gallery)

Rudolph von Hammerstein
(Courtesy A.S.K. Brown)

William Harcourt (National Portrait Gallery)

Jean-Baptiste Jourdan (Courtesy A.S.K. Brown)

Gerard Lake (National Portrait Gallery)

Francis Rawdon-Hastings, 2nd Earl of Moira (National Portrait Gallery)

Henry Phipps, 1st Earl of Mulgrave
(National Portrait Gallery)

Sir James Murray (National Portrait Gallery)

Jean-Charles Pichegru (Courtesy A.S.K. Brown)

Graf Ludwig von Wallmoden-Gimborn
(Courtesy A.S.K. Brown)

The Austrian attacks fluttered out as Coburg lost his nerve. It is quite likely that he knew of the prevailing sentiment in Vienna and realised that the Austrian Netherlands was no longer worth shedding Austrian blood over.

He retreated and established his headquarters at Braine-l'Alleud, just south of Waterloo.[23] The French lost about 5,000 men, the Coalition 1,500. Because Coburg retreated, the French claimed the victory.[24] They would claim another victory upon the same ground in 1815 – Ligny. And like Blucher in 1815, Coburg had at least retreated northwards, towards Brussels, rather than eastwards and home.

There was some hope in the duke's mind that they might establish a defensive position on the line between Waterloo and Ghent. On 28 June the road from Brussels to Nivelles was guarded by two battalions and ten squadrons established at Nivelles under the command of Generalmajor Otto; from Brussels to Charleroi by six companies and ten squadrons under the orders of Generalmajor Nauendorf, with his headquarters at Genappe. On the Coalition right, the Dutch detachment of the Hereditary Prince of Orange-Nassau (about 13,000 men) was headquartered at Roeulx. But Pichegru was marching up the river Scheldt, intent on capturing Oudenarde to the duke's left rear. Pichegru's orders were to capture Oudenarde, then wheel right to link up with Jourdan's victorious army advancing northwards from Charleroi. But then on 30 June Pichegru unaccountably retired the way he had come, without molestation. Unknown to the Coalition, the National Convention had decided upon an invasion of England, and so directed Pichegru to capture some Channel ports instead – Ostend, Nieuwpoort and Walcheren. He marched initially for Ostend, and Moira's force – marching the other way, as we have seen – managed to dodge him and made its way to Ghent, and then Alost and finally Malines to join the duke's army.

Unaware of Pichegru's change of orders, and in desperation over his allies, the duke wrote to Henry Dundas from Renaix on 28 June:

> I think it my duty to acquaint You for His Majesty's Information with the real state of affairs in this Country, as well as with the very critical Situation, in which an unfortunate Series of Events have placed me with His Majesty's Troops under My Command. From the moment that the Emperor's Determination of quitting the Army, and returning to Vienna was known, a visible Dejection has shewn itself among the Austrian Troops, but particularly among the Officers, who have publickly held a language expressive of the most anxious wish to terminate the war, even by abandoning a Country, to the preservation of which, it appears from the Emperor's own Conduct that He was at least indifferent. Before the Prince of

Waldeck was named Quarter Master General, He had Himself held a similar language, which appeared to be dictated by the known sentiments of Baron Thugut whose Creature he is.

The Suspicious to which this kind of language could not but give rise, have been in no small degree strengthened by an attentive Observation of the Conduct which the Austrians have pursued of late. Proposed Movements have been desisted from, without any sufficient Cause, Advantages have not been pushed, but have been followed by Retreats, and every pretext has been laid hold of to withdraw the Austrian Troops from West-Flanders, except the Corps under the Command of General Clerfait, which it was indispensably requisite, should remain while appearances were necessary. Every thing belonging to the Austrian Government has been sent from Brussels to Cologne and from thence to Vienna, long before the last Check, or before there was any probability of the Enemy's being able to get possession of that Town.

The unfortunate action of the 26th furnishes likewise fresh ground for suspicion as the Army retreated as soon as Intelligence was received of the Surrender of Charleroi, though had it succeeded in defeating the Enemy, Charleroi must have immediately fallen again into our hands. The situation in which I find myself with His Majesty's Troops under my Command is extremely precarious.[25]

On 1 July the duke rode the 40 miles (64km) across to Braine-l'Alleud – on the very edge of the 1815 Waterloo battlefield – for a council of war with the other Coalition commanders. It was agreed that the duke's and Clerfayt's armies should swap positions, so that the British were closer to the Channel, and the Austrians closer to the other Austrian contingents.

There were those who chose to interpret this as a concentration of armies closer to their bolt-holes in the event that the situation became even worse. To a direct question about Austrian intentions, the Archduke Karl responded: '[we] have no orders from His Majesty [the emperor] to quit the Low Countries … They feel … obliged to defend the country as long as human force will allow them, and to all extremities.'[26]

The duke had no sooner arrived back in Renaix when he received a letter from Coburg advising him that the Austrians were retiring all along the line, and that he should do the same:

> As in the present situation of affairs all retrograde movements become dangerous from the armies being so dispersed as to prevent a Cooperation of Measures, it is necessary to fix upon and to occupy a position in which we can and will remain… The following should be the distribution of the Troops:
> 1st. From Antwerp to Malines, The British Troops and all those in the pay of Great Britain, the Garrison of Antwerp included,

which place will be entirely evacuated by Austrian Troops, and the Garrison join General Clerfait's Corps.

2nd. The whole of Clerfait's Corps will be formed from Malines to Louvain behind the Dyle.

3rd. The Nine Battalions and the Light Troops both Infantry and Cavalry under Generals Kray and Froelick which formed the Corps at Tournay and at Maulde will march towards Brussels, taking with them the weak Garrison of that place, then through Louvain, and leaving that place to the right will post themselves behind the Dyle.

4th. The Corps at present under the Command of the Hereditary Prince of Orange will march in two Columns behind the Dyle, and will form so as to leave Wavre to the right of it. The left Column may proceed through Brussels, the right to Mont St. Jean from whence they can march to their destination.

5th. On the day that these Movements take place, the Corps which His Serene Highness the Prince of Coburg commands in person will march from Mont St. Jean to Wavre, the next day it must join Lieutenant General Quosdanowich and proceed to Gembloux whilst Lieutenant General Beaulieu marches to Boissieres and to the Forest of Mehaigne. The Corps at Nivelles and Gemappes must remain there as long as they are necessary to cover these movements and afterwards join the principal Corps.[27]

Tournai, Oudenarde, Ghent and Mons had all just fallen to the French; only Valenciennes, Le Quesnoy and Condé remained in Coalition hands.[28] Ostend had been evacuated but a Coalition garrison still held Nieuwpoort. In accordance with Coburg's orders, the British fell back to Grammont on 3 July and then to Lombeke on the 4th; Ghent was evacuated and immediately occupied by the French.

The Prince of Orange-Nassau with a 17,000-man Austro-Dutch force fought a failed minor action against a portion of Armée de Sambre-et-Meuse (Lefebvre's and Morlot's division plus Dubois' cavalry reserve, 22,000 men) at Mont St Jean on 6 July. Of the action, Général de brigade Jean Soult later wrote:

> The divisions of Hatry and Mayer attacked Beaulieu in Sombreffe in vain. Championnet fought all day to take Marbais. Morlot advanced well to Genappe from Quatre-Bras. It was Kleber who led the left wing, namely the divisions of Duhesme, Lefebvre and Dubois, from Nivelles upon Braine-la-Leud (sic) and Mont-Saint-Jean. An Austrian corps was assembled there with the Dutch of the Prince of Orange. These two corps made a good show for a few hours and even pushed back a charge from the cavalry of Dubois, as well as the attack of General Morlot, who was on their left. But Lefebvre having arrived with his valiant vanguard, overthrew everything in an instant; the position was taken, and the Prince of

Orange was forced to retire by Waterloo to reach Brussels, after having experienced many losses.[29]

The Prince of Hesse-Philipstadt lost his life in a charge against General Dubois, the third in his family to die in this war. The French ended the day camped in and around the chateau of Hougoumont. They called the action the battle of Mont St Jean, a place-name that was soon forgotten to history - until 1815.

Coburg and the Prince of Orange-Nassau retreated northwards through Brussels, then eastwards through Wavre to Ramillies.[30] But there it was, in plain view; the Austrians were retreating eastwards, out of the Austrian Netherlands and in the direction of home. 'The fate of this wretched country is at length decided,' Harry Calvert wrote to his sister, 'and where are we to stop, who will venture to say?'[31] The duke went into a black mood and penned a vicious letter to Coburg on 7 July:

> I am at length driven to the necessity of openly stating to Your Serene Highness that the opinion which the British nation must have on the subject cannot be other than we are betrayed and sold to the enemy.[32]

The duke's mood was only matched by the weather:

> Just at the close of day there came on the most tremendous storm of Thunder, Lightning, and Rain, that the oldest Man there remembered ... Our Commander, fearful of the Bayonets attracting the Lightning, gave orders for them to be unfixed, and the Men to march with their Arms secured; which is carrying them under the arm, with the muzzle pointing to the ground, and thereby protecting from the wet, both priming and charge. In this very dreadful weather, and drenched condition, we continued our march the whole night ... It may be necessary to observe, that to every Regiment of Foot, are attached two light Brass Six-pounders, to each of which belong twelve Artillery-Men, and three Horses with their drivers; besides an Ammunition Waggon and Tumbril, to each Regiment, which were very heavily laden.[33]

The duke ordered the retreat to continue in accordance with his orders, in the direction of Malines and Antwerp. The crestfallen Lord Cornwallis, returned to the army after the disappointing conclusion to his negotiations with the Prussians, he must have been glad he had, as it were, dodged a bullet – by not being command of the army in Flanders. He sailed home from Antwerp on 10 July. 'Cornwallis goes to England without a plan,' Harcourt wrote, 'and declares he knows not what can be done. He is miserable and says the provoking part is that the Austrians have fled from the shadows and that this campaign is absolutely given away – *given*, not lost.'[34]

After the juncture with Lord Moira's force near Malines on 9 July, Major General David Dundas was appointed commander-in-chief of forces at Antwerp and on the left bank of the Scheldt. But the appearance of Moira's men did little to lift spirits. 'Explain to me the reason of the recruits joining the army without arms or any appointments necessary for soldiers,' Harry Calvert wrote to his friend Colonel Dalrymple. 'I am often asked the question and can't resolve it.'[35] Then a new problem was discovered. Lord Moira's local rank of lieutenant general made him senior to some of the existing officers of the army to whom he had to report.[36] Therefore he had to return home.[37]

This was British army block-headed adherence to rank and custom at its worst, and it deprived the force of a fine and popular commander. Lieutenant General Abercrombie (confirmed in his new rank on 25 April 1794) assumed command of Moira's old corps.[38]

The Duke of York took the opportunity to re-organise the entire army. He now had nine infantry brigades, five cavalry brigades and five companies of artillery, some 36,000 men all told. Whilst hardly goliath in size it was nonetheless a far cry from the tiny force he commanded in March 1793.

So reorganised, the British adopted a defensive line from Antwerp to Malines, on the western flank of the Dutch, who held the line to Louvain. The Austrians then continued the line through Tirlemont and Lander, to Liége. Clerfayt was at Namur, the Prince of Orange-Nassau at Louvain, Prince Coburg at Tirlement, Wallmoden at Lierre.

Pichegru re-occupied Brussels on 10 July in triumph but did not seriously engage the Coalition line in any numbers; he was under orders to relieve Valenciennes, Le Quesnoy and Condé.[39] Then the Dutch retired from Louvain and Malines fell to a small French brigade after a feeble defence. On 13 July the French attempted to cross the river Nethe, where General Wallmoden's Hanoverians beat them back for the loss of fourteen men. The French tried the same tactics again the following day at Walheim, but a British brigade (12th, 38th and 44th Foot) and a six-gun battery barred their passage.

The duke was ill in the middle of July and so could not attend yet another conference at Prince Coburg's headquarters. It was not until 20 July that he heard the outcome; that a complete separation of the two armies had been agreed upon, and that the prince – without any communication - was marching his army eastwards to Maastricht. The duke was indignant. His left flank was completely exposed. He had no choice but to fall back again, this time into the United Provinces. Antwerp was evacuated on 23 July, and the retreat reached Rosendael, near Bergen-op-Zoom, about 22 miles (35km) north of Antwerp, in the morning of 25 July. There, the duke learned that Antwerp had fallen.

Nine 'white cockade' French émigré battalions, enlisted from French royalists, entered British service at that time, as did Baron Hompesch's Hussars, three squadrons of Germans commanded by French royalist officers.[40] The Baron also provided two companies of green-coated and rifle-armed Chasseurs (Jägers). Whilst in camp two additional British battalions, freshly arrived from Jersey, marched into camp – Lieutenant Colonel Lord Newark's 3rd Foot (the Buffs) and Lieutenant Colonel John Leveson-Gowers's 63rd Foot, 1,600 men in all. They were a welcome addition, for the constant retreating had played a serious effect upon British morale. The duke was forced to issue a general order on 24 July:

> It is with the utmost concern that H.R.H. the Commander-in-Chief has perceived the very scandalous height to which plundering and marauding of every species have gotten in the army under his command ... H.R.H. will put in arrest the first officer commanding a regiment in which any disobedience or inattention to orders is perceived.[41]

His Adjutant-General Craig was more candid in a private letter written to Colonel Hew Dalrymple at Whitehall:

> That we have plundered the whole country is unquestionable; that we are the most undisciplined, the most ignorant, the worst provided army that ever took the field is equally certain; but we are not to blame for it ... there is not a young man in the Army that cares one farthing whether his commanding officer, the brigadier or the commander-in-chief approves his conduct or not. His promotion depends not on their smiles or frowns. His friends (i.e. family) can give him a thousand pounds with which to go to the auction rooms in Charles Street and in a fortnight he becomes a captain. Out of fifteen regiments of cavalry and twenty-six of infantry which we have here, twenty-one are commanded literally by boys or idiots ... we do not know how to post a picquet or instruct a sentinel in his duty; and as to moving, God forbid that we should attempt it within three miles of an enemy.[42]

By August the super-confident French were facing the disheartened and dishevelled Dutch on their left, the 'most undisciplined, most ignorant, worst provided' British in the centre, and the reluctant and retiring Austrians on their right. For by this time the Austrians had completely separated from their Coalition partners. The duke was free to fight the coming campaign without their confining theories concerning cordons and general air of lethargy. But he still had the Dutch as allies – for better or worse.

Chapter 15

Defending the United Provinces

Farewell to the Austrian Netherlands
The isolated garrison of Nieuwpoort had been left far behind. It was held for the Coalition by 2,000 Hanoverians and around 500 French émigrés. As the Duke of York retreated out of Belgium, it was inevitable that Nieuwpoort would be exposed to a French siege as part of Pichegru's orders to establish French coastal bases.

The Duke of York wrote to Henry Dundas to ask what he should do with Nieuwpoort, and to warn him not to leave the émigrés exposed to capture. This letter crossed with one of 3 July from Dundas to General Diepenbroick, the commander at Nieuwpoort, in which he promised to help with any evacuation, but made it clear that he wanted to hold the port if at all possible.

Général de division Moreau sent a brigade under Général de brigade Vandamme to attack the port, and they arrived outside Nieuwpoort on 6 July. The town was defended by fifty-four Austrian artillerymen, twenty-seven Hanoverian artillerymen, 1,736 infantrymen of the 5. and 10.Infanterie-Regiments, 240 Loyal Emigrants, thirty-seven British troops and various volunteer companies. After a siege lasting two weeks, the garrison was forced to surrender on 18 July. Whilst the 1,700 Hanoverians were taken prisoner, the émigrés were forced into the ditch outside the fort and executed.[1] The French then moved east to besiege Sluys. Despite the lack of mercy shown to captured émigrés, cordial off-duty relations existed between the British and French troops:

> Whatever enmity may be in the hearts of the rulers of nations or conductors of war against each other, there seems to be little animosity between individuals of the different armies. Since the 17th the advanced posts of the French army have been established on one side of the river Neethe, and ours on the other; the river

is about thirty or forty paces wide; the cannon are planted on both sides ready for attack or defence; yet the men walk about, or carelessly lay on the bank on each side, and frequently converse with each other. Several of the French have stript and swam over to our men, bringing with them gin and other liquors, and after drinking with each other with the utmost frankness and cordiality, swim back again to their posts. This familiarity was, however, strictly forbidden as soon as known.[2]

The frontier of the United Provinces was defended by five fortresses; Bergen-op-Zoom, Breda, Bois-le-Duc, Grave and Nijmegen. The first four were more-or-less in a straight line running from south-west to north-east, all about 20 miles (32km) apart, whilst Nijmegen was located to the north somewhat and only about 7 miles (11km) from Grave. The duke established his headquarters at Rosendael and dispersed his army between Bergen-op-Zoom and Breda, securing the Channel end of the defensive line. The Dutch army, less immediately threatened by the likely advance of the French, secured the line between Breda and Bois-le-Duc. The country between the latter place and Nijmegen was left relatively undefended. That there were too few men for this length of front line was patently clear to Adjutant-General James Craig:

> The moment the Austrians retire over the Rhine the Frenchmen have sufficient force to attempt all three passages at once [i.e. Bergen-op-Zoom, Breda and east of Bois-le-Duc] and it will be utterly impossible for us to resist them.[3]

The duke eventually came around to this viewpoint and realised that he had accidentally fallen into the Imperial way of thinking, all penny-packets of troops and a cordon system. So, he proposed a new plan to the stadtholder and the Hereditary Prince of Orange-Nassau at a conference held in Breda on 27 July, which involved entrusting the fortresses to the Dutch, whilst his own army formed a concentrated central reserve. His intended position was on the line of the River Aa between Bois-le-Duc and a marshy area south of Nijmegen known as the Marais de Peel.[4] But the prince was worried this placed the British too far away from Bergen, and therefore the duke agreed to march no farther than Oosterhout, 8 miles (13km) north of Breda-for now.

The British tents were struck at 01.00 hours on the morning of 4 August and the army marched towards Breda, and in the afternoon camped on a plain near Osterhout. Around them they could see the remains of redoubts and entrenchments which had been erected in the time of the Duke of Marlborough. The weather had turned very hot and dry, almost Mediterranean in aspect. The Brigade of Guards had experienced a pleasant march:

> The country through which we passed this day, is not exceeded in culture or fertility by any we have yet seen. Numberless little hamlets and cottages, shaded with verdant groves, with fields or meadows between, filled with all the luxuriance of nature's bounty, among which are great quantities of hops. The peasants of both sexes were all busily employed, some reaping, others mowing, all in their several employments; the children homely clad, but strong and hearty, diverting themselves with innocent amusements, form a most complete and finished picture of rural industry, innocence, and happiness. The weather has been exceeding hot yesterday and to-day, and as we march always in the heat of the day it is very fatiguing for troops carrying so much luggage as the British generally do.[5]

The French were busy reducing the coastal fortresses in Belgium and their march north must wait a few more weeks. In the short lull the the British soldiery turned sightseers. Corporal Brown noticed some alarming local customs in Breda:

> On that part of the common nearest Breda are a great number of criminals hung in chains, four of whom have been lately executed, one broke upon the wheel, and three hung. One was chained up alive to a high post resembling a crucifix; one chain goes round under his arms, one round his loins, and a third round his ancles [sic]; and in that posture it is said that he lived three days, and part of the fourth. I could not learn to any degree of certainty the several crimes of these men. There are also the remains of a great many more unfortunate wretches scattered up and down this Golgotha; as also the fragments of several wheels and instruments of torture. Our soldiers were ordered to take down the carcases and bury them, which they did, and burnt the gallows, posts, &c. to which they had been suspended.[6]

The approach of the French did not necessarily excite universal approbation in the United Provinces. Those of the upper classes felt themselves gravely threatened:

> The people of property... left Breda, taking with them all their valuables into the interior parts of Holland, to secure them, if possible, from the rapacity of the republican army; so great was the panic struck into the minds of the people by French plunder and fraternization, that they fled with the utmost precipitation, taking with them their wives and families, and whatever valuable effects they could, though many seemed quite at a loss where

to find an asylum from plunder or the guillotine, and would frequently express a wish to live in 'happy England'. For it was now well known that the French had entirely changed their conduct with their success; after planting their tree of liberty, they treated those to whom they had just given their liberty, as a conquered people, and imposed the most heavy contributions, under pain of the guillotine, and their exactions they levied with the most summary military execution.[7]

A new country meant new monetary systems, and the one in which the British found themselves did not work to their advantage:

The army being now in Holland, it is necessary that they should be informed that the money they now have diminishes in its value, and that the weights and measures increase almost in an equal degree. The French crown, which was paid five shillings, and for which they received sixty-five sous and one leier in Brabant, in Flanders, passes only for fifty-six in Holland; this deficiency will be made up to them in the purchase of bread and butcher's meat.[8]

Five shillings was a small fortune to a private. Ten pounds was a small fortune to a subaltern. Forty pounds per head may not sound a lot today, but it too must have seemed an absolute fortune when levied upon ten general officers to pay for a grand dinner to celebrate the duke's thirty-first birthday on 16 August. Over 150 guests attended and for a few hours the war might have been a million miles away. Things were not quite so swell in the lower ranks, where army punishments constantly reminded the men about the immediacy of the war:

At 8 a.m. in the morning the whole of the British army assembled in front of the encampment to see a soldier (belonging to the 8th Light Dragoons) shot for mutiny, the army was drawn up in two lines - the prisoner after being conducted along the first line under a strong escort (of Horse and Foot) was taken to a small eminence in front of both lines (whereas gravel was already made) when after a few minutes in prayer, he gave the signal and met his fate with a calm resignation - he was accompanied to the place of execution by his brother, a private soldier in the same regiment, this unfortunate youth was no more than 16 years of age.[9]

With no dangers immediately present, the duke re-organised his army again, primarily due to a lack of general officers for brigade commanders, but also because reinforcements had arrived. Major General Henry Phipps (better known as Lord Mulgrave) had landed at Flushing, in advance of a brigade despatched from England for the defence of Zealand. His troops arrived on 26 August - the 31st (Huntingdonshire), 34th (Cumberland), 79th (Cameronian Volunteers), 84th (York and Lancaster) and 85th Regiments of Foot. He was able to create four 'corps' (although the term was not then used to describe a permanent formation) under Hammerstein, Wallmoden, Erskine and Abercrombie. Two fresh batteries of Hessen-Cassel artillery had also arrived with twenty guns, including eight 12-pounders.[10]

On 27 July the duke issued an interesting order concerning the formation of his infantry battalions on the battlefield, based upon contemporary Austrian practice and perhaps influenced by his uncertainty over the quality of the newly-arrived regiments in particular:

> His Royal Highness the Commander-in-Chief orders the formations of the battalions of infantry of the army under his command to be in three ranks, but with the following regulations, which are at all times to be observed:
>
> When the battalion forms for action, the third rank is instantly to be formed into two divisions, and two ranks, each under the command of an officer. When the army or corps to which the battalion belongs is in two lines, those divisions will form on the rear of the centre of each wing of their battalions at the distance of fifty paces. When there is no second line, the two divisions joined together, a captain is appointed to the command of them; and being then in one body, it forms a reserve each to its own battalion, at 200 paces in the rear of the centre; in this manner these divisions form a reserve or second line, which may be used either in lengthening the first line by being carried to either flank, or as a corps-de-reserve to strengthen any point may be necessary.[11]

These instructions were designed to ensure that each battalion always had a central reserve. Given that battalion commanders tended to put their most reliable men in the third (i.e. rear) rank (to act as both back-stop and encouragement) this proposal ensured that the best men were positioned to 'strengthen any point as may be necessary'. The nett result was British battalions fighting in two-deep line (rather than the Continental three-deep lines) but for different reasons than the well-known two-deep line insisted upon by Wellington.

Coalition intelligence-gathering throughout the campaign was, on the whole, poor. Glances over to the 'other side of the hill' were few and far between. The fluid state of the French command structure and frequent re-organisation of the French armies did not help; but the Coalition could expect little information from inhabitants along the Franco-Belgian frontier, unless they happened to be royalists. Occasionally however, they received intelligence from deserters (probably royalist sympathisers) worth its weight in gold, as Harry Calvert recorded:

> An officer, who deserted from the enemy's 9th Regiment of Hussars, informs us that the force of the enemy's armies of the north, including those of the Ardennes and the Moselle, amounts to 240,000 men, which, according to his account, are disposed of in the following manner: 50,000 are engaged in the investment of the towns of Valenciennes, Le Quesnoy and Condé; 20,000 are employed at Nieuport and Ostend, or quartered in different parts of the Netherlands. Of the remaining 170,000, 60,000 are in the environs of Antwerp, of which 2000 are advanced towards Rosendael, but the gros of the army is encamped about a league on the other side of Antwerp, on the road to Malines. The cavalry of this corps he does not estimate at more than 3500, and they are generally very badly mounted; the chief reliance of their army is on their artillery, which is numerous, well-appointed, and ably served.[12]

In reality, the French armies now facing the northern frontier were the old foe l'Armée du Nord and the new Armée de Sambre-et-Meuse. Pichegru commanded Armée du Nord with six divisions (Souham, Moreau, Lemaire, Despeaux, Bonnaud and Delmas) and a large artillery park. Each division had anywhere from one to three large brigades, each brigade typically having six to eight infantry battalions, one or two cavalry regiments, and an artillery company. Each battalion had attached two 'battalion guns' (typically 4-pounders) served by regimental gunner volunteers.[13] It's paper strength on 19 July was 77,000 men with 232 cannon. Jourdan commanded Armée de Sambre-et-Meuse, a massive formation with eleven divisions, 92,000 men and nearly 300 cannon. L'Armée de la Moselle (farther to the east) was commanded by Jean René Moreaux, four divisions with 48,000 men and 109 cannon.[14] In all the 217,000 men available in the theatre was not a far cry from the deserter's stated 240,000; but what was really telling was the number of French artillery pieces (over 600) compared to the duke's meagre 36,000 men and 117 cannon.[15]

Pichegru's l'Armée du Nord remained the main threat to the Anglo-Dutch. Le Quesnoy fell to them on 16 August. With a major obstacle in his rear now gone, the way was now clear for Pichegru to advance into the United Provinces. Three days later a picquet of fifty French hussars was surprised by the Black Hussars (in Dutch service) after which two Frenchmen deserted and reported that Pichegru was a day's march away.[16]

In 24 August a strong force of 1,000 Coalition cavalry fanned out on patrol to gather intelligence about the whereabouts of Pichegru. The Hanoverians under Oberstleutnant Linsingen set an ambuscade for

700 French cavalry which was ruined after a serjeant of the 16th Light Dragoons deserted to the enemy and gave away the plan. That same day a French deserter rode in and reported that an attack was imminent, so the entire British army stood to their arms for two days. Spying a French patrol, fourteen squadrons of Coalition cavalry advanced to their front on 26 August, but no attack was directed at the British.[17]

The only activity that day was a partial attack at Chaem, Ryberg and Galder, to cover the main French assault on Breda. On 27 August Harry Calvert wrote in his diary, 'something is in agitation in the enemy's camp. Whether the blow is to be struck at us or at the Prince of Cobourg, tomorrow or next day will probably decide.' Everyone was jittery. Four cavalry regiments were ordered to a plain in front of Gilze where they remained on patrol until 16.00 hours - 'expecting a visit from the French but on their not making their appearance, we returned to camp but were obliged to keep in readiness to turn out at a moment's notice.'[18]

Harry Calvert's presentiment was correct:

> August 28 — The enemy made a general attack on the outposts. Before noon, they carried and established themselves at the post of Strybeck. From the force they showed, it appeared to be their intention to attack our camp; and from the direction of their columns, it was evidently their plan to turn our left.[19]

This was much farther east than the duke thought likely and alarmed him considerably:

> In the evening, his Royal Highness assembled a council of war, where it was unanimously agreed that, as the object of the position of Ousterhout — namely, giving time to the Dutch to put Breda and Gertruydenberg in a state of defence, was accomplished, it would be imprudent to risk an action in the position, and give to the enemy the possibility of cutting our communication with Bois-le-Duc. The army marched at night, having been previously joined by the Hessians, and the next day, in the afternoon, encamped with their right to the village of Giersberge.[20]

The conclusion reached was that the army must retire again, behind the line of the River Aa. The army marched once more the next morning, and the headquarters moved to Berlikum, the bulk of the army being located between Bois-le-Duc and the Marais de Peel to the east.

The Austrians had by this time reached Maestricht, to all intents and purposes within a whisker of leaving the United Provinces. Prince Coburg had alienated all those in the Austrian Netherlands with any shred of loyalty to the empire by issuing an inflammatory proclamation, which read in part:

> Inexhaustible resources of France, its innumerable cohorts, the inactivity of a blinded people (the Belgians), who would not listen to the paternal voice of their good prince, and the secret practices of some of their ambitious representatives, are the causes which have caused the Imperial armies to retreat.[21]

The proclamation then proceeded to threaten to plunder the country before leaving it, on the grounds of withdrawing whatever the enemy might find for subsistence. Insofar as keeping Austria in the war, military persuasion had failed; accordingly, William Pitt resorted to political means. He sent Thomas Grenville and Lord Spencer to Vienna to plead for the Austrians to resume their efforts and to co-operate more closely with the British. Their appeals fell on deaf ears but did have some success in that Prince Coburg was relieved of the supreme command; command then devolved upon Clerfayt as the next most senior, there being no better candidate in sight. On the last day of August this news arrived at the duke's headquarters. By this stage the Austrians were so far away as to make the news feel irrelevant, and it excited little curiosity in the British camp.

Prince Coburg bade farewell to his troops on the Maas on 11 September and rode home to Coburg. Such was the depressed mood in the German states that his home town did not even cheer him on his arrival six days later. He resigned from the army and built himself a palace with lavish gardens (the Bürglaß-Schlösschen) where he lived out the remaining twenty years of his life.[22]

But the change in command created difficulties – the duke out-ranked Clerfayt, but the Austrians would not assent to giving the Englishman command over their troops. Then Lord Cornwallis, recently back in England, announced that he would – with reluctance – be prepared to assume the supreme command. The king acidly advised that he would not withhold his consent to this, but observed that: 'I own, in my Son's place, I should beg to allow to return home if the command is given to Lord Cornwallis.'[23] The duke's own feelings on the matter were plain. 'Should His Majesty be pleased to appoint Lord Cornwallis to the command, as is now proposed, I trust that His Majesty will graciously consent to my request to my permission to return to England.'[24] The machinations in the halls of power would continue for some weeks yet, while the campaign must still be decided one way or the other.

Picquets were posted at advanced posts along the River Dommel, the largest of which was at the little village of Boxtel, about 11 miles (18km) north of Eindhoven.

Boxtel

Boxtel

Général de division Pichegru advanced north from Hoogstaeten with 68,000 men at the start of September as if he was about to threaten Breda. Then he turned north-east, and advanced towards the British outpost at Boxtel, whilst a secondary force manoeuvred south-east to capture Eindhoven. The new Imperial commander Clerfayt, falling back on the Rhine, and therefore out of touch with goings-on in the United Provinces, suggested a general advance to re-capture Antwerp.

The duke called another council of war on 1 September with the Prince of Orange-Nassau and Beaulieu (representing the Austrians) to consider this idea. The duke was clearly excited with the idea of fighting alongside the Austrians once again, but the unwelcome news of the loss of Valenciennes (27 August) and Condé (29 August) squashed any hopes for a new offensive. Adjutant-General Craig, often pessimistic but usually pragmatic, had a difference of opinion with his chief, writing that: 'I could but help differing from His Royal Highness in one respect, which is being able to take up our winter quarters in Brabant and Flanders.'[25]

The Coalition front line along the river Dommel, nearly 9 miles (14km) long, was only very thinly defended. The region from Bois-le-Duc to Boxtel was occupied by the Hessen-Darmstadt brigade, British infantry and light dragoons, and six squadrons of emigrants. In and near Olland there were Hanoverians and Hessen-Cassel squadrons, one Hanoverian Grenadier-Bataillon and a Hessen-Cassel Fusilier-Bataillon; and at Sint-Oedenrode, where Generalmajor Hammerstein had his headquarters, ten squadrons of British and Hanoverian Dragoons, a Hanoverian Grenadier-Bataillon and the Hessen-Cassel Jäger-Bataillon, with a Hanoverian horse battery. From Breugel to Gerven, one battalion of emigres, two squadrons, one company of jägers and a horse battery of Hanoverian troops were posted. The remainder of the river chain, extending from Gerwen through Helmond to Back, was occupied by penny-packets of Hanoverians, and eight squadrons plus one battalion of émigrés under Generalmajor Linsingen. All of the infantry battalions were below half-strength. At no point existed any kind of defence in depth. Engineers dismantled most of the bridges over the Dommel, with the exception of those at Sint-Oedenrode. The locks at water mills were also removed so that the lowlands around Bois-le-Duc flooded. One of the few crossing places left across the Dommel was at Boxtel.

French troops clashed with Coalition outposts at Tilburg, Poppel, Bladel and Eersel on 7 September. Five days later a Hessen-Darmstadt patrol riding from Boxtel captured two French officers, who were discovered to belong to the Etat-Major (General Staff), and therefore valuable sources of information. Harry Calvert:

> The report they make is as follows: The army under General Pichegru's immediate orders is divided into four columns, of which one, consisting of about 8,000 or 10,000 men, is left to keep the garrison of Breda in check. Pichegru was yesterday in march with the other three, and was expected to take his headquarters at Oosterwyk last night: this force they estimate at about 50,000 men. He does not appear to be so well provided with artillery as their armies usually are, but he has a heavy train at Malines. The corps engaged in the reduction of Valenciennes and Condé consisted of nearly 50,000 men. They are marching in three divisions, two of which are destined to act on the Meuse, and one is expected very shortly to join Pichegru. The prisoners assure us that Pichegru's orders to attack his Royal Highness are positive.[26]

The French advance was improvised as new information came to hand. Instead of going straight to Fort Isabella near Vught, Bois-le-Duc was approached by a wide flanking movement to the east. Boxtel, Schijndel, Berlicum and Heeswijk were therefore important strategic points in the French advance. And Boxtel was the only practicable river crossing.

The duke knew that an attack would surely come; but not where. He guessed that it would come from Helmond in the south. But that is the one direction the French eschewed. They approached Boxtel from the west via Tilburg, Haaren and Esch, from the south via Best and from the southeast via Son, Wolfswinkel and Sint-Oedenrode. The three converged and attacked Boxtel at 14.00 hours in the afternoon of 14 September, with a division-sized force commanded by Général de division Antoine Guillaume Delmas in the van.[27] The village was defended by a brigade of Hessen-Darmstadt troops under Generalmajor Georg Emil von Düring:

> When the French approached Boxtel on the morning of the 14th, Generalmajor von Düring, who had gathered there scarcely 1,684 men, were set up in the following manner: The Hessen-Darmstadt and Hompesch Jägers, assisted by detachments of the two infantry battalions, occupied the embankment of the village with all the entrances, and had taken over Dommel-Waart with some advanced-guards. Behind each of the two bridges, over which the two roads leading to Oirschot and Eyndhoven run, two Hessen-Darmstadt guns were placted (under cover of a company), but the rest of the two line battalions were placed in reserve in the centre of the village. Of the cavalry a number of detachments were sent on

the roads leading to the enemy on the other side of the Dommel, but the remainder were behind.[28]

The French attack concentrated on the two vital bridges over the River Dommel, where the Hompesch Jägers were driven back across towards the Stapelen Castle. The Hessen-Darmstadt infantry kept the French at bay for several hours whilst Engineers destroyed the bridges. But at 16.00 hours another French division under Despeaux arrived and threatened the Coalition left flank. A detachment of 8e Hussards found a ford and rode around behind the defenders, taking many prisoners and forcing the remainder to flee. The defenders set fire to the mediaeval Barrier House on their route northwards out of town to slow the French pursuit. They fell back to Sint-Michielsgestel and then Middelrode on the River Aa, having lost nearly 750 men in the Hessen-Damstadt brigade alone.[29] Some 204 French émigrés serving with the Hompesch Jägers were rounded up and immediately executed.

The Hessians sensed that war-weariness was affecting the performance of the high command:

> On the 14th ... the Duke was unable to escape from his lethargic apathy. All that happened was due to the command of the Hessen-Darmstadt officer commanding Boxtel, Oberst von Werner in Saint Oedenrode, to which two squadrons of English dragoons and a half-riding battery were sent to defend the town to the utmost, and small detachments posted on the crossings over the Aa in front of the main army were instructed to assert their positions to the last man... Although the enemy still attacked Boxtel's post most vividly on the same afternoon, and the [Hessians] were only able to assert themselves with great difficulty, the Duke was unable to take either the outpost line from the Dommel back or provide from the main position a proper corps in support of those outposts. Instead, two squadrons of Prince Frederick and two squadrons of Hanoverian Dragoons were detached to Saint Oedenrode and one English battalion to Vucht, which, however, was stopped at Boxtel, as the bridge of St. Michael's had meanwhile been burned down.[30]

The sleepy men of the Reserve were awakened at about 22.30 hours and ordered under arms. Lieutenant General Abercrombie's Reserve comprised the best troops available; the Brigade of Guards, the light dragoons and the 3rd Infantry Brigade, and he was given orders to retake Boxtel.[31] Three Hanoverian grenadier battalions and a company of Jägers accompanied them.

The already-tired men marched from the Reserve camp (between Dinther and Uden) at 23.00 hours and stopped at 02.00 hours not having covered many miles, at which point Abercrombie sent a messenger to headquarters with the intelligence that Hammerstein had evacuated Sint-Oedenrode, and therefore the French might get behind and cut off any force marching to Boxtel. The Duke replied that Abercrombie must consult with Hammerstein and act according to his directions.

The march resumed at 05.00 hours and they passed through Schijndel, where the 42nd Highlanders were left as a reserve. The flanks of the column were protected by the Coldstream Guards on the south side and the 12th Foot with a detachment of the 1st (Royal) Dragoons in Sint-Michielsgestel on the north side. The light dragoons of Major General Richard Vyse led the advance. As the column approached a forested area between Hermalen and Langenberg (about 3 miles or 5km west of Schijndel) the light dragoons encountered the advanced elements of Delmas' division just after sunrise. This was in fact a brigade commanded by the Belgian-born Général de brigade David Hendrik Chassé.[32] Boxtel was still two-and-a-half miles (4km) away to the west but was clearly in French hands. The ever-cautious Abercrombie made a reconnaissance and believed he had run into Pichegru's main force, so he sent an aide to the duke to seek further instruction.[33]

The duke ordered him to push on, but to be prudent. Captain Roger Morris of the Coldstream Guards recorded the initial skirmishes with the French:

> We formed our line in a Lane leading out to the Heath – Wood & Enclosures in our Front, & at no great distance on our Right Flank – we advanced our 2 Batt'n guns & a 12 P'r (of which 2 accompanied us, & 2 Howitzers, but the latter were left in Moddeven) & fired some shot into the wood, in front, in which we saw the French Rifle men, who fire many ineffective shots at us – they were soon driven off, as was a French Howitzer placed at the Corner of the Wood. A Large body of French Cavalry were soon on the Plain who attracted several Shot from us, which I believe did them little mischief. While we were occupied with them, the Enemy brought a Gun to their Right, which (from a Masqued situation) they made to bear upon Our Battalion.[34]

Lieutenant & captain George Bristow's company of the 1st Foot Guards was sent forward to skirmish, supported by light companies of the 33rd and 44th Foot and cavalry on the flanks. Abercrombie observed what he thought were large quantities of chasseurs protecting them and ordered the recall. But Captain Bristow and his men were too far advanced and were cut off and taken prisoner in the confusion. It was at this point Abercrombie decided that the prudent thing to do would be to retreat, which he did having lost thirty men to skirmishing. The French force immediately in front of him was in fact far inferior to Abercombie's, both in numbers and quality, and a determined attack upon them would surely have been successful.[35] When detachments from the French 3e and 8e Régiments de Hussards (commanded by Chassé) turned to follow the British, the retreat threatened to turn into a rout, but the situation was saved by the 1st Foot Guards and 33rd Foot, who formed up in line and fired disciplined volleys which drove back the French hussars:

> When he (Sherbrooke) had obtained the rank of Lt-Col., he served under the Duke of York in Flanders, and during this unfortunate and memorable retreat, the 33rd was appointed to cover it... Two regiments of French Cavalry were seen coming down with the intention of charging the 33rd... Col. Sherbrooke faced his Regt to the rear and gave the word 33rd 'Steady'. In this awful crisis not a man moved, but with determined fortitude they awaited the attack. When the first French Regt. was within 50 yards the command was given to Fire!'- the steady coolness of the men gave it full effect... men and horses were precipitated to the ground – those who were neither unhorsed nor wounded, halted and attempted to retreat, but before they had gained a very short distance a second volley completed the work of destruction and the whole Regt. lay stretched on the ground. The second Regt witnessing the dreadful over-throw faced about and were seen no more.[36]

The British retired to Schijndel, where the 42nd Highlanders joined the light dragoons as the rearguard, then marched eastwards back to the Reserve camp. The French did not pursue past Schijndel, but a French cavalry patrol stumbled upon a company of the 12th Foot at Voet (just north of Schijndel) and captured them wholesale. Abercrombie returned to safety by 14.00 hours with the loss of ninety men, including forty-nine prisoners-of-war taken from the 12th Foot, along with two cannon and three officers.[37]

Boxtel was the low-water mark for the British forces in Flanders. Two French divisions sent to an obscure village on a river bend - with the singular aim of securing a crossing point - had blunted the best British brigades and forced the entire British army to fall back 'one more river'. The duke did not provide sufficient support to Hammerstein's outposts at Dommel, then neither he nor Abercrombie were aggressive enough in the face of the small French column.[38] Abercrombie retired quickly at Schijndel after offering little resistance.

The duke was so spooked he believed that he could no longer hold the line of the Aa. It probably did not help that William Windham, the Secretary at War, was present at the conference when retreat was decided; and recorded that: 'I certainly took all pains to make him [the duke] adopt that resolution [to retreat].'[39]

It would not have helped that Windham was, at the time, one of the leading proponents for a change in the command.[40] From a letter Windham later drafted, we learn that the duke was opposed to a retreat but allowed himself to be talked into it by Abercrombie, Craig and Windham.[41] He had lost all confidence in his own decision-making and had descended to the same defeatism as the Austrians. His official despatch home took all the blame upon himself. His days as commander-in-chief were now numbered.

Chapter 16

Every Disgrace and Misfortune

Nijmegen

The same defeatism was seeping down to all levels. The duke was not happy with the state of discipline of the army:

> In order to put a stop to that scandalous and too prevalent practice of plundering, his Royal Highness gave this day in public orders a pointed address to the officers of the army, and another caution to the men; at the same time empowering the Provost to execute on the spot any one whom he might detect in the commission of that act of disobedience.[1]

The army retreated towards Grave in the afternoon of 15 September. The Hessen-Cassel units, as always the most disciplined of the duke's troops, had by this time a dim view of their British allies:

> As usual, there was a great deal of disorder on this march, with not only a great number of English baggage and pack-horses wandering everywhere, clogging the narrow roads in the villages, but also, favoured by the darkness of the night, many English soldiers rank and file left and allowed themselves in every town the grossest debauchery. Thus, this retreat once again provided the very picture of an army that was on the run for defeat; it was not until the 16th that those stragglers found themselves back in the camp... The combined loss of the army, with the exception of a few left on guard, amounted to a total of 1,200 men killed, wounded, and imprisoned, and the Hessen-Darmstadt brigade had lost proportionately the most.[2]

After spending two nights in the open, the force crossed a bridge of boats constructed under the supervision of the Royal Engineers and took up a position on the River Meuse, with the duke's headquarters at Wijchen. Harry Calvert was despatched off to the east to find Clerfayt, and the 37th Foot under the command of Major Joseph Baird and some Loyal Emigrants were left on the south side of the river as the garrison of Grave.

The Austrians were by now on the River Roer, about 60 miles (96km) away. Clerfayt offered to link his right flank with the British left at Venloo, about 30 miles (48km) south of Grave; but he had no intention of resuming the offensive. Prince Frederik of Orange-Nassau begged the duke to post a detachment within Fort Crevecoeur, an important post at the confluence of the Meuse and the Aa, promising to relieve it within three days. The duke obligingly sent three companies of the Hessisches Leichte-Infanterie-Bataillon, but the place was surrounded by the rapidly-following French and the Dutch gave up relief efforts. The light infantrymen were taken prisoner and paroled home to Hessen-Darmstadt.

The duke had to devise a plan for holding over 60 miles (96km) of river with only 34,000 men. That same day, William Windham wrote a private letter to William Pitt suggesting that the Duke of York be made commander-in-chief at home and replaced by Lord Cornwallis in the field.[3] For a week Pitt vacillated over the matter, suggesting one thing one day and then the opposite the next. His final view formed, Pitt bucked up the courage to face the field commander's father – the King. On 11 October he penned a lengthy letter to his sovereign which contained a startling recommendation:

> [We intend to] propose to the Dutch government to offer the Duke of Brunswick the joint command of both Your Majesty's forces and theirs, and of any other which may serve within the Republic. Mr Windham seems confident, from the result of his conversations with the Duke of York, that His Royal Highness would feel no difficulty in acting under the Duke of Brunswick.[4]

Pitt believed the campaign to be too far gone to plunge Cornwallis into an unenviable, probably unwinnable position; the old warrior deserved a better last hurrah. As to the Duke of York coming home to act as commander-in-chief – well, that would require him to have a close working relationship with Windham (as Secretary at War), a man who did not hold him in any high regard. 'In plain words, the Duke of York and Mr Windham acting in the same Department together would never submit to the official orders and business that I am in the daily Routine of doing.'[5] Thus Pitt, in control-freak mode, pulled the strings to his advantage; Cornwallis could rest on his laurels and the duke would stay in Flanders. In so doing he was forced to put forward the only other 'Prince of the Blood' felt suitable for the Anglo-Dutch command – King George's brother-in-law, the elderly and dithering Duke of Brunswick. The Brunswicker declined the offer, as we shall see in due course.

At least Pichegru could bask in the knowledge that his career (and life) were probably safe – his advancing army was at the Dutch frontier and pressing the Coalition back everywhere. The peasant boy from the Jura had become, at thirty-three years of age, *Sauveur de la Patrie*. But militarily he was more of a Grant than a Lee, relentlessly determined rather than nimble, ever pushing his men onwards rather than leading them forward. Dogged as always, he followed the British slowly (on 16 September the French were still on the Dommel, and on 18 September only just across the Aa) and established his own headquarters at Bois-le-Duc on 19 September, before detaching forces to besiege Breda.

Nieuwpoort, Sluys, Ghent and Ypres had been abandoned to the enemy. On 27 September Lord Mulgrave's force at Flushing returned to England, ordered to the West Indies. To replace them, the raw 78th (Highland, or the Ross-shire Buffs) and 80th regiments of foot arrived at Flushing from Guernsey.[6] Also arriving were major generals Nisbett Balfour and the Honourable John Thomas de Burgh, in response to the duke's plea for more general officers. Since Lord Cathcart's departure in July, the army had only one major general (Stewart) available for five line infantry brigades. 'Woolly' Erskine was in very poor health (he would go home at the end of October, being 'quite worn out,' and die at home five months later). The unpopular Henry Fox was largely engaged in staff duties and therefore unable to command his 'Little Brigade'.[7] This could have been acceptable if regimental level leadership was of a high calibre, but it was the opposite. Harry Calvert wrote that 'the field officers are many of them boys, and have attained their rank by means suggested by government at home, which, I am sure, have never directly or indirectly received the smallest countenance from the commander-in-chief in this country; consequently his Royal Highness cannot be responsible for their youth and inexperience.'[8]

Sensing that his son's spirits were low, the king wrote a touching letter on 3 October:

> Keep up your spirits, remember that difficulties are the times that show the energy of character; and as the rest of Europe seems blind to the evils that await the unprosperous conclusion of this business, it is my duty and that of my country by the greatest exertion to attempt to save Europe and society itself.[9]

The 'unprosperous conclusion' appeared one step closer on 2 October when Clerfayt fell back across the Rhine. This was the point of no return. The Austrians would not be seen again in this campaign. 'You can not be surprized at our having lost all confidence in the Austrians', Henry Clinton wrote home from Nijmegen on 6 October. 'We are now drawing by degrees to our Winter quarters, and the sooner an end is put to this disastrous Campaign I think the better.'[10] With their left flank 'in the air' the duke's force continued its retreat north:

> The Austrians under General Clairfait [sic] having been defeated, and consequently exposed our left flank uncovered, which the enemy seemed inclined to turn, and being also in great force on our right, near Battenburg, at which place they seem preparing to cross the river; his Royal Highness thought it expedient to contract his army to a more central point, as it was impossible to defend the vast extent which it now occupied. Accordingly, the principal part of the forces were drawn towards Nimeguen [Nijmegen], where a bridge had previously been thrown over the Waal, and the heavy baggage have already passed.[11]

'For God's sake press for the sending out of more artillery, men and drivers,'[12] the duke wrote home as he surveyed the miles of river to be defended by his handful of remaining artillery pieces. The nature of the countryside, however, provided opportunities for the Royal Engineers to exercise some delaying tactics:

> All the enemy still remain in quiet possession of Dreumel, but I understand by cutting the Dyke of the Waal near Drujten, the whole of the Country between that, and the Meuse as high as Apeltern, can be laid under water, and this precaution has already been taken, and if it succeeds, the more of the Enemy that have passed the better.[13]

Such tactics may explain the frosty welcome exhibited by the locals, and Corporal Brown wrote disparagingly of the Dutch on 6 October:

> We were cantoned in a number of small villages, and received in general but very indifferent treatment from the inhabitants, who by the bye, if we may judge from appearances, are no friends to us, and give Old England but little thanks for expending her blood and treasure in defending them from the incursions of the Carmagnols, whom they would certainly make more welcome than us: indeed many of them say so to our face, and we have had every reason to believe that what they say is true.[14]

Occasionally this 'indifferent treatment' became something far more serious, as recorded by Lieutenant & Captain Roger Morris of the Coldstream Guards the same day (6 October):

> A Dutch Boor fired from a house on a follower of the Army with[ou]t the Smallest provocation – the Consequence of which was breaking open the house in order to arrest the Criminal – this was a work of

time as he had taken every precaution to barricade the Door – when it was effected (& indeed during the operation he fired several Shot[s], & the house being entered & several Shot[s] having been fired at & returned by him in the hay loft, Serg't Malpas, drill Serg't of the Grenadiers attempted to seize him, when the Boor stabbed him to the heart with a Snickersee, of which he immediately died – the house was then set of fire by a quick match which forced him to bolt out, when he was immediately taken & almost as soon hung upon a tree in the next Orchard.[15]

On the night of 9 October, a British sortie from Nijmegen to surprise French outposts was ruined after the Dutch inhabitants of several villages the British passed through rang their church bells to alert the French.[16] With these attitudes in place it is easier to explain the rapidity with which fortresses defended by the Dutch capitulated.

The French crossed the Meuse on 8 October and Bois-le-Duc fell two days later after offering no resistance whatsoever,[17] and Venlo on 27 October having at least making a show of it. The British maintained forward posts at Grave and Nijmegen, and the French attacked the British garrison at Druten, on the south bank of the Waal about 11 miles (18km) west of Nijmegen, on 19 October. It was held by several companies of the 37th Foot and the Rohan Hussars. The inexperienced recruits of the 37th mistook the advancing French 9e Hussards for their German compatriots and withheld their fire until it was too late. Ten officers and staff [18] and 402 rank-and-file were taken prisoner in the ensuing confusion. The 37th Regiment of Foot practically ceased to exist.[19] To add insult to injury, they lost a colour in this action:

> Craig had expressed misgivings about the extent of our line, not without reason, for early on October 19th the regiment was attacked in great force … All accounts agree that the regiment put up a stout resistance and behaved admirably, especially the Light Company which was on picquet, Lieutenant Waddams, who was badly wounded, handling it skilfully. Despite their greatly superior numbers the French were held for some time, but Rohan's, after a stubborn defence were ousted from Appelthoorn and badly mauled by cavalry in retiring. This allowed the French to outflank the Thirty-Seventh and Hope had therefore to evacuate Druten and retire along a narrow dyke. The regiment had gone some way safely enough when some hussars appeared on its flank. Rohan's Hussars had picquets there and French Hussars were easily mistaken for their émigré countrymen with their sky-blue breeches and dolmans, especially as many of our men were recruits of little experience. The mistake was disastrous; the hussars,

charging in, caught the Thirty-Seventh at a great disadvantage, the confined space allowing them no room to 'form'. They fought stubbornly, however, securing the respect of the French by their refusal to surrender when hopelessly placed. This defence of their Colours was particularly gallant; one was being carried off when a sergeant knocked its captor off his horse with his pike and rescued the Colour.

Eventually Hope himself with about 60 men managed to fight their way out and get back to Wundt near Nimuegen, being appreciably assisted by the 55th, but eight officers, nearly 400 men, one Colour and both battalion guns were lost. Many missing men re-joined later on but such losses reduced the regiment to a handful, too weak for further active participation in the campaign. Calvert, writing some days later, exonerated Hope: 'he had acted as he thought for the best,' if there was the 'want of a little experience', but we had copied the Austrians in extending our outposts too much.[20]

In August and September three freshly-raised and newly-arrived British regiments (87th, 88th and 89th Foot, all raised in Ireland) had formed the garrison of Bergen-op-Zoom, whilst most of the Hanoverian and Hessen-Cassel infantry regiments remained in West Flanders. They were not a very soldierly lot, as described by Surgeon James McGrigor of the 88th:

> Indeed the 87th, or Irish heroes as they termed themselves, came in from the army soon after our landing, and a curious spectacle they presented. They were a fine body of men, but most unsoldier-like to behold; for although the majority of them had muskets, they were without accoutrements, and the usual kit of soldiers; and so soiled and dirtied were their coats, that it was difficult to discover they had ever been of a scarlet colour. The fact was, this unformed corps was hurried from Dublin, where they were raised, to the scene of action; and their irregularities rendered them more formidable to their friends than to their enemies.[21]

'The new levies which successively joined the Army were, with a few honourable exceptions, of the most wretched description,' a newspaper of the time recorded. 'The 78th and 80th were well composed, well equipped and efficient. The 85th, 87th and 89th were in appearance a disgrace to any service and the laughing stock of all who beheld them.'[22] Lieutenant & Captain Roger Morris of the Coldstream Guards provided a comical description of the 89th Foot at this time:

> A Ragamuffin crew, whose appearance beggared all description. The Centry [sic] at the Guardroom door had neither shoes, or

stockings, & the whole picquet, from their rags & filth, had more the appearance of a jail delivery, than anything else.[23]

They were also very sickly. Typhus fever broke out in Bergen-op-Zoom, putting nearly a third of the garrison in hospital. In this fragile state the 87th, 88th and 89th Foot were put aboard ship on 9 October and sailed to Dordrecht, from which place from where they marched to Gorkhum, which along with Dort was being used as a hospital town by British forces. They then marched up the Waal to Nijmegen, reaching it on the 17th and 18th.[24]

On 21 October the duke moved his headquarters farther north, to Arnhem. As a last-gasp measure he despatched the German-speaking Colonel George Don to Prussian headquarters to defend the line of the Rhine as far as Bonn. Mollendorff considered the war over and told Don that he considered the Treaty 'was at an end and that he wanted nothing to do with any plan of co-operation with the Duke of York or Clerfayt.'[25] The last remaining ally was, or so it seemed, gone. But then, on 28 October, Clerfayt rode over to Arnhem and, out of the blue, offered a fresh Austrian division, 7,000 men under Feldmarschalleutnant Franz von Werneck, due to arrive at or near Arnhem by 1 November. The two leaders agreed that a combined offensive south from Nijmegen could therefore commence on 3 November.

The duke fed additional troops into Nijmegen in anticipation of imminent action, even though his Adjutant-General thought the place indefencible. 'Have little reliance on Nymegen. The town is in no state of defence in any one particular, and there are natural defects in the exterior position, which I fancy are not to be remedied by art.'[26]

The garrison of Nijmegen comprised a diverse range of detachments of units (British, Hanoverian, émigré and Dutch) commanded by an Irish peer, Major General the Honourable John Thomas de Burgh. The cathedral in Nijmegen was so large that three battalions quartered there without difficulty. Gin was dirt cheap and the garrison was drunk every night. 'Liquor being very cheap, the inhabitants who sold or gave them any, expressed the greatest astonishment on seeing an English soldier drink off ten or a dozen glasses of raw gin, as fast as it could be poured out for him; and would lift up their hands and eyes in amazement to see him unaffected by the strength of the liquor; the people of this part being themselves very moderate drinkers.'[27] With drunkenness came sickness. The town sits on the south bank of the Waal (which was 400 yards wide at that point) and communications with the northern (Coalition) side of the river was via a bridge of boats constructed by the Royal Engineers, over which hospital carriages creaked daily, bound for

Arnhem. One of the reinforcing regiments was the newly-arrived 88th Foot, the Connaught Rangers. Their commanding officer, Lieutenant Colonel Frederick Keppel,[28] kept a journal:

> 31st – at five in the morning we crossed a bridge of boats which is made over the Waal ... the duty was so hard that the men had not a night in bed. The enemy did not appear except their sharp shooters. They had got possession of a windmill in a high spot of ground but too far distant to fire into the town. They were not idle for to our astonishment, on the morning of Nov. 2nd we discovered their first parallel at a windmill about 1200 yards from the ramparts.

The French attacked the southern outposts at Nijmegen on 27 October and commenced a siege on the first day of November, the same day that Werneck was due. But Werneck was still 10 miles (16km) to the east, and 'could not arrive until the 5th, in time for a battle on the 6th or 7th.'[29] Then the plan became muddled out of all comprehension. The duke, Wallmoden, Werneck, Prince Fredrik of Orange-Nassau and Craig rode from Arnhem to Nijmegen to observe the French dispositions, and to the surprise of all Wallmoden dissented to the proposed break-out from Nijmegen, whereupon Werneck presented a new plan. His own division, reinforced, would cross the Rhine at Wesel and attack the French from the east. No mention was made of British cooperation from Nijmegen. Craig refused to sign this plan and both Wallmoden and Werneck were affronted. It says something of the Duke of York's fragile state of mind that he gave Werneck approval to proceed. The garrison of Nijmegen had to hold out until the 8th or 9th of November, at the earliest.

The French operated to a very different timetable and had completely encircled the south of Nijmegen by 4 November. But they were suffering from sickness to an even greater degree than the Coalition troops:

> From several wounded men that were brought in prisoners, we learned, that the French army in camp, before the town, was in a dreadful situation, in consequence of the continued heavy rain; that great numbers were daily dying of fluxes, fevers, &c. caught by being continually in wet clothes, and lying upon wet straw in their tents, and that great murmuring prevailed in their army, in consequence of not being allowed to go into winter quarters; but that Pichegru had promised them the town of Nimeguen for their quarters in a very few days.[30]

This might explain why a sortie by Coalition troops ordered by Wallmoden (but under the immediate command of de Burgh in person) on that day easily cleared the French from a section of entrenchments. The attack went in with unloaded muskets and at bayonet-point:

> 4th [November] – At three o'clock we were ordered again to our alarm posts without noise and then found there was to be a sortie which consisted of the 8th, 27th, 28th, 55th, 69th [sic 63rd] and 78th Regts. We were to act as reserve. We saw the commencement from the ramparts, which was the prettiest show I ever saw in my life. They had got into the enemy's works when we were ordered to an advanced lunette to cover the advancing of the cavalry, where we remained all night. The French were driven from their works, but owing to these cowardly rascals the Dutch, no mischief was done to them.[31]

French casualties were heavy, and no prisoners were taken. De Burgh's assault force had twelve men killed and 172 wounded, with another twenty missing.[32] Despite this local success, by 6 November the French had guns in positions that could knock out the bridge of boats.[33]

Seeing no relief in sight, de Burgh held a council of war where it was decided to evacuate Nijmegen: 'When it was known that the town was to be evacuated our soldiers began to plunder and many of them were very justly put to death by the Dutch,' Keppel recorded.[34] Most of the garrison had evacuated the town by 22.00 hours on the night of 6/7 November (except the 88th, who had been forgotten about)[35], but all British troops were across to the north side of the Waal the following morning, at which point the bridge of boats was destroyed. This left only a flying bridge for the evacuation of the Dutch. However, at daylight on the 8th a lucky shot carried away the top of the mast to which the hawser was attached, and it drifted slowly but inevitably upon the hinge of its fixed end around to the French side with 400 Dutch troops on board, who were immediately taken prisoner, along with their commander, General Hache.

Upstream, Werneck built his bridge across the Rhine, but only managed to get two battalions across before Pichegru attacked and forced the Austrians to dismantle the bridge. The operation was over.

New Broom

The British were now nearly all on the north bank of the Waal, defending from the river-banks as the weather turned to winter.[36] The commissariat had broken down. 'The distressed situation of the army for cloathing was at this time very great,' an anonymous officer wrote, 'some regiments having lost the whole of their necessaries by their transports falling into the hands of the enemy, and many of the soldiers had hardly a coat to wear.'[37] 'I wish to God you would send us, but it must be immediately,' Craig wrote to the War Office on 3 November, '20,000 pairs of good shoes ... we will pay for them.'[38] This last statement was extraordinary, since the army had been starved of money as well as all else. To take into account the loss of senior officers either wounded, sick, or departed for home, the Duke of York re-organised his infantry brigades for the fourth time on 13 November.

On 18 November a severe frost set in, as both sides watched and waited. 'There is now such a scarcity of news and everything seems to be at so complete a stand still,' Major Henry Clinton wrote home to his father.[39] The British army defended a 25-mile line of the river Waal, with fourteen battalions spread out between Wadonoijen in the west and Oosterhout in the east. Five regiments were in reserve behind Oosterhout. Two small stone and earthen fortresses (Fort Saint-André and the fortified village of Oise-sur-Bommel) were defended by about 2,000 Coalition troops, the last two remaining Coalition positions on the south bank of the Waal. The Dutch were at Gorcum on the right, and the Hanoverians and Hessen-Cassel were on the British flanks.

Everywhere, troops were digging in for winter. The duke had 21,000 infantrymen in the United Provinces, of which 11,000 were sick.[40] The British general hospital at Rhenen reported thirty to forty deaths each day. Major General Alexander Stewart was extremely sick and would die of illness by mid-December. Working parties toiled in the freezing conditions to complete defences along the line of the Waal, near Nijmegen. None of the newly-arrived regiments had greatcoats or tents.

The French, on the other hand, did not appear to be settling down into winter quarters:

> Their posts are strengthened and are exceedingly attentive on the left bank of the river, and it is imagined that as soon as Graave has surrendered, attempts will be made to pass the Waal at various points. The enemy have assembled near 150 boats (which, as they are the property of the inhabitants, are probably small ones, and must have been secreted from our notice) in the canal which empties itself into the Rhine between Emmerik and Schenckenschans; they have many boats and the materials for the construction of a bridge at the village of Druten, and they are employed in the construction of vessels in the basin of Nymegen.
>
> The fire at Graave has been uninterrupted and heavy these last six-and-thirty hours. I am assured the enemy have sixty-two pieces of ordnance before the place. They have thrown a bridge over the Meuse at a place called Overlangel. General Moreau, who commands the siege, has his quarters at Ravenstein. Barracks are being erected for the cavalry on the heaths between Breda and Bois-le-Duc.[41]

Newly promoted Général de division Macdonald (temporarily commanding Souham's division) ordered Reynier, commanding his old brigade, to seize the two Coalition forts on the south bank of the Waal. As the French approached Oise-sur-Bommel the garrison abandoned the village rather than fight, leaving their artillery behind. The same thing occurred on their approach to Fort Saint-André. By 28 December, the south bank of the Waal was free of Coalition troops.[42]

The British privates grumbled about their quartermasters and their officers, the regimental officers grumbled about their brigade staff, whilst those at brigade headquarters 'croaked' about the army headquarters. But one unidentified 'croaker' at or very close to the duke's headquarters went one step farther, and wrote a damning letter to his close friend and confidant, Lord Cornwallis:

> Despised by our enemies, without discipline, confidence or exertion amongst ourselves, hated and more dreaded than the enemy, even by the well-disposed inhabitants of the country, every disgrace and misfortune is to be expected… Whatever measures are adopted at home, either removing us from the continent or remaining, something must be done to restore discipline, and the confidence that always attends it.[43]

Lord Cornwallis neither disclosed the author nor responded directly.[44] However he did pass a copy along to Henry Dundas. It must have crossed his mind that the letter was a prompt to reinvigorate the idea of Lord Cornwallis coming out as supreme commander-in-chief (since the letter did not advocate the recall of the duke); but Cornwallis no longer wanted the post, rightly considering it a poisoned chalice. The Duke of Brunswick had declined the formal offer made in October:

> The Prince of Brunswick has declined the command that was offered. I concluded he would; for I think no officer with a grain of character to lose, would risk it on the co-operation of the Prussians and Austrians, and I trust no minister with a grain of sense will persevere in bestowing the riches of our country on these deceitful mercenary bankrupts.[45]

Henry Dundas discussed the letter with Pitt. The Prime Minister mulled over the matter for a few days, then on Sunday 23 November, sat down in his study at Holwood House and wrote the longest and most difficult letter he had ever written to his king:

> Under these circumstances Mr Pitt is reluctantly compelled to submit to Your Majesty his deliberated opinion that the continuance of the Duke of York in command can be attended only with the most

disadvantageous consequence to His Royal Highness himself; and that, considering the prejudices which he has to encounter, there is little prospect of his having the benefit of that hearty co-operation on the part of the Dutch which is so necessary at the present crisis. On these grounds alone Mr Pitt would humbly implore Your Majesty to put an end to the Duke of York's command for the sake of His Royal Highness as well as that of the country.[46]

In the course of the lengthy letter, Pitt did not offer an alternative supreme commander, other than pointing out that Abercrombie could be given command of the British contingent, and Wallmoden the shrinking Hanoverian corps. His proposal solved nothing, and in fact created more potential problems through command disunity (as indeed proved to be the case). Two days later Pitt nervously attended King George's private Closet, at which the matter was not even mentioned. The Prime Minister wrote to the king again the following day, enclosing a draft recall despatch to the duke. The king replied in writing – he would, reluctantly, assent to Pitt's proposal. And so, Dundas' letter of recall dated 27 November was despatched to Arnhem:

> I am commanded to signify to Your Royal Highness, His Majesty's pleasure that you should take the earliest opportunity of returning to England, leaving the command of His Majesty's British forces in the hands of such British officer as may be next in seniority to Your Royal Highness.[47]

This dismissal arrived at British headquarters in Arnhem at midnight on Monday 1 December. The duke handed over command to General Wallmoden-Gimborn as the senior officer and Lieutenant General Harcourt for the British troops in the morning of 2 December, and rode away with a small retinue, bound ultimately for home. He would not return during the campaign.

Lieutenant Lewis Tobias Jones of the 57th Foot recorded what was probably a near-universal sentiment:

> Here the British army lost a father and a friend, who had endeared himself to them by his humanity, justice, and benevolence. The army felt themselves very much obliged to their commander, and his Royal Highness had every reason to be so to them, and expressed himself so in the handsomest manner on his taking leave; for there was no duty, let it be ever so dangerous or fatiguing, but was done with chearfulness, and pleasure; there was a wonderful good understanding between all ranks, from headquarters down to the lowest; and one circumstance is to be mentioned, and which perhaps never happened before, nor ever will again, in any army,

that is that there was not a tatler, or tale bearer, in the whole army, or even a person suspected.[48]

It will be remembered that the Commander-in-Chief of the British army was this time was Lord Amherst, nearly 78 years old and a dotard. The lack of any military input to the previous correspondence of Pitt and Dundas is acutely obvious, with the two civilians meddling in military affairs probably even unaware of their own shortcomings. Pitt, first of all, not even thinking (or realising) that an alternative supreme commander might be needed, then suggesting having two. This was followed by Dundas not even knowing whom the next in seniority to command His Majesty's forces on the continent might be, in the largest war fought in his lifetime.

The duke went home to his estate at Oatlands, and to Frederica. After a few week's rest he received notification of his next appointments from his father:

> Mr Windham is to notify my son the Duke of York as Field Marshal and insert it in this night's Gazette besides sending the usual notifications to the Secretary of State's office. At the same time he is to have a letter of Service placing him on the Home Staff, which will give him naturally the command, which has till now been entrusted to Lord Amherst.[49]

The pointlessness of allowing the senile Lord Amherst to retain the commander-in-chief role was now so obvious to all; the campaign's loss was the army's gain. The British Army benefitted from this appointment very brilliantly.[50] The duke's 'family' nearly all assumed that he would return after wintering at home; at least they did so until Saturday 6 December, when the morning's mail contained orders for them too, to return home; they all departed on the 8th. Harry Calvert received a letter from the duke which concluded with the following enigmatic statement:

> With regard to my situation, and what I have learned of the intentions concerning me, you will hear more by another opportunity. Remember me to all friends.[51]

Harry Calvert returned home, straight to his chief's side as Deputy Quartmaster-General at Horse Guards, ultimately rising to Adjutant-General of the Forces in 1799. The duke looked after his Flanders 'family' with great affection, loyalty to his friends being one of his most endearing qualities. He appointed Robert Brownrigg his Military Secretary on return home, and then Quartermaster-General of the Forces in 1803.[52]

The British troops in Flanders at this time looked as unlike the serried ranks of trim redcoats seen at Horse Guards Parade in early 1793 as it was possible to be:

> The regimental cloathing of the greater part part of the troops being worn out, it was curious to see what shifts some of the soldiers were put to, to keep themselves warm and comfortable — one would have on, a huge pair of Dutchman's wide breeches to his regimental jacket; another would have a large full trimmed Burgomaster's coat on, by way of surtout, and another, to his red jacket would have sewed, a pair of wide black or brown sleeves with long hanging cuffs; with other curious contrasts of cloathing equally diverting; so that from the motley appearance of some of the troops, it would have been a difficult matter even for an Englishman just arrived to tell to what nation they belonged; all that was necessary here, was to keep the arms and ammunition in good order, as very little attention was paid to dress. The highlanders at this time, from the severity of the weather, were under the necessity of leaving off wearing their kelts, or short petticoats, and were furnished with pantaloons or close trowsers, which were much more comfortable for them.[53]

Many men were dressed in clothing donated to the army by the citizens of Arnhem.[54] This is not surprising given the state in which many of them had been sent out from home:

> The 38th, 40th (South Lancashires) and 55th are almost naked, many of their coats hanging together in pieces. A great number of recruits have joined the Regiments who never had any but the slop clothing they received when they were raised. Most of these recruits are in the most wretched state imaginable. Hundreds of them have only linen trousers, without stockings or drawers and only thin slop jackets without waistcoats. Flannel waistcoats and drawers would be of infinite utility, as would, above all, good comfortable greatcoats; indeed it hardly seems possible that the men can stand the severity of their duty without them.[55]

Rag-tag they may have looked, but it seems at least they were well-fed:

> The allowance of beef to our troops was encreased half a pound per day, in consequence of their hard duty and the excessive cold; a soldier's daily allowance now was per day, beef 1 lb. bread 1 lb. and spirits half a pint; with this allowance and potatoes, greens, &c. for which they foraged, they made out a tolerable good living, as coffee being very plentiful it was sold by the soldiers wives, and a man might for a penny, have an excellent breakfast of coffee, but he must find his own bread and butter. The bread was in general of

a very indifferent kind, being made of (what is called in England) buckwheat, which makes very black bread.[56]

As the weather deteriorated daily, they could expect limited offensive action from the French. This was a reasonable assumption, since the French were as exhausted as the Coalition. Souham's divisions were cantoned around Nijmegen, Bonnaud's between the Meuse and the Waal, and others around Grave and Bois-le-Duc. None showed any immediate signs of moving. Lieutenant General Harcourt endeavoured to build a second bridge over the river at Arnhem, to improve the army's imperfect communications with that important base, but the Dutch lacked all eagerness to help. Perhaps the winter of 1794 would follow the same pattern as the winter of 1793, as was customary in war on the Continent with months of inactivity.

The National Convention in Paris did not agree. They no longer saw any need to adhere to eighteenth-century notions of how wars were to be fought. Général de division Moreau (in temporary command of the Armée du Nord due to another of Pichegru's absences) was hustled back to activity. Winter Quarters were to be a thing of the past. The French attacked across the river Waal at Helderonkirk in boats on 11 December:

> At six o'clock in the morning on 11th December, with the help of the dark night and a dense fog, the [French] succeeded in taking the Battery No. 4 at Gent, although the guard under Captain Prizelius of the 9th Infantry Regiment had strengthened their position. Then Major Bacmeister, with a battalion of the 9th Infantry Regiment, hastened to attack the enemy. But the Major was badly wounded, and the attack was reduced by the enemy turning over the conquered guns and using them against our own troops. General von dem Bussche, who had arrived at the resulting tributary, attacked twice with detachments of the 1st and 14th Infantry Regiments but the enemies did not retreat. However, when General-Major von Bothmer also approached Bemmel with the 1st and 3rd Grenadier Battalion and the battalion of the 6th Infantry Regiment, the enemy left the battery before Bothmer could attack, after they had spiked the guns and thrown the three-pounder with all the ammunition into the water. Returning to the other shore, however, they opened a violent cannon fire from there. On that occasion, General von der Bussche was hit by a cannonball… which took away his right hand and 'passed so close' that the good old gentleman soon surrendered to it.[57]

The valiant Major Bacmeister was wounded and captured. Having killed seven and wounded fifteen Hanoverians, the French 'returned over the water and laughed at them.'[58] Another raid up-river from the first occurred two days later. Then a severe frost set in, and the rivers all froze. The fog was so dense that it was frequently impossible to see across the river. The troops resorted to shouting abuse across the river at each other. The French called the British 'Jack-roast-bif' or 'Jean Taureau'[59]. The redcoats were less elegant. 'Damn'd king-killing sons of bitches', 'crapauds' and 'paper money scroundrels' were popular.

On 22 December the river froze over, and on Christmas Day the snows started. 'In my life I never felt anything to equal the cold,' Lieutenant Colonel Frederick Keppel noted.[60] Sentry duty was reduced from two hours to one to prevent the risk of frost-bite. With the cold came sickness, and the army started to shrink in the field as the hospitals filled.

Wallmoden and Harcourt were appalled on 18 December when a message arrived at British headquarters from Henry Dundas, filled with more civilian nonsense; seven battalions were required to be released for service in the West Indies. Indeed, the 40th, 44th and 63rd Foot were to march to Helvoetsluys immediately. Harcourt was astonished and wrote to Dundas seeking further clarification. Did the Secretary of State for War not understand their situation? Seven battalions were the equivalent of two brigades, and those selected were some of the numerically strongest on the line. Dundas was depending upon the fact that Alvinczi's Austrians to the east, held in position by a £100,000 subsidy from Whitehall, would fill the gap. Stricken with anxiety, Harcourt wrote to Dundas begging further urgent instructions.[61]

This news, the weather, and indeed the entire situation made for a miserable Christmas. Some made the best of it they could. The Grenadier battalion of the Guards packed into two large barns, where the officers served roast beef and potatoes and plum pudding to all, wives and children included. Lord Charles Fitzroy arranged for two hogsheads of porter to liven the mood.[62] It snowed heavily all day.

Henry Dundas's ridiculous return orders became forgotten on 27 December. A force of 12,000 French under Général de division Delmas attacked over the Waal towards the Dutch garrison at Fort St Andre, Bommelwaart (26 miles or 42km west of Nijmegen) and drove them out for the loss of 1,600 men. Many fugitives ran 4 miles (7km) over the ice to Utrecht. General Constrant commanding at that place asked the nearby Hessen-Cassel garrison under Generalmajor von Dallwigk for assistance. Dallwigk immediately ordered the II/Garde-Grenadiere to Tuyl and the Grenadiere Bataillon von Lelong to Meteren:

> Evidently the staff officer commanding Mettern had neither sent out any patrols nor had he taken adequate safety measures, for

even before the commander-in-chief Generalleutnant von Dallwigk had arrived there, French hussars suddenly burst into this place in the pursuit of the fleeing Dutchmen. The alarm was immediately struck, and the battalion assembled with the greatest rapidity and order on the road to Geldermalsen.[63]

The French captured Tuyl but were stopped by Dallwigk's Hessen-Cassel troops at Meteren. Nevertheless, this gave the French command of another crossing point over the Waal.

Major General David Dundas led a force comprising ten battalions and six squadrons to Geldermalsen (24 miles or 39km west of Nijmegen) in order to drive the French out of the Bommel region. He had with him the brigades of Major generals Robert Laurie, Lord Cathcart, Andrew Gordon and Würmb with the 19th, 27th, 28th, 33rd, 42nd and 80th Foot, six squadrons of light dragoons and 150 hussars, the Loyal Emigrants, two battalions of the Hessen-Cassel Garde-Grenadiere-Regiment and three of grenadiers, and four squadrons of the Hessen-Cassel Prinz Friedrich-Dragoner-Regiment. Each man was ordered to carry three days provisions:

> [29 December] This night the troops for tomorrow's attack marched in three columns to their respective destinations, in order to be ready to begin the attack early in the morning; the frost continued with unabated rigour and the troops had not any covering during the night, but this did not in the least diminish their ardor as they marched to the scene of action and cheared each other with the greatest degree of spirit …
>
> [30 December] The right column consisting of four British battalions and the hussars of Rohan, under the command of Lord Cathcart, marched by the villages of Haasden and Rumb, to take Tiel in the rear; the other British column went by the village of Metteren, and the Hessian column proceeded to Waardenbourg, near which place the two latter joined at daybreak; the column under Lord Cathcart could not get up in time, the road by which he was to have marched being found so impassable, that he was under the necessity of going a considerable way about; however, General Dundas finding on his arrival at Waardenbourg, that the enemy had abandoned that place in the night, and had retired to join their countrymen the third column to come up, but immediately to push on with what troops he had, and begin the attack upon Tiel; this was done, and with such spirit and impetuosity, that notwithstanding the great strength of the place, the batteries which flanked the approach of our troops, the abbatis of fruit trees that were made, and the number of troops who defended it, the place was carried on the first attack by the two columns (British and Hessians) and the enemy were driven back

across the ice with the loss of a confiderable number of men, and four pieces of cannon, which they had brought over the preceding day; the loss on our part was very trifling confidering the nature of the attack and the numbers of the enemy, which greatly exceeded ours.[64]

It was purely a local success, causing the French to lose 600 casualties to the Anglo-Hessian tally of fifty-four men lost. But the long march in arduous conditions had exhausted the men, and the ease by which the French had tumbled back across the frozen Waal had not gone unnoticed; they could just as swiftly traverse back again. Dundas was ordered to withdraw northwards as the position could not be defended in the long term.

New Year's Eve was a dismal day. The frost was very severe, and a thick fog hung over the entire front. The sun was barely visible all day. There, on the frozen Waal, the year ended:

> 31st. Everything was quiet. Thus ends the year 1794, a most unprosperous one for the allied army. May the next be more fortunate.[65]

PART 4 – 1795: THIS MOST UNHAPPY EXPEDITIONARY FORCE

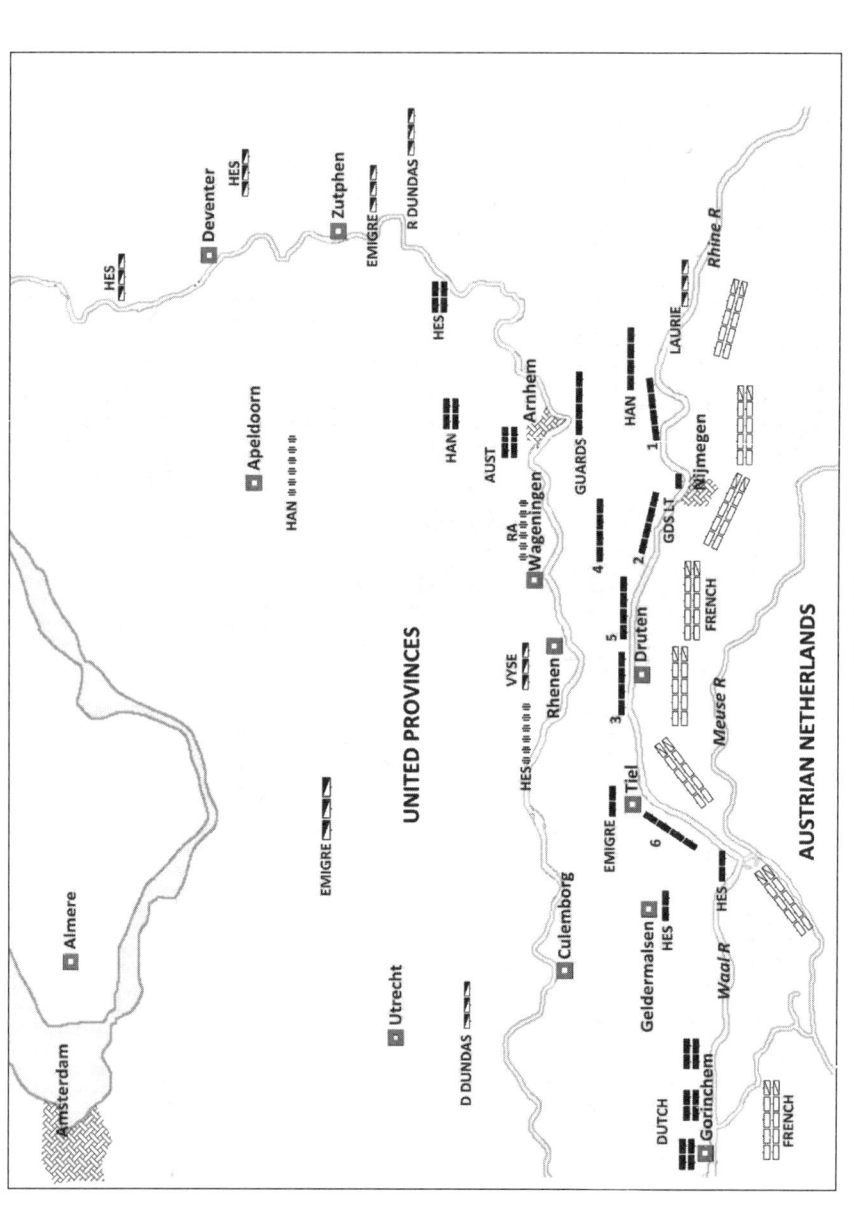

The Waal River

Chapter 17

Winter on the Waal

Geldermalsen

New Year's Day dawned with the River Waal completely frozen over. The duke's army shivered in its cantonments, cursing the wretched war. From 07.00 hours until lunchtime what sounded like a heavy cannonade could be heard at some distance to the rear. It was later confirmed as a celebration of the New Year in Amsterdam and Utrecht.

The Hanoverian infantry contingent, originally 14,000 strong, had fit for service at this time 4,650 men and 211 officers. The two battalions of Guards could muster 318 men; the 9.Infanterie-Regiment just seventy-nine men under arms.[1] The Hanoverian cavalry, on the other hand, was still in very serviceable condition.[2]

The Coalition right wing was crumbling. Grave capitulated, and the French siege-forces were therefore now available for service along the Waal. Four French divisions faced the Dutch between Breda and the Bommeler Waart. Souham's old division, now commanded by rising star Général de division Macdonald, occupied the ground between the Waal and the Meuse eastwards from Tuyl. Moreau's divisions faced Alvinczi's Austrians from the Pannarden Canal (east of Nijmegen) down to the Rhine.

On 3 January, an intensely cold day, the rivers froze, and the following day the French attacked across the Waal again. The Dutch, tired beyond measure of the war, retired without firing a shot. The 33rd Foot skirmished with a raiding party at Meteren, 6 miles (9km) west of Tuyl, during which the French got 200 men and two cannon across the ice. The French were now entrenched on the north side of the Waal and Major General David Dundas sent the 11th Light Dragoons, 33rd, 42nd and 78th Foot as a rear-guard to the south of Geldermalsen to hold them in place whilst he got the guns and baggage away. A detachment of French Hussars was allowed to get too close to the picquet-line (once again, they were mistaken for Royalist cavalry), the picquets of the 78th Foot were dispersed, Major General Robert Laurie was wounded, and two battalion guns were captured. The 42nd Foot charged the cavalry in fine style and recaptured the guns. Both sides then separated as it got dark.[3] The Royal Artillery was ordered to destroy all limbers and carriages. All guns that could not be carried away were spiked and the ammunition destroyed.

The thaw began on 6 January. 'The thaw is very great on the continuance of which our fate depends,' Keppel wrote. 'Tonight I presume will decide, as for fear of a thaw they must either bring over a very large force or retire. The former most likely.'[4]

The last conference of the Coalition commanders in the United Provinces was held in Utrecht the evening of 7 January. Attending were the Stadtholder, the Hereditary Prince of Orange-Nassau, Lord St. Helens,[5] Generals Alvinczi, Wallmoden, and Harcourt, and Colonel Calvert. All was doom and gloom. The United Provinces yielded to their fate. The Stadtholder and the princes of the House of Orange-Nassau and a small group of adherents took refuge in England, leaving from Scheveningen aboard a fishing boat on the night of 18 January. The States-General concluded peace with France – or rather, submitted to becoming a French client state.

All this news would of course take time to filter down to the freezing men defending the River Waal. The army began to retire from the Waal on the same day as the conference - 7 January. Large bonfires were set in the British lines to deceive the French as Dundas' men quietly filed away northwards towards Beuren, leaving many sick men behind. Corporal Brown of the Guards visited the hospital at Rhenen:

> Part of the church, and a large building resembling a monastry [sic] adjoining, has been converted into an hospital since August last, for the whole of the British army. The hospital, as well as every other place, are filled with soldiers, and no trade of any kind appears. Several large temporary hospitals have been erected in the fields adjoining. The great mortality which has lately pervaded this army, added to the shameful abuse and neglect in several of the hospital departments, has made it a perfect Golgotha. Upwards of four thousand men having been buried here within the last three months. At this time near half the army are sick, and the other half much fatigued with hard duty. This is now the tenth day since any of us has had a night's rest or had time to undress.[6]

Surgeon McGrigor of the 88th Foot later wrote, 'The want of system in our hospitals, and the inexperience of medical officers in the duties in which in after years they became so expert, were at this time very striking.'[7]

The advancing French were beginning to outflank the British position, and so the last actions of the war in this theatre still had to be fought. Lieutenant General Abercrombie and Generalmajor Hammerstein were ordered to attack southwards towards Tuyl with their Anglo-Hanoverian brigades supported by some Austrian reserves. Major General David Dundas was to support the attack with his brigade from Beuren. But Dundas' brigade had not reached Beuren; he found all the outposts driven in, and the enemy in force in the neighbourhood. After reconnoitring with the Uhlans Britanniques and the light companies, and part of the 27th Foot, he realised that the French garrison defending the dyke at Lingen was less than 800 men, so he determined to drive them out. Lord Cathcart brought up the remainder of the 14th and 27th Foot and some artillery. The 14th formed on the ice, the 27th across a farm enclosure on the right, and the artillery on the dyke. They marched in that order, driving the enemy before them. The French crossed the frozen river and re-formed at Geldermalsen, and from there kept up a heavy fire of musketry and grape. The British line advanced without a halt. The 27th Foot changed direction as it approached the mill, charged the village across the ice beyond the burnt bridge, and took the cannon. The 14th Foot entered the town on the right. The French retreated precipitately but returned and renewed the attack. In an echo of Riflemen in a later war of the era, the French *voltigeurs* were proving to be expert snipers:[8]

> In this action, the enemy's rifle-men particularly singled out our officers, which they might very easily do, as the parties were frequently within a few yards of each other, and the rifle-men were frequently heard to cry out, 'Prenez garde!' before they fired; numbers of them were put to death by the bayonet in the houses and other lurking places, where they had taken a situation for firing upon our people without running any risk themselves. Colonel Buller observing so many officers drop, desired those to whom he had an opportunity of speaking, to take off their epaulettes, as he rightly judged that it was by those distinguishing badges, the enemy were enabled to single them out, though he neglected to take off his own, and received his death wound.[9]

Cathcart's little force was compelled to retreat when French reinforcements arrived. The 28th Foot under the teenage Lieutenant Colonel Edward Paget[10] arrived as reinforcements and covered the retreat until 23.00 hours, losing sixty-eight men doing so, out of a total casualty list of nine killed (including the commanding officer of the 27th, Lieutenant Colonel John Thomas Buller) and 125 wounded. Dundas retired to Beuren. Abercrombie and Hammerstein had been too far away to offer any assistance. Buurmalsen was the last significant British action of the war.

Half-Starved Carmagnols

The French attacked across the Waal in six heavy columns in the morning of 10 January. The columns attacking Pannerden and Ghent were repulsed. The same could not be said of the columns which crossed the ice between Tuyl and Nijmegen. The right-hand column defeated the Hanoverian garrison on the river-bank north of Nijmegen and immediately turned left to march down-river towards Major General James Coates' picquet at Lent (200 men of the 40th, 59th and 79th Foot):

> A corporal and a small party were instantly dispatched to the brigade for a reinforcement (three miles off) but it was too late, as the enemy were plainly perceived coming in several directions, and they had already possessed themselves of the high road, to the amount of several hundreds, shewing every disposition to surround and cut us off. The troops were now ordered to retire into a small redoubt on the right, close to the river side, on which the enemy began their fire, which was immediately returned by our troops and became very warm on both sides. When it was seen from the heights of Nimeguen, that we were likely to maintain our situation in the redoubt, they opened the heavy cannon of the fortifications upon us, which entirely commanded our situation, and at the same time, determined to dislodge us, they poured over the ice from Nimeguen, a large body of troops who took us in the rear. In this critical situation, nothing remained for us but to make the best of our way to the brigade, and as a discharge of musquetry was heard in all directions, we concluded the enemy had crossed both on our right and left. Our retreat therefore began, through those who had already attacked us, and was made in the best possible order; the enemy closing in upon us, shouting and using every means of intimidating our troops, but durst not approach near the point of the bayonets.[11]

The picquet retreated to Elst, the 59th Foot under brevet Major William MacLeod having been particularly hard hit, losing thirty-six men. A tragi-comic episode in the aftermath demonstrated that the French were as starved as the Coalition troops:

> A grenadier in the retreat this day being hard pressed by the enemy, was under the necessity of leaving behind him the camp

kettle of his mess which happened to be full of beef. This glorious prize soon attracted the eyes of the half starved carmagnols, who thought proper to quit the pursuit of the soldier, and immediately commenced a formidable attack upon the kettle of beef, which though only intended for a mess of six Englishmen, was eagerly beset by upwards of twenty hungry Frenchmen, who were furiously contending for this invaluable treasure within 100 yards of one of our field pieces; the gun being loaded with grape, was levelled for the contending Frenchmen and with such fatal certainty, that of the whole group, not more than four or five were left unhurt to relate to their comrades the story of the English kettle of beef.[12]

These constant attacks at varying points succeeded in keeping the British off-balance. That same day Major General de Burgh's brigade, plus the 16th Light Dragoons and Salm Chasseurs, marched from Amerongen to Tuyl then back to Rhenen on a false alarm, exhausting the men. It was now clear that the Coalition would have to withdraw from the line of the Waal. Men were still dying in large numbers, and Corporal Brown recorded the method of burial:

The manner of burying the dead soldiers here is adapted to the circumstances of the times: in a field appointed for that purpose, a large hole is dug in the ground, from twelve to twenty feet square, more or less, and twelve or fourteen feet deep; here the coffins are piled regularly one above another, from the bottom to within a foot or two of the surface; then they begin another row, complete that to the top, and so on till the hole is full, when they cover the whole over with earth, and then dig another. They are not many days in filling a hole, and the excessive severity of the frost prevents any smell from arising, which otherwise would be intolerable.[13]

By 12 January the Anglo-Hanoverian army was across the River Leck running westwards from Arnhem towards Culemborg. The Waal belonged to the French. The next few days were quiet. Then momentous news arrived, as recounted by an anonymous officer of the 59th Foot:

Our immediate march out of Holland, was this day finally determined on to the great joy of the army, who were heartily tired of remaining so long exposed to the severest inclemency of the weather in so cold a climate, and by the daily diminution of their numbers by sickness and death; which of course rendered the duty of the survivors extremely severe and indeed almost insupportable.[14]

The French attacked along the entire line of the Leck from Arnhem to Rhenen on 14 January. The most serious attack was at Rhenen, which was repulsed by the Brigade of Guards and the Salm Light Infantry. The Guards had two officers wounded and a few men wounded and missing in the action:

> In these engagements it was observed that the French were generally very much intoxicated, as all the prisoners which were made, owed their captivity to that circumstance, particularly their officers, who set the laudable example by drinking large bumpers of liquor mixed with gunpowder, which they supposed rendered them invincible; [whereas] our troops were allowed a quantity of liquor after an action.[15]

The march orders were drafted the night of 14 January. Ralph Dundas' cavalry brigade was ordered to march to Driesbergen, and then via Amersfoort to a position between Nijkerk and Bunschoten. David Dundas' column was to retire from Duurstede and Culemborg to the plains around Amersfoort. Von Dallwigk's Hessen-Cassel division was ordered from Amerongen to Barneveld; and Abercrombie's large column from Amerongen and Rhenen towards the villages of Lunteren, Renswoude, Scherpenzeel, De Glind Soest, Hoevelaken, and Stoutenburg.[16] Nearly 250 British sick in the hospital at Rhenen were destined to be accidentally left behind. But at least they might expect some succour from their French captors. Over 4,000 men had been buried there in the previous four months, virtually all from disease.

That same night, 14 January, the mercury registered minus ten degrees. A British regiment tried to enter the gates of Amersfoort and was denied entry. Troops by the score were deserting, many heading west towards England, or east towards Hanover. Most were never heard from again. The retreat could not come soon enough.

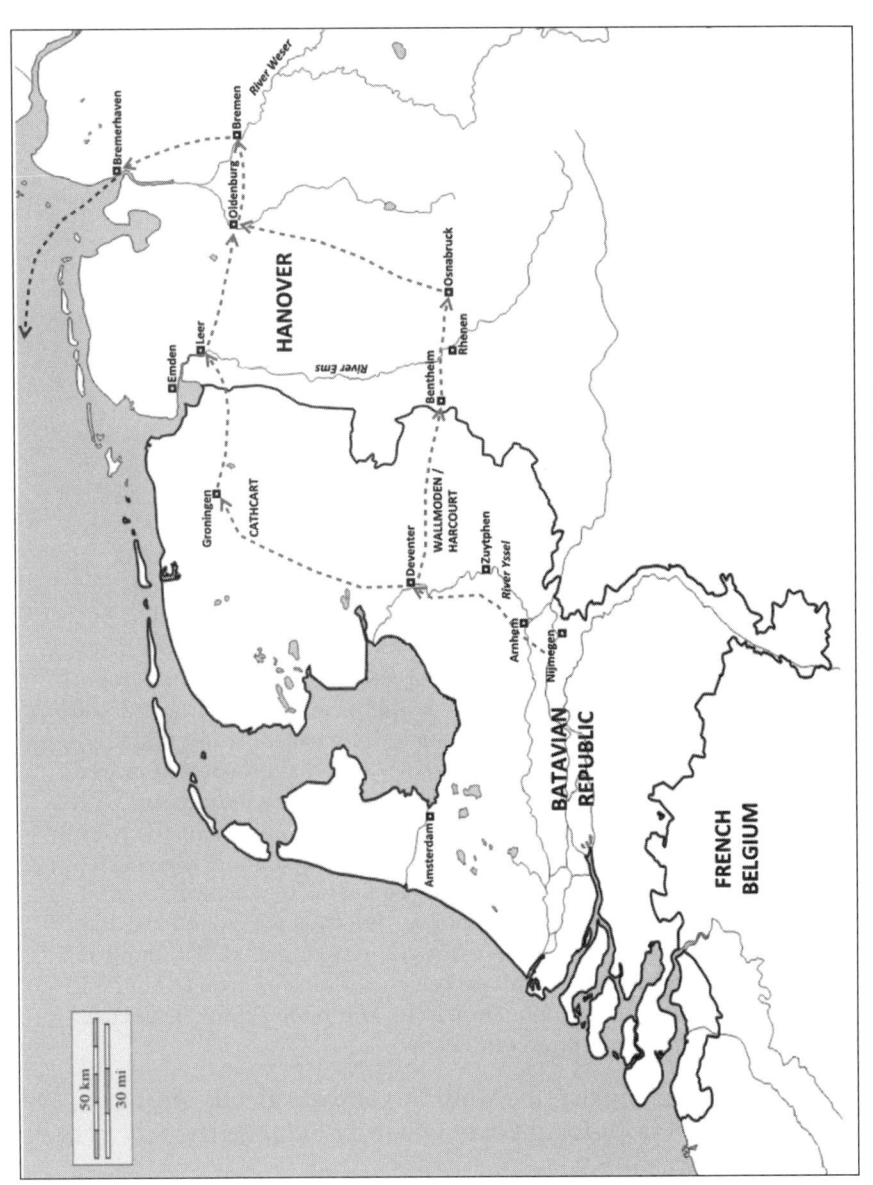

The Retreat to Bremen, January–March 1795

Chapter 18

Retreat to Bremen

Legions of Vultures
The retreat began at 04.00 hours on 16 January:

> The brigade of guards, and Colonel Strutt's brigade of the line were ordered to march at four o'clock and assemble at Lunteron, and await the orders of Major-general de Burgh: we accordingly marched at the appointed hour, and after a very tedious journey, about three o'clock in the afternoon reached the verge of an immense desert, called the Welaw; when, instead of having gained a resting place for the night as we expected, were informed that we had fifteen miles further to go. Upon this information many began to be much dejected, and not without reason; for several of us, besides suffering the severity of the weather and fatigue of the march, had neither ate nor drank anything except water that day.
>
> For the first three or four miles such a dismal prospect appeared as none of us was ever witness to before; a bare sandy desert with a tuft of withered grass, or solitary shrub, here and there: the wind was excessive high, and drifted the snow and sand together so strong, that we could hardly wrestle against it; to which was added, a severity of cold almost insufferable. The frost was so intense, that the water which came from our eyes, freezing as it fell, hung in icicles to our eyelashes, and our breath freezing as soon as emitted, lodged in heaps of ice about our faces, and on the blankets or coats that were wrapped round our heads.[1]

By the night of 16 January, the army was already greatly strung out and straggling. The troops fought over whatever lodgings they could find:

> We doubled up with the men of the 8th Regiment but we had nothing to eat, and the same to drink. I myself got at bit of biscuit, a bit of cheese, an onion and a glass of gin. Unfortunately there were two casks of gin in the barn where the men were, of cause they breached it, of course they got drunk, and the two regiments

quarrelled. The 8th are a very disorderly set, but also encouraged by their officers. Lt. Colonel Dawson behaved very silly that night; we all littered down together round the kitchen fire.[2]

The morning of the 17th brought stark reality to the scene. The 88th found they had already lost nine serjeants, nine drummers and 135 rank-and-file, 'we suppose them to have been lost by the inclemency of the weather.'[3] An attempt to quarter troops in the town of Zutphen that night was opposed by the locals, who turned out with pitchforks and elements of the Dutch Guards. At Batham a foraging party of the 1st Dragoon Guards was attacked by a number of farmers, some armed with muskets and others with pitchforks.[4] Scenes witnessed upon the retreat were all horror:

> Near a cart, a little further on the common, we perceived a stout looking man, and a hearty young woman, with an infant about seven months old at the breast, all three frozen and dead. The mother had most certainly expired in the act of suckling her child, as with one breast exposed, she lay upon the drifted snow, the milk, to all appearance, in a stream drawn from the nipple by the babe, and instantly congealed, the infant seemed as if its lips had but just then been disengaged, and it reposed its little headupon the mother's bosom, withan overflow of milk frozen as it trickled from the mouth; their countenances were perfectly composed and fresh, resembling those of persons in a sound and tranquil slumber.[5]

What was left of the Coalition army rendezvoused at the line of the river Ijssel, between Zutphen and the sea two days later. There they encamped to wait for stragglers. Lieutenant Colonel Keppel recorded that 'the plunder and outrages committed by the British in the different villages thro' which they retreated was so enormous as to stamp infamy on the name of Englishmen forever and render them odious to the Dutch.'[6]

The Dutch garrison of Bergen-op-Zoom capitulated to the French the following day, thus surrendering the British 87th Foot under Lieutenant-Colonel Lord Dungarvan which had formed part of the garrison. The entire battalion went into captivity. The French treated them well, allowing the battalion to keep their baggage and horses. However they took a shine to Lieutenant Colonel Lord Dungarvan's horse, and took it anyways, paying him the equivalent of £30 in Assignats in compensation.[7]

Pichegru entered Utrecht on 19 January with thirty men and was instantly greeted by 1,500 Dutchmen wearing national cockades.[8] The French also occupied Arnhem at noon the same day. On 23 January the 8e Hussards and the 15e Régiment d'Infanterie de Ligne famously captured the ice-bound Dutch fleet, anchored between the island of

Texel and Den Helder, about 50 miles (80km) north of Amsterdam. It seems likely however that the fleet had been ordered to surrender beforehand, and the Hussars merely crossed the ice to negotiate the terms of surrender.

Meanwhile the situation on the Ijssel was becoming grimmer by the day:

> Our numerous hospitals which were lately so crowded, are for the present considerably thinned. Removing the sick in waggons, without cloathing sufficient to keep them warm in this rigorous season, has sent some hundreds to their eternal home; and the shameful neglect that prevails through all that department, makes our hospitals mere slaughter-houses. Without covering, without attendance, and even without clean straw, and sufficient shelter from the weather, they are thrown together in heaps, unpitied, and unprotected, to perish by contagion; while legions of vultures, down to the stewards, nurses, and their numberless dependants, pamper their bodies and fill their coffers with the nation's treasure.[9]

On 21 January Major Frederick Beckwith of the 37th Foot entered Arnhem under a flag of truce with £500 in his pocket for the succour of the Coalition sick left at Rhenen. He dined with Général de brigade Vandamme who showed him 'great civility' and promised to to provide 'every attention to the situation of the sick.' The French subsequently moved them all to Nijmegen - surely an improvement in their situation.[10]

After waiting for stragglers, the Coalition army resumed its retreat eastwards on 27 January. The Brigade of Guards and brigades of Lieutenant General Abercrombie and Colonel Strutt remained behind for twenty-four hours to cover the retreat, convey such stores as could be sent to Bentheim, and burn those that could not. Deputy Quartermaster-General Colonel Robert Brownrigg[11] managed to get all the ammunition sent on, and as many sick and wounded as could be moved. Some 600 sick men at Deventer, Zwoll and Zutphen, too sick to move, were left behind with medical staff under the command of Major Charles McMurdo of the 3rd Foot.[12]

It rained torrentially all day on 28 January as the British set a course for Osnabrück whilst the German forces made for Munster. A lack of wagons meant that 362 British sick at Zutphen had to be left behind. A detachment under Major General Lord Cathcart (27th, 28th, 80th, 84th Foot and 15th Light Dragoons) made a circuitous detour of more than 170 miles (274km) well away from the rest of the army to the east of the Zuider Zee. Their mission was to go to West Friesland to stir up support for the House of Orange-Nassau, but also to reduce the dependency of the army on a single line of retreat and sustenance.

The first elements of the British retreat crossed the border on 30 January. Abercrombie's advanced posts were at Borkelo, Goor, Delden and Almelo; the 15th Light Dragoons were at Otmarch; de Burgh's brigade was at Bentheim; Strutt's brigade at Northorn, Nienhuys and Velthuysen; while the main body was in cantonments from Rheine to Emden. This meant that some regiments were now in Hanover. It was not England, but at least it was friendly territory:

> We this morning quitted Bentheim, with regret; the people of this town were proud to own themselves subjects of King George, and we had the pleasure to observe at one of the inns in the town, the King's Head for the sign; also on the guide posts to shew the roads (as in England) was inscribed G.R.; this, with the civility and even friendship of the inhabitants, gave great pleasure to every individual.[13]

General Wallmoden was probably glad to be home but owed his old commander-in-chief some hard truths. 'Your army is destroyed,' he wrote to the duke on 3 February. 'The officers, their carriages, and a large train are safe, but the men are destroyed. The army now has no more than six thousand fighting men, but it has all the drawbacks of thirty-three battalions; and consumes a vast quantity of forage.'[14] The 33rd Foot, under Lieutenant-Colonel Arthur Wellesley, formed the rear-guard along with the Light Battalion of the Guards. On 8 February a thaw set in, and all the rivers rose.

The French, being as cold, poorly-supplied and exhausted as the Anglo-Hanoverians, pursued at a snail's pace. Both sides were inutterably war-weary and homesick:

> Is it said the French Army have received orders to drive us from the Territories of the Republick of Holland; as they cannot be more anxious to get rid of us, than we are to be off, I fancy there will not be much driving necessary, in the business.[15]

By the end of January, the Anglo-Hanoverians had advanced to Kampen and Zwolle on the River Yssel, near where it empties into the Ketelmeer. Then rumours arrived of a treaty with Prussia,[16] and with it the suggestion (incorrect as it turned out) that the line of demarcation would be determined by the actual territory occupied by France at the conclusion. No more needed to be said; the Armée du Nord sprang into action. Général de division Macdonald's divisions invaded Groningen, leaving those of Général de brigade Vandamme and Général de division Moreau on the Yssel.

Macdonald, attacking eastwards from Groningen, hit Lord Cathcart's fortified headquarters at Winschoten (about 16 miles or 26km south of Emden) on 27 February but was easily repulsed. Général de brigade Jean Reynier repeated the attack two days later, and finding his brigade out-numbered, Cathcart decided to withdraw. In any event he had found absolutely no local support for the Dutch royal cause, so his mission was pointless. He withdrew his little force eastwards towards Bremen.

Meanwhile, 50 miles (80km) to the south, the main British columns reached the Hanoverian town of Ems in Osnabrück on 5 February and paused. Although subjects of the same king, the locals nonetheless behaved as civilians have done as long as there has been warfare. The price of everything increased – sugar from 16 to 20 Thalers a pound, hair powder from 6 to 9 Thalers.[17] On 16 February Lieutenant General Abercrombie reviewed de Burgh's tattered brigade, 'thought us very ragged about the breeches, hoped to see us in the course of a few days more like soldiers.'[18] On 20 February:

> The Light Companies of the [6th] Brigade and an Emigrant Regiment were formed into a unit under Lieutenant-Colonel Forbes Champagné [80th Foot] as a rearguard. During one withdrawal Champagné had a narrow escape when he was chased by French Hussars across a river until the ice gave way and he spent a most uncomfortable half-hour in the semi-frozen water before he managed to scramble up the bank. When the Light Companies tried to make a stand it was found, somewhat belatedly, they had no ammunition and Cathcart ordered them to make the best retreat they could: by forming line when the French got too close they reached the protection of the main body of the rearguard.[19]

On 23 February General Wallmoden urged a reinforcement of the north-south position along the River Ems, and the army was split in two. The Right Wing was placed under the command of Major General David Dundas with Lord Cathcart's isolated brigade, Sombreuille's Emigrants, the 3rd and 4th Brigades and Dundas' own brigade of cavalry. The much stronger Left Wing was to be commanded by Lieutenant General Abercrombie with advanced posts under lieutenant colonels Hay McDowall and William Gooddy Strutt, the 1st, 2nd and 5th Brigades, the Brigade of Guards, the cavalry brigades of Laurie, Vyse and Ralph Dundas, plus the reserve artillery.[20]

On 24 February the French advanced upon Nienhuys and Velthuysen, which were defended by Lieutenant Colonel Strutt's advanced guard

(Loyal Emigrants, plus detachments of Rohan's and Bouille's émigrés). They were obliged to fall back to Nordhorn for the loss of 100 men.[21]

In late February the troops heard that Major General Fox had gone home never to return, 'to the joy of the whole army.'[22] The frost and snow returned on the last day of February, and the countryside was so poor and thinly populated that the troops had to be quartered all over the countryside, meaning that many went missing from being either forgotten or lost.

At the end of February Generalleutnant Friedrich Adolf Riedesel arrived at Bentheim with five battalions of Brunswick infantry and a corps of mounted chasseurs, joining the Hessen-Cassel and Hanoverians there.[23] They were there because a British subsidy had paid for them to be there. But they had no heart for this failed war; and the Anglo-Hanoverians had neither the provisions to feed them nor the cash to pay them, let alone the ammunition to supply them. The Brunswickers unsurprisingly abandoned Bentheim and withdrew back to Rheine upon the first advance of the French.

The British cabinet decided to withdraw the troops from the continent on 8 March. Lieutenant General Harcourt received the news three days later, along with advice that transports for 23,000 men were on their way. Hanover, Hesse-Darmstadt and Hesse-Cassel were to be left to their own devices, defended by not much more than the tattered remnants of their armies in the aftermath of this failed campaign.

By mid-March the British were cantoned around Osnabrück in Hanover, where the population received them much more coolly than the reception had been at the beginning of February. Prussian troops had arrived from the east to hold the line of the Ems, and to the Hanoverians, the British were abandoning the country whilst fellow Germans now defended them. To add further discomfiture, the Prussians would not lift a finger to aid their former Coalition allies.

With the weather improving, the French made one last thrust at the Coalition outposts between the Rivers Dunkel and Vechte on 13 March. One column got bogged down in rough country and made no impact, but the other three (about 10–12,000 men) were far too strong for the meagre Coalition garrisons in Gronau, Bentheim and Schüttorf.

Riedesel's retiring Brunswickers found themselves in danger of encirclement and lost 220 men fending off the French attackers. A tiny garrison left in Bentheim Castle commanded by Leutnant Friedrich du Plat of the Hanoverian 3.Grenadier-Bataillon kept the French at bay for a while but were permitted to retreat with all their arms in the morning of 14 March. They rejoined the rest of Wallmoden's force, now withdrawn to the east bank of the Ems.

Wallmoden was in a quandary. He had only 14,000 men with which to defend over 100 miles (160km) of frontier, and 6,000 of those men were under orders to return to England. He complained to General Harcourt, begging the British to stay until Prussian intentions were clear. But Harcourt could do nothing. He was under orders to bring the army home.[24]

Homeward Bound

The British retreat re-commenced northwards to Bremerhaven via Bremen on 22 March. Two days later 100 sail of transports arrived off Bremerhaven. The army marched into Bremen from 25 March onwards, and isolated units and stragglers continued to stream into the place for days afterwards. Lieutenant General Abercrombie established his headquarters there and the Brigade of Guards found quarters in the town; the rest of the army had to make do in surrounding villages. Officers bought food and wine in preparation for the sea voyage. 'There was very old Hock to be sold at the rate of two guineas per bottle, that was 300 years old.'[25] Abercrombie boarded a ship for home on 1 April.

The army was divided into four classes,[26] each with a separate embarkation date and destination:

1st Class (Colonel William Morshead) – Royal Artillery (part), Foot Guards, Royal Waggon Train, Royal Military Artificers – bound for Greenwich

2nd Class (Major General Hon. John Thomas de Burgh) – 12th, 27th, 28th, 40th, 54th, 57th, 59th, 79th, 80th, 84th Foot, Loyal Emigrants – bound for Portsmouth and Gosport

3rd Class (Major General Charles Gordon) – 3rd, 14th, 19th, 33rd, 38th, 42nd, 53rd, 63rd, 78th, 88th Foot – bound for Harwich and Yarmouth

4th Class (Major General James Coates) – 8th, 37th, 44th, 55th, 85th, 89th Foot – bound for Sunderland and Tynemouth

On 5 April Lieutenant General Harcourt took the salute at Bremen, his last official act as commander-in-chief. The 4th Class was the first to embark and sail, being the most collected in Bremen when the orders were issued. The experiences of the 3rd Class were fairly typical. They boarded their transports on 8 April, dropped down to the Beacon (about eight leagues from Bremerhaven) on 15 April, then weighed and set sail on 26 April. The 3rd Class arrived off Sunderland on 30 April and disembarked at Harwich on 7 May.[27] The 2nd Class was the last to embark, not sailing until 1 June. Two years to the day from their first engagement at Famars, 8 May 1795, the Brigade of Guards started to disembark at Greenwich.

Altogether around 15,000 men embarked, meaning that some 6,000 must have perished or become lost since leaving the line of the Waal. The cavalry and horse artillery were, at the insistence of King George, destined to stay on in Hanoverian territory to defend the Electorate until November 1795 under major generals Ralph Dundas, Richard Vyse, Colonel Richard Wilford and the German-speaking Lord Cathcart.

About three weeks after disembarkation, the 37th Regiment of Foot held its first inspection since returning from the Continent, at Sunderland on 4 June 1795. They were able to muster just four officers, one quartermaster, one surgeon, one surgeon's mate, twenty-one serjeants, six drummers, and 140 other ranks fit for duty. Another thirty men were sick present, whilst 179 were still sick in hospital. A further nine officers, twenty-one serjeants, twelve drummers and 523 men were absent, prisoners-of-war. Unsurprisingly, four officers were absent on recruiting parties.[28] Notwithstanding that the regiment had lost some 400 men as prisoners at Druten on 19 October 1794, the general attrition and rate of sickness were probably fairly representative of the regiments returned from the Continent at this time.[29]

But such were the growing demands of other theatres of war, in particular the West Indies, that it was rushed back up to a strength of over 1,500 men with raw recruits and despatched to the West Indies under Abercrombie's expedition to re-capture the Windward Islands on 28 September. The fleet was utterly dispersed by storms and they ended up on the Isle of Wight, subsequently being sent to Gibraltar.

Their companion regiments in the old 1st Infantry Brigade – Fox's 'Little Brigade' - had common experiences. The 14th Foot landed at Harwich from Bremen on 7 May 1795, quartered at Warley in Essex in June, then proceeded to Nursling near Southampton in July, where it was ordered to embark on the first Quiberon expedition, but was driven back to Southampton due to contrary winds. Subsequently it embarked, over 1,200 strong, at Southampton for the West Indies on 30 September, sat at anchor until mid-November, and on departing was driven back to port by the storms. A second departure in early December was equally disastrous, however one transport with a company of the 14th aboard made it through and reached Barbados eleven weeks later. The rest of the 14th went into barracks at Cowes and re-embarked in early February, to reach Barbados in April 1796. The 53rd Foot landed in Norwich from Bremen in May 1795, marched to Southampton in late August and absorbed the 107th and 109th Foot to become over 1,100 men strong. Setting sail in mid-November, it too suffered the same division; four companies under Major Thomas

Brisbane arrived on Barbados in March 1796, whereas the remainder wintered in Hilsea and joined the rest of the battalion in the West Indies in the spring of 1796. In such manner were most of the Flanders regiments brought back up to strength and despatched – in great haste and in dramatic circumstances – to the West Indies. This left precious few regiments at home for further action on the Continent.

The doughty Loyal Emigrants, who had established an excellent fighting record, sailed for the Isle of Wight but soon found themselves back in France. They sailed with d'Hervilly's Royalist force as part of the disastrous assault upon Quiberon on 27 June 1795. On 21 July the survivors, twelve officers and eighty-five men, sailed back to England where they absorbed the remainders of other émigré regiments and settled down to garrison duty in Lymington, although their numbers were relatively low. In 1797 they were again shipped off, this time to Portugal, as part of Lieutenant General Charles Stuart's defensive force at Lisbon.[30] There they stayed until 1801, when at the Peace of Amiens, they made one last voyage to Jersey, where they were disbanded on 24 August 1802.

As the last British transports sailed away from Bremerheven, the Hanoverians and Hessians were of course on their own. The former had lost heavily in the campaign; 597 men killed, 3,460 men wounded, and 5,649 men missing.[31] The remaining men re-organised at Oldenburg, Quackenbruck, Hoya and other barracks-towns and recruited back up to strength. The Hessen-Cassel, Hessen-Darmstadt and Brunswick contingents cantoned in Hanover also, but were secretly in negotiations with the Prussians, intending to return home as part impending peace negotiations.

The Prussians, almost against expectations, had had some recent success on the Rhine. They stopped the French advance at Kaiserslautern in May 1794 and again at the same place in September 1794 with a combined force of Prussians, Austrians and Hessen-Darmstadters. But then they remained passive for the rest of the campaign. The Moselle valley came under French control. Trier was lost in early August 1794 and Koblenz fell in October. At that point the Prussian commander-in-chief Möllendorff gave up the Palatinate and withdrew his troops over to the right bank of the Rhine. In February 1795, the main Prussian army retreated to Westphalia at about the same time as the British did, while peace talks with France were well under way. The signed the first treaty of the Peace of Basel with France on 5 April 1795.[32]

Wallmoden wrote to the Duke of York on 16 April 1795 advising him of the treaty and that he had been requested by the Prussians to evacuate East Friesland. The duke ordered Wallmoden to comply and take up a position along the River Weser, and under no account to allow the Prussians to enter Hanover. He was also to prevent the Hessen-Cassel and Brunswick troops from dishonouring their subsidiary obligations, using force if necessary.

On 28 August 1795, the third treaty of the Peace of Basel was signed, between France and the Landgraviate of Hesse-Cassel. By September it was clear to all that hostilities were over and that all subsidiary troops could go home. The British and émigré cavalry had spent the spring and summer in Bremen and Lower Saxony, restoring the condition of the horses. After a month of waiting at anchor off Bremen, the British cavalry finally arrived home around Christmas 1795. Only the Loyal Emigrants sailed for England; other émigré regiments were disbanded and the stateless Frenchmen either joined other armies or made their way home as best they could.

The Hanoverian army would not take the field again until 1796 (as a 'Corps of Observation') and then exist in relative peace until French troops under Lieutenant-Général Édouard Adolphe Mortier occupied the electorate's capital at Hanover on 4 June 1803. The remaining Hanoverian troops withdrew to the north bank of the Elbe, into the Duchy of Saxe-Lauenburg, but were soon forced to surrender. It was then disbanded under the terms of the Convention of Artlenburg - the surrender of the Electorate of Hanover to Napoleon's army, signed at Artlenburg on 5 July 1803 by Oberbefehlshaber Wallmoden-Gimborn. It disbanded the Electorate of Hanover and instigated its occupation by French troops. Many of the Hanoverians took refuge in England and formed one of the British army's finest corps during the Napoleonic era – the King's German Legion.

In 1803 the Landgraviate of Hessen-Cassel was raised to the Electorate of Hesse; Landgrave William IX was elevated to Imperial Elector, with the title William I, Elector of Hesse. This title did not survive long, for in 1806 Cassel became the capital of the new Kingdom of Westphalia, with Napoleon's younger brother Jérôme Bonaparte it's king. Elector William I was dispossessed. Westphalian troops, lacking motivation and regional identity, fought for France in many campaigns; they proved to be generally reliable but in qualitative terms a shadow of the former Hessen-Cassel army.[33] William I was restored in 1813.

The Landgraviate of Hesse-Darmstadt was a member of the Holy Roman Empire. Upon the dissolution of the Holy Roman Empire in 1806, Landgrave Louis X joined the Napoleonic Rheinbund (Confederation of the Rhine)[34] and took the title of Grand Duke of Hesse. The Rheinbund collapsed in 1813 and the Landgraviate was restored in 1814. Along with Hanover and Hessen-Cassel, it joined the German Empire in 1871.

Chapter 19

Ringed with Enemies

The Austrian Netherlands had remained a high priority in the minds of *Comité de Salut Public* in Paris. The long open border, flat geography, adjacency to Britain and the Channel ports, occupation by the Austrians and proximity to Paris, ensured its pre-eminence in military planning. But it is sobering to reflect that the Austrian Netherlands was in fact only one of seven theatres of war absorbing the attention of French war strategists. Ranking perhaps second in importance was the **Rhineland and the Rhine** frontier. Unlike Belgium, this was hilly and often mountainous country, with generally stronger forts than existed along the Franco-Belgian border. The shape of the war here was a complex set of manoeuvres and counter-moves with no clear outcome. It was only with the freeing of French divisions in Belgium as the Austrians faded from view that sufficient French troops could transfer to the Rhine for fresh offensives. The Prussians retired from the war, but the Austrians defended the Rhine with a tenancity sadly lacking in the Austrian Netherlands. The year 1794 ended with both armies locked in a series of sieges.

Next (working geographically) came the **Alpine theatre**. The mountainous nature of the terrain - which allowed key passes to be held by relatively small forces – lack of forage, and difficulty of manoeuvre ensured that this theatre largely played out a 'phoney war'. The French posture in the Alps was defensive, and the Piedmontese made no effort to intervene. It would take a Bonaparte to demonstrate how alpine passes could be put to offensive use.

The **Mediterranean theatre** was a complex one and encompassed events as far away as Corsica (invaded by the British in February 1794) as well as southern invasions of French territory, of which there was one – at Toulon. Royalist revolts broke out in southern France in mid-1793, in significant places such as Bordeaux, Marseilles, Avignon,

Lyon, Toulouse and Toulon. The Sardinians and French clashed near Nice in June without result. The infant French Republic, desperate for troops in every direction, stripped men from the Alpine front to deal with this latest threat.

Floating off Gibraltar with the Royal Navy Mediterranean Fleet – twenty-three ships of the line, fourteen frigates and 12,000 sailors – Vice-Admiral Sir Samuel Hood had orders to blockade Toulon and Marseilles, and if possible, engage and defeat the French Mediterranean fleet. Fifteen ships-of-the-line and nine frigates set sail from Gibraltar on 27 June 1793, led by Hood in the 100-gun *HMS Victory*, and anchored off Toulon on 16 July, expecting to be joined by sixteen ships from Britain's new Bourbon ally, Spain, and seventeen French royalist ships. By 25 August nothing had happened; the French fleet wisely declined battle against a larger force.

Meanwhile in Toulon, Jacobins had attempted to whip up support for the revolution but failed. The population rose against them and jailed them on 18 July. Nailing their true colours to the mast, the General Committee in Toulon declared the Republican regime illegal on 12 August. In nearby Marseilles, troops under General Carteaux were 'dealing with' the anti-Republican elements. He summoned General Lapoype's division back from Italy to discourage Toulon, whose General Committee realised that it had six weeks' worth of food in the larders. Some outside help was required.

A delegation from Toulon boarded *HMS Victory* on 22 August 1793 and offered the French fleet at anchor and the naval base to the British, in return for protection. This was far more than Hood had ever expected, and he immediately accepted; on the condition that Toulon declared her support for the Bourbons, which of course was immediately forthcoming. The General Committee advised the French fleet of their impending annexation by the Royal Navy, at which point some sailors decided to queer the Committee's pitch by seizing Fort Balaguier in protest. Many sailors deserted over the following days, dissolving into the countryside to either join the Republicans, or go home.

Hood's fleet contained elements of regiments pressed into service as marines, military budget cuts in the pre-war years having led to a shortage of ship-borne troops. These troops prepared to disembark late on 27 August; little did they know they were about to spend four months entrenched around a French city, defending French citizens from their own Republican army.

To cut a long story short, the Anglo-Spanish occupying force was sent packing during a night assault on 17 December 1793, in which Général de brigade André Masséna and Chef de Bataillon Napoleone

Buonaparte were prominent. British commander Lieutenant General Charles O'Hara ended the expedition as a prisoner-of-war. The Anglo-Spanish force and any civilian who also wished to depart did so on 19 December. For the Toulonnais who had remained behind, the defeat was catastrophic. In the two weeks after the Republican capture of Toulon, 300 residents were shot without trial; 282 were guillotined. Many of them were merely the old, sick or poor, too slow to snap a berth on the departing Coalition fleet.

The **Spanish theatre** has longed received scant, if any recognition in English-language histories. In fact, it barely even received any attention from Paris. The mountainous barrier that was the Pyrenees ensured that any offensives occurred at the eastern or westernmost extremities of the range. In the east the French made heavy weather of reducing the Spanish frontier fortresses, a campaign in which Charles Pierre François Augereau was prominent.[1] In the west the French captured San Sebastian and Tolosa, at which point they ran out of supplies and Bon-Adrien Jeannot de Moncey assumed command.[2]

The sixth theatre was an internal battleground – the dissident regions of western France, **Brittany** (Bretagne) and the **Vendée**. These areas saw perhaps the most ferocious and blood-thirsty fighting of the entire war. Chouan and Vendéean rebels in Brittany and Normandy commenced a violent action in March 1793 that ultimately tied down 40,000 French troops. The pro-royalist population formed immense guerrilla[3] bands, using the bocage country to their advantage against Republican forces sent to quell them. Scorched-earth policies were common. Genocide was also one of the tragic outcomes. The historian François Furet wrote that the repression of the royalists in the Vendée 'not only revealed massacre and destruction on an unprecedented scale but also a zeal so violent that it has bestowed as its legacy much of the region's identity ... The war aptly epitomizes the depth of the conflict ... between religious tradition and the revolutionary foundation of democracy.'[4]

Last, but by no means least, was the war carried to the French possessions in the **West Indies**, most particularly the Windward and Leeward Islands (Îles du Vent). Lieutenant General Sir Charles Grey led a British expedition to capture Martinique, St Lucia and Guadeloupe in early 1794, which enjoyed early success, but later on catastrophic failure due to the arrival of Republican Commissioner Victor Hugues (who created a Franco-native army) and the decimation of Grey's force by Yellow Fever. By the end of 1794 Guadeloupe was back in French hands, and St Lucia was only months away from sliding out of Britain's grasp.

The **Naval theatre** is not fundamental to this work, but this discussion of other theatres is incomplete without mention of the one great naval battle of the war, the Glorious First of June. The first serious naval confrontation between Britain and France during the war was the result of an attempt to prevent a convoy of provisions reaching a starving France from North America. Landlocked by enemies on all sides, and with a large percentage of the rural population serving in the Republican armies, France could not feed her people and looked to her possessions in the West Indies and allies in the United States.

The Royal Navy Channel Fleet passed the winter of 1793–94 anchored between Torbay, Plymouth and Portsmouth. This was common practice in the age of sail; rough weather and extreme cold were deadly enemies to wooden ships and the men who crewed them. Admiral Richard, Earl Howe, the 68-year-old younger brother of generals William and George Howe, commanded the fleet and was anxious to strike a blow against the French Republic in the spring. On 26 December 1793, two French ships of the line under Rear-Admiral Pierre Jean Van Staebel sailed from Brest. Within their care were 117 convoy ships bound for the West Indies and North America, sailing to bring back supplies for an encircled and starving France. Howe guessed that they would return in four month's time and planned an expedition for the beginning of May 1794, with three objectives - firstly, to intercept the French convoy returning from North America; to engage the French Atlantic Fleet if it puts to sea; and to convoy a British fleet of 99 merchantmen bound for the East Indies, the West Indies and Newfoundland.

The French convoy fleet sailed fully-laden with grain from Norfolk, Virginia, on 11 April 1794, although their departure and arrival date at Brest could not be known to the Royal Navy for some weeks. Howe collected his fleet and merchantmen at St Helens on the Isle of Wight in April 1794 and prepared to sail at the beginning of May.

As the name indicates, the battle was fought on 1 June 1794. The day dawned clear as the two fleets sat at anchor some 4 miles (7km) apart, about 300 miles (480km) west of Ushant. Howe signalled: 'Are you ready to renew the action?' Every Royal Navy ship affirmed, and at 07.15 hours Howe signalled that he intended to attack the French centre. After an hour's break for breakfast – the fleet had been on action stations for three days and the men were exhausted – the fleet bore up. The French van opened fire on Howe's fleet as it approached, and at 09.20 the French centre opened fire. Therein followed about six hours of confused action. Three Royal Navy ships were totally dismasted, against eleven or twelve French ships. Ten French ships were left behind, but only six were captured. *Vengeur du Peuple* sank at about 18.15 hours, but HMS *Alfred*, HMS *Culloden* and HMS *Rattler* were on hand to take the 400 survivors off.

French losses are difficult to state with certainty, but were probably around 3,000 in the battle itself, and another 3,500 captured. Both sides claimed victory, but there were merits and demerits from either angle. Howe had captured seven vessels, but had failed to intercept the grain convoy, and had allowed the French Atlantic Fleet to escape back to port. Furthermore, he had good reason to feel dissatisfied with several of his captains, who had been slow to deploy on the day, and one who had ignored his orders altogether and sailed in parallel line to the French fleet rather than attacking directly. French Admiral Louis Thomas Villaret de Joyeuse's fleet had taken heavy losses, but his untried Republican navy had fought with great tenacity, most of his fleet were able to put back into port for repairs, and the grain convoy was safe.

Howe arrived in Portsmouth on 12 June to great acclamation. London was illuminated for three nights to celebrate the victory. Technically he had forced a draw, but in a broader sense he had achieved two great things - the first naval battle deep out to sea, well out of reach of land; and the first battle to use a tactic of deliberately cutting the enemy line, rather than fighting in line abreast as was then the fashion. This cutting of the line led to disruption of the enemy line and the ability to cripple an enemy vessel by attacking from several directions in the ensuing melee. It formed the cornerstone of Royal Navy tactical doctrine for the remainder of the war, to be perfected by a 35-year-old Royal Navy captain then serving in the Mediterranean, Horatio Nelson.

Chapter 20

Torpor and Treachery

The War of the First Coalition, at least as it pertained to the Austrian Netherlands and the United Provinces, thus ended with a whimper.[1] Rarely had a war been so inappropriately named:

> A Coalition implies some power of coalescing. But among the four Powers there was far more of disunion than union. In fact, England was the sole link between these wrangling confederates … Grenville … averred that the German princes turned towards England as an inexhaustible milch-cow. The animal in this case could dictate her terms; and thus the relations of the three Powers resembled those of a rich but somewhat exigent employer to grumbling and distrustful employees. Holland also, in return for her sacrifices in men and money, demanded from Austria a better frontier on the side of Dutch Flanders and Maestricht, to which the Viennese Court opposed a quiet but firm resistance.[2]

Whitehall was under no illusion as to the weakness of the First Coalition. 'They well knew the incurable jealousies of the Houses of Hapsburg and Hohenzollern, the utter weakness of the Holy Roman Empire, the poverty or torpor of Spain, Sardinia, and Naples, the potent distractions produced by the recent partition of Poland, and the Machiavellian scheme of the Empress Catharine II to busy the Central Powers in French affairs so that she might have a free hand at Warsaw.'[3] They laboured on, however, under the misconceptions that the finances of France must be exhausted and about to break down; and that the rule of the Jacobins – blood-thirsty, tyrannical and uncompromising – must certainly collapse at any time.

No exertion on the part of the Coalition after Dunkirk was ever going to be good enough. For the French were fighting a different war altogether, as one historian commented:

> The English Ministers knew little of what was going on in France, and therefore failed to understand that the desperadoes now in power at Paris were wielding a centralised despotism, compared with which that of Louis XIV was child's play.[4]

William Pitt constantly believed that the French social structure was on the verge of breaking up. 'Here again the miscalculation was perfectly natural in an age which regarded kings, nobles, and bishops as the fixed stars of a universe otherwise diversified only by a dim Milky Way.' Such notions were easily dispelled. The French had harnessed two potent forces - democracy and nationality – and created a platform for becoming the leading power in Europe. Their vast conscripted citizen armies, led on by talented young generals who were more afraid of the guillotine than the enemy, were playing in a different league altogether to the ponderous, inflexible Coalition armies led (for the most part) by aged veterans from another era.

Whitehall contributed to the disasters by indirect means as well as direct. They weakened the British force in Flanders by sending large drafts of troops to the West Indies, Toulon and Corsica to confront France everywhere a front could be made, a useless diffusion of meagre resources. Corsica was occupied in the spring of 1794, yet little or no use was made of that island for expeditions against the Riviera or the south of France, which might easily have stirred royalist revolt in those anti-Republican provinces.

The year 1794 promised to retrieve the failures of the first campaign and to wear down the French defences. Austria was liberally subsidised, and Prussia snared by a treaty which, with better management, might have brought a second highly-efficient army into Flanders. In April 1794 the hope that 340,000 coalition troops would advance on the north and north-east frontiers of France appeared quite possible. The victories of April and early May seemed about to open the way to Paris. Earl Howe's victory, the Glorious First of June, ensured Royal Navy supremacy in the Channel. Corsica and French holdings in the West Indies were under the Union Jack. Brittany and la Vendée were aflame. In early May 1794 the collapse of the Jacobins seemed imminent.

That all changed by the end of May. The victory at Tourcoing sent French confidence into the stratosphere, whilst having the opposite effect on the Coalition. Even the Coalition victory at Tournai four days later did not change the equation. The emperor gave up and rode back home to Vienna, taking his talented chief-of-staff Mack with him. Prussia and Austria relaxed their efforts at the very moment that France sensed blood. Both were distracted by the Polish Question. The 62,000 Prussians promised (and paid for) required a line of march so rigid as to furnish the Prussian generals with good excuses for refusing to march – it would have placed them across the front of the French columns now pressing northwards. Great Britain got nothing in return for the subsidies paid.

The British army found little glory in Flanders and the United Provinces. Totally unprepared for war, insignificant in numbers (at least initially) and poorly recruited and supplied, it played second-fiddle to stronger continental armies for the first year of the war, only taking a more senior role when the Austrians lost heart - not to mention one of their most valuable territories, the Austrian Netherlands. Britain had lost its closest ally on the continent, the Dutch Republic, and a pro-British administration would not be seen in Amsterdam until 1814.

The National Convention in Paris had called the nation to arms; why could not Great Britain? Parliamentary distrust of the army, the ingrained conservatism of the English character, and the political ferment which marked the years 1794–5 explained why not. Any proposal to merge line troops, militia, and volunteers as the French had done would have seemed madness. Protests against the facilities given to the loyal to arm and drill themselves had occurred spontaneously. Conscription might well spell revolution. It would take Great Britain until 1914 to cross that particular bridge. No, the army must make do with volunteers of any class prepared to endure every hardship for a pittance, and enthusiastic amateurs for officers, the results of which created the army of 1793–1795:

> It was easy for a man with influence to obtain command and most had neither ... ability nor enthusiasm; some lacked courage and four were tried by Court Martial for cowardice after a single skirmish. Drunkenness was rife and the Colonels, some young and many owing their ranks to patronage and jobbery, were not the men to enforce discipline or even to realise its necessity. In addition, there was an acute lack of drivers for the artillery, then civilians; a corrupt commissariat, which cheated the troops of food and pay and sold the animals' forage; and finally an almost useless medical corps manned by the dregs of the profession. All these contributed to the makings of the tragedy which befell this most unhappy expeditionary force.[5]

By the time British infantry was available in respectable numbers it was by-and-large reduced to miserable trench duty, followed by a winter retreat on a par with Corunna or the Berezina.

The cavalry had more satisfying outings, winning plaudits for its dash at Willems and Cateau. In fact, April and May 1794 might be considered the British cavalry's finest performance in the entire period of 'The Great War.' A number of future Peninsula generals first drew their blades in Flanders as junior dragoon officers, but it would be 1813 before the British army was able to put a sizeable cavalry force in the field once more.

As to relations with the armies of Coalition partners, the Prussians were so little seen as to allow any particular opinion to be formed. The Austrians, admired as the very ideal of professional soldiery in early 1793, grew steadily more reviled by the British in direct proportion to their commitment to the campaign. By late 1794 most British officers seemed glad to see the back of them. Nonetheless the Imperial Army contained some excellent regiments. The infantry regiment Nr.20 (Graf Kaunitz-Rietberg) and cavalry regiments Nr.1 (Leopold Hussars) and Nr.16 (Blankenstein Hussars) in particular constantly excelled in the service.

It seems at no point in the entire campaign were Dutch troops trusted by the British. Letters and journals are full of references to the 'cowardly' Dutch, which we can temper by seeing that the country was wavering, fighting a war that many Dutchmen did not believe in.[6] Junior British officers of 1794 who commanded brigades, divisions and corps in 1815 must surely have carried strong prejudices against the Dutch (and Belgians too) which they probably filtered down to the lower ranks, tainting English-language views of Wellington's Dutch-Belgian allies at Waterloo that are only now being re-assessed and corrected.

The Hanoverians served solidly and quietly without earning the press inches of their British partners-in-arms. The Hanoverian infantry earned some early criticism from British diarists,[7] but it will come as no surprise to scholars of the Peninsular War to learn that the Hanoverian cavalry was uniformly excellent. The contingents from Hessen-Cassel and Hessen-Darmstadt were, perhaps, the best of the duke's troops, always committed to professionalism and frequently appalled by the behaviour of their British allies. The officers of the German-speaking contingents displayed an equally high standard of conduct. Hammerstein and Würmb as two notable examples deserve praise for their part in a losing cause.

Which brings us to the units of the British army. The Guards did their duty at all times and served as a role-model for the army. The three battalions of the 1st Infantry Brigade (14th, 37th and 53rd) started roughly but after six months became quite dependable. The loss of the 37th at Grave was either sheer bad luck, or bad officering – probably the latter. As to the other infantry regiments, it was pot luck. The newly-raised regiments from Ireland (87th, 88th, 89th) were a rabble. Of the rest, the 12th, 27th, 28th, 33rd, 40th and 55th had their moments in the sun. The Royal Artillery, always too few in numbers to make a real difference, were as professional as always – *Ubique*.[8] Parcelled out to infantry battalions in tiny numbers to direct battalion guns, it is a great shame that British artillery doctrine at the time did not do justice to their skill.

The greatest acclaim is due to the British cavalry, serving in their singularly most successful campaign of the era. Given 'good cavalry country' they were unstoppable in April and May 1794. This must be tempered by the fact that the troops opposed to them were markedly inferior. Nonetheless, they had many talented officers in their ranks – Robert Laurie, John Mansel, Ralph Dundas, Stapleton Cotton, Denis Pack, William Payne, Robert Long and John Le Marchant. The fact that they won two actions virtually on their own is a testament to their contribution to the campaign.

The Duke of York received most of the blame for the failure in Flanders, although few stopped to consider that at the outset, he had been a 29-year-old with no previous campaign experience; and had been required to learn everything on the job. This was not necessarily a barrier to success. Frederick the Great and Napoleon fought campaigns without having commanded a battalion in action.[9] His seven years of staff experience in Prussia was more than most other British generals could lay claim to. His greatest failing, in all likelihood, was his lack of *hauteur*. The future Duke of Wellington and Robert E. Lee could reduce subordinates to jelly with withering stares and stern silences. The Duke of York never could; his natural affability would not allow it. To quote Alfred Burne, 'if he had been less of a gentleman, he would have been more of a general.'[10] The famous nursery rhyme carrying his name was almost certainly aimed at an earlier duke (Flanders being largely dead flat) but popular culture has given him the aura of indecisiveness and incompetence, which is largely unjust. There were many reasons for Coalition failure in the campaign. Imperial interference, outdated strategic ideas, poor coordination between the allied nations, lack of experience with large armies over large geographic areas, appalling conditions and meddling from politicians were equally to blame.

The British Army had been neglected for many years, and the Duke of York found his true metier as an administrator and reformer in his new role as Commander-in-Chief from 10 February 1795. Everything he saw wrong and sought to fix had been learned the hard way – in Flanders and the Austrian Netherlands. His reforms created the army that won the Peninsular War and the Waterloo campaign. Over the next twenty years he used his power and influence as a Prince of the Blood to transform the ill-disciplined rag-tag army of Flanders into the victors of Maida, Talavera, Martinique, Salamanca, Vitoria, Nivelle and Toulouse. In this he was aided considerably by his hard-working staff, his 'family' – Harry Calvert, Robert Brownrigg, William Wynyard, David Dundas, Charles Craufurd, Herbert Taylor; Flanders veterans all.

The burgeoning industrial revolution played a part that cannot be ignored. Britain could produce *materiel* at a rate no other European power could touch. Saltpetre, essential to produce gunpowder, was another overlooked factor. The British conquest of Bengal in 1757 led to Britain securing 70 percent of the world's saltpetre production; not only did Britain have more of it than anybody else, but also at a higher quality. British military invention (more specifically, utilisation thereof) drastically outstripped French practice; shrapnel, rocket artillery, rifles, the percussion cap.[11] But technology was nothing without the leadership to employ it, with youth and vigour in contrast to the creaky torpor of the Coalition generals of 1793–1795. In this regard the duke found gold, with Arthur Wellesley (the future Duke of Wellington) commanding an expeditionary force at age 39, John Stuart and John Moore at age 47, and William Cathcart at age 50.[12] Under the duke's stewardship the British Army grew from 133,000 men in 1795 to a peak of 367,000 in 1813, necessitated by a war fought on many global fronts and by 1813 entering it's twentieth year.[13] By that time most officers taking commissions were from the middle-class; contrary to myth, nobles represented only two percent of the army's officer corps.

Ultimately the British army achieved success by emulating the French revolutionary army. It was as well that it was commanded by a man who knew first-hand just what that required. Sir John Fortescue believed that the Duke of York did 'more for the army than any one man has done for it in the whole of its history.'

Whilst it would take a few years to become evident, the road to Waterloo started at his appointment. And Waterloo was a critical juncture, since history is written by the winners. For Europe, the wars of the French Revolution – which morphed into the Napoleonic Wars – would dictate the course of the twentieth century. France would emerge after 1815 as a country unrecognisable from its pre-1789 form; the revolution had fulfilled its promise in every sense of the word. After 1815, her wings plucked, she was reduced to a second-rate power - at least temporarily. Primacy in Europe had transferred to the United Kingdom and by extension, her empire. The other big winner in 1815 was German nationalism, although this would take until 1870 to acquire political form. Austria would fade for the next hundred years, as would Spain. Russia, unengaged in Flanders and somewhat mysterious to those in the west, would become involved after 1799 and be one of the 'big five' powers by 1815.

As the century progressed France recovered its pride and power; Germany unified and coveted primacy on the continent; the Austro-Hungarian Empire clung onto whatever prestige it could as glories faded; and Russia grew unimaginably large, populous and secretive in the east. The United Kingdom, armed with the vast resources of a world-wide empire but a small and highly-professional army, considered itself strong enough to counter all perils by threats and subsidies alone.

Fast forward to 1914, and the fields of Flanders. *Quod severis metes.*[14]

APPENDICES

Abbreviations

Rank abbreviations have been used in the Appendices in the interests of saving space.

Battalion	batt
Brigadier-general	BG
Captain	Capt
Chef de bataillon	CdB
Colonel	Col
Companies	co
Feldmarschall	FM
Feldmarschalleutnant	FML
Feldzeugmeister	FZM
Field-marshal	FM
General	Gen
Général d'àrmee	GdA
Général de brigade	GdB
Général de division	GdD
General der kavallerie	GdK
Generalmajor	GM
Lieutenant	Lt
Lieutenant Colonel	LtCol
Lieutenant General	LG
Major	Maj
Major general	MG
Oberst	Ob
Oberstleutnant	ObLt
Squadrons	sq

Appendix I

The Crimp Riots

Victories such as the Glorious First of June gave the Royal Navy prestige in the eyes of the British public, even if they did not guarantee a rush of recruits. But the Royal Navy was fortunate. In wartime, it was permitted to acquire man-power by press-ganging, provided that the man so pressed had previous sea experience – a rule that was somewhat often loosely or creatively applied. But the army – tellingly, never the Royal Army – did not have such legislatively-supported methods to boost its ranks. Considered unpopular due to the strict discipline, perceived unattractiveness of garrison duty in boring or unhealthy locations and the perception of being a civil enemy due to its enforced usage as a police force, the army always had difficulties in recruiting. As a remedy it resorted to crimps, civilian agents who forcibly recruited men for the army, earning a share of the bounty along the way. Never mind that crimping was technically illegal; their bases of operation were known as crimp-houses, often little more than prisons in which recruits could be bound and restrained until they were led handcuffed before a justice of the peace to be sworn in – whether they consented or not.

By 1794, with the battles in Flanders and the mosquitoes in the West Indies taking their toll, bounties were as high as 30 pounds per head. London was an especially popular crimping ground, due to the large population and density of potential manpower. Royal Navy press-gangs prowled the docks, whilst army recruiters set up in ale-houses (euphemistically called 'rendezvous houses') and relied on crimps to bring in recipients for the King's Shilling:

> One of the great evils of war is the encouragement given to deceit, fraud and cruelty in procuring recruits for the service. When the war is itself unpopular, the bounties to recruits rise in proportion to the general reluctance to enlist… The recruiting houses in London, kept by crimps and kidnappers, were the general scenes of enormities committed in this atrocious and inhuman traffic. Debauchery and intoxication, the general means of seduction into the engagement; force, cruelty and sometimes perjury, the remedy against repentance

in the moment of returning sobriety and reflection; these evils will ever exist as long as the present recruiting system is continued.[1]

In early August 1794, the City of London militia ballots were underway. The Whigs, who were in opposition, put forward an anti-militia bill, which stirred civil unrest. The last date for appeal by anyone who had been balloted was set for 19 August:

> The militia ballots are) … a link of that chain of innovation on the rights of the people which characterise the present administration, and another attempt to convert the government of the country into an absolute monarchy and introduce a military government.[2]

George Howe was found lying bound and dead in the street outside the King's Arms public house, a notable crimp-house, at 14.00 hours of 15 August. He apparently had died whilst trying to escape. Justice of the Peace and MP Richard Brinsley Sheridan, an Irish-born playwright and noted Whig, arrived and signed a warrant for the search of surrounding crimp-houses in the area. An angry crowd gathered around him, and the Royal Horse Guards were called in to disperse them. The inquest into his death the following day resulted in Justice Sheridan demanding a search of all crimp-houses, which was refused by the Bow Street magistrate's office. A noisy crowd gathered outside the King's Arms and other crimp-houses near Charing Cross. Parties of the Horse Guards and Coldstream Guards were marched to the area and stood guard all night to keep the peace.

The Court of Lieutenancy at the Guild Hall heard ballot appeals. A large crowd gathered outside, chanting: 'Down with the recruiting houses!' The Lord Mayor, Peter Le Mesurier, ordered the masses back to their own wards. Somehow, and accidentally, the Militia Bill and Crimping issues had become intertwined, which was unfortunate since the former was a logical process with the right of substitution or appeal, whereas the latter was little more than arbitrary and semi-sanctioned kidnap. Handbills appeared, plastered to walls around London, falsely claiming that men could be kidnapped and shipped to Canada as pressed recruits. A mob attacked the White Horse public house in Whitcomb Street. Rumours spread that the Horse Guards had trampled rioters, which is probably untrue.

The trials of alleged rioters commenced on 20 August. With Coldstream Guardsmen behind him, Lord Mayor Le Mesurier read the Riot Act, but the crowd refused to disperse, chanting: 'Liberty and no crimps!' and 'No war! No soldiers!' He ordered the Guards to clear the streets, which they did without incident.

APPENDIX I

Riots broke out all over London; Holborn, Golden Lane, Middle Moorfields, Whitecross Street, Hackney, Tower Hamlets and Spitalfields. Six county cavalry regiments were ordered to stand by and rode to Vauxhall in the event they would be needed for crowd control. Mobs attacked constables in Bride Lane and Shoe Lane. A further detachment of Coldstream Guards from the Tower was ordered out on patrol, and another 100 men of the Honourable Artillery Company was ordered to Mansion House. A public meeting was held at Founders Hall to discuss the Militia Act. The Lord Mayor banned the meeting and the crowd was forced to disperse. Fires broke out in Saffron Hill, King Street, Holborn and Deptford. Someone tried to set fire to the Light Horse Volunteer headquarters but failed. Thirty Coldstream Guardsmen from the Tower and a troop of cavalry from Epping arrived to protect special constables, who were being sworn in by Bow Street. But little else happened; the authorities were back in control. The Home and War Secretaries had deliberately kept the army involvement low-key to avoid inflaming the anti-army sentiment any further. Hence the six cavalry regiments at Vauxhall were never used. Some twenty-three accused rioters were committed to trial, of which four received the death sentence. The Crimp Riots were over.

Some 38,563 men enlisted in the British army in 1794, against 18,596 soldiers killed or died on service. Battle casualties accounted for 2,202 (or 12 per cent) – the rest were mainly fever victims in the West Indies. Curiously, this recruitment number is higher than any of the years 1805, 1806, 1811 or 1812, when the threat from Napoleon or the cascading successes of Wellington in the Peninsula made 'going for a soldier' a more compelling career-choice. Just how many of these 38,563 men were snared by crimps history does not relate.

Appendix II
Biographies

France

Johann Nikolaus Luckner (1722-1794)
A Bavarian, Nikolaus Luckner served in various continental armies before joining the French in 1763. Such military career paths were not unusual in the eighteenth century. Made a marshal in 1791, he was appointed second commander of the Armée du Nord in 1792. The National Convention became unhappy with the subsequent slow progress of the 70-year-old commander. Luckner asked to be dismissed and was summoned to Paris where a guillotine rather than a pension awaited him. He was executed on 4 January 1794.

Adam Philippe, Comte de Custine (1740-1793)
Custine was born into minor aristocracy in Metz and served in the royal army in the Seven Years' War and in the American War of Independence. Despite suspicions against him, he led successful campaigns by the Army of the Vosges in 1792. Re-assigned to the command of the Armée du Nord in January 1793, he fatally failed to capture the besieged fortress of Condé. The Revolutionary Tribunal was not impressed and brought a charge of treason. He was guillotined in Paris on 28 August 1793.

Jean Nicolas Houchard (1739-1793)
Houchard was a fervent French patriot. Born in Lorraine, brave to a fault, and wounded in action many times, he was however a limited field commander – 'brave and stupid.' He replaced Custine as commander-in-chief of the Armée du Nord after Custine's execution. Despite victories against the British at Hondschoote and the Dutch at Menin, he was accused of cowardice for failing to pursue his beaten foes. He tore his shirt off to display his many wounds at his trial; it did him no good. The Revolutionary Tribunal sent him to the guillotine on 17 November 1793.

Charles-François du Périer Dumouriez (1739-1823)

Another aristocrat, Dumouriez was born at Cambrai in the Austrian Netherlands. He allegedly received twenty-two wounds during the Seven Years' War, but then suffered thirty years of unfulfilled ambition in the peace-time army. That all changed in 1790 when he became French military adviser to the new Belgian government (Belgian independence being something close to his heart). He became French Minister of Foreign Affairs then won a major victory over the Austrians at Jemappes. But he had enemies at home, and after defeat at Neerwinden, he went over to the allies. He lived the rest of his life in exile and died in England in 1823.

Auguste Marie Henri Picot de Dampierre (1756-1793)

This promising young officer was born in Paris and studied the tactics of Frederick the Great in Prussia. Sympathetic to the revolution, he was made lieutenant-colonel of dragoons in 1791 and rose quickly. He commanded a division at Valmy and a wing of the army at Jemappes. Elected commander of the Armée du Nord on 8 April 1793, he confronted British forces in May 1793 but was hideously wounded by a cannon-ball and died at Valenciennes on 11 May 1793.

Jean-Baptiste Jourdan (1762-1833)

A private at age 15 and a Général de division by age 30, Jourdan was named as the commander of the Armée du Nord on 25 September 1793. Three previous commanders had already been sent to the guillotine for 'inadequacy'. Brought before the Committee of Public Safety in January 1794 for refusing to carry out an impossible order, Jourdan escaped with his head, but was dismissed. He was re-appointed in May 1794 and won the battle of Fleurus. A Marshal's baton under Napoleon awaited him. He died in Paris in 1833.

Jean-Charles Pichegru (1761-1804)

Another of France's young patriots, Pichegru was born in the Jura and attended Brienne, where he taught mathematics to Napoleon. Elected lieutenant-colonel at the revolution, he was a général de brigade by 1793, then commander-in-chief of the Armée du Rhin, where he scored numerous victories. Appointed to replace Jourdan in the Armée du Nord in 1794, Pichegru eventually drove the allies across the River Waal, then captured Amsterdam in January 1795. A Hero of the Revolution, he shocked the nation by conspiring for the return of King Louis XVIII. He was permitted to retire in disgrace but was arrested and later found strangled in prison in 1804.

Great Britain
HRH Prince Frederick, Duke of York and Albany (1763-1827)
The second son of King George III, born in London. He was gazetted colonel at the age of 17, major general at age 19, and lieutenant general at age 21. Somewhere along the way he lived in Hanover for six years where he learnt to speak German. Promoted to full general just after sailing for Flanders, the duke commanded the British portion of the Coalition army until returning home in late 1794. The following year his father promoted him commander-in-chief of the British Army. He commanded in the field only once more, in 1799. As commander-in-chief he is remembered as the great reformer of the army in the early part of the nineteenth century.

Gerard Lake, 1st Viscount Lake (1744-1808)
A stern guardsman, Lake was born in Harrow and served in the Seven Years' War and in North America. Appointed to command the Brigade of Guards in February 1793, he commanded the army at Linselles and went home in April 1794. He later served in the Irish Rebellion (where he developed a reputation for cruelty) but won lasting fame as commander-in-chief in in India. Ennobled as Viscount Lake, a lifelong gambler, he died broke in London in 1808.

Sir William Erskine, 1st Baronet (1728-1795)
The son of a colonel, Erskine served in the War of the Austrian Succession, the Seven Years' War, and the American War of Independence. An old campaigner, he was on the Duke of York's staff from the outset of the Flanders Campaign, and commanded the army during the Duke's absence at Christmas 1793. He commanded the right wing of the army in 1794 and later the Coalition II Column. He died in Scotland in 1795.

Sir Ralph Abercrombie (1734-1801)
Considered one of the better British generals of the era (a reputation could be argued not wholly deserved), Abercrombie was born in Scotland, served in the Seven Years' War but stayed home to avoid the American War of Independence as he sympathised with the Americans. Appointed to command a brigade in the first expeditionary force despite his age and poor eyesight, he stoically served with the army for the entire campaign. He later commanded in the West Indies and in Egypt, where he was mortally wounded and died a soldier's death on 28 March 1801.

William Harcourt, 3rd Earl Harcourt (1743-1830)

A member of the aristocracy, born in Berkshire, Harcourt served in the Seven Years' War and the American War of Independence. He commanded the British cavalry in Flanders and later succeeded the Duke of York as commander of the British troops during the retreat and evacuation. He later became the Governor of the Military College, and a field-marshal. He died in Berkshire in 1830.

Austria

Prince Friedrich Josias von Sachsen-Coburg-Saalfeld (1737-1815)

Born in Coburg, the son of a duke, Coburg (as he was commonly called) served in the Seven Years' War and later against the Ottomans, after which he was appointed field-marshal. Given overall Coalition command in Flanders, he won several early victories, after which Coalition disunity caused events to turn sour. After losing at Fleurus, and in accordance with his country's wishes, he led the Austrian army out of the Netherlands and resigned his commission. He died in Coburg in 1815.

François Sébastien Charles Joseph de Croix, Count of Clerfayt (1733-1798)

A Walloon by birth, Clerfayt spent his military career in the service of the Habsburgs, fighting mainly the Ottomans. In 1792 he commanded the Austrian contingent in the Duke of Brunswick's army. A string of early successes was reversed at Wattignies in October 1793. Clerfayt succeeded Coburg in supreme command in late 1794, defeated Jourdan at Höchst and relieved Mainz, but Austria's role in the war was all but over. A talented general, but slow and conservative, Clerfayt died in 1798.

Johann Peter Beaulieu (1725-1819)

Another Wallonian, Beaulieu was born in Brabant. 'As a young man, his bold and fiery character combined with his great energy and constant activity had made him well-suited to the military life.'[3] After many early successes against the French, he commanded the Austrian left wing at the reverse at Jemappes in November 1792. Disliked by Coburg, he found himself dismissed after the defeat at Fleurus in June 1794. Beaulieu then went on to command Austrian armies in northern Italy facing Napoleon. He died in Austria in 1819.

Baron József Alvinczi de Borberek (1735-1810)
Hailing from Transylvania, Alvinczi served in the Seven Years' War, the War of Bavarian Succession, and the Ottoman War. He commanded divisions at Neerwinden, Landrecies and Fleurus in 1793. Appointed to command the Army of the Upper Rhine, he was recalled to Vienna in 1795. He later found fame commanding Austrian armies fighting Napoleon at Arcole and Rivoli. He died in 1810.

Dagobert Sigismund, Count von Wurmser (1724-1797)
Wurmser was another example of the polyglot nature of the Austrian high command. Born in Stasbourg, he started his career in the French army, then switched to Austrian service in 1750. Action in the War of the Bavarian Succession followed. By 1793 he was a general of cavalry, commanding the Imperial Army of the Rhine. His sphere of operations did not take him in to Flanders. Wurmser was another who later faced Napoleon in Italy, at Castiglione. He died in Vienna in 1797.

Karl Mack von Leiberich (1752-1828)
'The unfortunate General Mack' of history. Mack was nonetheless intelligent, active and brave. Another Bavarian, barely 40 years old at the start The Flanders Campaign, he was made Imperial quartermaster-general (chief of staff) largely on his own merits. Coalition failures saw him fall into disfavour with the largely noble-born Imperial staff. The surrender of his entire army to Napoleon at Ulm in 1805 earned him his sobriquet. He died in Austria in 1828.

Erzherzog Karl Ludwig Johann Joseph Laurentius, Herzog von Teschen (1771-1847)
Better known to students of the Napoleonic era as the Archduke Charles, Karl was the third son of the Emperor Leopold II. He started his military career in the Austrian Netherlands in 1792 at the age of 21 and swiftly gained a reputation as a talented commander and strategist. After carrying out major reforms in the Austrian army, he inflicted the first major battlefield defeat upon Napoleon at Aspern-Essling in 1809. He died in Vienna in 1847.

Hanover

Wilhelm von Freytag (1720-1798)
Aged 73 in 1793, Freytag was old for a field command even by eighteenth-century standards. As a field-marshal commanding the Hanoverian

contingent of the Coalition army, Freytag had a poor relationship with the Duke of York. Wounded and captured at Dunkirk, he gave in to age and relationship issues in early 1794 and handed command of the Hanoverians over to Wallmoden. He died in Hanover in 1798.

Johann Ludwig, Reichsgraf von Wallmoden-Gimborn (1736-1811)
Born an illegitimate son of King George II in Hanover, he was given command of the Hanoverian Garde du Corps in 1759 and became a major general in 1761. In early 1794 he assumed command of the Hanoverian contingent in Flanders following the departure of Freytag, and in December 1794 assumed joint supreme command after the departure of the Duke of York, on the proviso that he could not issue orders directly to British troops. A great collector of art and literature, Wallmoden died in Hanover in 1811.

Hessen-Cassel

Ludwig von Wurmb (1736-1813)
Born into nobility, Wurmb made his name commanding the Hessen-Cassel Jägerkorps during the American War of Independence. In 1792 he was given command of the Hessen-Cassel contingent of the coalition and the rank of major general. He was wounded at Tourcoing, leading from the front as was his customary style. In 1806 he reluctantly took service with the new Kingdom of Westphalia as général de division, and again won distinctions under Napoleon. He died in 1813.

Prussia

Charles William Ferdinand, Duke of Brunswick, Prince Elector of Brunswick-Wolfenbüttel (1735-1806)
Charles was born in Saxony. After receiving a broad education, he entered the Hanoverian army and served in the Seven Years' War, winning plaudits at Minden. In 1764 he married Princess Augusta, elder sister of King George III of Britain, cementing a formal relationship between Brunswick and Great Britain. Ascending as Duke of Brunswick and Prince Elector of Brunswick-Wolfenbüttel in 1780, he was later made a field marshal in the Prussian army. He was supreme commander of the combined Austro-Prussian forces that invaded France in 1792, however his advance was exceptionally timid. He was fatally wounded at Jena in 1806 and died at Hamburg. His son, Friedrich Wilhelm, was killed at Quatre Bras in 1815.

Alexander Friedrich von Knobelsdorff (1723-1799)

Born into a military family in East Prussia, Knobelsdorff served as a cavalryman in all the campaigns of Frederick the Great, being neither wounded nor taken prisoner. He was appointed to command the Prussian contingent in March 1793 after the Duke of Brunswick fell ill, along with promotion to generalleutnant. Knobelsdorff died in Saxony in 1799.

Netherlands

Willem V, Prince of Orange-Nassau (1748-1806)

William (Willem) was born at den Haag, the only son of stadtholder William IV. Made Captain-General of the Dutch army at the time of his accession at age 18, his pro-British outlook led the Netherlands into the First Coalition against France in 1793. After the Batavian Revolution he sought exile in London and died in Brunswick in 1806. His son, the future King William I, acceded to the throne of the United Netherlands in 1813. His eldest grandson Willem (later King William II) commanded Wellington's I Corps at Waterloo.

Appendix III

Commanders of the Armée du Nord 1791-1795

Maréchal Jean-Baptiste Donatien de Vimeur, comte de Rochambeau, 14 December 1791 – 18 May 1792
Maréchal Nikolas Luckner, 19 May – 11 July 1792*
Lieutenant-général Gilbert du Motier, marquis de Lafayette, 12 July – 19 August 1792**
Lieutenant-général Charles-François du Périer Dumouriez, 18 August – 28 September 1792
Lieutenant-général Anne François Augustin de La Bourdonnaye, 28 September – 25 November 1792
Lieutenant-général Francisco de Miranda, 16 November 1792 – 1 February 1793
Lieutenant-général Charles-François du Périer Dumouriez, 2 February – 4 April 1793**
Général de division Auguste Marie Henri Picot de Dampierre, 6 April – 8 May 1793***
Maréchal de camp François Joseph Drouot de Lamarche, 8 – 27 May 1793
Lieutenant-général Adam Philippe, Comte de Custine de Sarreck, 28 May – 16 July 1793*
Général de division Charles Edward Jennings de Kilmaine, 17 July – 10 August 1793
Général de division Jean Nicolas Houchard, 11 August – 23 September 1793*
Général de division Florent Joseph Duquesnoy, 24 – 25 November 1793
Général de division Jean-Baptiste Jourdan, 25 September – 9 November 1793
Général de division Florent Joseph Duquesnoy, 10 – 14 November 1793
Général de division Jean-Baptiste Jourdan, 15 November 1793 – 12 January 1794

Général de division Jean Henri Becays Ferrand, 13 January – 8 February 1794

Général de division Jean-Charles Pichegru, 9 February – 18 October 1794

Général de division Jean Victor Marie Moreau, 19 October – 4 December 1794

Général de division Jean-Charles Pichegru, 5 December 1794 – 20 March 1795

Général de division Jean Victor Marie Moreau, 21 March 1795 – 29 March 1796

* went to the guillotine.
** went over to the Coalition army.
*** killed in action.

Appendix IV

The British Expeditionary Force 1 May 1793

Staff

HRH Frederick, the Duke of York, commanding.
Military Secretary: Lt & Capt Edwin Hewgill, Coldstream Foot Guards
Aides-de-camp: Capt Charles Cregan Craufurd, 2nd Dragoon Guards; Lt & Capt Henry Clinton, 1st Foot Guards; Lt & Capt Harry Calvert, Coldstream Foot Guards; Capt William Lord Bentinck, 11th Light Dragoons
Adjutant-General: Col Sir James Murray
Quartermaster-General: Capt & LtCol John St Leger, 1st Foot Guards
Engineers: Col John Moncrieff RE

Cavalry (Major General Robert Laurie)

Regiment	Officers	NCOs	Privates + Musicians	Total Men
11th Regiment of (Light) Dragoons (2 sq)	11	19	204	234
15th (King's) Regiment of (Light) Dragoons (2 sq)	9	17	204	230
16th (Queen's) Regiment of (Light) Dragoons (2 sq)	10	18	204	232
TOTAL	30	54	612	696

Brigade of Guards (Major General Gerard Lake)
Brigade-major: Capt Lloyd Hill, 1st Foot Guards
Aides-de-camp: Lt & Capt Francis Gerard Lake, 1st Foot Guards; Capt Robbert Fagel, Dutch service

Regiment	Officers	NCOs	Privates + Musicians	Total Men
1st Regiment of Foot Guards	22	36	496	554
Coldstream Regiment of Foot Guards	22	31	502	555
3rd Regiment of Foot Guards	20	34	495	549
Flank Battalion of Foot Guards	17	22	363	402
Artillery	7	2	112	121
Artificers	2	3	84	89
TOTAL	90	128	2052	2270

1st Infantry Brigade (Major General Ralph Abercrombie)
Brigade-major: Capt John Hope, 13th Light Dragoons
Aide-de-camp: Capt Patrick Tytler, 56th Foot

Regiment	Officers	NCOs	Privates + Musicians	Total Men
14th (Bedfordshire) Regiment of Foot	18	23	494	535
37th (North Hampshire) Regiment of Foot	20	29	497	546
53rd (Shropshire) Regiment of Foot	24	26	496	546
Flank Battalion of the Line	16	17	365	398
Artillery	2	1	46	49
TOTAL	80	96	1898	2074

Appendix V

The Hanoverian Auxiliary Corps April-June 1793

Feldmarschall Wilhelm von Freytag, commanding the Hanoverians
General Johann Ludwig, Reichsgraf von Wallmoden-Gimborn, commanding the Hanoverian cavalry
Generalleutnant Georg Wilhelm von dem Bussche, commanding the Hanoverian infantry
Generalmajor Johan Friedrich von Minnigerode of the cavalry
Generalmajor von Bussche of the infantry
Generalmajor Viktor von Treuw, commanding the Hanoverian artillery
Generalmajor von Diepenbroick of the infantry
Generalmajor Rudolf von Hammerstein of the infantry
Engineers: Maj Howgriwe
Adjutant-General: Col von Sporchen
Quartermaster-General: Lt Col Kintze

Infantry

Regiment	Date Mustered	Field Officers	Officers	Staff	Serjeants	Corporals Privates + Musicians	Artillerymen	Guns	Total Men
1. Grenadier-Bataillon	2 April 1793	1	20	12	43	654	28	2	753
I, II/10.Infanterie-Regiment von Diepenbrock	5 April 1793	4	28	15	81	1162	49	4	1354
I.II/4.Infanterie-Regiment von Bothmer	16 May 1793	2	29	14	71	947	55	4	1353
2. Grenadier-Bataillon	18 May 1793	1	20	7	44	632	28	2	751

Infantry *(cont.)*

Regiment	Date Mustered	Field Officers	Officers	Staff	Serjeants	Corporals Privates + Musicians	Artillerymen	Guns	Total Men
3. Grenadier-Bataillon	24 May 1793	1	20	4	43	638	25	2	747
Garde-Regiment zu Fuß	29 May 1793	2	30	15	67	1015	55	4	1352
I, II/5.Infanterie-Regiment von der Beck	29 May 1793	2	27	15	64	989	54	4	1344
I, II/6.Infanterie-Regiment von Hammerstein	31 May 1793	2	26	14	80	1067	51	4	1350
I, II/11.Infanterie-Regiment von Taube	1 June 1793	2	30	15	81	1091	55	4	1354
TOTAL		17	230	111	574	8195	400	30	10358

Cavalry

Regiment	Date Mustered	Field Officers	Officers	Staff	Serjeants	Corporals Privates + Musicians	Total Men
9. Leichte-Dragoner-Regiment	1 April 1793	3	16	12	13	277	338
10. Leichte-Dragoner-Regiment	1 April 1793	3	16	5	12	272	308
1. Cavallerie-Regiment	4 April 1793	3	16	11	13	273	338
4. Cavallerie-Regiment	4 April 1793	2	16	5	12	268	306
Leibgarde-Cavallerie-Regiment	29 May 1793	3	14	12	17	234	314
2. Cavallerie-Regiment	29 May 1793	2	16	6	12	231	318
5. Cavallerie-Regiment	29 May 1793	2	16	8	6	257	319
7. Cavallerie-Regiment	29 May 1793	3	16	12	5	266	326
TOTAL		21	126	71	574	2078	2567

APPENDIX V

Artillery

Regiment	Date Mustered	Field Officers	Officers	Staff	Serjeants	Corporals Privates + Musicians	Guns	Total Men
Train	1 June 1793	3	4	6	14	526	20 x 6pdr 8 x 4pdr	553
Reserve	1 June 1793	0	4	4	6	382	4 x 3pdr 2 x 7pdr how	396
TOTAL		**3**	**8**	**10**	**20**	**908**	**34**	**949**

Appendix VI

The Hessen-Cassel Auxiliary Corps June-July 1793

Generalleutnant Baron von Buttlar, commanding the Hessen-Cassel troops
Generalleutnant Ludwig von Würmb, commanding the Hessen-Cassel infantry
Generalleutnant von Dalwigk, commanding the Hessen-Cassel cavalry
Generalmajor von Schmidt of the Hessen-Cassel cavalry
Generalmajor von Borcke of the Hessen-Cassel infantry
Generalmajor von Coehenhausen of the Hessen-Cassel infantry
Quartermaster-General: Major Engelhardt of the artillery
Assistant Quartermaster-General: Kapitan Dollmar of the artillery

Kavallerie (Generalmajor von Dallwigk)

Regiment	Date Mustered	Field Officers	Officers	Staff	NCOs	Privates + Musicians	Total Men
Gensd'armes	1 July 1793	3	15	12	54	375	459
3. Dragoner-Regiment Prinz Friedrich (GM von Schmidt)	8 July 1793	3	18	13	59	617	710
Karabinier-Regiment (Ob von Kruse)	11 July 1793	3	15	11	47	372	448
TOTAL		9	48	36	160	1364	1617

APPENDIX VI

1. Division (Generalmajor von Wurmb)

Regiment	Date Mustered	Field Officers	Officers	Staff	NCOs	Privates + Musicians	Artillerymen	Guns	Total Men
3. Grenadier Bataillon Von Wurmb (ObLt von Wurmb)	29 June 1793	3	12	10	44	382	27	2	501
I/Infanterie-Regiment Prinz Karl (ObLt von Hanstein)	29 June 1793	3	16	12	60	475	33	2	618
Gensd'armes (Ob von Schlotheim)	1 July 1793	3	15	12	48	367	0	0	478
I/Füsilier-Regiment von Lossberg (Ob von Lengerke)	1 July 1793	2	16	11	60	475	28	2	610
II/Füsilier-Regiment von Lossberg	1 July 1793	3	17	11	60	476	27	2	616
TOTAL		14	76	56	272	2175	115	8	2823

2. Division (Generralleutnant von Buttlar)

Regiment	Date Mustered	Field Officers	Officers	Staff	NCOs	Privates + Musicians	Artillerymen	Guns	Total Men
Jäger-Bataillon (Ob von Prüschenk)	7 July 1793	2	8	7	27	150	-	-	212
1. Grenadier Bataillon von Eschwege (Ob von Eschwege)	7 July 1793	3	15	11	43	380	27	2	493
I/Infanterie-Regiment Erbprinz (Ob von Biesenrodt)	7 July 1793	3	19	10	58	449	27	2	614
II/Infanterie-Regiment Erbprinz	7 July 1793	3	14	12	58	448	27	2	608
I/Infanterie-Regiment von Kospoth (Ob von Stein)	7 July 1793	3	16	11	59	462	27	2	609
II/Infanterie-Regiment von Kospoth	7 July 1793	3	16	11	58	449	27	2	608
TOTAL		17	88	62	303	2338	135	10	3144

Source: Ditfurth

Appendix VII

The French Garrison of Valenciennes 30 May 1793

Garrison Commander: Général de division Jean Henri Becays Ferrand
Généraux de brigade: Jean Boillaud, Charles-Victor Beauregard
Director of Defences: Chef de brigade David-Alexis de Tholosé

1er Brigade
1e Bataillon de la Cote d'Or
Grenadiers de la Cote d'Or
1e Bataillon de la Charente

2e Brigade
1/87e (Dillon) Régiment d'Infanterie de Ligne
2/87e (Dillon) Régiment d'Infanterie de Ligne
Bataillon de la Seine-Inferieure
Bataillon des Grenadiers de Paris

3e Brigade
le Bataillon des Deux-Sevres
Detachment of 2e Bataillon des Deux-Sevres
2e Bataillon de l'Eure

4e Brigade
1/73e (Royal-Comtois) Régiment d'Infanterie de Ligne
2/73e (Royal-Comtois) Régiment d'Infanterie de Ligne
le Bataillon de Mayenne-et-Loire
Bataillon des Granvilliers

5e Brigade
1/29e (Dauphin) Régiment d'Infanterie de Ligne
2/29e (Dauphin) Régiment d'Infanterie de Ligne
2e Bataillon Permenant de Valenciennes

6e Brigade
Bataillon de Loir-et-Cher
le Bataillon de la Nievre
4e Bataillon de Ardennes
Gardes Nationale de Valenciennes – three battalions

Cavalry
Detachment of 25e Régiment de Cavalerie
Detachment of 26e Régiment de Cavalerie
Dragons de la Republique

Artillery
Detachment of le Régiment de Artillerie à Pied
Detachment of 3e Régiment de Artillerie à Pied
4 companies of Cannoniers formed by the residents of Valenciennes
1 company of Cannoniers de Douai
8 companies of Cannoniers de Paris

Source: Nafziger

Appendix VIII

The Duke of York's Command 13 August 1793

HRH Prince Frederick, Duke of York and Albany – commander-in-chief
Feldmarschall Wilhelm von Freytag (Hanoverian) – second-in-command

Second Line (GdK Graf Ludwig von Wallmoden-Gimborn)

HANOVERIAN COLUMN (GL Georg von dem Busche)

1st Hanoverian Brigade (GM Graf George von Oyenhausen)
1. Leib-Cavallerie Regiment (2 sq)
4. Cavallerie Regiment (2 sq)
7. Schwere Dragoner-Regiment (2 sq)

2nd Hanoverian Brigade (GM Rudolph von Hammerstein)
Garde-Regiment zu Fuß (2 batt)
5. Infanterie-Regiment 'von Hohorst' (2 batt)
10. Infanterie-Regiment 'von Diepenbroick' (2 batt)

3rd Hanoverian Brigade (GM August von Diepenbroick)
4. Infanterie-Regiment 'von Bothmer (2 batt)
6. Infanterie-Regiment 'von Hammerstein' (2 batt)
11. Infanterie-Regiment 'Graf von Taube' (2 batt)

Hessen-Cassel Division (GM Ludwig von Wurmb)

Hessen-Cassel Infantry Brigade (GM Johann Friedrich von Coenhausen)
Infanterie-Regiment 'von Losberg' (2 batt)
Infanterie-Regiment 'Erbprinz' (2 batt)

1st Hessen-Cassel Cavalry Brigade (GM Georg von Dalwigk)
Carabinier-Regiment (3 sq)
Gensd'armes-Regiment (3 sq)

2nd Hessen-Cassel Cavalry Brigade (GM August von Schmidt)
Dragoner-Regiment 'Prinz Friedrich' (5 sq)

CORPS DE RESERVE (FML Graf Eduard d'Alton)

1st Division (GM Fabry)
Grün-Laudon Freikorps (Austrian, 6 co)
O'Donnell Freikorps (Austrian, 1 batt)
Tyroler Jägers (Austrian, 2 co)
Jägers (Hesse-Darmstadt, 2 co)
Loyal Emigrant Regiment (Émigré, 1 batt)
k.k. Husaren Regiment Nr. 16 'Blankenstein' (Austrian, 3sq)
k.k. Chevauléger Regiment Nr. 18 'Karaczay' (Austrian, 1 sq)
9. Leichte Dragoner Regiment 'König' (Hanoverian, 2 sq)
10. Leichte Dragoner Regiment 'Prinz Wallis' (Hanoverian, 2 sq)

2nd Division (MG Ralph Abercrombie)
Guards Flank Battalion (flank companies from all three Foot Guards regiments)
Line Flank Battalion (flank companies from 14/37/53 Foot)
1. Grenadier-Bataillon (Hanoverian)
2. Grenadier-Bataillon (Hanoverian)
3. Grenadier-Bataillon (Hanoverian)
1. Grenadier-Bataillon 'von Eschwege (Hessen-Cassel)
3. Grenadier-Bataillon 'von Wurmb' (Hessen-Cassel)
k.k. Infanterie Regiment Nr.33 'Sztaray' (Austrian, 1 batt)

1st British Cavalry Brigade (MG Ralph Dundas)
7th (Queen's Own) Regiment of (Light) Dragoons (2 sq)
11th Regiment of (Light) Dragoons (2 sq)
15th (King's) Regiment of (Light) Dragoons (2 sq)
16th (Queen's) Regiment of (Light) Dragoons (2 sq)

Artillery (Maj William Congreve)
Royal Artillery (5 co)

Appendix IX

The Duke of York's Command at Dunkirk 25 August 1793

BRITISH CORPS (MG Ralph Abercrombie) - 5,200 infantry & 1,300 cavalry

Cavalry
Royal Regiment of Horse Guards (2 sq)
1st (King's) Regiment of Dragoon Guards (2 sq)
2nd (Queen's) Regiment of Dragoon Guards (2 sq)
3rd (Prince of Wales') Regiment of Dragoon Guards (2 sq)
1st (Royal) Regiment of Dragoons (2 sq)
2nd (Royal North British) Regiment of Dragoons (2 sq)
6th (Enniskillen) Regiment of Dragoons (2 sq)
7th (Queen's Own) Regiment of Light Dragoons (2 sq)
11th Regiment of (Light) Dragoons (2 sq)
15th (King's) Regiment of (Light) Dragoons (2 sq)
16th (Queen's) Regiment of (Light) Dragoons (2 sq)

Infantry
Guard Flank Battalion (flank companies from all three Guards regiments)
Line Flank Battalion (flank companies from 14/37/53 Foot)
1/1st Regiment of Foot Guards
1/Coldstream Regiment of Foot Guards
1/3rd Regiment of Foot Guards
14th (Bedfordshire) Regiment of Foot
37th (North Hampshire) Regiment of Foot
53rd (Shropshire) Regiment of Foot
Royal Artillery (5 companies)
Loyal Emigrant Regiment

HANOVERIAN CORPS (FM von Freytag) - 9,000 infantry & 1,600 cavalry

1st Cavalry Brigade (GM von Dachenhausen)
1. Leib-Cavallerie-Regiment (2 sq)
2. Cavallerie-Regiment (2 sq)

2nd Cavalry Brigade (GM Graf von Deynhausen)
5. Cavallerie-Regiment (2 sq)
7. Schwere Dragoner-Regiment (2 sq)

3rd Cavalry Brigade (GL Georg von dem Busche)
1. Cavallerie-Regiment (2 sq)
4. Cavallerie-Regiment (2 sq)

1st Infantry Brigade (GM August von Diepenbroick)
2. Grenadier-Bataillon
3. Grenadier-Bataillon
Fuss-Garde Regiment (2 batt)

2nd Hanoverian Brigade (GM Rudolph von Hammerstein)
4. Infanterie-Regiment 'von Bothmer' (2 batt)
6. Infanterie-Regiment 'von Hammerstein' (2 batt)
11. Infanterie-Regiment 'Graf von Taube' (2 batt)

3rd Infantry Brigade (Ob von Klinkowstrom)
5. Infanterie-Regiment 'von Hohorst' (2 batt)
10. Infanterie-Regiment 'von Diepenbroick' (2 batt)

Detached Brigade
1. Grenadier-Bataillon
9. Leichte-Dragoner-Regiment 'König' (2 sq)
10. Leichte-Dragoner-Regiment 'Prinz Wallis' (2 sq)

HESSEN-CASSEL DIVISION (GM Ludwig von Wurmb)

Hessen-Cassel Infantry Brigade (GM Johann Friedrich von Cochenhausen)
HK Infanterie-Regiment 'von Losberg' (2 batt)
HK Infanterie-Regiment 'Erbprinz' (2 batt)

HK 1. Grenadier-Bataillon 'von Eschwege'
HK 3. Grenadier-Bataillon 'von Wurmb'

1st Hessen-Cassel Cavalry Brigade (GM Georg von Dalwigk)
HK Carabinier-Regiment (3 sq)
HK Gensd'armes-Regiment (3 sq)

2nd Hessen-Cassel Cavalry Brigade (GM August von Schmidt)
HK Dragoner-Regiment 'Prinz Friedrich' (5 sq)

AUSTRIAN CORPS (General-Feldmarschalleutnant Edouard d'Alton)

1st Division (GM Fabry)
Grün-Loudon Freikorps (6 co)
O'Donnell Freikorps (1 batt)
Tyroler Jägers (2 co)
Jägers (Hesse-Darmstadt, 2 co)
k.k. Husaren Regiment Nr.16 'Blankenstein' (3 sq)
k.k. Chevauléger Regiment Nr.18 'Karaczay' (1 sq)
k.k. Infanterie Regiment Nr.33 'Sztaray' (1 batt)

Appendix X

Freytag's Dispositions South of Dunkirk 5 September 1793

Maisonblanche
Generalmajor von Wangenheim with the 10. Infanterie-Regiment and the 4. Cavallerie-Regiment

From Croixrouge to Crochte and Crochte to Grand Millebrügge
Generalmajor von Hammerstein with the 11. Infanterie-Regiment, one battalion 4. Infanterie-Regiment, one company Loyal Emigrants, the 7. Cavallerie-Regiment and two squadrons of Hessen-Cassel Prinz Friedrich Dragoner-Regiment

Between Crochte and Esquelbecq
5. Infanterie-Regiment, the 2. Cavallerie-Regiment and three squadrons of Hessen-Cassel Prinz Friedrich Dragoner-Regiment

Esquelbecq and along the Yser
Two battalions of k.k. Linien-Infanterie-Regiment Nr. 35 (Brentano), the II/Garde-Regiment zu Fuß, the 6. Infanterie-Regiment and the 2. and 3. Grenadier-Bataillons

Wormhoudt
The Avantgarde commanded by Generalmajor Fabri - 1. Grenadier-Bataillon, two companies Grün-Loudon's Freikorps, three companies of Loyal Emigrants, k.k. Kavallerie-Regiment Nr. 16 Husaren (Blankenstein), two squadrons of the 9. Leichte-Dragoner-Regiment and the British 16th Light Dragoons

Herzeele
Oberst von Prüschenk with the Hessen-Cassel Jäger-Bataillon, two companies of Grün-Loudon's Freikorps, and one squadron of the 5. Cavallerie-Regiment

Houtkercque and Watou
Each village had two companies of Grün-Loudon's Freikorps and a detachment of Blankenstein Husaren

Poperinghe
Oberst von Linsingen with the I/ Garde-Regiment zu Fuß, I/4. Infanterie-Regiment and two squadrons of the 10. Leichte-Dragoner-Regiment

Hondschoote
A detachment of infantry and cavalry commanded by Major von Hugo, guarding 14 captured cannon and 300 French prisoners of war.

Source: *Geschichte der Königlich-Hannoverschen Armee*, vol. I, pp.258-259.

Appendix XI

The Duke of York's Command at Le Cateau 16 April 1794

Strengths shown are as per the official return dated 1 April 1794:

1st Cavalry Brigade (MG William Harcourt)
1st (King's) Regiment of Dragoon Guards (3 sq) [311]
5th (Princess Charlotte of Wales') Regiment of Dragoon Guards (3 sq) [326]
6th (Princess Royals) Regiment of Dragoon Guards (3 sq) [335]

2nd Cavalry Brigade (MG John Mansel) (Ralph Dundas from 26 April)
Royal Regiment of Horse Guards (2 sq) [215]
3rd (Prince of Wales') Regiment of Dragoon Guards (2 sq) [208]
1st (Royal) Regiment of Dragoons (2 sq) [213]

3rd Cavalry Brigade (MG Robert Laurie)
2nd (Queen's Bays) Regiment of Dragoon Guards (2 sq) [216]
2nd (Royal North British) Regiment of Dragoons (2 sq) [205]
6th (Enniskillen) Regiment of Dragoons (3 sq) [306]

4th Cavalry Brigade (MG Ralph Dundas)
7th (Queen's Own) Regiment of (Light) Dragoons (2 sq) [316]
11th Regiment of (Light) Dragoons (2 sq) [322]
15th (King's) Regiment of (Light) Dragoons (2 sq) [314]

Brigade of Guards (MG Gerard Lake)
1/1st Regiment of Foot Guards [860]
1/Coldstream Regiment of Foot Guards [811]
1/3rd Regiment of Foot Guards [834]
Guards Flank Battalion [860]

1st Infantry Brigade (MG Ralph Abercrombie)
16th (Queen's) Regiment of (Light) Dragoons (2 sq) [322]
14th (Bedfordshire) Regiment of Foot [600]
37th (North Hampshire) Regiment of Foot [594]
53rd (Shropshire) Regiment of Foot [593]

Emigrés
Uhlans Britanniques [244]
Loyal Emigrants [1378]
York Rangers [514]

Artillery
Royal Artillery (5 co) [480]
Royal Military Artificers [76]

Appendix XII

French Forces at Tourcoing, 17-18 May 1794

Compiled from a variety of incomplete and occasionally conflicting sources. French strengths shown are at 14 May 1794. Approximate strength: 78,000 infantry, 5,300 cavalry, 28 large-calibre guns. Battalion guns and gunners attached to battalions not shown in the overall strengths (quantities uncertain).

FRENCH ARMÉE DU NORD (GD Souham)

DIVISION SOUHAM (GB Daendels)
Avantgarde (CdB Rubry)
2e Régiment de Chasseurs à Pied [456]
1er Bataillon des Tirailleurs [1034]
5e Régiment de Chasseurs à Cheval [273]

Division Jardon (GB Jardon))
Avantgarde (CdB Simon)
3e Régiment de Chasseurs à Pied [955]
31e Division de Gendarmes à Pied [446]
4e Bataillon des Grenadiers [842]
29e Demi-brigade d'Infanterie de Ligne (CdB Patissier)
1/29 Demi-brigade d'Infanterie de Ligne [873]
2/29 Demi-brigade d'Infanterie de Ligne [832]
3/29 Demi-brigade d'Infanterie de Ligne [854]
199e Demi-brigade d'Infanterie de Ligne (Col Rivas)
1/199 Demi-brigade d'Infanterie de Ligne [801]
2/199 Demi-brigade d'Infanterie de Ligne [890]
3/199 Demi-brigade d'Infanterie de Ligne [927]

Cavalry (CdB Dumont)
20e Régiment de Cavalerie [336]

MACDONALD DIVISION (GB Macdonald)
Avantgarde (Maj D'Argent)
4e Bataillon des Tirailleurs [757]
5e Régiment de Chasseurs à Cheval [167]
3e Demi-brigade d'Infanterie de Ligne (CdB Englebert)
5e Bataillon de l'Aisne [952]
1/2e Régiment d'Infanterie de Ligne [942]
5e Bataillon de la Cote-d'Or [914]
24e Demi-brigade d'Infanterie de Ligne (CdB Fosses)
10e Bataillon des Volontaires Nationaux [609]
2/12e Régiment d'Infanterie de Ligne [835]
3e Bataillon de la Somme [902]
68e Demi-brigade d'Infanterie de Ligne (Col Beauretour)
2e Bataillon de Loire-et-Cher [875]
2/34e Régiment d'Infanterie de Ligne [890]
13e Bataillon des Volontaires Nationaux [829]
200e Demi-brigade d'Infanterie de Ligne (CdB Cazalon)
2e Bataillon de l'Yonne [900]
21e Bataillon des Volontaires Nationaux [946]
7e Bataillon du Nord [918]
Cavalry (CdB Jaucourt-Latour)
2e Régiment de Carabiniers
Artillery (6 guns)
11e Artillerie à Cheval (6x4pdr)

MALBRANCQ DIVISION (GB Malbrancq)
Advanced Guard (CdB Druot)
3e Bataillon des Tirailleurs [1,067]
3e Bataillon des Fédéralés [901]
2/19e Régiment d'Infanterie de Ligne [810]
29e Artillerie à Cheval [6x4pdr]
Det/19 Régiment de Chasseurs à Cheval [31]
150e Demi-brigade d'Infanterie de Ligne (CdB Fabus)
1er Bataillon de l'Aisne [928]
2/81e Régiment d'Infanterie de Ligne [897]
2e Bataillon des Basses-Alpes [910]
Cavalry (CdB Trubard)
19e Régiment de Cavalerie [244]

DEHAY DIVISION (CdB Dehay)
Advanced Guard (CdB Dereix)
1er Bataillon de Chasseurs à Pied [948]
1/30e Division de Gendarme a Pied [263]
2/30e Division de Gendarme a Pied [265]
27e Demi-brigade d'Infanterie de Ligne (CdB Rzemar)
1er Bataillon du Pas-de-Calais [853]
1/14e Régiment d'Infanterie de Ligne [870]
11e Bataillon des Fédéres [989]
Det/19e Régiment de Cavalerie [100]
23e Demi-brigade d'Infanterie de Ligne (CdB Geraud)
2e Bataillon du Pas-de-Calais [724]
1/12e Régiment d'Infanterie de Ligne [735]
1er Bataillon du Calvados [743]
Cavalry (CdB Thierry)
9e Régiment de Hussards [299]
Det/19e Régiment de Cavalerie [100]
Artillery (CdB Delpire)
Artillerie à Pied (6x12pdr, 6x8pdr)
Artillerie à Cheval (4x8pdr)
2e Régiment d'Infanterie de Légère (4 co) [405]

MOREAU DIVISION (GD Moreau)
Vandamme Division (GB Vandamme)
Advanced Guard (CdB Toussant)
Det/21e Régiment de Chasseurs à Cheval [52]
8e Régiment de Hussards [116]
1er Bataillon de l'Egalite [916]
Brigade Harcourt (CdB Harcourt)
Det/21e Régiment de Chasseurs à Cheval [52]
9e Bataillon du Pas-de-Calais [707]
6e Bataillon des Fédéres [850]
1er Bataillon de la Marne [786]
3e Bataillon de la Marne [818]
Brigade Gauthrin (CdB Gauthrin)
4e Bataillon du Nord [951]
1/16e Régiment d'Infanterie de Ligne [701]
2/45e Régiment d'Infanterie de Ligne [686]
1er Bataillon de l'Ille-de-Vilaine [763]
2e Bataillon de l'Ille-de-Vilaine [606]

Desenfans Division (GB Desenfans)
Avantgarde (CdB Ducroix)
Bataillon des Chasseurs de Mont Cassel [708]
3e Bataillon des Chasseur-Tirailleurs [637]
14e Bataillon des Chasseurs à Pied [918]
Brigade Trousseau (CdB Trousseau)
2/1er Régiment d'Infanterie de Ligne [596]
2/22e Régiment d'Infanterie de Ligne [803]
9e Bataillon de Paris [782]
5e Bataillon de la Seine-Inferieure [586]
Brigade Bouvoir (CdB Bouvoir)
5e Bataillon du Rhone-et-Loire [613]
2/24e Régiment d'Infanterie de Ligne [784]
ler Bataillon du Calvados [881]
Grenadier Bataillon [871]
Det/21e Régiment de Cavalerie [179]
Det/1er Régiment de Carabiniers [25]
Artillery
Artillerie à Pied (6x6pdr, 6x8pdr)
Artillerie à Cheval (4x6pdr)

DIVISION BONNAUD (GD Bonnaud)
Division Osten (GB Osten)
Advanced Guard (CdB Beaufont)
5e Régiment de Chasseurs à pied [983]
10e Bataillon du Pas-de-Calais [792]
27e Bataillon des Volontaires Nationaux [948]
Brigade Girard (CdB Girard)
2/90e Régiment d'Infanterie de Ligne [932]
ler Bataillon d'Eure-et-Loire [988]
8e Bataillon de la Meurthe [987]
Brigade Brenier (CdB Brenier)
ler Bataillon des Cotes-du-Nord [486]
4e Bataillon de l'Yonne [905]
1/102e Régiment d'Infanterie de Ligne [457]
PIERQUIN DIVISION (GB Pierquin)
1e Brigade (GB Salme)
5e Bataillon de Paris [806]
2e Bataillon des Ardennes [638]
1/54e Régiment d'Infanterie de Ligne [675]
3e Bataillon des Volontaires Nationaux [679]

15e Bataillon des Volontaires Nationaux [741]
23e Bataillon des Volontaires Nationaux [760]
Brigade Leclerc (ChB Leclerc)
1er Bataillon de Republicaine [734]
2/10le Régiment d'Infanterie de Ligne [589]
1/90e Régiment d'Infanterie de Ligne [879]
Brigade Noel (GB Noel)
1/83e Régiment d'Infanterie de Ligne [888]
1er Bataillon de Valenciennes [805]
1/25e Régiment d'Infanterie de Ligne [781]
1er Bataillon de l'Oise [838]
1/104e Régiment d'Infanterie de Ligne [544]
3e Bataillon de l'Yonne [722]

DIVISION COMPÉRE (GB Compère)
Brigade Trudeau (ChB Trudeau)
5e Bataillon Franc [364]
1/71e Régiment d'Infanterie de Ligne [833]
8e Bataillon de Paris [827]
17e Bataillon des Volontaires Nationaux [958]
Brigade Roget (ChB Roget)
4e Bataillon des Fédéres [750]
3e Bataillon de l'Aube [845]
1er Bataillon de la Somme [807]
12e Compagnie d'Artillerie Légère [96]
Artillery
Det/27e Compagnie d'Artillerie Légère [27]
28e Compagnie d'Artillerie Légère [79]
Det/6e Régiment de Artillerie a Cheval [104]

DIVISION THIERRY (GB Thierry)
Demi-brigade de l'Allier (ChB Flavier) (2,921)
1er Bataillon de l'Allier
2e Bataillon de la Manche
7e Bataillon du Pas-de-Calais
Brigade Beauvoir (ChB Beauvoir)
8e Bataillon des Fédéres [964]
10e Bataillon de Calvados [976]
3e Bataillon des Chasseurs Francs [941]
1er Régiment de Cavalerie [475]
26e Compagnie d'Artillerie Légère (6x4pdr) [51]
1er Compagnie Cannoniers de la Charente (3x4pdr) [76]

CAVALRY (GB Baillot)
Brigade Scholtenius (ChB Scholtenius)
5e Régiment de Hussards [385]
6e Régiment de Hussards [360]
10e Régiment de Hussards [248]
Brigade Bouquet (ChB Bouquet)
13e Régiment de Chasseurs à Cheval [382]
14e Régiment de Chasseurs à Cheval [199]
13e Régiment de Dragons [434]
Brigade Jaucourt-Latour (ChD Jaucourt-Latour)
1er Régiment de Carabiniers [334]
7e Régiment de Cavalerie [438]
13e Régiment de Cavalerie [479]
Det/25e Régiment de Cavalerie [97]
Gendarmes a Cheval [48]

Parc de Artillerie (GdB Elbe)
Gunners of diverse regiments [496]
Cannoniers Volontaires du 1er de la Moselle [755]
5e Bataillon de la Meurthe [967]
Artillerie à Pied (6x12pdr, 6x8pdr, 6x4pdr)
Artillerie à Cheval (4x8pdr).

Appendix XIII

Coalition Forces at Tourcoing, 17-18 May 1794

Feldzeugmeister Prince Josias von Coburg, commanding.
Approximate strength: 62,100 infantry, 11,700 cavalry, 28 large-calibre guns. Battalion guns not shown in the overall strengths (quantities uncertain).

NORTHERN COVERING COLUMN (FZM Clerfayt)
(16,601 infantry; 3,451 cavalry)
Advanced Guard (GM Hammerstein) (Hanoverian/British)
3. Grenadier-Bataillon
I/14.Leichtes-Infanterie-Regiment 'Von Diepenbroick'
55th (Westmoreland) Regiment of Foot
Loyal Emigrants
Leibgarde-Cavallerie-Regiment (2 sq)
9. Leichte-Dragoner-Regiment 'der Königin' (2 sq)
10. Leichte-Dragoner-Regiment 'von Linsingen' (2 sq)
Hessiches Gensd'armes (2 sq)

Column Troops (FML Stein, FML Sztarray, FZM Hohenlohe-Kirchberg)
Austrian
Grün-Laudon Freikorps (6 co)
Hessisches Jägers (1 co)
Tyroler-Scharfschützen (2 co)
Feld-Jäger-Korps de Loup (2 co)
I/k.k. Linien-Infanterie-Regiment Nr. 3 'Erzherzog Karl'
II/k.k. Linien-Infanterie-Regiment Nr. 3 'Erzherzog Karl'
I/k.k. Linien-Infanterie-Regiment Nr. 9 'Graf Clerfayt'
II/k.k. Linien-Infanterie-Regiment Nr. 9 'Graf Clerfayt'
I/k.k. Linien-Infanterie-Regiment Nr. 26 'Schroder'
II/k.k. Linien-Infanterie-Regiment Nr. 26 'Schroder'

I/k.k. Linien-Infanterie-Regiment Nr. 33 'Graf Sztaray'
II/k.k. Linien-Infanterie-Regiment Nr. 33 'Graf Sztaray'
I/k.k. Linien-Infanterie-Regiment Nr. 38 'von Württemberg'
II/k.k. Linien-Infanterie-Regiment Nr. 38 'von Württemberg'
k.k. Kavallerie-Regiment Nr.1 Dragoner 'Kaiser Franz II' (6 sq)
k.k. Kavallerie-Regiment Nr.16 Husaren 'Blankenstein' (6 sq)
k.k. Kavallerie-Regiment Nr.25 Dragoner 'Graf Latour' (4 sq)

British
12th (East Suffolk) Regiment of Foot
8th (King's Royal Irish) Regiment of (Light) Dragoons (2 sq)

Hanoverian (GM Wangenheim)
II/14.Leichtes-Infanterie-Regiment 'Von Diepenbroick'
4. Grenadier-Bataillon 'von Lasfeld'

Hessen-Darmstadt
Hessisches I/Landgraf Infanterie-Regiment
Hessisches II/Landgraf Infanterie-Regiment
Hessisches Leichte-Bataillon
Hessisches Leib-Regiment
Hessisches Chevauxlegers-Regiment (2 sq)

Artillery
6 x 12-pounders, 6 x 6-pounders, 1 x howitzer.

NO.1 COLUMN (GL Goerg von dem Bussche-Hardenberg) (Hanoverian) (3,000 infantry; 1,000 cavalry)

1. Grenadier-Bataillon
I/1.Infanterie-Regiment 'von Scherther'
II/1.Infanterie-Regiment 'von Scherther'
I/4.Infanterie-Regiment 'von Bothmer'
II/4.Infanterie-Regiment 'von Bothmer'
I/6.Infanterie-Regiment 'Von Hammerstein'
II/6.Infanterie-Regiment 'Von Hammerstein'
I/9.Infanterie-Regiment 'Duering'
II/9.Infanterie-Regiment 'Duering'
I/11.Infanterie-Regiment 'Graf von Taube'
II/11.Infanterie-Regiment 'Graf von Taube'
1. Leib-Cavallerie-Regiment (2 sq)
2. Cavallerie-Regiment 'Prinz August' (2 sq)

4. Cavallerie-Regiment 'vom dem Bussche' (2 sq)
5. Schwere-Dragoner-Regiment 'von Ramdohr' (2 sq)
7. Schwere-Dragoner-Regiment von Oeynhausen' (2 sq)

NO.2 COLUMN (FML Otto) (8,847 infantry; 1,068 cavalry; 10 large-calibre guns)

Austrian (GM Kaim, GM Werneck)
Jägers (1 co)
2/O'Donnell's Freikorps (6 co)
Grenadierbataillon Rouviere
Grenadierbataillon Ulm
Grenadierbataillon Manesy
I/k.k. Linien-Infanterie-Regiment Nr. 20 'Graf Kaunitz-Rietberg'
II/k.k. Linien-Infanterie-Regiment Nr. 20 'Graf Kaunitz-Rietberg'
III/k.k. Linien-Infanterie-Regiment Nr. 20 'Graf Kaunitz-Rietberg'
I/k.k. Linien-Infanterie-Regiment Nr. 57 'Josef, Graf Colloredo'
II/k.k. Linien-Infanterie-Regiment Nr. 57 'Josef, Graf Colloredo'
Pioneers (half co)

Hessen-Cassel (GM Montfrault)
I/HK Garde-Grenadiere
II/HK Garde-Grenadiere
HK Grenadier-Bataillon 'von Germann'

Cavalry Brigade (MG David Dundas)
6th Regiment of Dragoon Guards (3 sq)
11th Regiment of (Light) Dragoons (2 sq)
k.k. Kavallerie-Regiment Nr. 2 Husaren 'Kaiser Franz II' (6 sq)

Artillery
8 x 12-pounders, 2 howitzers.

NO.3 COLUMN (Duke of York) (9,493 infantry; 1,292 cavalry; 18 large-calibre guns)

Brigade of Guards (MG Lake)
1/1st Regiment of Foot Guards
1/Coldstream Regiment of Foot Guards
1/3rd Regiment of Foot Guards
Foot Guards converged light battalion

1st Infantry Brigade (MG Henry Fox)
14th (Bedfordshire) Regiment of Foot
37th (North Hampshire) Regiment of Foot
53rd (Shropshire) Regiment of Foot

Austrian
1/O'Donnell's Freikorps
I/k.k. Linien-Infanterie-Regiment Nr. 23 'Granduca Fernando III di Toscana'
II/k.k. Linien-Infanterie-Regiment Nr. 23 'Granduca Fernando III di Toscana'
I/k.k. Linien-Infanterie-Regiment Nr. 56 'Wenzel, Graf Colloredo'
II/k.k. Linien-Infanterie-Regiment Nr. 56 'Wenzel, Graf Colloredo'
Pioneers (half co)

Hessen-Cassel
I/HK Leib-Infanterie-Regiment
II/HK Leib-Infanterie-Regiment

1st Cavalry Brigade (MG Richard Vyse)
15th (King's) Regiment of (Light) Dragoons (2 sq)
16th (Queen's) Regiment of (Light) Dragoons (2 sq)
k.k. Kavallerie-Regiment Nr. 2 Husaren 'Kaiser Franz II' (4 sq)

Royal Artillery
4 x 12-pounders, 4 x 6-pounders, 6 x howitzers

Austrian Artillery
4 x 12-pounders.

NO.4 COLUMN (FML Kinsky) (9,172 infantry; 3,494 cavalry)

Austrian (FML Schmerzing, GM Heister, GM Milwsk, GM Kerpen, GM Lothringen-Vaudémont, GM Wenkel)
Tyroler-Scharfschützen (1 co)
Slavonier-Freikorps (4 co)
I/k.k. Linien-Infanterie-Regiment Nr. 7 'Freiherr von Schroder'
II/k.k. Linien-Infanterie-Regiment Nr. 7 'Freiherr von Schroder'
III/k.k. Linien-Infanterie-Regiment Nr. 7 'Freiherr von Schroder'
I/k.k. Linien-Infanterie-Regiment Nr. 11 'Michael, Graf Wallis'
II/k.k. Linien-Infanterie-Regiment Nr. 11 'Michael, Graf Wallis'

APPENDIX XIII

III/k.k. Linien-Infanterie-Regiment Nr. 11 'Michael, Graf Wallis'
II/k.k. Linien-Infanterie-Regiment Nr. 11 'Michael, Graf Wallis'
k.k. Kavallerie-Regiment Nr.4 Dragoner 'Karakzay' (6 sq)
k.k. Kavallerie-Regiment Nr.17 Husaren 'Erzherzog Leopold' (4 sq)

Hessen-Cassel (GL von Würmb, GM Dallwick)
HK Leichtes-Infanterie-Bataillon Lentz (2 co)
I/HK Füsilier-Regiment von Kospoth
II/HK Füsilier-Regiment von Kospoth
HK 2. Grenadier-Bataillon 'von Eschwege'
HK 3. Grenadier Bataillon 'von Wurmb'
HK Leib-Dragoner-Regiment (5 sq)

Reserve Cavalry (MG William Erskine) (Followed No. 4 Column in error)
1st Reserve Cavalry Brigade (MG Ralph Dundas)
Royal Regiment of Horse Guards (Blue) (2 sq)
2nd (Queen's Bays) Regiment of Dragoon Guards (2 sq)
3rd (Prince of Wales') Regiment of Dragoon Guards (2 sq)
1st (Royal) Regiment of Dragoons (2 sq)

2nd Reserve Cavalry Brigade (MG William Harcourt)
1st (King's) Regiment of Dragoon Guards (2 sq)
5th (Princess Charlotte of Wales) Regiment of Dragoon Guards (2 sq)
2nd (Royal North British) Regiment of Dragoons (2 sq)
6th (Enniskillen) Regiment of Dragoons (2 sq)

Artillery
? x 12-pounders, ? x 6-pounders.

NO.5 COLUMN (Archduke Karl) (14,042 infantry; 4,007 cavalry)

Austrian (FML Alvinczy, FML Buglach, GM Nelms, GM Finke, GM Kray von Krajow und Topolya, GM Radowicz)
Tyroler-Scharfschützen (4 co)
Grenz-Scharfschützen (4 co)
Grenadierbataillon Malovitz
Grenadierbataillon Retz
I/k.k. Linien-Infanterie-Regiment Nr. 55 'Graf Murray'
II/k.k. Linien-Infanterie-Regiment Nr. 55 'Graf Murray'
I/k.k. Linien-Infanterie-Regiment Nr. 59 'Jordis'

II/k.k. Linien-Infanterie-Regiment Nr. 59 'Jordis'
k.k. Kavallerie-Regiment Nr. 2 Husaren 'Kaiser Franz II' (8 sq)
k.k. Kavallerie-Regiment Nr. 10 Kurassier 'Zeschwitz' (6 sq)
k.k. Kavallerie-Regiment Nr.16 Husaren 'Blankenstein' (6 sq)
k.k. Kavallerie-Regiment Nr. 37 Dragoner 'Coburg' (4 sq)

Émigré
Uhlans Britanniques (4 sq)

United Provinces
Regiment Erzprins van Orange
Orange-Nassau Infanterie Regiment No. 1
Infanterie Regiment No.3 'Van Dopff'
Infanterie Regiment No.7 'De Bons'
Infanterie Regiment Regiment No.14 'Hessen-Darmstadt'
Infanterie Regiment de Gumoëns
Infanterie Regiment Hirzel
Cavalerie Regiment 'Van der Duijn' (4 sq)

Artillery
? x 12-pounders, ? x 6-pounders, ? x howitzers.

Appendix XIV

Lord Moira's Reinforcements at Ostend June/July 1794

REGIMENT	FROM	EFFECTIVES*
19th (1st Yorkshire North Riding) Regiment of Foot	Netley camp	515
27th (Enniskillen) Regiment of Foot (Lieutenant Colonel John T Buller)	Netley camp	522
28th (North Gloucestershire) Regiment of Foot	Netley camp	586
40th (2nd Somerset) Regiment of Foot (Lieutenant Colonel Stephen Bromfield)	Netley camp	638
42nd (Royal Highland) Regiment of Foot	Netley camp	490
54th (West Norfolk) Regiment of Foot	Netley camp	524
57th (West Middlesex) Regiment of Foot (Lieutenant Colonel Hay MacDowall)	Netley camp	560
59th (2nd Nottinghamshire) Regiment of Foot	Netley camp	577
1/78th Regiment of Foot	Guernsey	?
87th Regiment of Foot (Lieutenant Colonel John Doyle)	Netley camp	774
88th Regiment of Foot (Lieutenant Colonel Frederick Keppel)	Jersey	?
89th Regiment of Foot	Netley camp	474
Royal Artillery/ Royal Irish Artillery	Waterford	184
8th (King's Royal Irish) Regiment of (Light) Dragoons (detachment)	Ireland	~120
16th (Queen's) Regiment of (Light) Dragoons (detachment)	England	~120

* Corporals and privates. Allow another 10 per cent for officers, sergeants, staff and musicians.

Appendix XV

The Duke of York's Command 15 August 1794

HRH Prince Frederick, Duke of York and Albany – commander-in-chief
Adjutant-General: Major General James Henry Craig
Deputy Adjutant-general: Lieutenant Colonel Charles Craufurd
Quartermaster-General: Major General Hon. Henry Fox
Deputy Quartermaster-General: Lieutenant Colonel Robert Brownrigg

AVANTGARDE (GM Rudolph von Hammerstein)

1st Brigade (GM von Linsingen)
HK Jäger-Bataillon [182]
HK Füsilier-Regiment von Lossberg [218]
Hanoverian Jägers [208]
Rohan's Light Infantry [504]
1. Grenadier-Bataillon (1 batt)
Rohan's Hussars (6 sq)
9. Leichte Dragoner-Regiment 'der Königin' (2 sq) [349]
10. Leichte Dragoner-Regiment 'Prinz von Wallis' (2 sq) [358]
Irvine's Hussars (4 sq) [264]
Hanoverian Reitende Artillerie

2nd Brigade (GM Georg von Düring)
Hompesc's Hussars (2 sq)
Salm Hussars (2 sq)
Choiseul Hussars (4 sq)
Carneville Hussars (2 sq)
Uhlans Britanniques (2 sq) [207]
Hessiches Regiment-Chevauxlegers (4 sq) [469]
Hessiches Leib-Grenadiere (1 batt) [672]
Hessiches Infanterie-Regiment 'Landgraf' (1 batt) [673]
Hessiches Leichtes-Infanterie-Bataillon (1 batt) [676]
Loyal Emigrant Regiment (2 batt) [1,202]

Hompesch's Chasseurs à Pied (1 co)
York Rangers [394]
Hessiches Jägers (1 co) [130]

FIRST LINE (GdK Graf Ludwig von Wallmoden-Gimborn)

Cavalry (LG William Harcourt)

1st Cavalry Brigade (MG Ralph Dundas)
Royal Regiment of Horse Guards (Blues) (2 sq) [192]
2nd (Queen's) Regiment of Dragoon Guards (2 sq) [232]
3rd Regiment of Dragoon Guards (2 sq) [160]

2nd Cavalry Brigade (MG Richard Whyte)
1st (King's) Regiment of Dragoon Guards (3 sq) [309]
5th (Royal Irish) Regiment of Dragoon Guards (3 sq)

Infantry (GL von Buttlar)

1st Infantry Brigade (GM Hundert)
3rd (East Kent) Regiment of Foot, or the Buffs
63rd (West Suffolk) Regiment of Foot
85th Regiment of Foot

2nd Infantry Brigade (MG Alexander Stewart)
2nd (Queen's Royal) Regiment of Foot
19th (1st Yorkshire North Riding) Regiment of Foot
54th (West Norfolk) Regiment of Foot

3rd Infantry Brigade (GM von Scheither)
12th (East Suffolk) Regiment of Foot [859]
38th (1st Staffordshire) Regiment of Foot [518]
55th (Westmoreland) Regiment of Foot [725]

7th Infantry Brigade (GM von Hanstein)
40th (2nd Somerset) Regiment of Foot
57th (West Middlesex) Regiment of Foot
59th (2nd Nottinghamshire) Regiment of Foot

Hessen-Cassel Division (GL Georg von Dalwigk)

Hessen-Cassell Infantry Brigade (GM von Maydel)
HK Garde-Grenadiere (2 batt) [1,050]
HK Leib-Infanterie-Regiment (2 batt) [842]
HK Infanterie-Regiment 'von Kospoth' (2 batt) [984]

Hanoverian Division (GL Georg von dem Busche)

1st Hanoverian Infantry Brigade (GM Ludwig von Scheither)
1. Infanterie-Regiment 'von Scheither' (2 batt)
6. Infanterie-Regiment 'von Hammerstein' (2 batt) [902]
9. Infanterie-Regiment 'Sachsen-Gotha' (1 batt)

2nd Hanoverian Infantry Brigade (GM Prinz Adolph Friedrich, Duke of Cambridge)
4. Infanterie-Regiment 'von dem Busche' (2 batt) [996]
Garde-Regiment zu Fuß (2 batt) [1,130]

Hanoverian Cavalry Division (GL Johann von dem Busche)

1st Hanoverian Cavalry Brigade (GM Prinz Ernst)
Garde du Corps (2 sq) [300]
1. Leib-Cavallerie-Regiment (2 sq) [293]
4. Cavallerie-Regiment 'von dem Busche' (2 sq) [304]

2nd Hanoverian Cavalry Brigade (GL Johann von dem Busche)
2. Cavallerie-Regiment 'Prinz Ernst' (2 sq) [308]
5. Dragoner-Cavallerie-Regiment (2 sq)
7. Dragoner-Cavallerie-Regiment 'Graf von Oeynhausen' (2 sq) [290]

SECOND LINE (LG Sir William Erskine)

3rd Cavalry Brigade (MG David Dundas)
1st (Royal) Regiment of Dragoons (2 sq) [215]
2nd (North British) Regiment of Dragoons (2 sq) [206]
6th (Inniskilling) Regiment of Dragoons (2 sq) [223]

5th Cavalry Brigade (MG Richard Vyse)
6th Regiment of Dragoon Guards (3 sq) [313]
8th (King's Royal Irish) Regiment of (Light) Dragoons (2 sq) [247]
14th (Duchess of York's Own) Regiment of (Light) Dragoons (1 sq)

Infantry Brigade (MG Nisbet Balfour)
8th (King's) Regiment of Foot
33rd (1st Yorkshire West Riding) Regiment of Foot
44th (East Essex) Regiment of Foot

Infantry Brigade (MG Charles Graham)
25th (Sussex) Regiment of Foot
27th (Enniskillen) Regiment of Foot
28th (North Gloucestershire) Regiment of Foot

4th Infantry Brigade (MG Henry Fox)
14th (Bedfordshire) Regiment of Foot [676]
37th (North Hampshire) Regiment of Foot [631]
53rd (Shropshire) Regiment of Foot [654]

Hessen-Cassel Cavalry Brigade (GM August von Schmidt)
HK Gensd'armes-Regiment (2 sq)
HK Carabinier-Regiment (3 sq) [393]
HK Leib-Dragoner-Regiment (5 sq) [518]

RESERVE CORPS (LG Ralph Abercrombie)

HK Dragoner-Regiment 'Prinz Friedrich' (5 sq) [650]

4th Cavalry Brigade (MG Robert Laurie)
7th (Queen's Own) Regiment of (Light) Dragoons (2 sq) [295]
11th Regiment of (Light) Dragoons (2 sq) [309]
15th (King's) Regiment of (Light) Dragoons (2 sq) [272]
16th (Queen's) Regiment of (Light) Dragoons (2 sq) [306]

Brigade of Guards (MG Samuel Hulse)
1/1st Regiment of Foot Guards [837]
1/Coldstream Regiment of Foot Guards [757]
1/3rd Regiment of Foot Guards [780]
Guards Grenadier Battalion (4 co)
Guards Light Battalion (8 co)

Hessen-Cassel Grenadier Brigade (GM Ludwig von Wurmb)
HK 1. Grenadier-Bataillon 'von Eschwege' [428]
HK 2. Grenadier-Bataillon 'von Germann' [431]
HK 3. Grenadier-Bataillon 'von Wurmb' [433]
2. Grenadier-Bataillon 'von Drieberg'
3. Grenadier-Bataillon 'von Heimburg'

Artillery
Royal Artillery (22 x 6-pdr cannon)
Hessen-Cassel Artillery (8 x 12-pdr cannon, 8 x 6-pdr cannon, 4 x howitzer)
Hanoverian Artillery (17 x 6-pdr cannon, 5 x 7-pdr howitzer, 2 x 30-pdr howitzer, 3 x 3-pdr cannon)

GARRISONS

Bergen-op-Zoom and Steenbergen
87th (The Prince of Wales's Irish) Regiment of Foot
88th Regiment of Foot (Connaught Rangers)
89th Regiment of Foot

Sas-van-Gent and Hulst (Hanoverians)
4. Grenadier-Bataillon 'von Lasfeld'
9. Infanterie Regiment 'Sachsen-Gotha' (1 batt)
11. Infanterie Regiment 'Graf von Taube' (1 batt)
14. Leichtes-Infanterie-Regiment 'von Diepenbroick' (1 batt)

PRISONERS OF WAR

Nieuwpoort (Hanoverians) (GM August von Diepenbroick)
5. Infanterie Regiment 'von Hohorst' (2 batt) [916]
10. Infanterie Regiment 'von Diepenbroick' (2 batt) [1,183]

Sluis (Hanoverians)
11. Infanterie Regiment 'Graf von Taube' (1 batt) [1,101]
14. Leichtes-Infanterie-Regiment 'von Diepenbroick' (1 batt)

Ypres (Hessen-Cassel) (GM Heinrich von Borck and Georg von Lengerke)
Gensd'armes-Regiment (1 sq)
Infanterie-Regiment 'Erbprinz' (2 batt) [1,006]
Infanterie-Regiment 'Prinz Karl' (2 batt) [1,023]
Infanterie-Regiment 'von Losberg' (2 batt) [1,014]

Troops in the United Provinces under the command of the Duke of York on 31 July 1794 (all figures are rank & file only)

Hanover infantry	5,958
Hanover cavalry	1,670
Hessen-Cassell infantry	2,886
Hessen-Darmstadt infantry	1,366
Hessen-Cassell cavalry	324
Baden infantry	215
Other foreign troops	2,000 approximately
Total foreign troops	15,800

APPENDIX XV

British	
Guards	3,600
14th, 37th & 53rd Foot	2,100
12th, 38th & 55th Foot	2,400
8th, 33rd & 44th Foot	2,550
Ten regiments with Moira	5,692
3rd & 63rd Foot	1,507
80th Foot	800
British cavalry	3,300
Total British troops	**21,949**
Sub-Total	37,749
Less those supposed to be taken at Nieuwpoort	(2,000)
GRAND TOTAL	**35,749**

Troops in the United Provinces under the command of the Duke of York on 15 September 1794 (all figures are rank & file only)

CAVALRY	Off	Sgts	Musicians	Rank&File
British	165	231	72	4,274
Hanoverian	112	184	44	1,365
Hesse-Cassel	46	116	23	860
Hesse-Darmstadt	10	36	0	280
TOTAL	**333**	**567**	**139**	**6,779**

INFANTRY	Off	Sgts	Musicians	Rank&File
British	583	924	511	19,734
Hanoverian	143	273	213	3,284
Hesse-Cassel	135	403	160	3,029
Hesse-Darmstadt	44	93	0	1,327
TOTAL	**905**	**1693**	**884**	**27,374**
GRAND TOTAL	**1,238**	**2,260**	**1,023**	**34,153**

Sources: von Sichart, *Geschichte der Koniglich-Hannoverschen Armee* Hannover, 1871.

Appendix XVI

The Coalition Garrison of Nijmegen 1 November 1794

Major General Hon. John Thomas de Burgh, commanding

7th (Queen's Own) Regiment of Light Dragoons
15th (King's) Regiment of (Light) Dragoons
Leibgarde-Cavallerie-Regiment
2. Cavallerie-Regiment (2 sq)
7. Cavallerie-Regiment (2 sq)
9. Cavallerie-Regiment (2 sq)
10. Cavallerie-Regiment (2 sq)
3rd (East Kent) Regt. of Foot, or the Buffs
8th (King's) Regiment of Foot
27th (Enniskillen) Regiment of Foot
28th (North Gloucestershire) Regiment of Foot
1/42nd (Royal Highland) Regiment of Foot
55th (Westmoreland) Regiment of Foot
59th (2nd Nottinghamshire) Regiment of Foot
63rd (West Suffolk) Regiment of Foot
78th (Highland) Regiment of Foot (Ross-shire Buffs)
88th Regiment of Foot (Connaught Rangers)
89th Regiment of Foot
Damas Cavalry (2 squadrons)
Choisseul Hussars (3 squadrons)
Irving's Hussars
Rohan's Hussars
Hompesch's Hussars (2 squadrons)
Regiment De Gumoëns (Swiss, in Dutch service)

Appendix XVII

Reorganisation of the British Infantry Brigades 13 November 1794

Brigade of Guards (MG Samuel Hulse)
1/1st Regiment of Foot Guards
1/Coldstream Regiment of Foot Guards
1/3rd Regiment of Foot Guards
Guards Grenadier Battalion (4 co)
Guards Light Battalion (8 co)

1st Infantry Brigade (MG James Coates, vice MG Alexander Stewart, ill)
3rd (East Kent) Regiment of Foot, or the Buffs
40th (2nd Somersetshire) Regiment of Foot
55th (Westmoreland) Regiment of Foot
59th (2nd Nottinghamshire) Regiment of Foot
79th (Cameronian Volunteers) Regiment of Foot

2nd Infantry Brigade (possibly Lt-col Sir Charles Ross Bt., vice MG Hon. John Thomas de Burgh, wounded)
8th (King's) Regiment of Foot
37th (North Hampshire) Regiment of Foot
44th (East Essex) Regiment of Foot
57th (West Middlesex) Regiment of Foot
88th (Connaught Rangers) Regiment of Foot

3rd Infantry Brigade (MG Nisbett Balfour)
12th (East Suffolk) Regiment of Foot
33rd (1st Yorkshire West Riding) Regiment of Foot
42nd (Royal Highland) Regiment of Foot
78th (Highland, or the Ross-shire Buffs) Regiment of Foot

4th Infantry Brigade (possibly Col Welbore Ellis Doyle, vice MG Henry Fox, on staff)
14th (Bedfordshire) Regiment of Foot
38th (1st Staffordshire) Regiment of Foot
63rd (West Suffolk) Regiment of Foot
80th Regiment of Foot

5th Infantry Brigade (Col William Goody Strutt)
19th (1st Yorkshire North Riding) Regiment of Foot
54th (West Norfolk) Regiment of Foot
84th (York and Lancaster) Regiment of Foot
89th Regiment of Foot – Lieutenant-Colonel Lord Blayney

6th Infantry Brigade (MG Lord Cathcart)
27th (Enniskillen) Regiment of Foot
28th (North Gloucestershire) Regiment of Foot
53rd (Shropshire) Regiment of Foot
85th Regiment of Foot

Appendix XVIII

British Regiments Present in Flanders 1793-1795

REGIMENT	ARRIVED	DEPARTED	SUCCESSOR REGIMENT (2018)	BATTLE HONOURS AWARDED
Royal Regiment of Horse Guards	June 1793	November 1795	The Household Cavalry Regiment (The Blues and Royals)	B W
1st (King's) Regiment of Dragoon Guards	July 1793	December 1795	1st The Queen's Dragoon Guards	B
2nd (Queen's) Regiment of Dragoon Guards	May 1793	December 1795	1st The Queen's Dragoon Guards	W
3rd Regiment of Dragoon Guards	May 1793	November 1795	The Royal Scots Dragoon Guards (Greys and Carabiniers)	B W
5th Regiment of Dragoon Guards	July 1793	December 1795	The Royal Dragoon Guards	B
6th Regiment of Dragoon Guards	September 1793	November 1795	The Royal Scots Dragoon Guards (Greys and Carabiniers)	W
1st (Royal) Regiment of Dragoons	June 1793	November 1795	The Household Cavalry Regiment (The Blues and Royals)	B W
2nd (North British) Regiment of Dragoons	July 1793	December 1795	The Royal Scots Dragoon Guards (Greys and Carabiniers)	W

325

British Regiments Present in Flanders 1793-1795 *(cont.)*

REGIMENT	ARRIVED	DEPARTED	SUCCESSOR REGIMENT (2018)	BATTLE HONOURS AWARDED
6th (Inniskilling) Regiment of Dragoons	June 1793	December 1795	The Royal Dragoon Guards	W
7th (Queen's Own) Regiment of (Light) Dragoons	May 1793	December 1795	The Queen's Royal Hussars (Queen's Own and Royal Irish)	B W
8th (King's Royal Irish) Regiment of (Light) Dragoons	June 1794 [M]	December 1795	The Queen's Royal Hussars (Queen's Own and Royal Irish)	
14th (Duchess of York's Own) Regiment of (Light) Dragoons	May 1794	December 1795	The King's Royal Hussars	
15th (King's) Regiment of (Light) Dragoons	April 1793	December 1795	The Light Dragoons	V W
16th (Queen's) Regiment of (Light) Dragoons	April 1793	February 1796	The Queen's Royal Lancers	B W
1/1st Regiment of Foot Guards	March 1793	May 1795	The Grenadier Guards	L
1/Coldstream Regiment of Foot Guards	March 1793	May 1795	The Coldstream Guards	L
1/3rd Regiment of Foot Guards	March 1793	May 1795	The Scots Guards	L
Foot Guards composite Grenadier Battalion	March 1793	May 1795		
Foot Guards composite Light Battalion	March 1793	May 1795		
8th (King's) Regiment of Foot	June 1794	May 1795	1st Battalion, The Duke of Lancaster's Regiment (King's, Lancashire and Border)	

APPENDIX XVIII

REGIMENT	ARRIVED	DEPARTED	SUCCESSOR REGIMENT (2018)	BATTLE HONOURS AWARDED
12th (East Suffolk) Regiment of Foot	May 1794	May 1795	1st Battalion, The Royal Anglian Regiment	
14th (Bedfordshire) Regiment of Foot	March 1793	May 1795	1st Battalion, The Yorkshire Regiment	T
19th (1st Yorkshire North Riding) Regiment of Foot	June 1794 [M]	May 1795	2nd Battalion, The Yorkshire Regiment	
27th (Enniskillen) Regiment of Foot	June 1794 [M]	May 1795	1st Battalion, The Royal Irish Regiment	
28th (North Gloucestershire) Regiment of Foot	June 1794 [M]	May 1795	1st Battalion, The Rifles	
33rd (1st Yorkshire West Riding) Regiment of Foot	June 1794	May 1795	3rd Battalion, The Yorkshire Regiment (14th/15th, 19th and 33rd/76th Foot)	
37th (North Hampshire) Regiment of Foot	March 1793	May 1795	1st Battalion, The Princess of Wales's Royal Regiment (Queen's and Royal Hampshires)	T
38th (1st Staffordshire) Regiment of Foot	April 1794	May 1795	3rd Battalion, The Mercian Regiment (Staffords)	
40th (2nd Somerset) Regiment of Foot	June 1794 [M]	May 1795	2nd Battalion, The Duke of Lancaster's Regiment (King's, Lancashire and Border)	
42nd (Royal Highland) Regiment of Foot	June 1794 [M]	May 1795	The Black Watch, 3rd Battalion, The Royal Regiment of Scotland	

British Regiments Present in Flanders 1793-1795 *(cont.)*

REGIMENT	ARRIVED	DEPARTED	SUCCESSOR REGIMENT (2018)	BATTLE HONOURS AWARDED
44th (East Essex) Regiment of Foot	June 1794	May 1795	1st Battalion, The Royal Anglian Regiment	
53rd (Shropshire) Regiment of Foot	March 1793	May 1795	Either 3rd or 5th Battalion, The Rifles	N T
54th (West Norfolk) Regiment of Foot	June 1794 [M]	May 1795	1st Battalion, The Rifles	
55th (Westmoreland) Regiment of Foot	April 1794	May 1795	1st Battalion, The Duke of Lancaster's Regiment (King's, Lancashire and Borders)	
57th (West Middlesex) Regiment of Foot	June 1794 [M]	May 1795	1st Battalion, The Princess of Wales's Royal Regiment (Queen's and Royal Hampshires)	
59th (2nd Nottinghamshire) Regiment of Foot	June 1794 [M]	May 1795	2nd Battalion, The Duke of Lancaster's Regiment (King's, Lancashire and Border)	
63rd (West Suffolk) Regiment of Foot	July 1794	May 1795	1st Battalion, The Duke of Lancaster's Regiment (King's, Lancashire and Border)	
1/78th Regiment of Foot	May 1794	May 1795	The Highlanders, 4th Battalion, The Royal Regiment of Scotland	

APPENDIX XVIII

REGIMENT	ARRIVED	DEPARTED	SUCCESSOR REGIMENT (2018)	BATTLE HONOURS AWARDED
79th (Cameronian Volunteers) Regiment of Foot	August 1794	May 1795	The Highlanders, 4th Battalion, The Royal Regiment of Scotland	
80th Regiment of Foot	July 1794	May 1795	3rd Battalion, The Mercian Regiment (Staffords)	
84th (York and Lancaster) Regiment of Foot	July 1794	May 1795	Disbanded in 1968 as the 2nd Battalion, York and Lancaster Regiment, after refusing amalgamation	
85th Regiment of Foot	August 1794	May 1795	Either 3rd or 5th Battalion, The Rifles	
87th Regiment of Foot	June 1794 [M]	August 1795	1st Battalion, The Royal Irish Regiment	
88th (Connaught Rangers) Regiment of Foot	June 1794 [M]	May 1795	Disbanded in 1922 as The Connaught Rangers	
89th Regiment of Foot	June 1794 [M]	May 1795	1st Battalion, The Royal Irish Regiment	
1st Battalion, Royal Artillery (Wright's Company, Wilson's Company, Winter's Company)*	Wright - March 1793 Wilson – June 1793 Winter – May 1793	May 1795	12th (Minden) Battery, RA	
3rd Battalion, Royal Artillery (detachments)	August 1793	May 1795	None	

329

British Regiments Present in Flanders 1793-1795 *(cont.)*

REGIMENT	ARRIVED	DEPARTED	SUCCESSOR REGIMENT (2018)	BATTLE HONOURS AWARDED
4th Battalion, Royal Artillery (Trotter's Company, Laye's Company, Shuttleworth's Company)*	Trotter – May 1793 Laye – September 1793 Shuttleworth – July 1794	May 1795	None	
Royal Irish Artillery (Arabin's Company, Wright's Company, Buchanan's Company)*	Arabin - June 1794 [M] Wright = - June 1794 [M] Buchanan – August 1794	May 1795	Became 7th Battalion, Royal Artillery in 1801	
Royal Engineers	March 1793	May 1795	Royal Engineers	

BATTLE HONOURS:

    L   Lincelles
    N   Nieuporte
    V   Villers-en-Cauchies
    B   Beaumont
    W   Willems
    T   Tournay
Spelling is that adopted by the War Office.
[M] unit which formed part of Lord Moira's force.

*   Royal Artillery companies sent to the continent were not employed as complete companies but split up to man battalion guns or to serve with the Park of Artillery.

Source: Anthony Baker, *Battle Honours of the British and Commonwealth Armies*.

Appendix XIX

The Nursery: Eminent British Officers Who Served in Flanders 1793-1795

Due to space limitations, individual service records are greatly abbreviated. Recommended sources for anyone wishing to study officer's later services in more detail are *Wellington's Brigade Commanders* (McGuigan & Burnham, Pen & Sword Books, 2017) and *Wellington's Peninsular War Generals & Their Battles* (Heathcote, Pen & Sword Books, 2010).

(* Denotes only held temporary command.)

Brigade of Guards

OFFICER	RANK 1793-1795	LATER SERVICE
William ANSON	Ensign/lieutenant & captain, 1st Foot Guards	Brigade and division* commander 1812-1814; general 1837; died 1847
Robert ANSTRUTHER	Lieutenant & captain, 3rd Foot Guards	Brigade commander 1808; Brigadier-general 1808; died 1809
Henry BAYLY	Ensign/lieutenant & captain, Coldstream Foot Guards	Brigade commander 1814; general 1841; died 1846
Henry Frederick CAMPBELL	Ensign/lieutenant & captain, 1st Foot Guards	Brigade commander 1809; brigade and division commander 1811-1812; General 1837; died 1856
Henry CLINTON	Lieutenant & captain/ brevet major, 1st Foot Guards	Divisional commander 1812-1814; divisional commander 1815; lieutenant general 1814; died 1829
William Henry CLINTON	Lieutenant & captain, captain, 1st Foot Guards	Brigade commander 1812-1813; GOC east coast of Spain 1813-1814; general 1830; died 1846

Brigade of Guards *(cont.)*

OFFICER	RANK 1793-1795	LATER SERVICE
George Duncan DRUMMOND	Lieutenant & captain, 1st Foot Guards	Brigade and division commander 1811; brigadier general 1811; died 1811
Kenneth Alexander HOWARD	Lieutenant & captain, Coldstream Foot Guards	Brigade commander 1811-1814; division commander 1813; general 1837; died 1845
Richard HULSE	Ensign/lieutenant & captain, Coldstream Foot Guards	Brigade commander 1809-1812; division commander 1812*; major general 1812; died 1812
John LAMBERT	Ensign, 1st Foot Guards	Brigade commander 1811-1814; division commander 1815; brigade commander 1815-1818; general 1841; died 1847
Peregrine MAITLAND	Ensign/lieutenant & captain, 1st Foot Guards	Brigade commander 1813-1815; division commander 1815*; brigade commander 1815-1818; general 1846; died 1854
George MURRAY	Ensign/lieutenant & captain, 3rd Foot Guards	Quartermaster-general 1808-1811; quartermaster-general 1813-1814; general 1841; died 1846
John MURRAY	Lieutenant & captain, 3rd Foot Guards; Lieutenant Colonel, 84th Foot	GOC east coast of Spain 1813; lieutenant general 1812; died 1827
Edward STOPFORD	Lieutenant & captain, 3rd Foot Guards	Brigade and division commander 1811-1812; brigade commander 1813-1814; lieutenant general 1821; died 1837
William WHEATLEY	Ensign/lieutenant & captain, 1st Foot Guards	Brigade commander 1812; died 1812
William WYNYARD	Lieutenant & captain, Coldstream Foot Guards; Deputy Assistant Adjutant-General	Deputy Adjutant-General to the Forces 1799; died 1819

Cavalry

OFFICER	RANK 1793-1795	LATER SERVICE
William Henry BENTINCK	Captain, 11th Light Dragoons; major, 28th Foot	Brigade commander 1808-1809; GOC east coast of Spain 1813; Commander-in-Chief India; general 1825; died 1839

APPENDIX XIX

OFFICER	RANK 1793-1795	LATER SERVICE
William ERSKINE	Captain/major/lieutenant-colonel, 15th Light Dragoons	Commanded cavalry division 1811-1813; lieutenant general 1811; died 1813
John Gaspard LE MARCHANT	Captain, 2nd Dragoons; major, 16th Light Dragoons	Cavalry brigade commander 1811-1812; major general 1811; killed in action 1812
John HOPE	Captain, 13th Light Dragoons	Division commander 1812; lieutenant general 1819; died 1836
Robert Ballard LONG	Lieutenant/captain, 1st Dragoon Guards	Cavalry brigade commander 1811-1813; lieutenant general 1821; died 1825
Terence O'Bryan O'LOUGHLIN	Lieutenant, 7th Light Dragoons	Cavalry brigade 1813-1814; lieutenant general 1825; died 1843
Denis PACK	Cornet, 14th Light Dragoons	Brigade commander 1810-1814; division commander 1813*; brigade commander 1815-1818; major general 1813; died 1823
William PAYNE	Captain/major/lieutenant-colonel, 1st Dragoons	GOC cavalry in Peninsula 1809-1810; lieutenant general 1811; died 1831
William Henry PRINGLE	Lieutenant, 16th Light Dragoons	Division* commander 1812-1813; lieutenant general 1825; died 1841
Robert Edward Henry SOMERSET	Lieutenant/captain, 10th Light Dragoons	Cavalry brigade commander 1813-1814; cavalry brigade commander 1815-1818; general 1841; died 1842
John SONTAG	Captain, Guides; deputy quartermaster-general	Brigade and division* commander 1809-1811; lieutenant general 1814; died 1816
Herbert TAYLOR	Cornet/lieutenant, 2nd Dragoon Guards	ADC to Duke of York; Private Secretary to King George III; brigade commander 1813-1814; lieutenant general 1825; died 1839
John Ormsby VANDELEUR	Captain-lieutenant/captain and major, 8th Light Dragoons	Brigade and division* commander 1811-1815; general 1838; died 1849
Robert Thomas WILSON	Cornet/lieutenant, 15th Light Dragoons	Brigade commander (Portuguese army) 1809-1810; general 1841; died 1849

Line Infantry

OFFICER	RANK 1793-1795	LATER SERVICE
Wroth Palmer ACLAND	Captain, 3rd Foot	Brigade commander 1808; lieutenant general 1814; died 1816
George BECKWITH	Captain and brevet lieutenant-colonel, 37th Foot	Commander-in-Chief in West Indies 1808; general 1814; died 1823
Andrew BLAYNEY	Major, 89th Foot	Expedition commander 1810; lieutenant general 1819; died 1834
Thomas BRISBANE	Captain, 53rd Foot	Brigade and division commander 1813-1818; General 1841; died 1860
John BYNG	Ensign/lieutenant/major, 33rd Foot	Brigade commander 1811-1814; brigade, division and corps commander 1815; Field-marshal 1855; died 1860
Alan CAMERON	Major/lieutenant-colonel, 79th Foot	Brigade commander 1809-1810; lieutenant-general 1819; died 1828
Robert CRAUFURD	Captain, 75th Foot; Liaison officer at Austrian headquarters	Brigade commander 1809-1810; Light Division commander 1811-1812; major general 1811; killed in action 1812
Gordon DRUMMOND	Lieutenant Colonel, 8th Foot	GOC Upper Canada 1814; general 1825; died 1854
James ERSKINE	Captain/brevet major, 37th Foot	Cavalry brigade commander 1809; lieutenant general 1813; died 1825
Ronald Crauford FERGUSON	Captain, 53rd Foot; major/lieutenant-colonel 84th Foot	Brigade commander 1808; general 1830; died 1841
William HOUSTOUN	Captain/major, 19th Foot	Brigade commander 1811; division commander 1811; general 1837; died 1842
William INGLIS	Captain, 57th Foot	Brigade commander 1810; brigade commander 1814; lieutenant general 1825; died 1835
James KEMMIS	Captain/brevet major, 40th Foot	Brigade commander 1809-1812; division commander 1809*; division commander 1811*; major general 1811; died 1820
Stafford LIGHTBURNE	Captain-lieutenant, 37th Foot	Brigade commander 1810; lieutenant general 1813; died 1827

APPENDIX XIX

OFFICER	RANK 1793-1795	LATER SERVICE
James McGRIGOR	Surgeon, 88th Foot	Surgeon-general in Peninsula 1811-1814; Director-general of Army Medical Service 1815-1851; died 1858
Kenneth MacKENZIE	Lieutenant, 14th Foot	Brigade commander 1815; lieutenant general 1821; died 1833
Edward PAGET	Lieutenant colonel, 28th Foot	Division commander 1808-1809; division commander 1811-1812; general 1825; died 1849
Henry William PAGET	Lieutenant-colonel-commandant, 80th Foot	Cavalry brigade commander in Peninsular 1808-1809; commanded Allied cavalry in the Waterloo campaign; Field-marshal 1846; died 1854
John Coape SHERBROOKE	Captain/major/lieutenant-colonel, 33rd Foot	Division commander 1809-1810; Governor-general of British North America; General 1825; died 1830
Charles William STEWART	Ensign/lieutenant/captain, 108th Foot	Cavalry brigade commander 1808-1809*; adjutant-general 1809-1812; General 1837; died 1854
Richard Hussey VIVIAN	Captain, 28th Foot	Cavalry brigade commander 1813-1814; cavalry brigade commander 1815-1818; lieutenant general 1830; died 1842
George Townsend WALKER	Captain/major, 60th Foot	Brigade commander 1811-1813; division commander 1811-1814*; General 1838; died 1842
Arthur WELLESLEY	Lieutenant colonel, 33rd Foot	Field marshal 1813; Prime Minister 1828-1830; Commander-in-Chief 1842; died 1852

Royal Artillery

OFFICER	RANK 1793-1795	LATER SERVICE
William BORTHWICK	Captain, Royal Artillery	CRA Peninsula 1810-1811; major general 1812; died 1820
Augustus Simon FRAZER	2nd Lieutenant, Royal Artillery	RHA commander 1815; Colonel 1825; Director of the Royal Laboratory; died 1835

335

Royal Artillery *(cont.)*

OFFICER	RANK 1793-1795	LATER SERVICE
William ROBE	Captain-lieutenant, Royal Artillery	CRA Peninsula 1812-1813; Colonel 1814; died 1820
George Adam WOOD	Lieutenant, Royal Artillery	CRA Netherlands 1813-1814; CRA Waterloo 1815; major general 1825; died 1831

Hanoverian

OFFICER	RANK 1793-1795	LATER SERVICE
Karl von ALTEN	Kapitan, 8. Cavallerie-Regiment	Brigade commander 1811-1812; division commander 1812-1814; division commander 1815; field marshal; Inspector-general of Hanoverian army; died 1840
Viktor von ALTEN	Kapitan, 8. Cavallerie-Regiment	Cavalry brigade commander 1813-1815; lieutenant general 1818; died 1820
Viktor von ARENTSCHILDT	2. Leutnant, Artillerie zu Fuß	Commanded Portuguese artillery 1809 to 1814; died 1841
Charles BEST	1. Leutnant, 14. Leichtes-Infanterie-Regiment	Brigade commander 1815; major general 1816
Georg von BOCK	Kapitan/major, Leibgarde Cavallerie-Regiment	Cavalry brigade and division* commander 1812-1814; major general 1810; died 1814
Georg von DRIEBERG	Kapitan, 10. Infanterie-Regiment; major, 2. Grenadier-Bataillon	Brigade commander 1809; Brigadier general 1808; died 1832
Heinrich von HINUBER	Kapitan, 14. Leichtes-Infanterie-Regiment	Brigade commander 1813-1814; division commander 1815; lieutenant general 1819; died 1833
Sigismund von LOW	Kapitan/major, Garde-Regiment zu Fuß	Brigade commander 1809-1813; general 1838; died 1846

Hessen-Cassel

OFFICER	RANK 1793-1795	LATER SERVICE
Wilhelm von DORNBERG	Kapitan, HK Leib-Grenadier-Garde	Cavalry brigade commander 1815; lieutenant general 1818; died 1850

APPENDIX XIX

Dutch

OFFICER	RANK 1793-1795	LATER SERVICE
Colin HALKETT	Lieutenant & captain, 2. Hollandsche Gardes	Brigade commander 1812-1813; brigade commander 1815; General 1846; died 1856

French

OFFICER	RANK 1793-1795	LATER SERVICE
David Hendrik CHASSÉ	Capitaine, Légion Franche Étrangère	French service 1788-1814; division commander 1815; general 1830; died 1849

Bibliography

Archival Sources
   The National Archives, Kew (NAK)
   WO 1/1056-1085 – War Office General Correspondence
   WO 4/291-292 – Secretary at War Out-Letters 1793-1794
   WO 17/1160 – Monthly returns 1796-1799
   WO 27/72 – Inspection returns 1792
   WO 27/74 – Inspection returns 1794
   WO 27/75 – Irish inspection returns 1794
   WO 27/77 – British & Irish inspection returns 1795
   University of Nottingham, King's Meadow
   Lord William Cavendish-Bentinck Papers:
      Pw Ja 441-456 – Papers relating to the Flanders Campaign 1793-4
      Pw Ja 610 – 7 May to 5 August 1793 Journal
      Pw Ja 611 – 5 August to 30 August 1793 Journal
      Pw Ja 612 – 3 September to 27 October 1793 Journal
      Pw Ja 617-622 – 1793-1794 Small notebooks re. Flanders campaign
      Pw Ja 623 – 1794 Notebook containing remarks about Lord Moira's expedition
   University of Michigan
   Henry Clinton Collection, Volume 235 - *Correspondence from his sons (William & Henry) from Flanders 1793-1794.*

Printed Primary Sources
Anon. *A Full, Accurate, and Impartial History of the Campaign, from the Beginning of January 1794 down to the Present Time*. London: T. N. Longman, 1794.
Anon. *An Accurate and Impartial Narrative of the War, by an Officer of the Guards*. Two volumes. London: Cadell and Davies; 1794.
Anon: *The Present State of the British Army in Flanders*. London: H. D. Symonds, 1794.
Anon. *A Journal Kept in the British Army from the Landing of the Troops under the Command of the Earl of Moira at Ostend*. Liverpool: 1795.
Brown, Robert. *An Impartial Journal of a Detachment from the Brigade of Guards, Commencing 25 February 1793, and Ending 9 May 1795*. London: John Stockdale, 1795.
Jones, Capt L.T. *An Historical Journal of the British Campaign on the Continent in the Year 1794; With the Retreat Through Holland in the Year 1795*. Birmingham: Swinney And Hawkins, 1797.

Combermere, Mary and Knollys, W. *Memoirs and Correspondence of Field-marshal Viscount Combermere, from his Family Papers.*
Graham, James J. *Memoir of General Graham.* Edinburgh: R. & R. Clark, 1862.
Le Marchant, Denis. *Memoirs of the late Major General John Le Marchant 1766-1812.* Staplehurst: Spellmount Ltd, 1997.
McGrigor, James. *The Autobiography and Services of Sir James McGrigor, Bart.* London: Longman, Green, Longman and Roberts. 1861.
Morris, Roger / Harrington, Peter (ed). *With the Guards in Flanders.* Warwick: Helion & Company Limited, 2018.
Ompteda, Christian. *In the King's German Legion: Memoirs of Baron Ompteda.* London: H. Grevel & Co., 1894.
Verney, Sir Harry Bt. *The Journals and Correspondence of General Sir Harry Calvert, Comprising the Campaigns in Flanders and Holland in 1793 And 1794.* London: Hirst And Blackett, 1853.
Randolph, Herbert. *Life of General Sir Robert Wilson.* Two volumes. London: John Murray, 1862.

Printed Secondary Sources

The Cambridge Modern History, History of the Wars of the French Revolution, from the Breaking Out of the War in 1792, to the Restoration of a General Peace in 1815: Comprehending the Civil History of Great Britain and France, During that Period.
Allison, *History of Europe from the Commencement of the French Revolution in MDCCLXXXIX to the Restoration of the Bourbons in MDCCCXV*
Burne, Alfred H. *The Noble Duke of York: the Military Life of Frederick Duke of York and Albany.* London: Staples Press, 1949.
Chandler, David. *Napoleon's Marshals.* London: MacMillan Publishing, 1987.
Coutanceau, Michel Henri. *La Campagne de 1794 à l'Armée du Nord.* Paris: Librairie Militaire R. Chapelot et cie Imprimeurs-éditeurs, 1903.
Crowdy, Terry. *French Revolutionary Infantry 1789-1802.* Osprey, 2004.
Demet, Paul. *We are Accustomed to do our Duty – German Auxiliaries with the British Army 1793-1795.* Warwick: helion & Company Limited, 2018.
Ditfurth, Karl Maximilian. *Die Hessen in den Feldzügen von 1793, 1794 and 1795.* J. Bohne, 1839.
Dupuis, Victor. *La Campagne de 1793 à l'Armée du Nord et des Ardennes.* Paris: Librairie Militaire R. Chapelot et cie Imprimeurs-éditeurs, 1909.
Dyer, Thomas Henry. *Modern Europe, from the Fall of Constantinople to the Establishment of the German Empire.* Five volumes. London: George Bell & Sons, 1877.
Fortescue, Hon. J.W. *British Campaigns in Flanders, 1690-1794.* London: MacMillan Company, 1918.
Glover, Michael. *Warfare in the Age of Bonaparte.*
Griffiths, Paddy. *The Art of War of Revolutionary France 1789-1802.* Aylesbury: Greenhill Books, 1998.
Haythornthwaite, Philip. *Who Was Who in the Napoleonic Wars.* London: Arms and Armour, 1998.
Hibbert, Christopher. *The French Revolution.* Penguin Books, 1982.

von Hinrichs. *Neue Bellona oder Beiträge zur Kriegskunst und Kriegsgeschichte*, Vol. IV. Österreichische Nationalbibliothek, 1808.

Hochedlinger, Michael. *Austria's Wars of Emergence, 1683-1797*. Routledge, 2015. Online version.

Jacques, Tony. *Dictionary of Battles and Sieges*. Melbourne: The Miegunyah Press, 2007.

Leopold, Albrecht & others. *Der Feldzug Der Preussen Gegen Die Franzosen in Den Niederlanden, Im Jahr 1793*. Three volumes. Berlin: Stendal, 1798.

Phipps. *The Armies of The First French Republic, and the Rise of the Marshals of Napoleon I*. Volume I. Uckfield: Naval & Military Press reprint.

Schrager, James. *The People's Chronology*. London: The Quorum Press, 1992.

Von Sichart, Louis Heinrich Friedrich. *Geschichte der Königlich-Hannoverschen Armee*. Hannover: Hannoversche Hofbuchhandlung, 1870.

Smith, Digby. *The Greenhill Napoleonic Wars Data Book*. London: Greenhill Books, 1998.

Von Sybel, Heinrich. *History of the French Revolution*. Four volumes. London: John Murray, 1867.

Treasure, Geoffrey. *Who's Who in Late Hanoverian Britain 1789-1837*. Mechanicsville: Stackpole Books, 2002.

Uglow, Jenny. *In These Times: Living in Britain through Napoleon's Wars, 1793-1815*. New York: Farrar, Strauss and Giroux, 2004.

Vincent, Benjamin. *Haydn's Dictionary of Dates*. London: Edward Moxon and Co., 1866.

Von Witzleben, A. *Prinz Friedrich Josias von Coburg-Saalfield, Herzog zu Sachsen*. Three volumes. Berlin: Königlichen Geheimen Ober-Hofruchdruckerei, 1859.

Theses

Gramm, Ernest Rainer. *Der Unglückliche Mack, Aufstieg und Fall des Karl Mack von Leiberich*. Dr. Phil. thesis. Universität Wien, 2008.

Parrish, Ricky Eugene. *The Military and Diplomatic Career of Jacques Étienne MacDonald*. Dr. Phil thesis. Florida State University, 2005.

Magazine Articles

Duffy, Michael. *A Particular Service: The British Government and the Dunkirk Expedition of 1793*. The English Historical Review, Volume XCI, Issue CCCLX, 1 July 1976, Pages 529-554.

Uppelschoten, Raymond. *De'ontzaggelikje Groote Passage van de Engelsche Armee*. Oudheidkundige Vereniging Flehite Amersfoort yearbook, 2013.

General Sources – British Army

Baker, Anthony. *Battle Honours of the British and Commonwealth Armies*. London: Ian Allen Ltd, 1986.

Barnett, Corelli. *Britain and Her Army*, p.236.

Burnham, Robert and McGuigan, Ron. *The British Army Against Napoleon*. London: Front Line Books, 2010.

Chartrand, René. *Emigre and Foreign Troops in British Service 1793-1802*. Botley: Osprey Publishing, 1999.

BIBLIOGRAPHY

Chichester, Henry Manners and Burgess-Short, George. *The Records and Badges of Every Regiment and Corps in the British Army*. London: William Clowes and Sons Ltd, 1895.
Fortescue, Hon. J.W. *A History of the British Army*. Uckfield: The Naval and Military Press Ltd, 2004. Five volumes.
Fortescue, Hon. J.W. *The British Army 1783 To 1802*. London: Macmillan & Co, 1905.
Guy, Alan J. *The Road to Waterloo*. London: National Army Museum, 1990.
McKenna, Michael G. *The British Army – And Its Regiments and Battalions*. West Chester, Ohio: The Nafziger Collection. 2004.
Norman, C.B. *Battle Honours of the British Army*. London: David and Charles Reprints, 1971.
Park, S.J. and Nafziger, G.F. *The British Military – Its System and Organization 1803-1815*. Cambridge, Ontario: Rafm Co. Inc. 1983.
Philippart, John. *The Royal Military Calendar, or Army Service and Commission Book*. London: A.J. Valpy, 1820. Five volumes.
Quartermaster-General's Department. *British Minor Expeditions 1746-1814*. London: Her Majesty's Stationery office, 1884.
Reid, Stuart. *Wellington's Officers, Volume 1*. Leigh-On-Sea: Partizan Press, 2008.
Reid, Stuart. *Wellington's Officers, Volume 2*. Leigh-On-Sea: Partizan Press, 2009.
Reid, Stuart. *Wellington's Officers, Volume 3*. Leigh-On-Sea: Partizan Press, 2011.
War Office. *A List of the Officers of the Army and Marines, with an index, a succession of Colonels, and a list of the Officers of the Army and Marines on Half-Pay* (London: War Office, 1791 to 1795).
The Field of Mars: Being an Alphabetical Digestion of the Principal Naval and Military Engagements of Great Britain and Her Allies, From the Ninth Century to the Peace in 1801. London: G. & J. Robinson, 1801. Two volumes.

Naval
Clowes, William Laird. *The Royal Navy: A History from the Earliest Times to the Present*. London: Sampson Low, Marston and Co., 1899. Seven volumes.
James, William. *The Naval History of Great Britain, from the Declaration of War on France in February 1793, to the Accession of George V in January 1820*. London: Harding Lepard and Co., 1826. Two volumes.

Regimental Histories
Almack, Edward. *The History of the Second Dragoons – Royal Scots Greys*. London: 1908.
Bray, Edward William. *Memoirs and Services of the 83rd Regiment, County Dublin, From 1793 to 1887*. London: Hugh Read Ltd, 1908.
Brereton J.M. and Savary A.C.S. *The History of the Duke of Wellington's Regiment (West Riding) 1702 To 1992*. Halifax: The Duke of Wellington's Regiment, 1993.
Cannon, Richard. *Historical Record of the 3rd or Buffs Regiment of Foot: Containing an Account of the Formation of the Regiment, and of its Subsequent Services to 1838*. London: Longman Orme & Co., 1839.
Cannon, Richard. *Historical Record of the 8th or The King's Regiment of Foot: Containing an Account of the Formation of the Regiment in 1685, and of its Subsequent Services to 1844*. London: Parker Furnivall & Parker, 1844.

BIBLIOGRAPHY

Cannon, Richard. *Historical Record of the 12th or East Suffolk Regiment of Foot: Containing an Account of the Formation of the Regiment in 1685, and of its Subsequent Services to 1847.* London: Parker Furnivall & Parker, 1847.

Cannon, Richard. *Historical Record of the 14th or Buckinghamshire Regiment of Foot: Containing an Account of the Formation of the Regiment in 1685, and of its Subsequent Services to 1845.* London: Parker Furnivall & Parker, 1845.

Cannon, Richard. *Historical Record of the 31st, or the Huntingdonshire Regiment of Foot; Containing an Account of the Formation of the Regiment in 1702, and of its Subsequent Services to 1850.* London: Parker Furnivall and Parker, 1850.

Cannon, Richard. *Historical Record of the 42nd, or the Royal Highland Regiment of Foot: Containing an Account of the Formation of Six Companies of Highlanders in 1729 and of the Subsequent Service of the Regiment to 1844.* London: Parker Furnivall and Parker: 1844.

Cannon, Richard. *Historical Record of the 53rd, or the Shropshire Regiment of Foot: Containing an Account of the Formation of the Regiment In 1755 and of its Subsequent Services to 1848.* London: Parker Furnivall and Parker, 1849.

Cannon, Richard. *Historical Record of the 71st Regiment, Highland Light Infantry: Containing an Account of the Formation of the Regiment, and of its Subsequent Services to 1852.* London: Parker Furnivall & Parker, 1852.

Cannon, Richard. *Historical Record of the 86th, or the Royal County Down Regiment of Foot: Containing an Account of the Formation of the Regiment In 1793 and of its Subsequent Services To 1842.* London: John W Parker, 1842.

Cannon, Richard. *Historical Record of the Fourth, or Queen's Own Regiment of Light Dragoons: Containing an Account of the Formation of the Regiment in 1685, and of its Subsequent Services to 1842.* London: Parker Furnivall & Parker, 1843.

Cannon, Richard. *Historical Record of the Sixth or Inniskilling Regiment of Dragoon's: Containing an Account of the Formation of the Regiment In 1689 and of its Subsequent Services To 1846.* London: Parker Furnivall and Parker, 1847.

Cannon, Richard. *Historical Record of the Seventh, or the Queen's Own Regiment of Hussars: Containing an Account of the Origin of the Regiment In 1690 and of its Subsequent Services To 1842.* London: John W. Parker, 1842.

Cannon, Richard. *Historical Regiment of the 13th Regiment of Light Dragoons: Containing an Account of the Formation of the Regiment In 1715 and of its Subsequent Services to 1842.* London: John W. Parker, 1842.

Cannon, Richard. *Historical Record of the Third, or King's Own Regiment of Light Dragoons: Containing an Account of the Formation of the Regiment in 1685, and of its Subsequent Services to 1846.* London: Parker Furnivall & Parker, 1847.

Cannon, Richard. *Historical Regiment of the 87th Regiment, or the Royal Irish Fusiliers.* London: Parker Furnivall, 1853.

Cannon, Richard. *Historical Record of the 88th Regiment of Foot, Or Connaught Rangers: Containing an Account of the Formation of Regiment in 1793 And of its Subsequent Services to 1887.* London: William Clowes and Sons, 1888.

Cannon, Richard. *Historical Record of the Life Guards: Containing an Account of the Formation of the Regiment in 1660, and of its Subsequent Services to 1836.* London: Longman Orme and Co., 1840.

Cannon, Richard. *Historical Record of the 10th, or the Prince of Wales's Own Royal Regiment of Hussars: Containing an Account of the Formation of the Regiment In 1715 And of its Subsequent Services to 1842.* London: John W. Parker, 1843.

BIBLIOGRAPHY

Cannon, Richard. *Historical Record of the 15th, or the King's Regiment of Light Dragoons, or Hussars: Containing an Account of the Formation of the Regiment In 1759 and of its Subsequent Services to 1841*. London: John W. Parker, 1841.

Cannon, Richard. *Historical Record of the 16th, or the Queens Regiment of Light Dragoons, or Lancers: Containing an Account of the Formation of the Regiment in 1759 and its Subsequent Services to 1841*. London: John W. Parker, 1842.

Cannon, Richard. *Historical Record of the 17th Regiment of Light Dragoons, or Lancers: Containing an Account of the Formation of the Regiment In 1759 and of its Subsequent Services to 1841*. London: John W. Parker, 1841.

Carter, Thomas. *Historical Record of the 44th, or the East Essex Regiment of Foot*. London: W.O. Mitchell, 1864.

Carter, Thomas. *Historical Record of the 26th or Cameronian Regiment*. London: W.O Mitchell, 1867.

Crooks, Major J.J. *History of the Royal Irish Regiment of Artillery*. Dublin: Brown and Nolan Ltd, 1914.

Danielle, David Scott. *Cap of Honour: The 300 Years of the Gloucestershire Regiment*. Stroud: Sutton Publishing Ltd, 2005.

De Ainslie, General. *Historical Record of the First or Royal Regiment of Dragoons*. London: Chapman & Hall, 1887.

Duncan, Francis. *History of the Royal Regiment of Artillery*. London: John Murray, 1879. Two volumes.

Everard, Major H. *History of Thomas Farrington's Regiment, Subsequently Designated the 29th (Worcestershire) Foot, 1694 to 1891*. Worcester: Littlebury & Company, 1891.

Ferrar, M.L. *A History of the Services of the 19th Regiment.... From Its Formation in 1688 to 1911*. London: Eden Fisher & Company, 1911.

Hamilton, Henry Blackburne. *Historical Record of the 14th (King's) Hussars from A.D. 1715 to A.D. 1900*. London: Longmans, Green, and Co., 1901.

Hamilton, Lt. Gen. Sir F.W. *The Origin and History of the First or Grenadier Guards*. London: John Murray, 1874. Three volumes.

Jameson, Captain Robert. *Historical Record of the 79th Regiment of Foot, or Cameron Highlanders*. Edinburgh: William Blackwood & Sons, 1863.

Jarvis, Brevet-Major. *Historical Record of the 82nd Regiment, or the Prince of Wales's Volunteers*. London: W.A. Mitchell, 1866.

Kane, John. *List of Officers of the Royal Regiment of Artillery, as They Stood in the Year 1763, With a Continuation to the Present Time*. Greenwich: Elizabeth Delahoy, 1815.

Kingsford, Charles Lethbridge. *The Story of the Duke of Cambridge's Own Middlesex Regiment*. London: Country Life, 1916.

Laws, M.E.S., *Battery Records of the Royal Artillery, 1716-1859*. (Woolwich: Royal Artillery Institute, 1952).

Mackinnon, Daniel. *Origin and Services of the Coldstream Guards*. London: Richard Bentley, 1833. Two volumes.

Mollo, John. *The Princes Dolls*. London: Leo Cooper, 1997.

Packe, Edmund. *An Historical Record of the Royal Regiment of Horse Guards, or Oxford Blues*. London: William Clowes, 1834.

Slack, Major James. *The History of the 63rd West Suffolk Regiment*. Publisher Unknown, 1884.

Smith, Henry Stooks. *An Alphabetical List of the offices of the 11th, or Prince Albert's Own Regiment of Hussars, from 1800 to 1850*. London: Simkin Marshall and Co., 1850.

Smythies, Capt R.H. Raymond. *Historical Records of the 40th (2nd Somersetshire) Regiment, from its Formation in 1717 To 1893*. Devonport: A.H. Swiss, 1894.

Sutherland, Douglas. *Tried and Valiant: The History of the Border Regiment*. London: Leo Cooper, 1972.

Trimble, W. Copeland. *The Historical record of the 27th Inniskilling Regiment, from the Period of its Institution as a Volunteer Corps, until the Present Time*. London: William Clowes & Sons, 1876.

Weaver, Lawrence. *The Story of the Royal Scots (The Lothian Regiment)*. London: Country Life, 1915.

Wilcox, Walter Temple. *The Historical Records of the Fifth Royal Irish Lancers, from their Foundation as Wynn's Dragoons in 1689 to the Present Day*. London: Arthur Doubleday & Co. Ltd, 1908.

Militia

Abstract of Three Acts of Parliament Namely, the Supplementary Militia, Cavalry, and Army and Navy. Government Printers, 1796.

Additional Rules and Orders to be Observed by the Embodied Militia. London: War Office, 1793.

Stevenson, J. *The London Crimp Riots of 1794*. International Review of Social History, 1971.

Magazines and Periodicals

The London Gazette online.

The Times online.

18th Century British Newspapers online. National Library of Australia.

19th Century British Newspapers online. National Library of Australia.

The House of Commons Parliamentary Papers online. National Library of Australia.

The British Military Library: Comprehending a Complete Body of Military Knowledge, and Consisting of Original Communications. London: Richard Phillips, various years.

Bulletins of 1793, 1794, 1795, 1796, 1797, 1798. London: A. Strachan, various years.

A Collection of State Papers Relative to the War against France. London: John Stockdale, Various Years. Eleven volumes.

The Monthly Army List. London: various years. Consulted extensively for the period 1788 To 1817.

The Naval and Military Magazine. London: T. Clerc Smith. Various years.

The New Annual Register, or General Repository of History, Politics and Literature. London: G.G. & J. Robinson, various years. Covers the period 1794 To 1815.

The Royal Military Chronicle or British Officers' Monthly Registers and Mentor. London: J Davies, various years.

The United Service Journal and the Naval and Military Magazine. London: Henry Cole Byrne and Richard Bentley, various years.

BIBLIOGRAPHY

Websites and Online Resources

17th-18th Century Burney Collection Newspapers. National Library of Australia. https://www.nla.gov.au/app/eresources/item/3304

18th Century British Newspapers Online. National Library of Australia. https://www.nla.gov.au/app/eresources/item/4314

The *Times* digital archive. http://gale.cengage.co.uk/times-digital-archive/times-digital-archive-17852006.aspx

The House of Commons Parliamentary Papers online. National Library of Australia. http://www.nla.gov.au/app/eresources/item/1642

Electric Scotland Website – 78th Regiment. http://www.electricscotland.com/history/scotreg/rosshire/

Keppell, Frederick. *Journal of Lt Colonel Fred. Keppell Commanding 88th Regiment 1794 & 1795*. Online at https://issuu.com/arcotiri/docs/keppel_bk

Nafziger, George. *Collection of Orders of Battle*. Available online at http://www.cgsc.edu/carl/nafziger.htm.

The House of Commons Parliamentary Papers online. National Library of Australia.

Doorn, Frank von. *De Slag om Boxtel*. 2013. Available online at http://www.muboboxtel.nl/CMS/wp-content/uploads/basistekst-21-def-20151114-DE-SLAG-OM-BOXTEL-kopie-2.pdf

Wills, Garry David. *British Battalion Guns in the Netherlands in 1794*. Smoothbore Ordnance Journal 6. Available online at https://www.napoleon-series.org/military/OrdnanceJournal/Issue6/SOJ-6-5_British_Bn_Guns.pdf

Notes

Foreward
1. Commanded, coincidentally, by the then Duke of York – James (1633-1701), eldest son of Charles II. Later King James II (1685-1688).
2. King Charles II sold Dunkirk back to France in 1662. But the sale was unpopular, and the sentimental attachment of Britain to Dunkirk ran deep, as we shall see.
3. The author includes in this the Imperial army's Hungarian regiments, of whom it is assumed understood some German, their language of command.

Conventions
1. Haythornthwaite, *Austrian Army of the Napoleonic Wars I - Infantry*, Osprey, 1986.

Prologue
1. The author has used the Germanic form of the name to more clearly distinguish between the King Frederick and the Prince Frederick.
2. Burne, *Duke of York*, p.22.
3. The Prussian method of discipline in the ranks was renowned for its harshness.
4. Letter of 7 October 1785, quoted in Burne, *Duke of York*, p.25.
5. ibid.
6. ibid, p.18.
7. ibid, p.26.
8. Letter dated 28 August 1791, ibid, p.33.
9. Huish, *Authentic Memoir of Frederick, Duke of York & Albany*, Volume 1, pp.13-14.
10. Now Buckingham Palace, although much enlarged.

Chapter 1
1. His older brother (also named Louis) died in 1761 when Louis-Auguste was seven.
2. His own father, the Dauphin, had died in 1765 when Louis-Auguste was eleven.
3. Von Sybel, *History of the French Revolution*, Vol.I, p.39.
4. Von Sybel, *History of the French Revolution*, Vol.I, p.1.
5. Eleven were Swiss, eight German, three Irish and one Belgian.
6. The previous Estates-General had been held in 1614.
7. Necker was restored on 19 July, but by then it was too late.
8. Von Sybel, *History of the French Revolution*, Vol.I, p.68.
9. John Hall Stewart, *A Documentary Survey of the French Revolution,* Macmillan, 1951, pp.105-6.

10. Tha National Guard, or Gardes Nationale, was a local militia formed in Paris; its strength was however considerably less than 80,000. Recruits were expected to pay for their own uniform and equipment, so it was strictly a middle-class corps, with nobles as officers.
11. Part of the Declaration was authored by Thomas Jefferson.
12. A Woman's March was held in Versailles on 5 October 1789 in protest of their exclusion.
13. Jews were not given similar rights until September 1791.
14. The Pope responded on 13 April 1791, declaring all elections under the Civil Constitution of the Clergy void and condemning the entire decree and its 'foolish form of Church government'. The Assembly in reply issued a decree that no message from the head of the Catholic church could be published, unless it had been sanctioned by the King.
15. Colonial Assemblies were given the right to uphold or abolish slavery at their discretion on 11 May 1791.
16. https://fr.wikipedia.org/wiki/D%C3%A9cret_de_D%C3%A9claration_de_paix_au_monde
17. The original version was the reverse image of today's French flag, with the red closest to the staff. The order was reversed in 1794.
18. Much of this information from Crowdy, *French Revolutionary Infantry 1789-1802*.
19. Dr. Guillotin in fact did not invent the device (it was designed by Antoine Louis, a surgeon) and was against the death penalty. He later unsuccessfully petitioned for the name of the device to be changed.
20. The last person to be guillotined in France was executed in 1977.
21. https://en.wikipedia.org/wiki/Declaration_of_Pillnitz
22. Over 1,200 émigré officers had left the French army, severely weakening its training and discipline.
23. Hochedlinger, *Austria's Wars of Emergence*, p.497.
24. Austria had reduced its army strength in August 1791 and the Emperor hoped that firm words and some sabre-rattling would suffice to detere the revolutionaries.
25. Tulard, Fayard, Fierro. *Histoire et Dictionnaire de la Révolution Française*. p.339.
26. Troop strengths are based upon Nafziger Orders of Battle for 1792.

Chapter 2

1. *The Bee, Or Literary Intelligencer*, Volume 9, 1792, p.ii.
2. ibid.
3. *Kentish Chronicle*, 8 May 1792.
4. On 8 June the Assembly ordered the raising of an army of twenty thousand volunteers to be camped outside Paris. King Louis vetoed this three days later.
5. The same Jarry who became first commandant of the Royal Military Academy at High Wycombe, which later became Sandhurst.
6. Luckner swapped to the command of the Armée du Centre at this time. Armand-Louis de Gontaut, duke de Biron became the new commander of the Armée du Rhin.
7. The Duke only authorised and issued it. It was actually ghost-written for him by a French émigré.
8. J.H. Robinson, ed., *Readings in European History*, Boston, Ginn, 1906, Vol II, pp. 443-445. The proclamation attracted humour and scorn in France, rather than the intended effect.
9. How very different to 1916!

NOTES

10. Marie Joseph L. Adolphe Thiers, *The History of the French Revolution*, with notes by F. Shoberl, p.53.
11. In the times before Corps d'Armée (army corps), armies used a variety of terms to describe formation sizes above a division. Line, column and rank were three such terms.
12. Comprising a black leather skull and peak, bearskin crest and a calfskin band painted to look like leopard-skin, casques resembled the Tarleton helmets worn by the British light dragoons.
13. https://erenow.com/modern/achronicleofthefrenchrevolution/56.html
14. Arthur Dillon (1750-1794) was born in England, a cousin of the murdered Théobald Dillon. He was found guilty of treason and guillotined in Paris on 13 April 1794.
15. Based upon a report in the *Kentish Chronicle*, 28 August 1792.
16. *The Cambridge Modern History*, pp.417-418.
17. Baines, *History of the Wars of the French Revolution, from the Breaking Out of the War in 1792, to the Restoration of a General Peace in 1815: Comprehending the Civil History of Great Britain and France, During that Period,* Philadelphia, 1819, Vol. I, p.123.
18. *The British and Foreign Review: Or, European Quarterly Journal*, Volume 17, 1844, p.628.
19. *Annual Register*, Volume 35, 1793, p.214.

Chapter 3

1. Parson James Woodforde, diary entry for 26 January 1793, quoted in Uglow, *In These Times*, p.28.
2. In the Budget of 1792 Pitt asked for 17,013 men as guards and garrisons in Great Britain; he reduced even that scanty force to 13,701 for the next six months.
3. *A Collection of State Papers*, Volume 2, 1794, p.190.
4. The militia had existed since 1660 but was only embodied in times of national emergency.
5. *The New Annual Register… for the Year 1793*, Volume 13, p.59.
6. On 2 December 1792 a meeting of Catholic delegates in Back-Lane, Dublin - ever after referred to as the 'Back-Lane Parliament' - prepared a petition to the King, asking for the franchise and some other privileges. It was signed by Roman Catholic archbishop of Dublin, Doctor Troy, by the bishop of Cork, Doctor Moylan, and by all the county delegates.
7. Hence why the British Army has never been the 'Royal Army'.
8. That there was no General-in-Chief of the British Army for the first three years of the American War of Independence is almost beyond belief.
9. Glover, *Peninsular Preparation*, p.40.
10. The Paget brothers are perfect examples of this policy. Edward Paget joined the army as a cornet in the Life Guards at age 17 and was a lieutenant-colonel commanding the 28th Foot at age 19. His elder brother Henry was made a temporary lieutenant-colonel at the age of 25 on raising the 80th Foot in 1793, then given a series of 'paper promotions' up through the system after returning from Flanders to ensure he was given permanent rank within the army.
11. Rose, *William Pitt and The Great War*, p.112.
12. At this time there were only seventeen permanent barracks in Great Britain. By 1805, there would be 168.
13. WO 17/835, Returns for Great Britain and Ireland 1 February 1793. These numbers are for privates and corporals only; allow another ten percent for senior NCOs,

NOTES

staff and officers. They also exclude the Life Guards, and the 54th/59th Foot in the Channel Islands.
14. The establishment of a regiment was its authorised strength measured in terms of corporals and privates, to which were added seniors NCOs, staff and officers.
15. There was no centralised recruiting at this time. Each regiment relied upon recruiting serjeants and officers spruiking the attractions of their regiment in market squares and taverns.
16. Whitehall's solution came on top of an earlier hare-brained idea to raise 100 new 'Independent Companies' of 100 men each to supplement the army, not to mention all the men being soaked up by the militia.
17. The Kingdom of Sardinia at this time also included Piedmont, Savoy and Nice, and was ruled from Turin.
18. Rose, *William Pitt and The Great War*, p.123.

Chapter 4

1. Napoleon's invasion of Russia in 1812 does not count as a coalition war, as no other European states sided with Russia in that conflict. Nor does the Peninsular War in Spain count, being considered somewhat remote and peripheral (at least on the continent).
2. After 1801, the United Kingdom of Great Britain and Ireland. Austria (and the Holy Roman Empire) was present in six, Russia five.
3. However, many in Vienna considered the Prince's Army and its officers unreliable.
4. For brevity, hereafter referred to as (Prince) von Coburg, or just Coburg.
5. Ompteda, *In the King's German Legion*, p.24.
6. ibid, p.23.
7. ibid, p.28.
8. Order of battle information derived from Nafziger. Artillery strengths not known.
9. Fédérés were recent republican volunteers for the Garde Nationale; later integrated, they changed to complexion of the Garde Nationale from constitutional monarchist to republican.
10. Order of battle information derived from Nafziger. Artillery strengths not known.
11. Volunteers were allowed to leave if they had given two month's notice to their commanding officer. Therefore many of these troops were not actually deserters.
12. Regiments were combined as follows: Leibgarde & 2. Cavallerie Regiment; Leibregiment & 4. Cavallerie Regiment; 5. & 7. Cavallerie Regiments; and 9. & 10. Cavallerie Regiments, Leichte Dragoner.
13. The Netherlands.
14. Burne, *Duke of York*, p.35.
15. Bijlandt was later court-martialled and sentenced to life imprisonment. His son Willem commanded a Netherlands brigade in Perponcher's division in the Waterloo campaign.
16. It would take the Revolutionary wars and a Napoleon to change all that.
17. Anon. *An Accurate and Impartial Account*, pp. viii-ix.
18. Although a composite Guards battalion comprising volunteers from all three Guards regiments had seen some service. But no single entire Guards battalion had ever been sent there.
19. Burne, *Duke of York*, p.35.
20. Brown, *An Impartial Journal*, p.2. The Brigade of Guards comprised the 1/1st Regiment of Foot Guards (Colonel Samuel Hulse) – 31 officers & 656 men; the 1/Coldstream Regiment of Foot Guards (Colonel Lowther Pennington –

NOTES

28 officers & 590 men; the 1/3rd Regiment of Foot Guards (Colonel William Grinfield) – 28 officers & 590 men; and four companies of the Guards Grenadier Battalion (numbers included above). The Foot Guards were an anomaly at this period in not being permanently organised into battalions. Instead they had more companies than ordinary line regiments and if needed for overseas service the requisite number of companies would be formed into one or more service battalions. The forming of composite Foot Guards battalions made up of companies from different regiments was quite common.

21. Serving in this brigade as ensigns were future Peninsular War generals Kenneth Howard (Coldstream Foot Guards), William Thomas Dilkes and the Honourable Edward Stopford (3rd Foot Guards).
22. Anon. *An Accurate and Impartial*, p.2.
23. Calvert, *Journals & Correspondence*, pp.22-23. A private of the Guards fell and broke his leg during boarding; not a single medicine chest or doctor could be found to assist him in the entire fleet.
24. Anon. *An Impartial etc*. p.6.
25. Brown, *An Impartial Journal*, p.4; Calvert p.21.
26. Henry Clinton letter dated 28 February 1793, Vol.235.
27. Burne, *Duke of York*, p.37.
28. ibid.
29. Secret letter from Secretary of State to Lake dated 23 February 1793, WO 4/291-292, NAK.
30. Letter of 28 February 1793, quoted in Burne, *Duke of York*, p.38.
31. Letter dated 2 March 1793, quoted in Burne, *Duke of York*, pp.38-39.
32. Calvert, *Journals & Correspondence*, pp.24-25. The Stadtholder was Willem V, Prince of Orange-Nassau.
33. Brown, *An Impartial Journal*, p.5.

Chapter 5

1. Calvert, *Journals & Correspondence*, p.31.
2. ibid, p.28.
3. Captain Jesse Wright's company, eight officers and 115 men.
4. Calvert, *Journals & Correspondence*, pp.33-34.
5. Brown, *An Impartial Journal*, p.6.
6. Craufurd was the elder brother of future Light Division commander Robert Craufurd.
7. Attachment to a letter from Secretary of State to James Murray dated 19 March 1793, WO 4/291-292, NAK.
8. Letter of 31 March 1793, quoted in Burne, *Duke of York*, p.40.
9. Letter of 31 March 1793, quoted in Burne, *Duke of York*, p.40.
10. Calvert, *Journals & Correspondence*, p.53. One of Dumouriez's staff who accompanied him was the young general Louis Phillippe, the son of *Général Égalité*. He would later become King Louis Phillippe I of France. *Général Égalité* immediately came under suspicion and ended up mounting the guillotine on 9 November 1793.
11. Calvert, *Journals & Correspondence*, pp.61-62.
12. Allison, *History of Europe*, p.243.
13. Calvert, *Journals & Correspondence*, pp.62-63.
14. Burne, *Duke of York*, p.41. In fact, Auckland had received notification from Grenville on 3 April that the King intended the capture of Dunkirk as a primary goal.

15. The ranks maréchal de camp and lieutenant-général ceased being used by the Decree of 21 February 1793. They were replaced by the ranks of général de brigade and général de division.
16. The village of Famars has recently been shown to contain the outlines of a gallo-roman fort and may in fact be the site of Caesar's Camp, once incorrectly identified as being farther south.
17. Calvert, *Journals & Correspondence*, p.53.
18. Probably men recruited in Jamaica, where the regiment had been in garrison from 1782 to 1791.
19. Calvert, *Journals & Correspondence*, pp.54-55.
20. Ompteda, *In the King's German Legion*, p.32.
21. Letter from Secretary of State dated 16 April 1793, WO 4/291-292, NAK.
22. Barnett, *Britain and Her Army*, p.236.
23. Calvert, *Journals & Correspondence*, pp.67-68.
24. Ompteda, *In the King's German Legion*, pp.33-34.
25. Burne, *Duke of York*, p.46.
26. Henry Clinton letter of 26 April 1793, University of Michigan, Vol.235.
27. Feldmarschall Franz Moritz, count von Lacy, the 'grand old man of the Austrian army' (1725-1801); and Johann Amadeus Franz de Paula Freiherr von Thugut (1736-1818). Thugut was a remarkable man. Born in Linz in 1736, the illegitimate son of an army paymaster who died young and left Thugut to the care of a domineering mother, he rose through the aristocrat-dominated diplomatic circles to become head of the foreign office in Austria. He never married, never socialised and did all work himself, rarely trusting others. He hated both France and Prussia passionately and believed that Austria should be rewarded for her exertions with territorial gains, split off from the minor German states.
28. Fortescue, *British Campaigns in Flanders*, p.196.
29. Burne, *Duke of York*, p.46.
30. He is remembered today as the man Napoleon captured - along with his entire army - at Ulm in 1805.
31. Letter from Secretary of State to James Murray dated 16 April 1793, WO 6/7-12, NAK.

Chapter 6

1. Hessen-Darmstadt and Hessen-Kassel.
2. Fortescue, *British Campaigns in Flanders*, p.193.
3. Ompteda, *In the King's German Legion*, pp.35-36.
4. Ompteda, *In the King's German Legion*, p.39.
5. McKinnon, *Coldstream Guards*, Vol II., p.35.
6. ibid.
7. The patch of forest exists even today, as does the forest track. It is within a National Park.
8. Burne, *Duke of York*, p.49. Yes, the very Blücher of Waterloo fame.
9. He was taken into Valenciennes where a surgeon tried to save him, but he died on the morning of 9 May. He was buried on Mont Joui, just west of Famars, under an impressive column, later relocated to Valenciennes.
10. Ensign Kenneth Alexander Howard, wounded in the thigh, would later command the Guards brigade in the Peninsula War
11. The Abbaye de Vicoigne, built in 1125, was destroyed in 1793 and never rebuilt.
12. Calvert, letter to his sister dated 4 June, p.79.
13. The future Emperor Ferdinand I (1793-1876). Morris, *With the Guards in Flanders*, p.19.

NOTES

14. Unlike infantry battalions, the number of troops in a cavalry regiment could increase ('augmentation') or reduce ('reduction') according to the exigencies of wartime need. Most regiments had six troops, a number had nine troops, while the 1st Dragoon Guards had twelve troops.
15. Troops existed for administrative purposes; in the field, troops were paired into squadrons commanded by the senior troop commander in each pairing. Surplus troops were usually left at home for the purposes of recruitment and training.
16. Duncan, *History of the Royal Regiment of Artillery*, Vol.II pp.55-56.
17. ibid, Vol.II p.79.
18. Normally the most senior regiment in any formation stood on the right, with the second most senior on the left. Left in front means that the left wing was leading the advance, with the most senior regiment therefore at the rear.
19. Mack was out of favour at the Imperial court, and his days as chief-of-staff were numbered.
20. Burne, *Duke of York*, pp.50-51.
21. Calvert, *Journals & Correspondence*, p.76.
22. *Geschichte der Königlich-Hannoverschen Armee*, vol. IV, p.217.
23. *Geschichte der Königlich-Hannoverschen Armee*, vol. IV, p.218.
24. Ompteda, *In the King's German Legion*, pp.48-49.
25. Oberst mack having been wounded earlier in the day.
26. ibid, p.53.
27. Brown, *An Impartial Journal*, p.21.
28. Later a Marechal d'Empire under Napoleon.
29. Later a Marechal d'Empire under Napoleon.
30. Chandler, *Napoleon's Marshals*, p.312.
31. Who later commanded the Light Division in the Peninsular War.
32. Based upon Morris, *With the Guards in Flanders*, pp.21-22.
33. This is probably Ferdinand Hans Ludolf von Kielmansegge, aged 16.
34. Ompteda, *In the King's German Legion*, p.43.

Chapter 7

1. Ompteda, *In the King's German Legion*, pp.55-56.
2. Brown, *An Impartial Journal*, pp.23-24.
3. Le Marchant, *Memoirs of the late…*, pp.17-18.
4. Calvert, *Journals & Correspondence*, p.80.
5. ibid, p.83.
6. ibid, p.88. The late king being Frederick the Great.
7. Clinton Letters, University of Michigan, Vol.235.
8. Brown, *An Impartial Journal*, p.30.
9. William Cavendish-Bentinck journal for 17 June 1793, Pw Ja 610.
10. Calvert, *Journals & Correspondence*, p.82.
11. William Cavendish-Bentinck journal for 18 June 1793, Pw Ja 610.
12. Brown, *An Impartial Journal*, pp.37-38.
13. Morris, *With the Guards in Flanders*, p.30.
14. Brown, *An Impartial Journal*, p.46.
15. Burne, *Duke of York*, p.59.
16. Ompteda, *In the King's German Legion*, p.57.
17. Wilson's and Shuttleworth's companies.
18. *The Diary of William Windham*, p.281.
19. Ompteda, *In the King's German Legion*, pp.57-58.
20. Demet, *We are Accustomed to do our Duty*, pp.28-29.

21. Mines were called, in the expression of the time, 'globes of compression'.
22. Morris, *With the Guards in Flanders*, p.33.
23. Calvert, *Journals & Correspondence*, p.95. Typically, a step promotion was given to every bearer of victory despatches.
24. Ompteda, *In the King's German Legion*, p.65.
25. Ompteda, *In the King's German Legion*, p.66.
26. ibid, pp.66-67. Prince József Antoni Poniatowski later became a Maréchal d'Empire under Napoleon.
27. Calvert, *Journals & Correspondence*, p.102. The quoted text is actually from Victoires, Conquetes, Revers, &c.

Chapter 8

1. The Revolutionary Tribunal was a court which was instituted by the National Convention for the trial of political offenders. It was the engine-room of the 'Reign of Terror'.
2. Allison, *History of Europe*, p.143.
3. Burne, *Duke of York*, pp.66-67.
4. William Knollys letter quoted in Uglow, *In These Times*, p.43.
5. Allegedly a site where Julius Caesar had struck camp in 51-50 BC, although there is good reason to believe his actual camp was 16 miles (26km) farther south.
6. Burne, *Duke of York*, pp.63-64.
7. The Duke's column was by this time 6,500 British, 11,000 Austrians, 10,600 Hanoverians and 7,700 Hessians. A total of 29,700 infantry, 5,400 cavalry, and 1,900 artillerymen.
8. Calvert, *Journals & Correspondence*, pp.106-107.
9. Brown, *An Impartial Journal*, pp.65-66.
10. Duke of York letter to King George dated 19 August 1793 quoted in Burne, *Duke of York*, p.68.
11. Herbert, *Life of General Sir Robert Wilson*, p.53.
12. Calvert, *Journals & Correspondence*, p.101.
13. Phipps, *Armies of the First French Republic*, Vol.I, pp.218-219.
14. Born Edward Dalton in Ireland in 1737, d'Alton was an adventurer who had served most of his life in the Austrian army.
15. Ditfurth, *Die Hessen in den Feldzügen von 1793, 1794 and 1795*, Vol.I, pp.98-99.
16. Duke of York letter dated 26 August 1793, quoted in Burne *Duke of York*, p.70.
17. Fortescue, *British Campaigns in Flanders*, p.229.
18. Later a temporary division commander under Wellington in the Peninsula.
19. According to Burne, these reinforcements were allegedly the repatriated former garrison of Valenciennes, who by the terms of surrender were supposed to be non-combatant.
20. Quoted in Demet, *We are Accustomed to do our Duty*, p.32.
21. Anon., *An Accurate and Impartial Narrative*, p.105.
22. Ompteda, *In the King's German Legion*, p.69.
23. On 14 September he learned that 'my promotion to captain and adjutant in place of Charles [i.e. Karl von] Alten has been forwarded to England.' Ompteda, *In the King's German Legion*, p.70. The rank was confirmed on 10 October.

Chapter 9

1. Prince Adolphus, Duke of Cambridge, the 19-year-old seventh son of King George III.
2. Dupuis, *La Campagne de 1793 à l'Armée du Nord et des Ardennes*, vol. I, p.446.

NOTES

3. ibid, pp.450-451.
4. *Geschichte der Königlich Hannoverschen Armee,* vol. IV, p.274.
5. *Dupuis, La Campagne de 1793 à l'Armée du Nord et des Ardennes,* vol. I, pp. 446-454.
6. Moncrieff was mortally wounded by a shot which carried away part of his skull behind the ear. He was found by Colonel St Leger of the Guards, wounded and stripped in the possession of the Austrians, who assumed by his blue uniform that he was a Frenchman. His supine form was allegedly robbed of his watch, money, epaulettes and silver buttons as he lay mortally wounded. He may have been a victim of friendly fire.
7. *Geschichte der Königlich Hannoverschen Armee,* vol. IV, p.276.
8. Later commanded a division in the French I Corps at Waterloo.
9. The garrison at Hondschoote actually consisted of a battalion of the 6. Infanterie-Regiment, the I/11.Infanterie-Regiment and the II/Hessisches Erbprinz Regiment and the heavy artillery on the right wing under Generalmajor von Hammerstein; and the Gardes, 1. Grenadier-Bataillon, the II/4.Infanterie-Regiment, the II/11. Infanterie-Regiment, a battalion of the 6. Infanterie-Regiment, a battalion of the Hessisches Gross und Erbprinz Infanterie-Regiment and the k.k. Linien-Infanterie-Regiment Nr. 35 under Generalmajor von Cochenhausen defending the left wing of the position. It was a substantial garrison for a small town, but the lack of posted sentries – which allowed the French to advance within a mile of the place undetected – was a disgrace.
10. Dupuis, *La Campagne de 1793 à l'Armée du Nord et des Ardennes,* vol. I, pp. 475-476.
11. The ground to the south of this position was very flat and uncovered, therefore giving all advantages to the defender.
12. Later the first Chief of the Prussian General Staff, died of wounds received at the Battle of Lützen in 1813.
13. Account from Leclaire in Dupuis, *La Campagne de 1793 à l'Armée du Nord et des Ardennes,* vol. I, pp. 481-482.
14. The 5. Infanterie-Regiment alone lost 507 men, two-thirds of its strength (mostly missing and prisoners) as well as two colours. Both the 5. And 6. Infanterie lost their commanding officers. Generalmajor von Diepenbroick was also wounded. Six cannon were left behind.
15. Adjutant-général Gay de Vernon wrote of 1,800 French casualties, which seems more realistic.
16. Duke of York letter to King George dated 18 September 1793, quoted in Burne, *Duke of York,* p.77.
17. François Claude Amour, Marquis de Bouillé (1739-1800), a former French general and leading royalist.
18. Duke of York letter to Prince of Wales dated 21 September 1793, quoted in Burne, *Duke of York,* p.73.
19. Duke of York letter to King George dated 18 September 1793, quoted in Burne, *Duke of York,* pp.73-75.
20. William Cavendish-Bentinck journal for September 1793, Pw Ja 622, Nottingham University.
21. James Russell diary, entry for 8 September 1793.
22. James Russell diary, entry for 10 September 1793.
23. *The Present State,* p.4.
24. Landrin was suspended on 13 September, arrested on 8 December and released from prison on 15 August 1794. He was re-instated as a captain in April 1795. He retired in 1797.
25. Duke of York letter to King George dated 10 September 1793, quoted in Burne, *Duke of York,* p.81.

NOTES

26. Many of the vessels in the fleet subsequently sailed for service in the West Indies with Sir Charles Grey early in 1794.
27. Duke of York letter to King George dated 31 August 1793, quoted in Burne, *Duke of York*, p.70.
28. Calvert, *Journals & Correspondence*, pp.130-131.
29. *The Present State*, p.3.
30. Calvert, *Journals & Correspondence*, p.143.
31. Although a small town, Cysoing stands on high ground half-way between Lille and Tournai, in excellent cavalry country – an arm in which the Coalition had a clear superiority over the French.
32. Duke of York letter to King George dated 15 October 1793, quoted in Burne, *Duke of York*, p.87.
33. The 14th Foot (300 men) were left at Courtrai, the 53rd Foot at Nieuwpoort.
34. Calvert, *Journals & Correspondence*, pp.154-155.
35. ibid, pp.155-156.
36. Phipps, *Armies of the First French Republic*, Vol.I, p.261.
37. Ferguson later commanded a brigade under Wellesley in Portugal in 1808.
38. Nieuport is the French spelling.
39. Duke of York letter to King George dated 25 October 1793, quoted in Burne, *Duke of York*, p.92.
40. Quoted in footnote, Burne, *Duke of York*, p.92.
41. William Cavendish-Bentinck journal for 28 October 1793, PW Ja 612. The Royal Engineers wore blue long-tail coats and cocked hats, so unfortunately indeed looked like Frenchmen; the uniform was changed to scarlet in 1812.
42. Hamilton, *The First Regiment of Foot Guards*, p.292.
43. Dundas letter quoted in Burne, *Duke of York*, p.96-97.
44. It was about this time that Lieutenant Colonel Robert Brownrigg of the 88th Foot was appointed Deputy Quartermaster-General in Flanders. He later became a great friend and protégé of the Duke.
45. William Cavendish-Bentinck journal for 22 November 1793, PWJa621. The Hessen-Cassel brigade was nearly 4,000 men strong.
46. Demet, *We Are Accustomed to do our Duty*, p.57. By Christmas the Baden battalion had lost 180 men to desertion and sickness. The Hessen-Darmstadt brigade proved equally porous.
47. The Hessen-Cassel brigade had over 3,100 men upon leaving Ostend, but by the time they returned to the continent in late March 1794 after this futile journey they had over 850 men sick.
48. Hamilton, *The First Regiment of Foot Guards*, p.293. The same address also urged his troops (largely Protestant) to respect the religious customs of their Catholic Austrian allies.

Chapter 10

1. Calvert, *Journals & Correspondence*, pp.167-168.
2. Burne, *Duke of York*, p.98.
3. DNB, Vol. 39, entry for Sir James Murray-Pulteney.
4. Quoted in Fortescue, *British Campaigns in Flanders*, p.202.
5. Letter to King George dated 3 December 1793 quoted in Burne, *Duke of York*, p.111.
6. Mack's reasons for leaving were nebulous; some related to his health, some related to his finances, some related to the burning down of his castle.
7. Gramm, *Der Unglückliche Mack, Aufstieg und Fall des Karl Mack von Leiberich*, thesis, p.159.

8. Mack was officially re-appointed on 22 February 1794, and with the rank of generalmajor.
9. This practice caused particular disaffection within the Guards regiments, as might be expected.
10. Quoted in Burne, *Duke of York*, p.105. The Bonnington baronetcy became extinct in 1738; quite possibly the author Burne refers to was a Bonnington descendant, Andrew Carmichael, who was a captain in the 16th Light Dragoons in 1793.
11. Allison, *History of Europe*, p.143.
12. Duke of York letter to King George dated 18 September 1793, quoted in Burne, *Duke of York*, p.78.
13. The British maritime effort at Dunkirk in 1793 was a far cry from 1940!
14. *Morning Chronicle*, edition of 10 September 1793.
15. The Chancellor was at the time the head of Imperial foreign affairs. Thugut was also a renowned Prussophobe.
16. Some British Guards officers recorded that the Hanoverian cavalry had refused to take part in the fight, although they recorded casualties. Some lingering distrust since the Hondschoote disaster seems a possible explanation. Condescension to foreigners is another.
17. Based upon a summary in Henry Clinton letter dated 17 December 1794, University of Michigan, Vol.235.
18. Brown, *An Impartial Journal*, p.89.
19. Henry Bunbury quoted in DNB entry for James Henry Craig.
20. Craig letter dated 21 January 1794, quoted in Burne, *Duke of York*, p.116.
21. Imperial Ambassador to the Court of St James Starhemberg confidentially informed Mack that he thought it highly doubtful that the Duke would return to the army upon his arrival in London.
22. Burne, *Duke of York*, p.113.
23. Gramm, *Der Unglückliche Mack, Aufstieg und Fall des Karl Mack von Leiberich*, thesis, p.162.
24. Burne, *Duke of York*, p.114.
25. Carnot letter to Pichegru dated 11 February 1794, quoted in Fortescue, *History of the British Army*, Vol.IV, pp.227-228.
26. The rank of lance-corporal did not exist at this time. Men selected to substitute for absent corporals were called 'chosen men'.
27. Calvert, *Journals & Correspondence*, p.187.
28. ibid, pp.396-397.
29. Möllendorf had just returned from overseeing the second partition of Poland.
30. The emperor's fear of radicalism bordered on paranoia. He set up one of the largest spy networks in Europe, and maintained a separation of powers between the Imperial War Council and his field commanders in order to avoid placing too much power in the hands of any individual.
31. Von Rollin had the Emperor's ear, being his former military tutor.
32. The ceremonial royal entry—the first official peaceable visit of a reigning monarch, prince, duke or governor into a city.
33. Mack had been promoted to general officer rank on 24 February 1794.
34. Brown, *An Impartial Journal*, p.94.
35. Calvert, *Journals & Correspondence*, p.185.

Chapter 11

1. Le Marchant, *Memoirs of the late etc.*, pp.34-35.
2. Herbert, *Life of General Sir Robert Wilson*, p.61.

NOTES

3. Burne, *Duke of York*, p.120.
4. Herbert, *Life of General Sir Robert Wilson*, p.98. Halberds were the pikes carried by serjeants, three of which formed a 'triangle' from which men to be flogged were tied.
5. As was common in the days before Napoleon devised the corps system.
6. Jourdan had been arrested after refusing to carry out an impossible order. He was acquitted and sent home, but later returned to the army.
7. Quoted in Burne, *Duke of York*, p.118.
8. Griffith, *The Art of War in Revolutionary France*, p.82.
9. This had been mooted at the start of 1793, but only carried out at the end of that year.
10. The term 'regiment' was thought to have royalist overtones. Oddly, the same sentiment did not seem to exist in the cavalry or artillery.
11. Based upon Witzleben, *Prince Friedrich Josias of Coburg Saalfeld*, vol. III, p.21.
12. Based upon Witzleben, *Prince Friedrich Josias of Coburg Saalfeld*, vol. III, p.26. Oberst Mack put forward the proposition that for 1794 all battalions ought to have four battalion guns rather than the current two or three, using captured French guns. It is doubtful this ever came into effect.
13. Manessy, Ulm and Rouviere. Details of the advanced guard's actions based upon 'Von D', "Feldzug der verbundenen Armeen in Flandern, im Jahre 1794", in 'Neues militairisches Journal' 9. Band 18. Stück (Hannover 1798) pp. 297-302, quoted at http://theminiaturespage.com/boards/msg.mv?id=426931
14. Duke of York despatch quoted in Burne, *Duke of York*, p.125.
15. On 19 April the Duke of York sent an officer and 40 men of the Brigade of Guards to Basieux to prevent the pillaging of the burning houses.
16. Herbert, *Life of General Sir Robert Wilson*, p.63.
17. The capture of enemy possessions could be a lucrative business. On 12 May 1794 the Duke of York issued a General Order offering a reward of 20 pounds sterling per cannon or howitzer taken; ten pounds for each colour; ten pounds for each tumbril; and twelve pounds for each horse. These were princely sums to the average infantryman.
18. As was customary for bearers of victory despatches, Clinton was rewarded with promotion, to the brevet of major.
19. Herbert, *Life of General Sir Robert Wilson*, p.66.
20. His next actions were undertaken in the belief that the French had captured the emperor, which was merely a false rumour.
21. Herbert, *Life of General Sir Robert Wilson*, p.68.
22. idid, p.71.
23. These were, Major William Aylett, Captain Robert Pocklington Lieutenants Edward Ryan, William Keir and Granby Calcraft, and Cornets Thomas Blount, Edward Butler and Robert Wilson. The same officers were later made Knights of the Military Order of Maria Theresa (1801).
24. This Beaumont is about 10 miles (16km) east of Maubeuge, and not to be confused with the Beaumont (or more correctly Beaumont-sur-Cambresis) where a battle was fought on 26 April.
25. In 1813, commander of all 335,000 Allied troops at the battle of Leipzig.
26. Burne, *Duke of York*, p.129.
27. Russell, diary entry for 26 April.
28. Russell, diary entry for 28 April.
29. Murray later commanded a division on the east coast of Spain in 1813. He was court-martialled for his actions at Tarragona but later acquitted.

NOTES

30. Royal Horse Guards 1st, 3rd and 5th Dragoon Guards, 1st Dragoons and 7th, 11th and 16th Light Dragoons.
31. Brown, *An Impartial Journal*, p.130.
32. Where Wellington defeated '40,000 Frenchmen in forty minutes' in 1812. Noting however that the French troops were somewhat superior in calibre at the later encounter.
33. Chapuis and his aide were described by a Guards officer as 'stout vulgar looking Chaps.' Morris, *With the the Guards in Flanders*, p.70.
34. Calvert, *Journals & Correspondence*, p.198.
35. Hammerstein received the thanks of the emperor and Prince Coburg for his actions, and was sent a gold sword as a gift from King George III. He was to prove one of the Coalition's ablest divisional commanders in the campaign.
36. Brown, *An Impartial Journal*, p.132.
37. Herbert, *Life of General Sir Robert Wilson*, p.73.
38. Lake had been appointed regimental Colonel of the 53rd Foot. He would not return during the campaign.
39. Duke of York letter to King George dated 6 May 1794, quoted in Burne, *Duke of York*, p.134.
40. Dispositions and movements based upon Coutanceau, *La Campagne de 1794 à l'Armée du Nord*, vol.II, pp.220-225.
41. *Memoirs and correspondence of field-marshal viscount Combermere, from his family papers*, by Mary viscountess Combermere and W.W. Knollys, pp.38-41.
42. Evidently the 2e Bataillon des Ardennes and the 1/34th Régiment d'Infanterie de Ligne of Salme's brigade.
43. *Memoirs and Correspondence of Field-marshal Viscount Combermere, from his Family Papers*, by Mary Viscountess Combermere and W.W. Knollys, pp.38-41.
44. Royal Horse Guards 2nd, 3rd and 6th Dragoon Guards 1st, 2nd and 6th Dragoons, and 7th, 11th, 15th and 16th Light Dragoons.

Chapter 12

1. In which the Hessen-Darmstadt contingent lost 220 men.
2. Duke of York letter to King George dated 13 May 1794, quoted in Burne, *Duke of York*, p.136.
3. Feldzeugmeister Kaunitz had repelled the first French attempt to establish a foothold north of the River Sambre, south-west of Charleroi. The French lost 4,000 men and the Austrians 2,800.
4. Events based upon Gramm, *Der Unglückliche Mack, Aufstieg und Fall des Karl Mack von Leiberich*, thesis, p.169.
5. Calvert, *Journals & Correspondence*, p.207.
6. Quoted in Glover, *Warfare in the Age of Bonaparte*, p.29.
7. Intention of the plan as quoted in Burne, *Duke of York*, p.138.
8. Quoted in Glover, *Warfare in the Age of Bonaparte*, p.32.
9. His neighbour Kinsky had brought his column forward on the 16th and so was nearer to the three main columns at dawn the following day.
10. Hamilton, *The First Regiment of Foot Guards*, p.303.
11. Mack, the Duke of York and the Emperor Franz, respectively. Coburg, as nominal commander-in-chief, seems to have largely an onlooker.
12. Much of this detail is based upon the account in *Neue Bellona oder Beiträge zur Kriegskunst und Kriegsgeschichte*, Vol. IV, 1808.

NOTES

13. The Coalition commanders were concerned that the mist might too easily conceal French troops in the close country. It did not occur to them that the mist might be to *their* advantage.
14. This included two squadrons of the British 11th Light Dragoons.
15. Successive occupations and looting had reduced Tourcoing (population 11,000) to a starving ruin. It had no military value other than the fact it guarded the Lille-Courtrai road.
16. 'Relation der am 17ten May 1794 zwischen den vereinigten Kaiserlich Königlich und Landgräflich Hessischen Trupen, unter Commando des Feldzeugmeisters Grafen Kinsky, und Generals von Wurmb gegen die Franzosen bei Bouvines und Chereng vorgefallenen Affaire', by an anonymous officer, probably the Hessen-Kassel Generalmajor von Wurmb. Quoted in http://theminiaturespage.com/boards/msg.mv?id=426931, translation by Geert van Uythoven.
17. Incredibly, Major General 'Woolly' Erskine, with sixteen British heavy cavalry squadrons from the duke's No. 3 column, had mistakenly followed Kinsky's column! They spent the day idly watching the action from afar.
18. 'Relation der am 17ten May 1794', quoted in http://theminiaturespage.com/boards/msg.mv?id=426931, translation by Geert van Uythoven.
19. 'Relation der am 17ten May 1794', quoted in http://theminiaturespage.com/boards/msg.mv?id=426931, translation by Geert van Uythoven.
20. 'Relation der am 17ten May 1794', quoted in http://theminiaturespage.com/boards/msg.mv?id=426931, translation by Geert van Uythoven.
21. Confusingly, not the same town that the duke's No. 3 Column marched from, although the two are only about 10 miles (16km) apart.
22. No. 4 Column commenced its march from Froidmont, about 10 miles (16km) south of Templeuve, where the duke's column started. The error was almost certainly due to bungled orders, rather than being 'lost in the dark'.
23. Brown, *An Impartial Journal*, pp.140-141.
24. Herbert, *Life of General Sir Robert Wilson*, p.83.
25. Coutanceau, *La Campagne de 1794 à l'Armée du Nord*, Partie 2 Tome 1, p.21.
26. This colonel is referenced in Burne, *Duke of York*, p.143.
27. Warner, *How Wars were Won*, p.92.
28. The archduke had in fact suffered an epileptic fit during the night, and his staff would not wake him until his doctor deemed him fit to resume command.
29. Certain writers have assumed treason from Kinsky'a actions. It is likely however that he waited for the Archduke Karl – a Prince of the Blood – to take the lead. But the Archduke was indisposed.
30. Four battalions, namely Colloredo and Kaunitz in front; the Hessen-Kassel Grenadier-Bataillon von Germann on the right, and one battalion of Kaunitz on the left flank. The cavalry rode behind in support.
31. The duke never got his two battalions back.
32. The account in Neue Bellona states: 'This incident is a proof of how much what is called the bravura of whole regiments often depends only on chance and favorable secondary circumstances. It was this Regiment Kaunitz, one of the most beautiful of the Imperial Army, that had a few days earlier, on the 10th of May at Bachy, by exceptionally stalwart bravery, earned the general respect of the army and a special thanksgiving of the Duke.'
33. Much of this narrative is based upon http://batailles-franco-anglaises.blogspot.com/2009/02/bataille-de-tourcoing.html and upon the account in Neue Bellona oder Beiträge zur Kriegskunst und Kriegsgeschichte, Vol. IV, 1808.
34. The duke had imagined his southern flank was securely covered by No. 4 and No. 5 Columns and had only expected an attack from the north.

NOTES

35. The duke later took to wearing a plain coat when on campaign, possibly on account of this incident.
36. Doggerel quoted in Burne, *Duke of York*, p.147.
37. The pursuing Frenchmen were led by François Desurmont, the son of the Mayor of Tourcoing.
38. Lieutenant Colonel Browne died at Lille the following day.
39. Gilbert Cimitiere served in the 48th Foot from 1796 until 1827, ending his days as a lieutenant-colonel. History records that, as the only captain left standing, he led the 48th out of the bloodbath at Albuera in 1811.
40. Herbert, *Life of General Sir Robert Wilson*, pp.87-88.
41. ibid p.88.
42. Brown, *An Impartial Journal*, p.144.
43. Surgeon William Turner.
44. Herbert, *Life of General Sir Robert Wilson*, pp.89-90.
45. The Hessen-Cassel Leib-Regiment lost 329 men in Lannoy, mostly captured.
46. Strongly suggesting that the retreat of the Guards was somewhat less dignified than the perfect order anecdoted by the regimental histories.
47. *Neue Bellona oder Beiträge zur Kriegskunst und Kriegsgeschichte*, Vol.IV, 1808, p.329.
48. ibid, p.330.
49. *Prinz Friedrich Josias von Coburg*, vol. III, pp.220-221.
50. Quoted in Burne, *Duke of York*, p.148.
51. Calvert, *Journals & Correspondence*, p.217.
52. Even then it is doubtful that such a plan could have succeeded.
53. The captured included most of the Hanoverian 1. Infanterie-Regiment, taken prisoner at Dottignies.
54. Seven of these lost guns were precious 12-pounders from the siege artillery.
55. *Encyclopaedia Britannica*, 1911, p.179.

Chapter 13

1. Quoted in Burne, *Duke of York*, p.149.
2. ibid, p.150.
3. Brown, *An Impartial Journal*, pp.153-154.
4. Russell diary, entry for 6 June 1794.
5. Order of battle information based upon Macdonald, p.30.
6. Calvert, *Journals & Correspondence*, p.222.
7. Based upon Herbert, *Life of General Sir Robert Wilson*, p.96.
8. Account of the battle based upon *Prinz Friedrich Josias von Coburg*, vol.III, p.230.
9. Herbert, *Life of General Sir Robert Wilson*, pp.96-97.
10. Captain Stafford Lightburne, later a brigade commander under Wellington, was court-martialled for 'misbehaviour before the enemy' on 22 May. He was acquitted, and the Duke of York censured the subordinate making the accusation.
11. As it turned out Kaunitz scored a victory on 24 May at Erquelinnes. But the council had already broken down before the news came in.
12. Waldeck was a brave and experienced soldier – he lost an arm at Thionville two years earlier – who had shown a liking for 'leading from the front'. Whether that quality suited him in his new role remained to be seen.
13. Calvert, *Journals & Correspondence*, p.233.
14. Duke of York letter to King George dated 6 June 1794, quoted in Burne, *Duke of York*, pp.155-156.
15. Russell diary, entry for 7 June 1794.

NOTES

Chapter 14

1. Rose, *Pitt and The Great War*, p.195. Britain was paying a subsidy of £50,000 per month for the 62,000 Prussians; in the end Whitehall funded the Prussian occupation of Poland.
2. The garrison of Ypres at this time comprised just over 5,000 men commanded by Generalmajor Paul von Salis, of which about half were Hessen-Cassel.
3. Based upon the account in *Geschichte der Königlich-Hannoverschen Armee*, vol. IV, pp.468-472.
4. Dalrymple was a fellow Guardsman and commandant of Chatham Barracks.
5. Calvert, *Journals & Correspondence*, p.245.
6. Four Austrian and six Hessen-Cassel battalions were taken prisoner and marched to Lille.
7. Anon., *A Journal Kept*, p.2.
8. Anon., *A Journal Kept*, p.5.
9. ibid, p.6.
10. Vrouws = women.
11. *Memoir of General Graham*, p.127.
12. *A Journal Kept*, p.11.
13. Lieutenant Colonel, later Colonel Thomas Pakenham Vandeleur (1768-1803).
14. Lieutenant Colonel, later Lieutenant General Sir John Doyle (1756-1834).
15. *A Journal Kept*, p.22.
16. Jones, *An Historical Journal*, p.88.
17. Chandler, *Napoleon's Marshals*, p.181.
18. Later a Maréchal d'Empire under Napoleon.
19. Later a Maréchal d'Empire under Napoleon.
20. Chandler, *Napoleon's Marshals*, p.22.
21. Later a Maréchal d'Empire under Napoleon.
22. Soult had five horses shot from under him during the battle.
23. On a scientific note, *l'Entreprenant*, a French reconnaissance balloon operated by the Aerostatic Corps, continuously informed Jourdan about Austrian movements during the battle.
24. Quite fortuitously as it turned out. Representative Sainte-Just was present and had drawn up a list of generals to be executed in the event that the Austrians won.
25. Witzleben, *Prinz Friedrich Josias von Coburg-Saalfeld*, vol.III, p.474.
26. Quoted in Burne, *Duke of York*, p.163.
27. Witzleben, *Prinz Friedrich Josias von Coburg-Saalfeld*, vol.III, p.486.
28. The sluices on the Scheldt near Valenciennes and Condé had been shut in order to flood the canals around those places, preparatory to French sieges.
29. *Mémoires du Maréchal-Général Soult*, Paris, 1854, pp.180-181.
30. In other words, from a future battlefield to a past battlefield.
31. Calvert, *Journals & Correspondence*, p.270.
32. Quoted in Burne, *Duke of York*, p.164.
33. Anon., *A Journal Kept*, pp.10-11.
34. Quoted in Burne, *Duke of York*, p.165.
35. Calvert, *Journals & Correspondence*, p.277.
36. Officers could hold 'local rank' which was superior to their 'army rank'.
37. Lord Moira left the army on 21 July.
38. Ironically, Abercrombie was one the officers to whom Moira had to report. Moira had six month's seniority as lieutenant-general on the Continent over Abercrombie.
39. Le Quesnoy fell to the French on 16 August, Valenciennes on 27 August and Condé on 29 August.

NOTES

40. Most of these émigré units were put into garrisons or kept in hand for a projected attack upon the Vendée. Only a few hussar regiments served with the duke's army. See Appendix XV.
41. *Memoir of General Graham*, p.150.
42. Quoted in Barnett, *Britain and Her Army*, pp.236-237. Presumably the boys included the 19-year-old Edward Paget (later second-in-command in the Peninsular, for a time) and the 23-year-old Arthur Wellesley (the future Duke of Wellington). They turned out alright.

Chapter 15

1. The Duke of York was later blamed for the fate of the émigrés, although the decision to hold the port was actually made by Dundas.
2. Brown, *An Impartial Journal*, p.181.
3. Craig letter to Evan Nepean quoted in Burne, *Duke of York*, p.170.
4. The site of heavy fighting in October 1944.
5. Brown, *An Impartial Journal*, p.173.
6. ibid, pp.187-188.
7. *A Journal Kept*, pp.46-47.
8. *Memoirs of General Graham*, p.154.
9. Russell diary, entry for 18 August 1794.
10. Demet, *We are Accustomed to do our Duty*, p.86.
11. *Memoirs of General Graham*, p.156. Although there is also evidence that the Brigade of Guards was given this order as early as 12 April and practised these movements prior to the opening of the campaign. Perhaps the line regiments adopted them after the Guards had time to demonstrate their soundness.
12. Calvert, *Journals & Correspondence*, pp.292-293.
13. In the 'all arms' nature of the brigades can be seen the genesis of Napoleon's later Corps d'armée system.
14. Strength and order of battle details derived from Nafziger.
15. The number of artillery pieces present with the duke's army seems to have somewhat uncertain due to the presence of battalion guns. The figure of 117 is based upon a return dated 28 October 1794 showing ammunition required for the British guns then in the field (seventy-two), then adding in twenty-seven Hanoverian guns and twenty Hessian guns derived from their returns.
16. *A Journal Kept*, p.52.
17. A Hanoverian officer allegedly deserted this day (Morris, *With the Guards in Flanders*, p.103).
18. Russell diary, entry for 27 August 1794.
19. Calvert, *Journals & Correspondence*, pp.306-307.
20. ibid.
21. *Memoir of General Graham*, p.171.
22. He was the grand-uncle of the future King Leopold I of Belgium, and therefore the great-great-granduncle of Queen Victoria.
23. Quoted in Burne, *Duke of York*, p.174.
24. ibid, p.175.
25. Craig letter to Evan Nepean quoted in Burne, *Duke of York*, p.177.
26. Calvert, *Journals & Correspondence*, p.323.
27. According to a return dated 19 July 1794, Delmas' division numbered about 6,600 men.
28. Ditfurth, *Die Hessen in den Feldzügen von 1793, 1794 und 1795*, Vol. II, p.252. The defenders of Boxtel were the Hessen-Darmstadt Leib-grenadiere and Landgrave-Regiment (840 men); Hompesch Jägers (200 men); Hessen-Darmstadt Jägers

NOTES

(76 men); a squadron of Hessen-Darmstadt Chevaulegers (78 men); Hompesch Hussars (200 men); Irvine Hussars (250 men); 4 Hessen-Darmstadt foot artillery and 3 Hanoverian artillery pieces. Total: 1,116 infantry, 528 cavalry and 7 guns.
29. The Leib-Grenadier-Bataillon lost 327 men, the Landgraf-Regiment 303.
30. Ditfurth, *Die Hessen in den Feldzügen von 1793, 1794 und 1795*, Vol. II, p.250.
31. Lieutenant Colonel Arthur Wellesley had temporary command of the 3rd Brigade, while John Coape Sherbrooke took command of the 33rd Foot.
32. Later a divisional commander of Netherlands troops at Waterloo.
33. Abercrombie presumably believed the intelligence gained from the two French prisoners two days earlier, that Pichegru was in the area with 50,000 men. In any event Abercrombie had very poor eyesight, so it is uncertain how he made any kind of observation at all.
34. Morris, *With the Guards in Flanders,* pp.110-111.
35. What Abercombie could not have known was that Pichegru had around 40,000 men in the vicinity, not far short of the intelligence gained from the French prisoners.
36. *The History of The Duke of Wellington's Regiment (West Riding) 1702-1992*, page 93, by J.M. Brereton and A.C.S. Savoury.
37. Much of the 'Battle of Boxtel' account is based upon '*De Slag om Boxtel*', Frank van Doorn, Dik Bol and Ruud van Nooijen, at http://www.muboboxtel.nl/CMS/wp-content/uploads/basistekst-21-def-20151114-DE-SLAG-OM-BOXTEL-kopie-2.pdf.
38. In a secret letter to Henry Dundas dated 17 September, the duke placed all the blame for Boxtel upon the Hessen-Darmstadt contingent, who he claims suffered 'a sudden Panick' leading to their precipitate withdrawal. Their casualty returns disagree with his assessment.
39. Quoted in Burne, *Duke of York*, p.182.
40. Indeed, Windham recorded in his diary that very day: 'I took what occasions I could to say something animating to the soldiers; but as that kind of eloquence has much chance in it, I did not always succeed. The Duke of York, in an attempt or two that he made, failed most miserably. It is one of the talents in which he is defective.' *The Diary of William Windham*, p.318.
41. The conference must have been held as Abercrombie's men were retiring, or immediately after their return, since the retreat was commenced about two hours after they arrived back in camp.

Chapter 16

1. Brown, *An Impartial Journal*, p.194.
2. Ditfurth, *Die Hessen in den Feldzügen von 1793, 1794 und 1795*, Vol.II, p.255.
3. Quoted in Burne, *Duke of York*, p.184.
4. ibid, p.188.
5. Quoted in Burne, *Duke of York*, p.189.
6. The 80th Foot was commanded by the Lieutenant Colonel the Honourable Henry Paget, later the Earl of Uxbridge and commander of the Allied cavalry at Waterloo. The ship they sailed on had just returned from the West Indies and had not been fumigated; as a result, about a third of the men went down Yellow Fever and other sicknesses.
7. Based upon Calvert, *Journals & Correspondence*, p.386.
8. Calvert, *Journals & Correspondence*, pp.385-386.
9. Quoted in Burne, *Duke of York*, p.189.
10. Henry Clinton letter dated 6 November 1794, University of Michigan, Vol.235.

NOTES

11. Brown, *An Impartial Journal*, p.196.
12. Quoted in Burne, *Duke of York*, p.190.
13. Henry Clinton letter dated 16 October 1794, University of Michigan, Vol. 235.
14. Brown, *An Impartial Journal*, p.193.
15. Morris, *With the Guards in Flanders*, p.116. 'Boor' was the British army corruption of Boer (farmer) but general applied to all Dutch men. A snickersee was a long knife.
16. ibid, p.117.
17. The Dutch garrison were paroled and allowed to return home. Several companies of the Loyal Emigrants were locked up in the citadel and left to starve.
18. Captains Baird, Henley and Duff; Lieutenants Mitchell, Thomson, Colquhoun, Murray and Wadman, and Quartermaster Duxall.
19. After the action they mustered 6 officers and 60 men. Quoted in Henry Clinton letter of 21 October 1794, University of Michigan, Viol. 235.
20. Quoted in https://forums.armchairgeneral.com/forum/historical-events-eras/napoleonic-era/156635-les-trophies-de-la-france/page3. Hope was Lieutenant-Colonel the Honourable Charles Hope; 'Waddams' was Lieutenant Francis Wadman.
21. McGrigor, *The Autobiography and Services*, p.24.
22. Vale, *the South Staffordshire Regiment*, p.37.
23. Morris, *With the Guards in Flanders*, p.123.
24. Keppel journal entry in October 1794.
25. Calvert, *Journals & Correspondence*, p.367.
26. ibid, p.366.
27. *A Journal Kept*, p.95.
28. Keppel was himself of Dutch extraction, being a great-grandson of the 1st Earl of Albemarle who had accompanied William of Orange to England in 1688.
29. Burne, *Duke of York*, p.192.
30. *A Journal Kept*, p.98.
31. Keppel journal, entry for 4 November 1794. The units involved were 120 men from each of the infantry regiments mentioned in the journal, plus the 15th Light Dragoons, Hanoverian Garde du Corps, and the Swiss de Gumoens regiment in Dutch service. The 59th Foot covered the retreat.
32. The newly-arrived 63rd and 78th Foot lost 148 men and seem to have been the most heavily engaged.
33. Captain Home Popham of the Royal Navy oversaw repair efforts on the bridge under fire for several days.
34. Keppel journal, entry for 6 November 1794.
35. The 88th still had not received orders to evacuate at 2.30 am, at which point they considered burning their colours to prevent them falling into the hands of the French. Then the order came.
36. The army was down to about 22,000 effectives, including 4,300 Hanoverians and 3,000 Hessen-Cassel troops. The Hessen-Damstadt contingent had almost ceased to exist, with only 384 effectives left. Demet, *We are Accustomed to do our Duty*, p.98.
37. *A Journal Kept*, p.109.
38. Quoted in Burne, *Duke of York*, p.185.
39. Henry Clinton letter dated 17 November 1794, University of Michigan, Vol.235.
40. The Brigade of Guards alone had 900 men sick on 17 November.
41. Calvert, *Journals & Correspondence*, p.409.
42. Parrish, *Macdonald*, p.41.
43. Quoted in Burne, *Duke of York*, p.196.

NOTES

44. Subsequent Cornwallis biographers have been unable to ascertain the author of the letter.
45. Calvert, *Journals & Correspondence*, p.388.
46. Quoted in Burne, *Duke of York*, pp.201-202.
47. ibid, p.206.
48. Jones, *Historical Journal*, pp.144-145.
49. King George letter to William Windham dated 10 February 1795, quoted in Burne, *Duke of York*, p.210.
50. The Duke of York served as Commander-in-Chief of the British Army from 1795 until 1809, and then from 1811 until his death in 1827.
51. Duke of York letter dated 8 December 1794 quoted in Calvert, *Journals & Correspondence*, p.411.
52. Unlike Continental armies, the British Army had no Chief-of-Staff position. The role was shared between the Adjutant-General and Quartermaster-General.
53. *A Journal Kept*, p.119.
54. Jones, *An Historical Journal*, p.146.
55. Vale, *the South Staffordshire Regiment*, pp.29-30.
56. *A Journal Kept*, p.122.
57. *Geschichte der Königlich-Hannoverschen Armee*, vol.IV, pp.452-453.
58. Keppel journal, entry for 11 December 1794.
59. Literally, John Bull.
60. Keppel journal, entry for 25 December 1794.
61. Fortescue, *British Campaigns in Flanders*, pp.392-394.
62. Morris, *With the Guards in Flanders*, p.133. Captain & Lieutenant Colonel Lord Charles FitzRoy (1764-1829) of the 3rd Foot Guards was on the duke's staff.
63. *Die Hessen in den Feldzügen von 1793, 1794 und 1795*, pp.319-320.
64. *A Journal Kept*, pp.136-137.
65. Keppel journal, entry for 31 December 1794.

Chapter 17

1. Ompteda, *In the King's German Legion*, p.75.
2. Indeed, the Hanoverian cavalrymen of the (later) King's German Legion developed an outstanding reputation for field-craft and taking care of their mounts in the Peninsula war of 1808-1814.
3. The 42nd Foot - the Black Watch - celebrated this rare action of infantry successfully charging cavalry by the insertion of a red hackle in their bonnets. The Royal Regiment of Scotland continue the tradition.
4. Keppel journal, entry for 6 January 1795.
5. Alleyne FitzHerbert, 1st Baron St Helens, British ambassador at the Hague.
6. Brown, *An Impartial Journal*, pp.214-215.
7. McGrigor, *The Autobiography and Services*, p.32.
8. Voltigeur = literally 'vaulter', French light infantryman.
9. *A Journal Kept*, pp.149-150.
10. Later a general and commander of the 1st Division in the Peninsula in 1812.
11. *A Jounal Kept*, pp.152-154.
12. ibid, p.155.
13. Brown, *An Impartial Journal*, p.217.
14. *A Journal Kept*, p.160.
15. *A Journal Kept*, p.161.
16. Uppelschoten, *De 'ontzaggelikje groote passage van de Engelsche Armee*.

Chapter 18

1. Brown, *An Impartial Journal*, pp.220-221.
2. Keppel journal, entry for 16 January 1795.
3. ibid, entry for 17 January 1795.
4. ibid, entry for 18 January 1794.
5. Jones, *An Historical Journal*, p.174.
6. Keppel journal, entry for 21 January 1795.
7. Assignats were the de facto currency in France during the Revolution; by 1795 they were declining sharply in value and practically worthless.
8. Morris, *With the Guards in Flanders*, p.150. Presumably the cockades referred to are the French (red, white, blue) and Dutch (orange).
9. Brown, *An Impartial Journal*, p.225.
10. Based upon Morris, *With the Guards in Flanders*, p.150.
11. In addition to becoming Quartermaster-general of the Forces, Brownrigg later became a lieutenant-general and Governor of Ceylon. He fought the Second Kandian War in 1815.
12. Jones, *An Historical Journal*, p.177.
13. *A Journal Kept*, p.175.
14. Quoted in Fortescue, *British Campaigns in Flanders*, pp.399-400.
15. Morris, *With the Guards in Flanders*, p.157.
16. In fact, the preliminaries leading up to the treaty signed on 5 April 1795, part of the Peace of Basel. In secret, Prussia recognized French control of the west bank of the Rhine, whilst France returned all lands east of the Rhine captured during the war.
17. Morris, *With the Guards in Flanders*, p.159.
18. Keppel journal, entry for 16 February 1795.
19. Vale, *the South Staffordshire Regiment*, p.38.
20. PwJa455, Cavendish-Bentick Papers, Nottingham University.
21. The émigré regiments were, by this time, practically worthless. Fortescue describes them thus: 'Most of these regiments were simply frauds, imposed upon the English Ministers by a band of unscrupulous adventurers.'
22. Keppel journal, entry for 23 February 1795.
23. Quoted in Jones, *An Historical Journal*, pp.180-181. These 2,289 troops were paid for by a British subsidy. Reidesel had previously served in North America during the Revolution.
24. Details of the French attack of 13-14 March based upon Demet, *We are Accustomed to do our Duty*, pp.105-108.
25. Keppel journal, entry for 29 March 1795.
26. 'Class' was the actual terminology used in the orders, although it merely represented groupings rather than quality.
27. Keppel journal, entries for the period 8 April to 7 May 1795.
28. Based upon WO 27/77, NAK.
29. The 80th Foot lost 228 dead in the retreat and discharged 210 men declared unfit for service upon arrival in England. The regiment had to be virtually rebuilt from scratch. On 1 June 1795 the 63rd Foot had 327 men sick and 22 left behind as prisoners in Germany. Most of the sick were later discharged.
30. Stuart had been sent to Portugal in January 1797 with 8,000 men to counter a threat by Bonaparte to place French and Spanish garrisons in Portuguese ports and fortresses until a peace with Great Britain was concluded.
31. *Geschichte der Königlich-Hannoverschen Armee*, vol.IV, pp.622-623.
32. Spain signed the second treaty on 22 July 1795.

NOTES

33. Although the Kingdom of Westphalia also included other territories, such as Braunschweig-Lüneburg.
34. An amalgamation of nine kingdoms and twenty-eight territories, with a combined population of fifteen million, with the requirement to provide 63,000 troops for Napoleon's armies.

Chapter 19
1. Later a Maréchal d'Empire under Napoleon.
2. Later a Maréchal d'Empire under Napoleon.
3. This word was not then in use, but appropriately describes the activities.
4. Furet, *A Critical Dictionary of the French Revolution*, p.175.

Chapter 20
1. The war would drag on in Northern Italy until October 1797, giving a certain young Corsican dynamo a chance to shine.
2. Rose, *William Pitt and The Great War*, p.204.
3. ibid, p.196.
4. ibid, pp.196-197.
5. Vale, *the South Staffordshire Regiment*, p.37.
6. We can probably find a later parallel in the performance of the Italians in the Second World War.
7. The Hanoverian infantry regiments were brought up to strength from raw recruits before the campaign opened and this no doubt affected their performance.
8. The Royal Artillery motto, which means 'everywhere'.
9. Even the Duke of Wellington only ever fought a single battalion level action – Boxtel.
10. Burne, *Duke of York*, p.226.
11. Although the percussion cap, invented in 1807, was not implemented until after 1834.
12. Respectively: In Portugal 1808; at Maida 1806; in Portugal and Spain 1808; in Hanover 1805.
13. After 1815 the British army shrank back to a more manageable 149,000 in 1816 and 100,000 by 1821.
14. As you sow, so you shall reap.

Appendix I
1. *New Annual Register*, 1795, p.264.
2. *New Annual Register*, 1794.

Appendix II
1. Boycott-Brown, Martin. The Road to Rivoli. London: Cassell & Co., 2001.

Index

A

Aalbeke, 160, 172, 175
Abercrombie, Ralph, 57, 59, 77, 98, 120, 128, 132, 144, 150, 181, 205, 211, 218–21, 246, 248, 252–53, 254, 256, 278
Adelepsen, 80
Agache, 95
Agathon Lézy, 175
Ainslie, George, 122
Albert, Prince, 24–25
Aldenhoven, 49
Allison, Archibald, 92, 126
Alost, 199, 201
Alvinczi, Baron Josef, 98, 148, 237, 243, 244, 280
American War of Independence, 5, 11, 62, 128, 276, 278–79, 281
Amerongen, 247–48
Amersfoort, 248
Amherst, Jeffery, 34, 35
Amiens, 39, 67, 258
Amsterdam, 41, 44, 143, 243, 252, 267
Andigny, 144
Annappes, 168
Annihilation Plan, 159, 161, 171
Antoinette, Marie, 4
Antwerp, 28, 44, 53–55, 59–60, 68, 197, 202, 204–6, 212, 216
Appelthoorn, 225, 226
Archduke Karl von Österreich, Herzog von Teschen, 50, 52, 162, 166, 168, 170, 173, 175, 183, 188, 200, 202, 280
Arentschildt, Ensign, 107
Argonne Forest, 20
Armée du Nord, 13, 17–18, 23, 25, 41–42, 44, 50, 52–54, 56–57, 113, 115, 147–48, 200, 212, 276–77
Augustus, 41
Aylett, William, 147

B

Bacmeister, Major, 236
Baird, John, 74
Baird, Joseph, 222
Balfour, Nisbett, 224
Barère, Bertrand, 29
Beaulieu, Johann Peter, 18, 26, 140, 203, 279
Beckwith, Frederick, 252
Beckwith, George, 57
Bellegarde, Heinrich von, 148, 168, 180, 188–89
Bentinck, Lord William, xi, 63, 73, 86, 112, 123
Bijlandt, Alexander van, 44
Biron, Armand-Louis de Gontaut, 16
Bosville, Thomas, 97
Bouchain, 57
Bournonville, 55
Brownrigg, Robert, 252
Buller, John Thomas, 246
Burne, Alfred, 93

INDEX

Bussche-Hardenberg, Georg von dem, 62, 69,106, 107, 155, 161, 164, 171, 183, 188, 236

C

Carnegie, John, 73
Chapman, Sir Thomas, 156–58
Chapuis, René-Bernard, 148–49, 152
Chatham Barracks, 57
Childers, John Walbanke, 73
Civalart, Ludwig Franz, 17
Clerfayt, François Sébastien Charles Joseph de Croix, 22, 26, 42, 70, 117, 154, 152, 161, 202, 203, 225
Clinton, Henry, 158, 231
Coates, James, 246, 256
Coburg, Friedrich Josias von Sachsen-Coburg-Saalfeld, 40–42, 49, 52–53, 63–64, 68, 70. 76, 82, 93–94, 102, 119, 126, 128–129, 131, 133, 134, 139, 154, 160, 173, 180, 183, 186, 188–189, 200–204, 279, 309, 314, 340, 349, 357–361
Colloredo, Nikolaus, 76
Congreve, William, 73
Conway, Henry, 35
Cotton, Stapleton, 269
Craig, Sir James Henry, 131, 183, 187, 206, 208, 216
Craufurd, Charles, 120, 127
Custine, Adam Philippe, 24, 92, 104, 276

D

Daendels, Herman Willem, 115
Dampierre, Auguste Picot, 25, 56, 67, 69, 70–72, 82, 83
Danton, Georges, 18
De Burgh, John Thomas, 224, 228
Diepenbroick, General von, 105, 107, 110, 207
Dillon, Arthur 14, 23
Dover, 57

Doyle, John, 198
Doyle, Wellbore Ellis, 197
Dragoon Guards (British), 36, 120, 122, 130, 132, 146–50, 155, 187, 251
1st, 132, 149, 251
2nd, 53, 84, 120, 130
3rd, 146–147, 150,
5th, 122, 148–149, 157
6th, 122, 155
Dragoons (British), xx, 16, 21, 84, 105, 107, 120, 130, 146, 153, 156
1st, 146, 219
2nd, 130
6th, 130, 156, 187
7th (Light), 130, 171
8th (Light), 153, 182, 194–195, 199, 210
11th (Light), 146, 155, 243
14th (Light), 197
15th (Light), 130, 138, 145, 146, 147, 150, 154, 155, 171, 173, 177, 179, 190, 252, 253,
16th (Light), 144, 148, 150, 155, 173, 176, 213, 247
Duke of Brunswick, Karl Wilhelm Ferdinand, Prince Elector of Brunswick-Wolfenbüttel, 15, 18, 20–23, 42, 54, 90, 132, 223, 232, 281–82
Duke of York (& Albany), HRH Prince Frederick, iv, vii, ix, xii, xix, xx, xxii, xxiii, 44, 45, 47–49 53–55 62 69 70 71 74 78 82 87 88 93–97 110–114 116 118–126 128–132 134 145–150 153–156 158 161 162 166 170–173 175 177 180–184 186 190 192 194 196 197 200–208 210 213 214 216 218–223 225 228 234 253 269 270 278
Dumouriez, Charles-François du Périer, 14, 18, 20, 21, 42, 55, 56, 83, 86, 277
Dundas, David, 128, 205, 238, 243, 245, 248, 254, 270

Dundas, Henry, 31, 34, 45, 57, 60, 64, 121, 122, 129–30, 150, 196, 234, 237, 239, 244, 246, 254
Dundas, Ralph, 72–73, 95, 248, 254, 257, 269
Dundas, Thomas, 121
Dunkirk Fever, 101
Dunkirk, 23, 25, 56, 60, 62, 67, 92–93, 95, 97–101, 103–5, 107, 111–14, 126–128
Düring, Georg Emil von, 128, 217
Durutte, Joseph, 107
Dutch forces, 95, 113, 191, 200, 203
Dutch garrison of Bergen, 251
Dutch Guards, 251
Duurstede, 248
Dyer, Thomas, 58

E

East Indies, 35–36, 38, 263
Eden, Sir William, 44
Edinburgh Castle, 57
Edmund, Viscount Dungarvan, 58
Egalité, 21, 29
Eindhoven, 214, 216
Eisenach, xxii
Elbeke, 154
Eld, George, 99
Elector of Hesse, 259
Electorate of Hanover, 40, 259
Electorate of Hesse, 259
Elonges, 26
Elst, 246
Emden, 253–54
Émigrés, 13, 15, 23, 42, 207, 216, 228
Emperor Franz I, 14, 72, 134, 186
Emperor Franz II, 26, 147
Emperor Leopold I, 12
Emperor Leopold II, 280
Empress Catharine II, 265
Ems, 254–55
Enghien, 39, 63
Englefontaine, 117, 119
Erbach, Count, 88

Erskine, Sir William, 97–98, 111, 130–31, 144, 156–58, 169, 180, 187, 211, 278
Erzherzog Karl Ludwig Johann Joseph Laurentius, 280
Erzherzog Leopold, 166
Escaut, 56–57, 67–68, 70, 87, 126, 128, 187–88
Esch, 217
Eschwege, 99, 167
Espierre brook, 165, 177, 179
Espierres, 154, 161–62, 172, 180
Esquelbecq, 101, 105
Esterhazy, 16, 49
Estreux, 74, 142
Eugen, Freiherr von Monfrault, 165

F

Fabry, 101
Fairfax, Sir Thomas, 34
Famars, 57, 78
Favereau, 142
Fawcett, Sir William, 35, 57
Ferguson, Ronald Crawford, 57
Ferrand, 79, 86, 88
Ferrand, Jean, 89
Ferraris, 69, 76–77, 82
Fézensac, Anne-Pierre, marquis de Montesquiou, 24
First Coalition, 16–19, 21, 23, 25, 27, 29, 38–39, 41, 265, 282
Fitzpatrick, Sir Jeremy, 196
Fleurus, 200, 277, 279–80
Foot Guards (British), xx–xxi, 37, 43, 47, 49, 53–54, 71, 74, 89, 94, 96, 219–20
  1st, 47, 89, 131, 162, 219, 220
  Coldstream, xx, xxi, xxiii, 47, 71, 72, 86, 96, 97, 99. 129
  3rd, 47, 49. 53, 71, 94, 96, 120, 150, 179
Forest of Mehaigne, 203
Forest of Raismes, 68
Fort Balaguier, 261

INDEX

Fort Crevecoeur, 223
Fort George, 36
Fort Isabella, 217
Fortescue, Sir John, 64, 76, 149, 270
Fox, Sir Henry, 156, 170, 176, 177, 186, 189, 255
Frederica, xix, xxiii, 234
Frederick, xix–xxiii, 18, 22, 42, 126, 269, 277, 282
Frederik, Prince of Orange-Nassau, 49, 169, 188, 223
Frederika Sophia Wilhelmina, xxii
French National Convention, 12
Freytag, Wilhelm von, 42, 69, 94, 98, 104–7, 130–31, 280–81
Friedland, 39
Fromentin, 142
Fromm, Oberst, 85
Fryars, 198
Furet, François, 262
Furnes, 67–68, 84, 98, 105, 110–12, 119–20, 122
Fursy, 164

G

Gardes Nationale, 10–11, 24, 42, 87, 141–42, 164, 182
Gardes Suisses, 5
Garnier, George, 58
Gay, Simon François, 108
Geisen, General, 144
Gelderland, 41
Geldermalsen, 238, 243, 245
Gemappes, 203
Gembloux, 203
Genappe, 201, 203
Genoa, 192
Gertruydenberg, 44, 49, 213
Gheluvelde, 164
Ghent, 9, 17, 59, 68, 128, 133, 196, 199, 201, 203, 224, 246
Ghyvelde, 98
Gibraltar, 35, 74, 78, 257, 261
Giersberge, 213

Gilze, 213
Glorious First of June, 263, 266, 273
Goguet, General, 142
Gordon, Andrew, 238
Gordon, Charles, 256
Gorkhum, 228
Göttingen, xx
Goullus, François, 102
Graave, 231
Graham, Charles, 197
Gravelines, 67
Greenwich, 46, 256
Grenville, Lord, 34, 37–38, 45, 130, 194, 265
Grenville, Thomas, 214
Grey, Sir Charles, 114, 116, 121–22, 196, 262
Grey's force, 121, 262
Groningen, 254
Guards battalions, 70, 243
Guards Flank Battalion, 54, 120
Guards, xxiii, 45–47, 49, 70–71, 78–79, 87–88, 94, 96, 110–11, 116, 130–31, 167–71, 176–79, 217–18, 236–37, 243–44, 248, 252–54, 256, 274
Guernsey, 36, 123, 224
Gunpowder Act, 33

H

Haag, 47, 282
Haaren, 217
Haasden, 238
Habsburgs, 40, 279
Hache, General, 230
Haddenhause, 161, 164
Hadik, Karl, Graf von Futak, 144
Halluin, 96, 119, 181–82
Hamburg, 281
Hammerstein, Rudolph von, 153, 164, 195, 211, 216, 219, 220, 245, 246, 268
Hanover, xx–xxii, 37–38, 40, 43, 130, 248, 253, 255, 258–59, 278, 280–81

371

Hanoverian troops, 40, 104, 107, 192–93, 216, 259
Hanoverians, 41–43, 59–60, 62–63, 69–70, 88–89, 104, 106–12, 118–20, 128, 131, 144, 152–53, 161, 164–65, 192–93, 227–28, 253, 255, 258–59, 280–81
Hanstein, Karl von, 123, 179
Happoncourt, 17
Harcourt, William Earl of, 84, 97, 125, 130, 155, 156, 204, 233, 236, 237, 244, 255, 256, 279
Harlebeke, 18
Harnage, William Henry, 72
Harville, 27
Harwich, 256–57
Haye Menneresse, 144
Hédouville, 104, 113–15
Heeswijk, 217
Helderonkirk, 236
Helvoetsluys, 46- 48, 57
Hempenpont, 175
Hermalen, 219
Herseaux, 164–65
Hessen-Cassel, xv, 43, 105, 166, 173, 231, 281
Hessen-Darmstadt, xv, 123, 166
Hessians, 42, 68, 90, 110, 128, 144, 152, 184, 186, 213, 218, 238
Highlanders (42nd Foot), 198, 219–20, 235
Hilsea, 258
HMS Alfred, 264
HMS Brilliant, 101
HMS Culloden, 264
HMS Martin, 57
HMS Racehorse, 46
HMS Rattler, 264
HMS Syren, 53
Hodgson, Studholme, 72
Hoevelaken, 248
Hohenlohe-Ingelfingen, Prince, 21, 41, 78, 94, 125
Holy Roman Emperor Franz, 4
Holy Roman Emperor Josef II, 7, 9
Holy Roman Emperor Joseph II, xxi
Holy Roman Emperor Leopold II, 12–13
Holy Roman Empress Maria Theresa, 4
Hondschoote, 98, 104–5, 107–12, 116, 276
Hood, Sir Samuel, 261
Horse Guards, 35, 157, 234, 274
Hotham, George, 57
Houchard, Jean Nicolas, 92, 100, 104, 107–13, 116, 276
Hougoumont, 204
Houtkerke, 104–5
Howard, Kenneth Alexander, 72
Howe, Earl, 263, 266
Howe, George, 274
HRH Prince Adolphus, 105
HRH Prince Frederick, 278
HRH Prince William Henry, 131
Hulse, Samuel, 154
Hunter, Peter, 197

I

Ijssel, 252
Imperial Army, 15, 41–42, 72, 101, 130, 138, 143, 160, 214, 268, 280
Inchy, 148
Ingelfingen, 20, 41
Ingelmünster, 159–60
Irish Militia Act, 33
Irish Parliament, 32
Irish Rebellion, 278

J

Jacobin Club, 8
Jacobins, 14, 125, 261, 265–66
Jeannot, Adrien, 262
Jemappes, 26–28, 277, 279
Jersey, 36, 206, 258
Jones, Lewis, 233
Jourdan, Jean-Baptiste, 100, 104, 108–9, 200, 212, 277

INDEX

K

Kaiserslautern, 258
Kaunitz-Rietberg, Count Franz von, 140, 147, 155, 165, 175, 176, 184, 191, 200, 268
Kellermann, François Christophe, 21–22, 24
Keppel, Frederick, 229, 230, 237, 244, 251
Kielmansegge, Ferdinand Hans Ludolf von, 80
King Friedrich Wilhelm II, xix, xx, xxi, 10, 12–13, 18, 21, 23
King Friedrich Wilhelm, xx, xxii, 12, 41, 132
King George II, 281
King George III, xix, 40, 131, 278, 281
King Louis Philippe I, 21
King Louis XV, 14
King Louis XVI, 3, 5, 7, 13, 29–30
King Louis XVIII, 277
Kinsky, Josef, Count von Wichnitz und Tettau, 145, 148, 162, 166–73, 175, 180, 183
Kléber, Baptiste, 90, 203
Knobelsdorff, Alexander von, 42, 68, 70, 71, 76, 282
Knollys, William, 94
Koblenz, 15, 258
Kray, Baron, 121, 143, 203

L

Lafayette, Marie Joseph Paul Roch Gilbert du Motier, 11, 13, 18, 29
Lake, Sir Gerard, xxi, 45–46, 48, 53, 71, 96, 97, 131, 150, 154, 278
Lamain, 186, 188
Lamarche, François Joseph Drouot de, 76, 79, 86
Lambusart, 200
Landgraviate of Hesse, 259
Landgraviate of Hessen, 259

Landrecies, 67, 134, 143, 145, 147, 153, 162, 192, 280
Landrin, Jean-Noël, 104–5, 107, 113
Langenberg, 219
Langeron, Count Louis Alexandre Andrault de, 95, 118
Lannoy, 113, 120, 154, 155, 160, 162, 169–73, 175–77, 179–80
Launay, 7
Laurie, Sir Robert, 130, 138, 238, 244, 269
Laye, 101
Le Marchant, Sir John, 269
Le Mesurier, Peter, 274
Leau, 52
Leclaire, Theodore Francois, 100, 105, 107–10
Lefebvre, François Joseph, 200, 203
Lengerke, 88
Lennox, Charles, xxi
Leveson-Gower, John, 206
Lightburne, Stafford, 57
Ligny, 200–201
Lilien, 26, 89
Lingen, 245
Linselles, 92–93, 95–99, 101, 132–33, 161, 181–82, 278
Linsingen, Karl Kristian von, 128, 212, 216
Lisle, 156–57, 161
London, xxiii, 31, 36–37, 43–44, 46, 51, 129, 264, 273–75, 278, 282
Long, Robert, 269
Longwy, 20, 25
Loos canal, 110
Loos, 120
Lord Amherst, 35, 234
Lord Auckland, 48, 55, 56
Lord Bonnington, 126
Lord Cathcart, 224, 238, 245, 252, 254
Lord Charles Fitzroy, 237
Lord Cornwallis, 187, 192, 194, 214, 223, 232
Lord Dungarvan, 251
Lord Grenville, 56

INDEX

Lord Howe, 197
Lord Malmesbury, 194
Lord Melbourne, xxiii
Lord Moira, 123, 194, 196–99, 205
Lord Moira's force, 123, 197–98, 201
Lord Mulgrave, 210
Lord Newark, 206
Lord Spencer, 214
Lord St. Helens, 244
Lothringen-Lambesc, Karl Prinz von, 188
Loyal Emigrant Regiment, 84, 119, 152–53, 194–95, 207, 223, 238, 254–56, 259
Luckner, Johann Nikolaus, 14, 17, 18, 24, 276
Luingne, 164–65
Lunteren, 248, 250
Lynch, Isidore, 21
Lyons, 192, 261
Lys, 96, 114, 154, 160–61, 164, 171–72, 175, 181, 184

M

Maas River, 143
Maas, 60, 214
Macbean, Alexander, 58
Macbride, John, 101
Macdonald, Etienne, 154, 172, 175, 187–89, 195, 254
McGrigor, James, 227, 244
Mack von Leiberich, Karl, 33, 63–64, 125, 129–30, 76, 133, 138, 159–60, 161, 186, 190–91, 280
Maestricht, 41, 49, 51, 205, 265
Maida, 270
Mainz, 11, 24, 37, 40, 90, 92, 279
Malbrancq, Philippe Joseph 154, 172, 175, 187–88, 195
Mansel, John, 97, 146, 147–50, 154, 269
Marbais, 203
Marceau, François, 200
Maresches, 76, 78

Marlborough, Duke of, 34, 45, 208
Marlière, 69, 71–72
Marly, 82, 86
Marne, 18
Maroilles, 148
Marquain, 17, 154, 171–72, 180–81, 186
Marquion, 94–95
Marseilles, 260–61
Martinique, 192, 262, 270
Maubeuge, 56, 67–68, 93, 116–17, 119, 122, 128, 140, 142, 160
Maulde, 68–70, 203
Mauvaix, 96
McDowall, Hay, 254
McMurdo, Charles, 252
Mehaigne, 203
Mélantois, 168
Menin, 67–68, 96, 113–16, 119–20, 123, 152–53, 158, 160–61, 164, 172, 181
Merveldt, 155
Messines, 114, 160
Meteren, 237–38, 243
Metternich-Winneburg, Franz, Graf von, 55
Metz, 21, 24, 276
Meuse, 14, 67, 200, 203, 212, 217, 223, 225–26, 231, 236, 243
Mezières, 160
Michielsgestel, 218–19
Minden, 281
Miranda, Sebastián Francisco de, 21, 41, 49, 52
Moddeven, 219
Moerdyk, 53
Möllendorf, Wichard Joachim Heinrich von, 132, 191, 194, 228
Moncey, Bon-Adrien Jeannot de, 262
Monck, George, 34
Mons, 16–17, 22–23, 25–28, 68, 116, 128–29, 169, 191, 203
Mont Halluin, 172, 175
Mont Houy, 57
Mont St. Jean, 203
Montaigu, Anne Charles, 200
Montesquiou, 24

Montmédy, 11
Montrecourt, 146
Moreau, Jean Victor Marie, 142, 152, 153, 172, 175, 183, 187, 212, 231, 243
Moreaux, Jean René, 212
Morlot, 203
Morris, Roger, 225, 227
Morrison, Sir George, 35
Mortier, Adolphe-Édouard-Casimir, 79, 259
Moselle, 14–15, 25, 41, 43, 64, 100, 119, 127, 200, 212
Moulin-Tonton, 176
Mouscron, 152, 160, 161, 164–65, 172, 175
Mouveaux, 170–73, 175–76, 181
Munich, 38
Murray, Sir James, 53, 60, 63–64, 101, 122, 125–26
Murray, John, 150, 177

N

Namur, 16–17, 25, 28, 128, 140, 143, 205
Nançay, 84
Naples, 39, 265
Napoleon, 21, 25, 27, 39, 76, 141, 162, 269, 275, 277, 279–81
National Convention, 24, 28–29, 32, 41–42, 52, 54–56, 87, 90, 192–93, 201, 267
Nauendorf, General, 201
Navarre, 22
Néchin, 128, 155, 188
Neerwinden, 52, 277, 280
Nienhuys, 253–54
Nieuwpoort, 68, 101, 112, 113, 114, 116, 119–22, 128, 152, 196, 201, 203, 207, 212
Nijkerk, 248
Nijmegen, 41, 208, 222, 224–26, 228–29, 231, 236–38, 243, 246, 252
Nivelles, 201, 203, 270

Nordhorn, 255
Nouvion, 148
Nursling, 257

O

Oedenrode, 216–17
Oeyenhausen, General von, 152
Oirschot, 217
Oise, 67, 160, 232
Oise-sur-Bommel, 231
Oisy, 148
Ompteda, Christian, 59, 62, 63, 69–70, 79, 82, 88, 101, 102
Orchies, 168
Orléans, Duc de, 21, 29
Orne, 109
Osnabrück, 252, 254–55
Osten, General, 155, 172, 187, 188
Ostend, 56, 62, 83–84, 87, 95, 101, 113–16, 121–23, 196–97, 201, 203
Osterhout, 208, 213
Overlangel, 231
Oyly, 150
Oyré, 90

P

Paget, Sir Edward, 10, 245
Pannarden Canal, 243
Passavaut, 20
Passchendaele, 194
Payne, Edward, 150
Payne, William, 269
Peace of Basel, 258–59
Perryn, James, 54
Petit Baisieux, 167
Philippeville, 67, 147, 160
Philipstadt, 204
Phipps, Sir Henry (Lord Mulgrave), 210
Pichegru, Jean-Charles, 141, 143, 146–48, 152, 153–54, 159–60, 194, 196, 201, 212, 217, 219, 229–30, 236, 277

Pierquin, General, 142, 155, 175
Pillnitz, 11–12, 192
Pitt, Sir William, 15, 17, 30–31, 34, 36, 37–38, 44–45, 93, 129, 130, 214, 223, 232–34, 266
Plymouth, 263
Poland, 10, 38, 90, 191, 194, 265
Polish Problem, 194
Polish Question, 267
Pomereul, 133
Poniatowsky, Prince, 90
Pont-à-Chin, 186, 189
Pope Pius VI, 8
Poperinge, 104
Poppel, 216
Portsmouth, 114, 256, 263–64
Portugal, 37, 39, 258
Potsdam, xx, xxii
Pottelberg, 154
Prémont, 144
Prestre, 67
Princess Friederike Charlotte Ulrike Katharina, xix
Prisches, 148
Privy Council, 31
Provence, 13
Prüschenk, Moritz, 105
Prussia, xix–xxii, 9–13, 15, 18–19, 37–41, 44, 127, 132, 266–67, 269, 277, 281
Prussian army, 20–21, 23, 40, 132, 187, 192, 194, 281
Prussians, 10, 12, 15, 18, 21–23, 41–42, 44, 68–70, 84, 191–92, 255, 258–60, 267–68
Pyrenees, 25, 64, 262

Q

Quackenbruck, 258
Quatre Bras, 281
Quérénaing, 78
Querimain, 78

Quesnoy, 67, 76, 93, 102, 114, 116, 140–41, 143, 203, 205, 212
Quiberon, 258
Quieverain, 70
Quosdanovich, Peter von, 200, 203

R

Raismes, 67–68, 70–72
Ramignies, 188–89
Ramillies, 204
Ramsay, William, 58
Rawdon, Francis (Lord Moira), 196
Regiments of Foot (British), 33, 57, 121, 153, 197–98, 204, 211, 226, 257
  8th, 195, 229, 243, 244, 245, 256
  12th, 194, 219, 220
  14th, 36, 57, 59, 62, 77, 89, 116, 139, 156, 177, 245, 257
  27th, 119, 245
  28th, 245
  33rd, 229, 243, 253
  37th, 57, 62, 116, 117, 130, 184, 222, 226, 252
  38th, 195
  42nd, 198, 219–20, 235
  44th, 205, 219
  53rd, 57, 62. 74, 119, 121, 184, 189, 190, 257
  55th, 153, 182, 195
  59th, 246, 247
  63rd, 209, 237
  78th, 243, 244
  80th, 238, 254
  84th, 252, 256
  87th, 199, 251
  88th, 229, 244, 256
  89th, 227, 228, 256
Reichenbach, 9–10
Renaix, 196, 200–202
Reningelst, 104
Renswoude, 248
Rexpoëde, 98, 104–8

376

INDEX

Reynier, General, 172
Rheinbund, 259
Riedesel, Friedrich Adolf, 255
River Aa, 208, 213, 218
River Dommel, 214, 216, 218
River Ems, 254
River Ijssel, 251
River Leck, 247
River Lys, 115, 131, 159, 187
River Maas, 44, 49
River Marque, 142, 155, 160, 162, 166–69, 172
River Meuse, 15, 222
River Rhonelle, 76
River Roer, 223
River Scheldt, 57, 59, 69, 82, 83, 128, 188, 189, 195, 201, 205
River Vechte, 255
River Waal, 225–26, 228–32, 236–38, 242–47, 257, 277
River Weser, 259
River Yssel, 253
Rochefort, 18
Rocroi, 67, 160
Roesbrugge, 104–5
Roeslaere, 114, 153, 195
Roeulx, 201
Roncheval, 155
Roncq, 152, 172, 175
Rosendael, 98, 208, 212
Ross, Alexander, 58
Roubaix, 169–71, 173, 175–79
Roucq, 96
Rouleur, 69
Rousbeke, 134
Royal Artillery, 36, 53, 70, 73–74, 82, 87, 101, 115, 139, 169, 184
Royal Navy, 30, 35–36, 38, 57, 64, 93, 98, 100–101, 261, 263–64, 273
Royal Waggon Train, 256
Ruel, 27
Ruhr, 49
Russell, James, 112, 149, 150
Russia, 37–38, 63, 194, 271

Rutherford, John, 120
Ryberg, 213

S

Sachsen-Teschen, Prince Albert Kasimir August Ignaz Pius Franz Xaver von, 105–6
Sackville, John Frederick, 7
Saing, 95
Sainghin, 152, 154–55, 160, 168–69
Saint Amand, 68–69, 71, 74
Saint Oedenrode, 218
Saint Quentin, 67
Saint Saulve, 69
Sainte-Menehould, 23
St Leger, John, 63
Sambre, 76, 117–18, 121, 133, 145, 191, 196, 200, 203, 212
Sapin-Vert, 176
Sardinia, 37, 265
Scharnhorst, David, 110, 153
Scheither (cavalry officer), 80
Schenckenschans, 231
Scherpenzeel, 248
Schijndel, 217, 219–20
Schloss Charlottenburg, xix
Schwartzenberg, Karl, 148
Sedan, 20, 67
Sens, 166
Sheridan, Richard Brinsley, 274
Sierck-les-Baines, 20
Silesia, xx, 9, 35
Somme, 67
Sontag, John, 100
Souham, Joseph, 101, 112, 142, 154–55, 171–72, 175, 183–84, 188–89, 195, 212, 243
Southampton, 196, 257
Spain, 37, 39, 261, 265, 271
Spanish Netherlands, 9
Spencer, Joseph, 171
Speyer, 24
Sporck, General, 105, 152

377

INDEX

St Amand by Pont, 162
St Amand, 118, 140, 160, 162, 168
St Lucia, 262
Staebel, Pierre Jean van, 263
Stahrenberg, Count, 55
Stapelen Castle, 218
Stasbourg, 280
Steenevorde, 104
Steinkerke, 110
Stenay, 67
Stewart, Alexander, 231
Strutt, Goody, 254
Strybeck, 213
Stuart, John, 270
Sunderland, 256–57
Swabia, 41
Swiss mercenaries, 7
Sztáray, Graf de Nagy-Mihály, 181, 182, 195

T

Talleyrand, Charles Maurice de, 14–15
Taureau, Jean, 237
Taylor, Herbert, 94, 270
Templeuve, 162, 169, 179–80, 188–90
Tennis Court Oath, 5
Téteghem, 100
Texel, 252
Thalers, 254
Thielt, 161–62, 164
Thierry, General, 154, 155, 158, 172, 175, 187–88
Thionville, 20
Thomas, George, 73
Thugut, Baron von, 63, 127, 133, 191–92, 202
Tiel, 238
Tielt, 195
Tilburg, 216–17
Tilleul, 175
Tirlemont, 9, 50, 52, 205
Torhout, 114, 195
Toufflers, 162, 169

Toulon, 64, 126, 192, 260–62, 266
Toulouse, 261, 270
Tourcoing, 113, 154, 159–65, 167, 169–77, 179–81, 183–84, 186–87, 189–90, 266, 281
Tournai, 16–17, 22–23, 59, 62, 72, 74, 119, 121–23, 140, 154–55, 158, 160, 180, 185–91, 193
Tourville, 133
Tower Hamlets, 275
Transylvania, 280
Trauttmansdorff, Ferdinand von, 132
Treffin, 167
Tressin, 155, 167–68, 173
Tréves, 140
Trevillian, William, 73
Trinity College, 32
Troisvilles, 148–49
Trouille, 26
Tuileries Palace, 11, 19, 29
Turenne, General, 85
Turnhout, 9
Tuscany, 39
Tuyl, 237, 243, 245–47
Tynemouth, 36, 256

U

Uden, 219
Ulm, 76, 280
Ulster, xx
United Netherlands, 38, 40, 282
United Provinces, 36, 38–41, 44, 48, 205, 207–9, 211–13, 216–17, 219, 221, 244, 265, 267
Untenburger, 85
Upper Rhine, 280
Ushant, 263
Utrecht, 9, 237, 243–44

V

Valence, Jean-Baptiste Cyrus de, 25
Valenciennes, 16, 18, 23–25, 55, 57, 67, 69, 74, 76, 79–83, 85, 87–93, 128, 140–41, 216–17

INDEX

Valmy, 16, 21, 23–24, 28, 40, 42, 277
Valotton, Charles, 33
Vandamme, Dominique, 104, 108, 113, 119, 121, 122, 152, 172, 181–83
Vandeleur, John Ormsby, 199
Varennes, 11
Vatican, 8
Vauban, 67, 68
Vaux, 144
Velthuysen, 253–54
Vendée, 90, 123, 126, 192, 262, 266
Venlo, 41, 223, 226
Verdun, 11, 20, 23
Versailles, 5–7
Veurne, 107
Vicoigne, 68–72
Vienna, xxi, 12, 14, 127, 132, 191, 201–2, 214, 267, 280
Vieuzac, 29
Villaret, Thomas, 264
Villers, 146–47
Villers-en-Cauchies, 137, 146–47
Vimeur, 13
Vincennes, 11
Vistula, 143
Vlamertinge, 104
Vosges, 25, 276
Vry-Bosch, 194
Vucht, 218
Vyse, Richard, 219, 254, 257

W

Waardenbourg, 238
Waart, 217
Waddams, 226
Wadonoijen, 231
Wagram, 39
Walcheren, 201
Waldeck, Georg Prinz zu Waldeck und Pyrmont, 133, 180–81, 188, 191, 196, 202
Walheim, 205
Wallis, Michael, 168
Wallmoden-Gimborn, Graf Ludwig von, 106, 108, 110, 120, 128, 131, 205, 229, 233, 237, 253, 254, 259, 281
Wangenheim, 106, 152
Wannehain, 155
War Office, 97, 231
Washington, George, 13
Wasquehal, 182
Waterloo, 47, 84, 156, 162, 201, 204, 268, 270, 282
Wattignies, 116–18, 128, 279
Wattrelos, 113, 162, 165–66, 170, 173, 175–76, 179–81
Wavre, 203–4
Wellesley, Arthur, 197, 270
Wellington, xxi, 162, 211, 269–70, 275
Wenkheim, General, 88, 159
Werneck, Franz Freiherr von, 133, 228–30
Wervicq, 119, 131, 133, 161, 164, 170, 172, 181, 183
Wesel, 229
West Flanders, 25, 93, 112, 140, 142, 152, 192, 196, 199, 227
West Friesland, 252
West Indies, 35–36, 114, 116, 121–22, 126, 257–58, 262, 266, 273, 275, 278
Weybridge, xxiii
Whitehall, 37, 120, 206, 237, 265–66
Whyte, Richard, 150, 153
Wijchen, 222
Wiklantitz, 191
Wilhelm IX of Hessen, 40
Willem V, 40, 42, 48, 282
Willems, 76, 151–52, 157–58, 172, 268, 282
Willemstadt, 48
Wilson, Henry, 171
Wilson, Robert, 138, 145, 146, 177, 190
Winckheim, Genreal, 68

Windham, William, 87, 221, 223, 234
Windward Islands, 257
Winneburg, 55
Winnezeele, 105
Winschoten, 254
Wissembourg, 127
Wolfswinkel, 217
Woolwich, 74
Wormhout, 102, 104, 105, 107
Wright, Jesse, 70–71, 85
Würmb, Ludwig von, 42, 99, 120–21, 167, 238, 268, 281
Würmb II, Oberst, 167
Wurmser, Dagobert Sigmund von, 41, 127, 280
Wynyard, Sir William, 270

Y

Yarmouth, 256
Ypres, 67–68, 98, 104, 107, 113–14, 119, 123, 128, 131, 133, 140, 194–96
Ysemberg, 110
Yssel, 254

Z

Zandvoorde, 131
Zedwitz, 80
Zuider Zee, 252
Zutphen, 251–52
Zwoll, 252, 253